The Dynamics of
Chinese Politics

Lucian Pye

The Dynamics of
Chinese Politics

 Oelgeschlager, Gunn & Hain, Publishers, Inc.
Cambridge, Massachusetts

International Standard Book Number: 0-89946-132-8 (cloth)
                                    0-89946-133-6 (paper)
Library of Congress Catalog Card Number: 81-14228
Printed in West Germany

Library of Congress Cataloging in Publication Data

Pye, Lucian W., 1921–
  The dynamics of Chinese politics.

  Bibliography: p.
  Includes index.
  1. China – Politics and government – 1976–
I. Title.
DS779.26.P93   951   81-14228
ISBN 0-89946-132-8   AACR2
ISBN 0-89946-133-6 (pbk.)

Jacket/cover design by Clifford Stoltze

To Mary,
Lyndy, Chris and Karen, and Ginny,
Sources of boundless joy.

Contents

Preface

The tension between consensus and faction is in large measure the most basic dynamic of Chinese politics. Pulling in one direction is the cultural imperative of conformity and consensus – within the ranks of the elite there should be only harmony and cooperation, never unseemly competition and disagreements. Yet there is an equal, if not stronger, cultural imperative that pulls in the other direction, which says that security is to be found only in personal, particularistic relations that ensure that one is not just a part of the common herd but that one has special ties with both superiors and inferiors.

In this book we seek to examine the ramifications of this basic contradiction that is the driving force for so much of Chinese political behavior. On the one hand, there is the ideal of unanimity, the principle of collective conformity, of never causing waves or being out of step. On the other hand, there is the irresistible compulsion to find security by seeking out special relationships. The consequence is that behind the curtain of consensus there is an endless process of forming and reforming of clusters and networks of officials, which at times consolidate into fairly coherent factions. Since all Chinese leaders know that this process takes place, those upholding the consensus of the moment tend to be quickly suspicious that others are acting against it, and therefore they are inclined to threaten the others and thereby cause them to do the very things they are suspected of doing.

Our approach in this book is a search for the general principles and patterns that underlie Chinese political behavior, particularly factional politics. Our focus is on the period beginning with the succession struggle following the rule of Mao Zedong and ending with Deng Xiaoping's successful removal of Hua Guofeng as both premier and chairman. We shall not seek to tell this story chronologically. That history will have to await the resolution of certain mysteries relating to specific events, decisions, and agreements. (We do, however, have a brief summary of those years on pp. 244–257.) Our analysis, nevertheless, does explain why Hua Guofeng, with all of his apparent advantages as Mao's designated successor and the leader who ordered the arrest of the Gang of Four, who had excellent contacts with rural cadres and the public security apparatus, who first dramatized the great goals of the Four Modernizations, and who personally heralded China's opening to the world by his tours of Europe and Japan, could not hold on to power; and why Deng Xiaoping, with an initially narrower power base, was successful in gaining domination.

The success of the one man and the failure of the other was not rooted in profound policy matters – on the record, Hua was even more verbally enthusiastic about the Four Modernizations than Deng, and in his desperate efforts to maintain his offices he was in some respects more "pragmatic." Hua's basic problem, beyond any limitation in wits and skill, was that, like most Chinese leaders, he found that he could not be a national leader without compromising the particularistic ties that lay at the base of his substantive power. Every effort Hua made to identify himself as a leader with interests greater than his particular web of cadres compromised his relations with them, created confusion as to exactly what and whom he represented, and failed to win him new supporters among those already committed to others. Our predicition is that Deng Xiaoping will in his turn be confronted with the same problem, for we see no reason to expect an end to factional politics – their dynamics are far too deeply rooted in the very essence of Chinese political culture.

Anyone with a feel for China's political culture will, for example, know why Chinese find nothing redeeming, only shameless conduct, in Jiang Qing's feisty behavior at her "trial."

My own claim to understanding Chinese culture stems partly from the fact that Hua Guofeng and I were born about fifteen miles from each other in the same year, he in February and I in October, and hence we grew up knowing the same Shanxi geographical and social landscape, the same villagers and city people, the same sounds, smells, and tastes – although in other ways our socialization was no doubt profoundly different. I must acknowledge that I have never met Hua Guofeng, although I have been privileged to have had several interesting hours of discussion with Deng Xiaoping.

As an antidote to possible sources of personal bias in my own experiences with Chinese society, I have used as the data for this book a series of extensive interviews with emigrés from China and primary and secondary literature on Chinese politics. As a part of the interviews, a questionnaire was used that incorporated items from several standardized scales for measuring operationalized concepts in social psychology. Because of cultural and situational considerations, it was clearly inappropriate to use the entire set of questions employed in any one of the scales. This has meant that except for the few cases where items rather than scales have been the bases for reporting findings, no quantifiable cross-cultural comparisons are possible. We therefore have used the items for essentially illustrative and suggestive purposes. The questionnaire results have value to the extent that they supplement other evidence; by themselves, they cannot either prove or disprove any proposition. The responses of the forty-four former PRC residents now living in Hong Kong reveal, however, that two decades of Maoist attempts to change Chinese character have seemingly failed to affect those dimensions of Chinese personality that motivate political factionalism. Attitudes about authority, trust, dependency, and other key sentiments measured in the questionnaire indicate strong propensities for precisely the kinds of behavior that generate factions. The uncertainty associated with the dramatic, but unpredictable, political changes now taking place in China can be expected to cause even greater efforts to establish the personal networks that give individual Chinese feelings of security and thereby produce factions in the polity.

L. W. P.

Acknowledgments

This book originated as a Rand Corporation Project AIR FORCE report prepared for a study project on "China's Strategic and Regional Roles and Asian Security." The author is indebted to Rand for supporting the rewriting and editing necessary to turn this report into a book. Richard H. Solomon, Head of Rand's Social Science Department, helped to conceptualize this project and provided administrative and intellectual support throughout the effort. Also at Rand, Nathan Leites and Steven I. Levine critically read the first version. George Tanham provided essential encouragement and guidance, and Mary Yanokawa coordinated the production of the draft manuscript with cheerful efficiency. David Rothberg helped to identify items for the questionnaire, and Sophia Lu-tao Wang made the initial translation of the questionnaire and contributed to the data analysis. John Dolfin, Director of the Universities Service Centre, and his staff helped to plan and organize the interviewing in Hong Kong, and Tuan Chi-hsien and Ko Liu-kai located respondents and helped administer the questionnaire and the interviews. Donald Morrison put the results into the computer and provided a voluminous printout.

The manuscript was carefully and thoughtfully read by Harriet B. Braiker, Thomas P. Bernstein, Richard Baum, Jürgen Domes, B. Michael Frolic, Merle Goldman, Harry Harding, Donald Klein, Richard

Samuels, and Lynn T. White, III, all of whom suggested improvements that have added substantially to the quality of the final version. Lola Klein patiently typed near-illegible handwritten drafts into immaculate manuscripts, and then equally patiently retyped all the subsequent drafts. Mary Pye, with sensitivity but uncompromising standards, edited the entire manuscript. Janet DeLand carefully went over the manuscript, made improvements, and saved me embarrassments.

In light of all of this gratefully appreciated help, it goes without saying that all the faults in this book are the sole responsibility of the author.

Chronology of the Post-Mao Years

1976

January 8	Zhou Enlai dies.
January 15	Deng Xiaoping gives eulogy in last public appearance before his second purge.
January 30	Hua Guofeng, fifth-ranking Politburo member, made "acting prime minister."
April 5	Tienanmen Incident – demonstration in memory of Zhou and against "radicals."
April 7	Deng Xiaoping stripped of all posts by Politburo, called an "unrepentant capitalist roader," and exiled to South China.
April 30	Reportedly Mao Zedong said to Hua Guofeng, "With you in charge I am at ease."
July 28	Earthquake destroys Tangshan.
September 9	Mao Zedong dies.
September 18	Hua Guofeng delivers memorial speech, saying, "The correctness or incorrectness of the

ideological and political line decides everything."

October 6   Wang Dongxing, acting under instructions from Hua Guofeng and Ye Jianying, "arrests" the Gang of Four (Mao's widow Jiang Qing, Zhang Chunqiao, Yao Wenyuan, and Wang Hongwen).

October 22   Hua made Chairman of the Party.

October 26   Hua reissues Mao's *Ten Great Relationships*.

1977

May 3   Deng writes letter to Hua and Party leadership asking to be rehabilitated and promising his loyalty.

July 16–21   Third Plenum of Tenth Central Committee meets, confirms Hua's appointment as Chairman of both the Party and the Military Affairs Commission, and reinstates Deng Xiaoping as a Vice-Chairman and a member of the Standing Committee of the Politburo.

August 12–18   Eleventh Party Congress meets, Hua gives opening address and declares the Cultural Revolution concluded, and Deng gives closing speech, calling for "less empty talk and more hard work."

    Standing Committee of Politburo, in rank order, Hua Guofeng, Ye Jianying, Deng Xiaoping, Li Xiannian, and Wang Dongxing.

September 9   Mao's mausoleum completed.

October 24   Third campaign against the Gang of Four and their supporters begins. Yu Quili declares need for wage incentives and major economic changes.

1978

February 18–23   Meeting of the Fifth National People's Congress (NPC) and the Fifth National Committee of the Chinese Peoples' Consultative Conference, preceded by the Second Plenum of

	the Eleventh Central Committee, at which Hua Guofeng announces ambitious Ten-Year Plan, with targets of 120 large-scale projects, 60 million tons of steel, and 400 million tons of grain by 1985. Ye Jianying elected Chairman of the NPC. Revised state constitution gives more freedom, including the Great Four Freedoms of "speaking out freely, airing views fully, holding great debates, and writing big-character wall-posters."
May	Sino–Vietnamese tensions rise, Chinese withdraw technicians from 72 projects, and Chinese ethnics begin to flee from Vietnam.
May 20–23	Zbigniew Brzezinski, President Carter's Assistant for National Security, visits China.
August 11–September 1	Hua Guofeng visits Romania, Yugoslavia, and Iran.
August 12	Japan and China sign Treaty of Peace and Friendship, which includes an "anti-hegemony" clause.
November	Democracy Wall Movement under way.
December 15	President Carter and Chairman Hua announce normalization of relations will take place on January 1, 1979.
December 18–22	Third Plenum of Eleventh Central Committee meets and proclaims the two slogans, "Seek truth from facts" and the "four basic principles," of Marxism-Leninism-Mao Zedong Thought. Chen Yun, an economic authority, added to the Standing Committee of the Politburo as Deng's ally. The verdict on the Tienanmen Incident is reversed and the Incident is declared to have been a revolutionary event; the termination of the campaign against Lin Biao and the Gang of Four is officially proclaimed.

1979

January 1	United States and China normalize relations.

January 29–February 4 Deng Xiaoping visits United States.

February 17 China invades Vietnam "to teach a lesson."

March Leading champions of democracy and free speech, including Wei Jingsheng and Fu Yuehua, arrested.

April Deng's supporters speak of an "adverse current" in the Party. China informs Soviet Union of its intention not to extend the 30-year Sino–Soviet Treaty of Friendship, Alliance, and Mutual Assistance due to expire April 11, 1980.

June 18–July 1 Second Session of Fifth National Peoples' Congress hears that ambitious goals of Four Modernizations have caused economic dislocations and that there is a need for three years of "readjusting, reforming, rectifying, and raising standards." Official support given to trade negotiations with the West and Japan.

October–December Deng calls for law and order, clamps down on dissent. Democracy Wall closes. Hua Guofeng visits France, West Germany, Britain, and Italy – the first such tour by a most senior Chinese official.

1980

February 23–29 Fifth Plenum of the Eleventh Central Committee rehabilitates Liu Shaoqi, appoints Deng's allies Hu Yaobang and Zhao Ziyang to the Standing Committee of the Politburo, and accepts the "resignation" of Hua's allies Wang Dongxing, Ji Dengkui, Wu De, and Chen Xilian. Hu Yaobang appointed Secretary General of Party, and Secretariat is reestablished in effort to separate Party and state functions.

March Economy remains sluggish, but hopes for improvements are raised by a call for the use of market forces, especially in agriculture, and the practices initiated by Zhao Ziyang in Sichuan.

April

Countering the move to "liberalize" the economy, the "Four Great Freedoms" are eliminated from the constitution.

July

Pictures of Mao taken down in Peking. Widespread cryptic attacks on Hua and extensive rumors of his impending fall.

September

Second Session of the Fifth National Peoples' Congress meets again; Zhao Ziyang replaces Hua as Prime Minister; six vice premiers, including Chen Yongqui, the model peasant from Dazhai, and Li Xiannian, leader of the veteran cadre faction, "resign." Increased press praise of market forces and criticisms of excessive central planning.

October

Major readjustment of economy necessary; cancellation of foreign contracts begins.

November

Gang of Four indicted on 48 counts, including causing the "death of 34,000."

1981

February

Announced budget deficit of 17 billion yuan for second year; further economic retrenchment and appeals for stronger central planning.

June 15

Sixth Plenum of Eleventh Central Committee finally meets after repeated postponements since January; accepts Hua Guofeng's "resignation" as Chairman; appoints Hu Yaobang to the post; and makes limited criticisms of Mao Zedong's contribution to the Party's history.

July 1

Sixtieth anniversary of the founding of the Chinese Communist Party finds Mao's immediate successor Hua Guofeng demoted, but the victorious Deng Xiaoping still has substantial opposition within the Party.

Romanized Forms of Chinese Names

Pinyin	Wade-Giles
Individuals	
Chao Gai	Ch'ao Kai
Chen Xilian	Ch'en Hsi-lien
Chen Muhua	Ch'en Mu-hua
Chen Yonggui	Ch'en Yung-kuei
Chen Yun	Ch'en Yun
Deng Xiaoping	Teng Hsiao-p'ing
Deng Yingchao	Teng Ying-ch'ao
Deng Zihui	Teng Tzu-hui
Duan Chunyi	Tuan Ch'ün-i
Guomindang	Kuomintang
Hong Xiuchuan	Hung Hsiu-ch'üan
Hu Qiaomu	Hu Ch'iao-mu
Hu Yaobang	Hu Yao-pang
Hua Guofeng	Hua Kuo-feng
Ji Dengkui	Chi Teng-k'uei
Jiang Qing	Chiang Ch'ing
Kang Sheng	K'ang Sheng
Li Desheng	Li Teh-sheng

Li Lisan	Li Li-san
Li Xiannian	Li Hsien-nien
Lin Biao	Lin Piao
Lin Zhuanxin	Lin Chuan-hsin
Liu Bocheng	Liu Po-ch'eng
Liu Shaoqi	Liu Shao-ch'i
Liu Xiangping	Liu Hsiang-p'ing
Lu Xun	Lu Hsün
Mao Yuanxin	Mao Yuan-hsin
Mao Zedong	Mao Tse-tung
Ni Zhifu	Ni Chih-fu
Nie Rongzhen	Nieh Jung-chen
Peng Dehuai	P'eng Te-huai
Peng Zhen	P'eng Chen
Pi Dingjun	P'i Ting-chün
Qiao Guanhua	Ch'iao Kuan-hua
Song Chang	Sung Ch'ang
Song Peizhang	Sung P'ei-chang
Tang Tsou	Tang Tsou
Wang Dongxing	Wang Tung-hsing
Wang Hairong	Wang Hai-jung
Wang Hongwen	Wang Hung-wen
Wang Renzhong	Wang Jen-chung
Wei Guoqing	Wei Kuo-ch'ing
Wu De	Wu Teh
Wu Guixian	Wu Kuei-hsien
Xu Shiyou	Hsu Shih-yu
Xu Xiangqian	Hsu Hsiang-ch'ien
Xu Yinsheng	Hsu Yin-sheng
Yang Zhijie	Yang Chih-chieh
Yao Wenyuan	Yao Wen-yuan
Ye Jianying	Yeh Chien-ying
Yue Xiao	Yueh Hsiao
Zhang Guotao	Chang Kuo-t'ao
Zhang Hanzhi	Chang Han-chih
Zhang Chunqiao	Chang Ch'un-ch'iao
Zhang Tiesheng	Chang T'ieh-sheng
Zhang Zhixin	Chang Chih-hsin
Zhao Ziyang	Chao Tzu-yang
Zhou Enlai	Chou En-lai
Zhou Peiyuan	Chou P'ei-yuan
Zhou Yang	Chou Yang
Zhu Ping	Chu P'ing

Cities, Provinces, and Places

Anhui	Anhwei
Beijing	Peking
Fudan	Futan
Fujian	Fukien
Fuzhou	Foochow
Gansu	Kansu
Guangdong	Kwangtung
Guangxi	Kwangsi
Guizhou	Kweichow
Hebei	Hopei
Heilongjiang	Heilungkiang
Henan	Honan
Hubei	Hupeh
Hunan	Hunan
Jiangsu	Kiangsu
Jiangxi	Kiangsi
Jilin	Kirin
Liaoning	Liaoning
Neimonggu	Inner Mongolia
Ningxia	Ningsia
Qinghai	Tsinghai
Shandong	Shantung
Shanghai	Shanghai
Shanxi	Shansi
Shaanxi	Shensi
Sichuan	Szechwan
Suzhou	Soochow
Tianjin	Tientsin
Xiang Xiang	Hsiang Hsiang
Xiangtan	Hsiang-t'an
Xinjiang	Sinkiang
Xizang	Tibet
Xunyi	Tsunyi
Yunnan	Yunnan
Zhejiang	Chekiang

Chapter 1

An Overview Analysis

The Chinese, whether Confucianists or Communists, have persistently believed that government should be guided only by ethical imperatives and ideological prescriptions, never by the dynamics of political contention. Indeed, one of the most distinct characteristics of the Chinese has been their uncompromising denial of legitimacy to the clash of power and values, of men and opinions, which nearly all other people accept as the normal basis for public life. In their escape from politics, most Chinese have steadfastly tried to idealize government – in the past by calling for a rule of benevolence and justice, and more recently by extolling the need for everyone to follow "correct solutions" and the collective leadership of the Party.

Usually, the Chinese openly admit to the existence of political contention in their society only when they are bewailing the evils of corruption, as for example, when they used to describe the venality of dishonest mandarin officials or as they now recount the horrors of the Cultural Revolution and the vile schemings of the Gang of Four. To describe and analyze political life without moral praise or condemnation is as unthinkable to the Chinese as it is second nature to people of most other cultures.

At times in Chinese history there were acknowledged conflicts between organized political forces, as in the struggles to establish a new dynasty, or between revolutionary and conservative elements in the modern era. Under Communism, they have come closer to recognizing that politics is a matter of power, and hence contention, as when they speak of different forms of "contradictions" or class conflicts between elements of the "five red categories" and the "five black groups," or the struggle between "two lines." These, however, are still all morality plays, theater cast in heroic dimensions, and have little in common with what other people have in mind when they speak of day-to-day, run-of-the-mill politics. Also, the Chinese, of course, at times violate their taboo about acknowledging the existence of ordinary politics, but rarely in serious discourse; and almost always when they do so it is in a risque mood, as though they were engaged in telling off-color jokes.

A consequence of the Chinese attempt to deny in public politics, and their resulting refusal to analyze openly or systematically their political processes, is that it becomes awkward for outsiders even to try to describe the realities of Chinese politics. Over the years, the Chinese have clearly preferred that others should follow their example and dwell on either the virtues of their political ideologies or their professed policy aspirations. During the era of Mao's rule, attention was thus focused on the intensity of revolutionary fervor and the heroic attempt to create a new "Maoist man"; and in the post-Mao years, analysis has been concentrated on the ambitions of presumably pragmatic policies. In both cases, foreigners have been provided with little information about the political activities that must certainly take place behind the wall of secrecy that the Chinese diligently erect around their political processes. Only when scandals erupt are people given a keyhole peek at political contests, and hence it seems almost scandalous that at other times the Chinese elite might also engage in politics.

This book seeks to penetrate that wall of secrecy. Not, however, in the spirit of exposing scandal – except to the extent that academics have an obligation at all times to puncture the pretensions of public men in any society. (The fact that the Chinese have such a peculiar distaste for publicizing politics will make it seem at times as though we were perversely rubbing their fur in the wrong way even as we treat them as we would any people – certainly any discussion of American politicians would call for more acerbic judgments.) Our purpose is far more innocent: It is a response to the growing need to know the actual dynamics of Chinese politics at a moment when the Chinese are becoming a part of the world, and it is to be hoped they will also gradually accept openly the fact that they, like everyone else, engage in the game of politics.

Although in comparison with the recent past, Chinese society under the command of Deng Xiaoping has become more open to outside influences and the Chinese have become somewhat less fearful about discussing Party and government activities, the dominant rule is still secrecy about politics. The search for efficiency and rapid modernization has in fact tightened the strictures against even hinting that Chinese decisionmaking might be influenced by a political process. The trial of the Gang of Four and of the five military leaders has revealed that the Chinese persist in believing that actions which in other societies would be seen as politics should be classified as criminal moves.

It is an anomaly that the most populous country in the world can be ruled by one of the most secretive political processes. One billion Chinese are in nearly total ignorance of how the critical thousand or so of the elite manage their country's affairs. Until recently it was routine for the National People's Congress to meet in the middle of Peking without either the Chinese public or the world at large knowing that a meeting was taking place. Yet an understanding of this veiled political process is profoundly important not only for the Chinese people but also for the stability of international politics. Much, therefore, rests upon the skill whereby educated speculation can penetrate China's secrecy in order to provide warnings about the direction in which Chinese politics is moving.

Up to a point, outside analysts have been remarkably adroit in fathoming the obscurities of the Chinese "public" scene. Somewhat paradoxically, the more the problem has been one of deducing precise figures, the more accurate has been the speculation. Quantitative estimates of various forms of production rest upon the more readily calculable parameters and variables provided by known technologies, engineering principles, and geographical and other given resources. Indeed, whenever the Chinese authorities have revealed such specific statistical information, it has been an occasion for self-congratulation by foreign analysts because the numbers have usually been fairly close to their own. Unfortunately, on the more basic matters of politics and national directions, speculative penetration is more difficult, and Chinese statements taken literally can be very wide of the mark.

There are numerous reasons for Chinese secrecy, ranging from the revolutionary practices of Marxism–Leninism to the traditions of ancient China, but one of the most fundamental is basic to Chinese political behavior: All who participate in elite affairs must acknowledge as imperative the maintenance of consensus. The requirement that everyone must appear to be in agreement with everyone else has the consequence of erecting a wall around Chinese politics. This pretense of agreement, seen from the outsider's perspective, becomes the make-believe that hides the presumed reality lying at the heart of Chinese secrecy. Thus, the need to shield what goes on from the eyes of others is only partly a function of an exaggerated sense of discretion and an overevaluation of the advantages of surprise; it also arises from the Chinese rulers' obligation to feign harmony. (Although the Chinese leaders have gone to great lengths to exterminate traditional Confucian values, and certainly they scorn the classical virtue expressed in the word *ho,* or harmony, their behavior is consistent with the belief that it is bad form, if not actually dangerous, for leaders to squabble publicly with each other.)

Ironically, what goes on behind the shield cannot be completely obscured, because the imperative of consensus makes it inherently dangerous for actors to participate in clandestine or private channels of communication; those who would modify the consensus therefore find it more prudent to employ the public media to hint at their preferred variations on the dominant themes of the day.

Indeed, as we shall see, one of the most striking paradoxes of Chinese politics is that the weak and vulnerable dissidents are not the ones who rely upon Aesopian language and code words – on the contrary, they must make their messages unambiguously blunt and explicit on wall posters. Rather, it is those in the ranks of the powerful who monopolize all the forms of esoteric communications.

This book will focus on how the Chinese elite, behind their conspiracy of consensus, carry out their politics and their decisionmaking. Our central hypothesis is that the fundamental dynamic of Chinese politics is a continuous tension between the imperative of consensus and conformity, on the one hand, and the belief, on the other hand, that one can find security only in special, particularistic relationships, which by their very nature tend to threaten the principle of consensus. These particularistic ties tend to produce factions, and therefore much of our study will be the examination of propositions about factional behavior. What are the bases of factions? What are the relationships between the rules of factional politics and public policies? In what ways do factional politics give both stability and instability to the Chinese system? Above all, what is the likelihood that the dynamics of factions will alter the current Chinese consensus about the Four Modernizations in domestic policies and antagonism with the Soviet Union in foreign relations?

The death of Mao Zedong and the "smashing of the Gang of Four" produced no decline in the tension in Chinese politics between the ideal of consensus and the reality of factionalism. The Chinese media, in steadily shriller tones, called for an end to factionalism, yet cadres at every level prudently sought the security inherent in those personal relations of trust that form the networks basic to factions in Chinese political culture. Increasingly, factional considerations affected relations among the principal leaders and among officials at all levels of the state and Party bureaucracies as "rehabilitated" cadres contended with cadres who profited during the Cultural Revolution. Even though diffuse and general agreement apparently existed about policy directions, strong particularistic differences produced inescapable lines of cleavage in the ranks of Chinese officialdom, according to patterns of trust and distrust. Nevertheless, the Chinese try to deny the existence, or certainly the significance, of factions; indeed, the idea of factions is threatening to the Chinese, as can be seen in the discomfort with which Chinese officials react to queries about factional relationships – queries that participants in most political systems would take to be the proper starting point for rational discussions.

The conventional method for analyzing Chinese politics has been to perform in-depth studies of practices and policies during quite discrete time periods. The vacillations of politics in the history of Chinese Communism simplify periodization and invite a case-study approach. But the very attractiveness of such an analysis also reveals its weakness: If the breaks between periods are so sharp, then what has been learned about one period may not tell much about another, or about the future. The application of such historically defined case studies to the study of factionalism within the Chinese Communist Party (CCP) would yield a series of quite different pictures of the dynamics of factions. The divisions in the 1920s would have accentuated differences in leadership responses to Moscow. Those in the 1930s highlighted communications problems between geographically separated elements: First, Mao in the mountains of Jiangxi and the others underground in Shanghai, and then the struggle between Mao and Zhang Guotao, each heading his respective army. After victory, policy issues divided the leadership with respect to the Great Leap; then radical passions during the Cultural Revolution and the succession struggle set the leaders against each other. Left uncertain is the fundamental question of which period provides the best guidance for understanding the present and the immediate future.

In approaching this problem, our study will deal with the phenomenon of factionalism in Chinese politics, looking to all periods for insights and generalizations that we judge to be of the greatest current relevance. We shall therefore not trace in detail the unfolding of particular cases of factional struggles; rather, we shall record conclusions about past practices that appear to be pertinent to understanding the nature of factionalism in Chinese political culture. These conclusions also reflect insights we obtained by interviewing people who had experienced political life in the People's Republic of China (PRC).

A major problem in attempting to penetrate the secrecy of Chinese politics is the maintenance of a proper balance between absorption with clues and concentration on the larger issues. Although we believe that our judgments are based on facts and a careful regard for detail, it seems wisest in communicating the results of our research to begin with a rather bold statement of our overview conclusions. It is hoped that such a statement will provide an orientation that will make it easier to appreciate the whole while we scrutinize the parts. In short, since we shall in the subsequent chapters examine in considerable detail the "trees," it is advisable at the outset to get a clear view of the "forest."

THE BASES OF FACTIONS

To understand the role of factions in Chinese politics, it is necessary to put out of mind the analogue of interest-group politics or even of bureaucratic politics in industrially developed societies. Factions in the CCP rarely, if ever, represent clearly defined institutional, geographical, or generational interests. This does not mean, however, that institutional, geographical, or generational considerations may not contribute to the formation and maintenance of particular factions.

The prime bases of factions are power constellations of clusters of officials who for some reason or other feel comfortable with each other, who believe that they can share mutual trust and loyalties, and who may recognize common foes. More often than not, the real motivation is that of career security and enhancement, whether it be at the lowest county or provincial committee level or among those on the Politburo and the State Council jockeying for greater influence. The glue that holds factions together can thus be either mutual career self-interest or the highly particularistic sentiments associated with personal ties in Chinese culture, that is, the spirit of *guanxi*. The concept of *guanxi*, which describes the intense personal bonds of acquaintanceship and mutual belonging that give vivid context to the networks of personal associations in Chinese culture, will be of central concern in this study; and those unfamiliar with the concept may want to turn early to pages 138–142, where it is discussed in detail.

Chinese factions lie between the extremes of the intimately knit cliques and the diffuse mass parties that are common in the politics of other countries. Although cadres are capable of being highly aggressive in protecting each other, the networks that shape factions in the PRC are not usually strongly motivated to assert generalizable political interests. Factions are thus more latent than manifest, more capable of bureaucratic obstructionism than of policy initiation or implementation, and generally diffuse and imprecise with respect to policy matters, except when it comes to pragmatic considerations of career and power.

Right at the outset we must briefly address the question of the relationship between policy choices and factional alignments in Chinese politics. Unquestionably, certain leaders do become identified with particular policies, and therefore their supporters are also inclined to champion these policies and oppose the policies of competing factions. Indeed, certain policies can become the trademark of particular factions. Similarly, the introduction of new policies can be interpreted as favoring the well-being of cadres in a particular faction and damaging those in other factions. In these respects, factions are related to policy.

Yet it would be quite incorrect to jump from these observations to the conclusion that factions are formed in response to policy preferences. Those who are actively engaged in political participation in China do not have the luxury of deciding their stand on new issues on the basis of an objective weighing of all the pros and cons. Quite the contrary, cadres are invariably hedged in and find themselves constrained by a host of past commitments, personal relationships, and obligations, so that the only realistic option they usually have is to go along with the position that appears to favor their faction's well-being. One has only to consider the marginal role that substantive policy issues can play in the decisions of American politicians concerning which of their party's presidential aspirants to support for nomination and to recognize that in Chinese politics personalized relationships are orders of magnitude more intense, leaving Chinese cadres far less elbow room for maneuvering, to understand why policy cannot be the prime basis for factions in China.

This same constraint also makes it inappropriate to refer to factions as "opinion groups." Such labeling would suggest that they are casually united on the basis of like thinking and are free to recombine into new groupings as new matters of opinion arise. The personal commitments, and the personal costs of breaking those commitments, are far too great to be governed by mere opinion.

Thus, Chinese factions are *not* formed primarily in response to policy issues, bureaucratic interests, generational differences, or geographical bases, although these considerations do play a part, and policy is indeed affected by the outcome of factional tensions. Neither are ideological considerations of prime importance, although in their differing collective orientations, the current political factions in the PRC do have certain policy biases. The prime basis for factions among cadres is the search for career security and the protection of power. The extraordinary force that holds together the networks of officials is the intense attraction of mutual dependency in Chinese culture between superiors and subordinates, each of whom needs the other for his own protection and each of whom is vulnerable to the other, which means that both must be loyal to each other. Thus, the strength of Chinese factions is the personal relationships of individuals who, operating in a hierarchical context, create linkage networks that extend upward in support of particular leaders who are, in turn, looking for followers to ensure their power.

THE DISTRIBUTION OF FACTIONS

On the rare occasions when factional strife punctures the veil of consensus, it usually appears as though the Chinese ruling elite is divided into contending groups. Furthermore, Chinese rhetoric about intra-Party conflicts invariably details struggles of "two lines." Yet such clear bipolar divisions in fact appear to be exceptions, occurring only at times of extreme crisis.

The more normal condition is a pattern of factional distribution in which groupings of officials are scattered within the hierarchy of Chinese politics. Much of the time the groupings are in a latent state, nurturing themselves by providing the individuals involved with increments of security as frequently as is necessary or possible.

In short, factions are made up of networks of personal associations of indeterminate membership. There are periods in which the networks are lax to the point of apparent non-existence; at other times, they are agitated into action, whereupon coalitions and alignments of networks take on the character of aggressive factions.

Leaders do not necessarily strive consciously to build up networks of followers – in fact, there is a taboo in the ethics of the CCP against precisely such endeavors, a taboo so strong that senior officials are not supposed to engage in explicit talent searches among the younger cadres. What happens instead is that the networks tend to take a hierarchical shape and eventually strive to attach themselves to particular leaders. Consequently, any leader who has had a successful career in the Party will inevitably find that he has developed a chain of potential supporters. Unless he acts to satisfy their needs, they will, in time, abandon him for another, more supportive leader. As a result he will be alone, and as his peers discover his vulnerability, competitors will arise to seek his downfall in order to use his position to satisfy their own networks of supporters.

THE MOBILIZATION OF FACTIONS

In Chinese politics a variety of stimuli can mobilize latent networks into active factions. There is, however, a public rule that no clandestine channels should be used for mobilization. (In the propaganda denouncing Chairman Mao's sometime heir-apparent, Lin Biao, the disclosure that he secretly organized the "571 Group" caused as much alarm as the allegation that he had also attempted three times to assassinate the Chairman.) Consequently, the mass media are the most commonly used means of signaling the intentions of leaders to activate their networks and to form broader coalitions.

The triggering signal can be a code-word attack upon another leader, and the test of factional strength is the extent of support for the attack. For example, in the two years following the "smashing" of the Gang of Four, in province after province leading provincial officials were singled out (never by name, but rather by cryptic designations) as appropriate objects of attack because they were alleged to have been "sworn followers" of the "ultra-rightists." The issue at stake was whether lesser cadres would quickly join in the attack and thereby swell the ranks of the attackers or defend the accused, whose real names everyone knew, by denying that they willfully championed the Gang. Worst of all, would they try to remain silent and uncommitted until it became clear who would prevail in the future? Everyone in China must have known the identity of "China's Khrushchev" and "that Party person in authority taking the capitalist road" long before he was finally revealed to have been "that renegade, hidden traitor, and scab, Liu Shaoqi." Similarly, during the three years in which the Chinese press reviled "that political swindler like Liu Shaoqi and his ilk," everyone knew that the objects of attack were in fact first Chen Boda and then Lin Biao. Thus during the campaigns against the followers of the Gang of Four, the press in the provinces attacked a long list of local leaders by code names. For example, in Jiangxi, it was "that rather influential person"; in Hebei, there was "that bad man of Paoting Prefecture"; in Liaoning, it was "that sworn follower" and "his sinister henchman" (who was none other than Mao's nephew); in Guangdong, it was "a major leading figure" and "another major leading figure"; in Suzhou, "the tiger"; in Hunan, "the scoundrel," "the drummer," and the "dog's head staff officer," to mention just a few.

At other times, the test of mobilizing capabilities is initiated by highly esoteric declarations of what is good or what is bad. The actual trial balloons range from attacks upon Beethoven and Confucius to ecstatic praise for the slogan "Seeking truth from facts" and for believing that in the nature of things, "one divides into two" rather than "two forms into one." The process is routine: A slogan is floated in the media, and then everyone watches to see who chooses to repeat it and who conspicuously ignores it.

At times the question raised for determining factional strength can actually be a matter of public policy. But even in such cases the process calls for symbolic expression, and indeed, ideological posturing is often a convenient method of symbolically expressing what everyone can deduce as a policy preference. Even such apparently ambiguous statements as "taking agriculture as a base and industry as the cutting edge" can be read as an unequivocal advocacy of more resources for the rural masses.

The reasons for the use of such cryptic code words and Aesopian language are, first, they usefully disguise the fact that the consensus is being challenged and hence reduce the likelihood of disorderly debate that could damage all elements of the elite; and second, they reduce the vulnerability of the initiators if their slogans do not catch on – those who first advocated them can simply pretend that nothing actually happened.

POLITICAL RHETORIC AND FACTIONS

The dynamics of factional politics encourage not only extensive use of symbolic language but also considerable exaggeration in Chinese political rhetoric. The underlying objective – to mobilize favorable elements and neutralize the opposition – encourages extremism in making denunciations and promises for the future. The far-fetched statements about how the crimes of the Gang of Four impeded progress in nearly every sphere and the equally unrealistic timetables for the Four Modernizations have had the same practical purpose: the mobilizing of factional support for fundamental power alignments. (For obvious but not particularly complimentary reasons, Westerners have found it easy to see through the exaggerations about the former but are more gullible about the latter.)

The need for exaggeration stems in part from the troublesome fact that realistic statements would fail to provide a satisfactory test of political loyalties, since people might agree with such statements merely out of common sense. Exaggerated rhetoric provides a symbolic dimension to politics, in the context of which people can clearly reveal that they are supporting particular spokesmen by repeating statements that cannot be confused with reality. (This can be seen from the spontaneous way in which the Chinese extend the logic of their factional loyalty testing to foreigners, classifying those who unquestioningly accept Chinese exaggerations as "friends" of China while treating skeptics not as unimaginative realists but as people to be distrusted.)

Thus the dynamics of factional mobilization can, on the one hand, impart great urgency and inordinate attention to ritualized formulations about matters that otherwise might seem trivial – for example, in prolonged discussions about who among contemporaries is a "Song Chang" (a model of a "revisionist" found in a traditional Chinese novel) or about the need to "find truth from facts." On the other hand, the same dynamics can trivialize what, if taken literally, would be world-shaking events – for example, the startling idea that "the bourgeoisie is right in the middle of the Party," or that "world war is imminent and conditions are excellent."

In short, the operations of factional politics provide clues, through the mass media, as to the actual play of forces within the elite, while at the same time these processes cause the media to be filled with outlandish distortions of reality. The task of the analyst is the same as that of the Chinese participant: He must seek to be hypersensitive to the former and impervious to the latter.

THE TACIT CHARACTER OF FACTIONS

The fact that factions are generally mobilized out of latent networks of associations, through the introduction of highly symbolic communications, suggests the loose structuring of these critical units of Chinese politics. The boundaries of factions tend to be exceedingly vague, and there is always considerable uncertainty as to whether certain officials in fact belong to one faction or another. Even at the core of factions, relations seem to be more tacit than explicit.

Consequently, when a faction comes under attack there tend to be two diametrically opposite reactions: Those at the periphery often choose to fade away, denying whatever associations they may have had, while those at the core seek to strengthen their bonds, taking on a siege mentality. For example, as the second round of campaigns against the remnants of the Gang of Four followers took shape in 1978, the Chinese press made dark hints about the enduring power of three factions – the "slip-away faction," composed of people who would drift away from meetings when the denunciations of the Gang's followers became vehement, a "swivel faction," which would adjust its posture to any change in the political climate, and a "wind faction," which pleaded that the past for which they were being attacked was "gone with the wind." At the same time, there were those who could not deny their association with the "Maoists" and who therefore had to hold on as best they could, necessitating not only a third round of campaigns but apparently endless ritualized attacks on the Gang of Four.

The same structural constraints appear to operate when a faction is on the rise, since there can be considerable uncertainty as to how the benefits should be distributed within the coalition. Those who lose out become disaffected, while those who benefit the most must hang together more tightly, for they will in due time become the targets of attack by the next emerging faction.

The tacit nature of factions is accentuated by the process of accretion whereby networks of associations are expanded at different times, under different conditions, and for different reasons. Thus, the very things that hold a faction together at one time may become the cause of dissension under changed conditions. Given the tortuous history of the CCP, nearly all power groupings appear to be composed of people who do not necessarily share the same interpretations as to whether particular past events were good or bad.

These considerations have been shaped by Mao Zedong's profoundly important decision that the CCP would not follow Stalin's practice of applying the death penalty in Party purges. Although we now know that thousands of people were "persecuted to death" during the Cultural Revolution, the dominant Chinese practice has been to stress rehabilitation through reeducation, which has meant that not only can purged victims be restored, but also every organization may contain people who have been hurt and who thus have scores to settle once an opportunity arises.

During the years of contention between Hua Guofeng and Deng Xiaoping, the latter – being himself unique in the history of Communism in having twice returned from being purged – had a natural appeal to not only all rehabilitated cadres, but also to every Chinese who had suffered during the turmoil of the Cultural Revolution, which according to Deng amounted to 100 million people. Hua's natural supporters were increasingly placed on the defensive. Thus the essentially tacit nature of cadre networks operated to favor the more aggressive posture of Deng and harmed the more passive Hua.

POLICY AND FACTIONS

As we have already indicated, it would be foolish to argue that policy issues do not influence factional alignments or that the outcomes of factional struggles have no consequences for policy changes. Clearly, there could have been no program of the Four Modernizations without the smashing of the Gang of Four. Yet it is worth stressing that foreign analysts have a propensity for exaggerating the role of policy issues in factional conflicts.

As a general principle, it can be said that there are no fixed rules in the relationship between policy and factional politics. Indeed, the relationship is tenuous and unpredictable partly because leaders who might otherwise be in complete agreement on the substance of an issue can find it unbearable to be personally allied with each other. On other occasions, leaders can bitterly contend over policies, not necessarily because of intellectual disagreements, but because they foresee that the effects of the policy will alter their respective power positions. Thus, for example, in 1979 Deputy Prime Minister Ji Dengkui and other leaders of the "Cultural Revolution faction" or the "whatever faction" opposed the agricultural policies of Deng Xiaoping, Zhao Ziyang, and Chen Yun of the "rehabilitated cadres faction" largely because the introduction of market opportunities for increasing rural family household earnings would have diminished the power and the relative material well-being of the rural cadres who were the strongest supporters of Ji and Hua Guofeng. The power and the income of such cadres become greater the more complete their control over all commune activities, hence their liking for the Dazhai model (a model production brigade of the Maoist era) and their fears that freer markets for individual peasants would produce households richer than those of the cadres themselves. If it had been possible to figure out some way whereby the rural cadres could have proportionately benefited from greater use of markets, then Ji and Hua would have had less need to oppose the agricultural policies proposed by Deng's associates.

It is no doubt true that in most political systems there is a strong tendency to pretend that policy issues are more central to power relationships than in fact is the case, thus downplaying the degree to which power struggles can have a logic of their own, untainted by policy considerations. However, for several reasons the gap in China seems to be greater than the norm.

First, as we have already observed, the mobilization of factions calls for the interjection of code-word signals into the mass media, and of course the articulation of policy preferences provides an abundance of symbols and slogans. In any particular situation it may be exceedingly difficult to judge whether the issues at stake are the putative policy alternatives or the power positions of the factions or some combination of these whose making is equally difficult to evaluate. According to several methods of measuring, it seems that the manipulation of symbols is usually more important for power considerations than for policy. Consequently, victors in power struggles may not always vigorously carry out their presumed policy preferences. At times, they will even adopt the policies of the vanquished, thereby showing contempt for them either by robbing them of their own creations (as Mao did after the Cultural Revolution by establishing Liu-ism without Liu in nearly every field) or by striving to demonstrate that they are not what their defeated critics had portrayed them to be (as Mao did in Yunnan when he Bolshevized the Party after defeating those with closer ties to Moscow).

Also, power would seem to be more basic than policy whenever the intensity of the struggle is completely out of proportion to the importance of the concrete issue, as often happens in the cultural realm. Similarly, power would seem to be the key issue whenever tangential matters for contention are readily introduced into the conflict, diverting attention from the initial policy issue.

Moreover, whenever the actual issue would lend itself to easy compromise but the factional parties stubbornly refuse to seek any compromise, it seems plausible that the symbolic expression of policy was in fact serving factional power purposes.

Another major reason for the inordinate gap between policy and power in China is the strong Chinese cultural view, reinforced by Communism, that policy should be a manifestation of wisdom and morality and therefore a pristine product of the leadership. Policy, by tradition, should never be tainted by the vulgar compromises of power considerations. In spite of the principle of the "mass line," the expression of policy is the prerogative of leadership. In Chinese politics there is almost no recognition of the legitimacy of what is taken to be the norm in most societies, namely, that policies may be routinely defined by the vector of all the forces concerned.

In other societies, where policy is more closely meshed with power, there is a tolerance for grotesque policies if they are the best that compromises along the lines of power can produce. In China, preposterous policies are not the products of compromise but the brainchildren of leaders who are so jealous of their own decisionmaking prerogatives that they do not even use the prudence to staff out their notions before announcing them as policy. This was the case not only with Mao, the Great Helmsman, but even with the "pragmatists" as they proclaimed the Four Modernizations.

Closely related is a third major consideration: In China, the principal makers of general policies are frequently not intimately associated with administrative responsibilities. Although the vice-premiers apparently divide responsibilities for the various ministries, there is not a close fit in the sense of specific individuals being legally accountable for particular bureaucratic tasks. Furthermore, there is little communication at the lower levels between ministries, so bureaucratic infighting does not preoccupy the attention of subordinates. Issues are passed up to the top of ministries, where they are then transmitted to the amorphous domains of the various vice-premiers, each of whom has every reason to be more concerned with maintaining harmony with his peers and protecting his own power than with fighting for the parochial policy interests of particular ministries, especially when he may have several ministries reporting to him. The key source of Chinese policies is the "Center"

(Zhongyang), composed of men who are powerful but institutionally vaguely defined, including the members of the State Council, the Standing Committee of the Politburo, the Politburo itself, and the Military Affairs Commission of the Central Committee. Yet when the key figures at the Center make their decisions, the institutional capacity in which they are acting is usually unclear, and hence at its very inception, policy tends to be somewhat divorced from administration and thus highly susceptible to symbolic manipulation.

The imperative of consensus and the concept of elite autonomy in decisionmaking, combined with the relatively weak institutionalization of the distinctive administrative structures, result in the generally weak articulation of institutional and specialized interests. Officials do not feel bound to defend the special interests of their domains of responsibility. It is this characteristic of Chinese politics that explains the otherwise completely implausible fact that the Chinese Air Force became a stronghold of the "radical" faction and defended such unlikely and counterinstitutional doctrines as "Man's will is supreme over machines"; or the equally absurd (by the standards of any theory of interest representation) fact that Shanghai, the most culturally sophisticated, industrially developed, and cosmopolitan city in China, could have been the power base for the most anti-industrial, pro-rural, primitive egalitarianist faction in Chinese politics.

For these and other reasons, the relationship between factional strife and the highest levels of decisionmaking seems to be an erratic one. In contrast, the relationship between factions and policy is somewhat closer at the level of implementation. The very fact that policies are often presented in highly symbolic forms, without having been administratively staffed out to determine their feasibility, means that confusion can reign as they are operationalized, and in this confusion there is often considerable room for factional considerations to prevail – and at times even for sly technocrats to ply their preferred policies.

Evidence that this is the case can be seen from numerous examples in which new policies have been proclaimed with apparent ease after a factional struggle, then a prolonged period has followed when every affected organization has had to hold extensive "discussions" and "meetings" about the directives, and then have come changes of personnel. It is at this final stage that factional maneuvering becomes intense and decisive for the careers of those involved. The degree of enthusiasm with which directives are welcomed is apparently more a function of calculations as to their likely effects on cadre personnel than of judgments of their inherent merit. Thus while many are praising the wishes of the Center, just as many are figuring out how to sabotage them. Since this situation is universally known to exist, it is taken for granted that implementation will call for the screening of personnel; and this, of course, can trigger factional conflicts as cadres seek to protect themselves and those they feel they can most trust. Once these conflicts have been resolved, there can follow an outburst of compulsive support for the program and in defense of the new consensus.

Thus the effect of factional politics on policy implementation is generally a cycle that begins with a phase of immobilism as cadres try to figure out how to operationalize general policies and try to judge the likely personnel consequences. (From 1972 to 1976, foreign observers thought they knew what the Mao–Zhou line of post-Cultural Revolution policies should involve, but little was done to introduce "pragmatic" programs; even after Mao's death and the arrest of the Gang of Four, nearly two years of immobilism followed before the dramatization of the Four Modernizations and outbursts of hurried actions.) Once the initial problems of personnel purging are resolved there may be widespread compulsive support for the programs as cadres seek to identify with the new consensus, but in time the effects of implementation can stimulate opposition and the stage will gradually be set for another round of factional strife.

For the outsider seeking to understand Chinese developments there are further pitfalls in focusing unduly on policy when analyzing Chinese politics. First, there is the danger that professed goals may not lead to appropriate corresponding actions. For example, since 1969 and the Sino–Soviet border clashes, the Chinese, first under Mao and then under Deng, have urgently proclaimed the imminent threat of war with the USSR, causing some analysts to conclude that Chinese policies are guided by the fear of such a war, yet since 1971 there has been a *decline* in Chinese defense expenditures, and the Chinese military came to have less influence than they had during the Cultural Revolution. Policy thus did not respond to the professed problem of the country.

Second, Chinese methods for trying to realize their policy objectives have often been counterproductive, and hence developments may be the opposite of what would be expected from analyzing the announced policy. An example of this danger was Mao's policies of stressing the primacy of grain production and of the goal of national and provincial self-sufficiency in feeding the huge Chinese population which, according to Nicholas Lardy, ultimately resulted in China becoming a net importer of grain, with 40 percent of its urban population dependent upon foreign imports, and the Chinese population as a whole eating less in 1980 than in the 1950s.

Finally, there is the obvious danger of idealizing proclaimed objectives and policies, especially when facts about actual practices are so scarce.

Leaving aside those who for ideological reasons wish to delude themselves, and others, about Chinese policy accomplishments, it is still easy for thoughtful analysts who are denied access to Chinese realities to take Chinese policy statements as reflecting actual or potential achievements. This was particularly the case in the exhilarating days when the first travelers brought back accounts of the new China, and some, who later learned better, concluded that China under Mao and the Gang of Four had policies appropriate not just for the Third World but even for America.

IDEOLOGY AND FACTIONS

In many respects ideological nuances seem to fit more closely with the dynamics of factional politics than do policy issues. This is largely because the language of Chinese politics is more attuned to ideology than to policy evaluation. Furthermore, there is a strong presumption in Chinese culture that it is the moral character of officials–that is, their ideological outlook–that is decisive for the success or failure of their work.

Accountability in the Chinese scene has not been as closely related to records of accomplishment or performance as are ideological attitudes. In contrast to the Soviet Union, up until 1979, China had not exerted heavy personal pressure on its plant managers and state farm officials to achieve expected production levels. The Chinese take for granted that some plants and communes will be better than others, and while they may wish that all might "learn from" the model ones, they are slow to punish those who are less efficient, nor do they readily transfer or demote ineffectual managers.

Failure is thus primarily associated with the personal failings of the individuals involved rather than with faults in the policy. Although the Chinese now speak of the "ten lost years" following the Cultural Revolution, they still only slowly and hesitantly specify the technical errors of policy, preferring instead to dwell ceaselessly on the "evils" of the Gang of Four and their corrupting influences at every level of society. While they speak of the "adverse current" in the spring of 1979 and the troubles caused by the "opposition faction," they do not allude to any specific matters of policy; instead they concentrate on the personal qualities of the faction's members, saying that their "thinking is ossified or semi-ossified." (Exactly how this identifies a particular faction is unclear, since it is a fairly accurate description of the mental state of all too many Chinese cadres after twenty years of Mao Zedong Thought.)

We may appear to be splitting hairs by dwelling on the differences between policy and ideology in their respective relationships to factional politics, since it is well known that in China ideology informs policy, and policy is supposed to be only the applied extension of correct ideological thought. Yet it is precisely this presumption that makes ideological issues the more sensitive and frequent form of factional conflicts. Thus, even at a time when policy is becoming more responsive to technical and rational considerations, and when the state of Chinese ideology is in a muddle, it is significant that questions about states of mind and general attitudes continue to be basic to factional identifications. The reason is not hard to understand: Even though there may be confusion over what to do with Mao's ideological legacy, there is no doubt that subjective attitudes are crucial in determining the strength of the chains of loyalty that hold the factions together. Ideological sloganizing will continue to endure in China as long as the cadres find such formulations more comfortable and efficient to use for subtly probing each other to find out where the other stands. Even those who would uphold pragmatic approaches must employ the ritualized formulations of "finding truth from facts."

In the past, the vacillations of Mao Zedong of course resulted in wide swings in ideological orientations, which produced dramatically sharp and extreme factional conflicts. Today there no longer exists in Chinese politics a comparable capacity to generate such extreme shifts in ideology. As far as can be determined, there are no elements within Chinese politics that would work for another cultural revolution as chaotic as the Cultural Revolution of 1966–1969. Even those who advanced during that period have no such desires, for today they wish only to hold on to their good fortune and not lose out either to those who are being rehabilitated or to a new, and politically unscarred, generation. It seems safe to conclude from what evidence exists that those identified with the "whatever faction" adhere to whatever Mao said only in order to preserve the legitimacy of their authority as faithful followers of Mao and not because they would dismiss the Four Modernizations and return to the simplistic "Maoism" of the mid-1960s.

All of this points to the conclusion that in spite of the erosion of ideology and the narrowing of likely ideological swings, ideological phrasing and sloganizing will continue to be critical for defining factional alignments. As long as the general consensus continues to be defined in ideological terms, and as long as deviation from the consensus is treated as a personal failing in attitude and outlook, variations in the expression of ideology will remain basic to Chinese factional politics.

MOTIVATIONS FOR FACTIONAL IDENTIFICATION

The continuing need for ideological sloganizing does not explain the motivations of those who form themselves into the different factions. Why do Party cadres, who pretend to uphold a consensus, feel the need to subtly align themselves, using as distinguishing words nuances of a no longer deeply felt ideology? Why can't the Chinese leaders behave as pragmatic Americans wish them to and unite in a common effort to modernize their country?

Part of the answer lies in the need for leaders to float code-word signals to determine the distribution of power within the leadership and, more particularly, to mobilize support to ensure their own security. Such indirect testing of the political waters is necessary because of the absolute taboo against any explicit forming of factions, especially by covert communication, and because of the almost equally strong feeling among the Chinese that no important meeting should take place at which the outcome is not preordained. Leaders need to know the relative distribution of strength among themselves as they tacitly work out ahead of time whose views should prevail at the formal meeting. If no prior agreement is possible, the meeting will lose its ritual quality, allowing actual confrontations to occur, which in turn will only make more explicit the formation of factions, since the pretense of consensus will have been compromised. Hence, in such circumstances, the effort is directed to postponing meetings.

This still does not explain the motivations of those who choose to align themselves into factions at the lower levels. On this point, our interviews and questionnaire study of a panel of refugees in Hong Kong are illuminating.

The monolithic structure of Chinese politics is apparently well understood by the common people, so that everyone with even the slightest degree of political consciousness has a vivid feeling that whatever happens at the Center will have consequences for them as the decisions are passed down through the chain of command. Not only Party members but even non-Party people are quite aware that their local cadres must respond to whatever happens above. Therefore, in order to buy insurance against the unexpected and to protect their own status, lesser cadres must take the initiative to establish personal contacts with officials at higher levels. This process apparently continues down to the lowest levels in communes and within factories.

The intensity of the search for identification with those more powerful seems to be heightened by the insecurity of a people who have strong anxieties about social isolation and need the reassurance of conformity. The uniformity of life in the PRC is not entirely imposed from above; people generally feel uncomfortable about being non-conformists. Even those who have become cynical about the national leadership retain a belief in the importance of solidarity and the avoidance of ostracism in their face-to-face relationships. Thus at every level there appear to be strong pulls toward the perceived trends of the day.

On the other hand, if one cannot become a part of the majority, it becomes even more critical to seek security among others in the same situation. The strong Chinese sense of hierarchy means that in any situation there will be some who are more insiders than others, and thus there will always be many who feel somewhat excluded and who will anxiously search for another focus for their group identity. This search, however, cannot be satisfied merely by associating with dissatisfied peers, because of the strong cultural need for authority and for identification with those more powerful than oneself.

The Chinese need for authority is an expression of deep cultural feelings about the comforts of dependency. (The existence of these feelings is graphically substantiated by our questionnaire.) There is a strong element in Chinese culture that insists that in return for deference and respect, authority should be protective, nurturing, and supportive of those below it. The Chinese appetite for dependence is seemingly insatiable; therefore, subordinates constantly demand more from their superiors and are always on the verge of concluding that their allegiance is unrequited.

Thus this feeling of dependency becomes a driving motivation for the creation of the networks of associations that become political factions. Leaders, of course, have their reasons for seeking liegemen, but the flow of energy for the making of factions is not just downward; there is an equally powerful, if not more powerful, flow upward from people craving the security of dependency.

The bonding glue of the relationships that make up the networks thus consists of highly particularistic sentiments of mutual indebtedness—a continuation of the traditional Chinese feeling of *guanxi*, a term no longer allowed in China, except to be denounced, but one that describes enduring sentiments.

In a peculiar, ironic fashion, this coupling of authority and dependency has left each free to exploit the existence of the other for its own purposes. Leaders do not feel that they must or even should "represent" the "interests" of their client-dependents; indeed, according to the ethics of Communist morality, it is entirely illegitimate for leaders to "represent" any particular interests more parochial than the right "class interests." Conversely, those in dependent circumstances can feel free to take advantage of their good fortune in having a protector to create their own lineages of power and authority. And what they are doing can be presented as legitimate in Communist ethics, for on the surface they are merely displaying the activist spirit expected of the good comrade. Hence a conspiracy of silence can protect the tacit exploitation of half-hidden relations whose visible dimensions can be presented as legitimate.

All of this means that the dynamics of factional formation in Chinese political culture operate with little regard for the agenda of policy issues and, even to a lesser degree, the state of ideology. Both leaders and followers seek each other out because of much more intense and intimate considerations. For these same basic reasons they will continue to find it convenient to create symbolic differences in the ideological domain.

THE CYCLICAL RHYTHM OF CHINESE POLITICS

The tensions between the imperative for consensus and the search for personal security in factional relationships contribute to a pronounced cyclical pattern in Chinese politics. The ascendancy of any particular leadership group—such as Zhou Enlai in Mao's last years, Hua Guofeng in the months after Mao's death, Deng Xiaoping two months later, or Zhao Ziyang in 1980—creates widespread expectations that with a new consensus great activities are about to take place. Then the threat of being left out and anxieties that change will create greater insecurities cause the coalescing of other networks and a challenge to the authority of the ascendant leaders. Since Chinese are masters of the art of protecting themselves in hierarchical relations, regardless of whether they are superiors or inferiors, they are soon able to inhibit change—whether it be the Deng forces countering Hua's exaggerated goals for the Four Modernizations or the veteran cadres in the winter of 1980 checking Zhao Ziyang's enthusiasm for industrial decentralization and markets.

Thus the next stage in the cycle is a form of political immobilism as cadres protect their domains and try to prevent the will of any leader from becoming absolute. Soon, however, rhetoric runs ahead of performance, for the domestic imperatives of consensus and the international imperatives of prestige require that all cooperate in feigning that nothing troublesome is taking place. Ritualistic assertions provide a screen for the intensifying power struggle. Code words are floated in hopes of mobilizing expanding networks of power.

Finally, some element in the leadership will be persuaded that it has the advantage, and with an outburst of ambitious pretension it will seek to define the new consensus. With the new consensus must come promises of great events for Chinese leaders usually need to create exciting expectations that will either win over all cadres or at least intimidate and paralyze any opponents. But such changes never seem to take place, and therefore whatever change there is only triggers the need for all who feel threatened to thus begin the process of opposition again.

There is in this way a repeating cyclical pattern: movement toward confrontation, then a standoff, then the overexhilaration of glimpsed victory, which in turn soon stimulates opposition, and then back to a new movement toward confrontation.

THE POST-GANG OF FOUR PATTERNS OF FACTIONS

The Cultural Revolution and the succession struggle surrounding the death of Mao Zedong and Zhou Enlai continue to define the basic pattern of factional divisions in Chinese politics. The vicissitudes of a decade and a half of power struggles have left deep divisions among the cadres who constitute both the elite and the mass membership of the CCP. The tension among them arises from the elementary fact that the political, and hence career, fortunes of some have declined in direct proportion to the successes of others. Consequently, by 1980 most cadres belonged to one of three, or possibly four, categories, each of which contains the kind of networks of trust that can be activated into factions. (Although the categories can be readily identified on the basis of career experiences, this does not mean that all cadres of a particular category are necessarily linked to the latent networks of that category. However, the presumption usually is that unless a particular cadre acts to counter the implications of his career background, it is valid to suspect that he is potentially associated with others in his category.)

The first category consists of a huge group of 50- and 60-year-old cadres, in their prime of life, who either joined the Party or significantly advanced in rank during the Cultural Revolution. They are generally no longer "radicals" or "Maoists" and willingly conform to the new consensus of support of the Four Modernizations, except when they perceive that specific innovations will threaten their power. However, they remain vulnerable because of their past records, and they feel threatened by each wave of campaigns against the Gang of Four and by the introduction in early 1980 of a new "rectification" program by Deng Xiaoping. The Peking show "trials" against the Gang of Four, and the subsequent local "trials," were designed to intimidate these cadres.

While their opponents persist in exaggerating the degree to which they are "leftists" or "radicals," they do find it both distasteful and personally disadvantageous to blatantly defame the memory of Mao Zedong. They wish to go slowly in de-Maoization, partly because it was Mao's purported statement, "With you in charge, I am at ease," that legitimized their principal figure, former Party Chairman Hua Guofeng, as the first ranking member of the Chinese hierarchy. This need to uphold some of Mao's sayings, especially those of an anti-Soviet and pro-egalitarian, pro-rural character, has made others call these cadres the "whatever faction," suggesting that they wish to uphold whatever Mao said. It is probably more accurate to think of these cadres as somewhat troubled over the suggestion that they opportunistically advanced during the now discredited Cultural Revolution, but not enough to abandon the benefits they gained. Hence they, more than most cadres, appreciate the demoralizing effects that would follow from the patricide of the father figure of the Chinese Revolution. (In all other developing countries, the destruction of the "founding father" has produced a sense of general guilt that is then relieved by widespread cynicism and avaricious corruption.) Since the bulk of these are rural cadres, they are most sensitive to the Chinese peasants' continuing respect for their deceased idol, who came from the peasantry, respected rural values, and favored the countryside over the city. Furthermore, the personal commitments of these rural cadres lie with the collectivized aspect of agriculture, since their status depends on the work-point system, and hence they have no enthusiasm for policies that will increase the private over the communal earning capacities of peasant households.

This category of cadres is also heavily represented in the PLA, a fact that helps to explain two apparently inconsistent developments: first, the remarkable patience of the PLA at a time when national defense has received the lowest priority of all the Four Modernizations, and the willingness of the PLA to continue to adhere to Mao's military doctrines; and second, Deng's decision in early 1980 to change the commanders of six Military Regional Areas and replace hundreds of commanders down to regimental level.

This first category of Cultural Revolution cadres has been the special target of Deng Xiaoping and the "rehabilitated" cadres who were purged during that turmoil. Their potential leadership was seriously weakened in early 1980 at the Fifth Plenum of the Eleventh Central Committee, when Ji Dengkui, a spokesman for the rural cadres, and Wang Dongxing, Mao's former bodyguard and the guardian of his words, were purged. They were further threatened as the Party prepared for its Twelfth Congress by Deng Xiaoping's dramatic success in arranging Hua's "resignation" first as premier (in favor of Zhao Ziyang) and then as chairman (in favor of Hu Yaobang). Although now a minority on both the Politburo and the Central Committee, they have the inexorable laws of life expectancy on their side, since they are not only the largest but also the youngest category of cadres. The very fact that they are under considerable attack from much older cadres has made them coalesce into the kind of friendship networks that provide the bases for effective political factions.

The second largest category of cadres is that of the "veteran cadres" who have survived all the twists and turns of the Party line, including, most importantly, the Cultural Revolution. These are generally master bureaucrats, skilled above all in the art of protecting themselves against criticism, regardless of any changes in political climate. In mutually helping each other avoid accountability and defuse responsibility, they tend to inhibit policy innovations. They also appreciate the dignity of authority and the danger that "pragmatism" and "experimentation," if carried too far, can become a license for opportunists. The effectiveness of these cadres in bureaucratically complicating the implementation of any decisions they feel will hurt them is probably unmatched by the bureaucrats of any other country. Understandably, they have been called by their opponents the "opposition faction." Their opponents have also sought to denigrate them by saying that their thinking is "ossified or semi-ossified," but generally they take a most un-Chinese attitude of believing that "sticks and stones may break my bones, but words will never hurt me."

Although the veteran cadres have no scruples about administering "pragmatic" policies, and they are generally not demonstrative believers in ideology, they are masterfully effective in ideological argumentation, and therefore they do not relish seeing one of their comparative advantages debased. Needless to say, they believe themselves to be as dedicated as anyone else to the interests of their country and its modernization, but they also understand that everyone must look after his own and his family's and his friends' well-being. They see Ye Jianying and Li Xiannian as their symbolic spokesmen, they appreciate the end of the emotional tensions of the Maoist era, and especially the Cultural Revolution, but they can hardly welcome Deng's increasingly frequent appeals for older leaders to step aside in favor of younger talent, who have not manifested admiration for their elders' skills. As Deng Xiaoping worked to consolidate his growing power in 1980, he succeeded in obtaining the "resignation" of Li as Vice-Premier while renaming him a Vice-Chairman of the Party. Any move at that time against Ye, however, would have been too provocative for the PLA, who remained, on balance, distrustful of Deng.

Finally, there are the more than 2.7 million "rehabilitated" cadres who were purged during the Cultural Revolution but whose cases have been reexamined and whose names have been cleared of "false charges." By early 1981 they constituted only about 7 percent of the Party membership, but they included, paradoxically, both the enthusiastically aggressive innovators and the most dissatisfied and complaining elements in Chinese politics. Understandably, the rehabilitated cadres have reacted in quite different ways to the trauma of their sufferings during the years of the Cultural Revolution. Some have come back with very clear ideas of what they believe was and is wrong with Chinese Communism; others are determined to vindicate their view that what they represented before the Cultural Revolution is what China needs today; still others are driven by a thirst for vengeance, while many are physically infirm and emotionally exhausted. In spite of these variations in reactions, the rehabilitated cadres have tended to separate into two distinct categories: the minority who have regained and even advanced in power, and the majority whose names have been cleared but who have not regained posts of influence.

The first of these cadres has at times been referred to as the "restoration faction" because under the guidance of their initial spokesmen, Chen Yun and Hu Yaobang, they have sought to rebuild the Party and government by following policies and practices used to restore China after the Great Leap. By late 1979 the infirm Chen Yun had given way to Zhao Ziyang, the most administratively vigorous of the rehabilitated leaders. There have been signs that elements within the "restoration faction" would welcome alliances with the veteran cadres in building a more authoritarian system, and they have attracted to themselves some cadres in the first two categories who agreed with them that the initial proclamations of the Four Modernizations were mostly fluff and rhetoric, and that realism demanded candid confessions that China was very badly off. No strong alliances, however, have been possible, because the general suspicion of those who did not suffer during the Cultural Revolution is still strong among the majority of the rehabilitated cadres.

The second category of rehabilitated cadres includes many who have fallen out of politics. Brought back from the countryside, they have found that others now occupy their desks and posts; even their homes have new occupants who feel no need to move. Some have gracefully gone into retirement, pleased that now that their names have been cleared, at least their children may have a better future. Those who remain politically active, however, have tended to become extremely critical, seeking vengeance against all who did not suffer as they did, and almost nihilistically finding fault with nearly everything in the past. The less vindictive of them believe that China must follow entirely new practices – hence they are at times called the "practice faction." The most constructive of them are the intellectuals concentrated in the Academy of the Social Sciences who have a strong faith that science and technology can provide a means to modernization, and who, with seeming disregard for political costs, suggest that anything should now be possible in China, even the questioning of socialism.

As easy solutions evade China, the majority of this category of rehabilitated cadres have become increasingly aggressive in calling for the purging of the surviving cadres. Being themselves unsure of exactly what kind of China would relieve their frustrations, they have concentrated on achieving "justice" by rehabilitating all who were ever purged, whether now alive or dead, and thereby explicitly attacking all those in the first two categories, and even some in their own category, as when they forced the rehabilitation of people purged before the Cultural Revolution when the Party was under Deng's control. Their success in rehabilitating Liu Shaoqi meant, of course, that all the unpurged cadres who had once joined in denouncing the "renegade capitalist-roader and scab" would be put on the defensive. After wavering briefly, Deng decided that the better strategy would be to employ intimidation against the bulk of the Party who had not suffered during the Cultural Revolution. Hence his decision to press, first, for the demotion of Hua Guofeng as Premier at the September 1980 meeting of the National People's Congress, and second, for the "trial" of the Gang of Four and six followers of Lin Biao – a spectacle calculated to "teach a lesson" to all Chinese that it was in the past, as it would remain in the future, exceedingly dangerous to oppose the power of Mr. Deng Xiaoping, regardless of whatever formal title he might have. By early 1980, many rehabilitated cadres were privately saying to American businessmen that Mao was "seven parts wrong and only three parts right," a reversal of the proportions of only a year earlier.

Deng Xiaoping was apparently caught between the increasingly conflicting demands of these two types of rehabilitated cadres, at times stressing the need for greater discipline and more pragmatic policies, and at other times accepting the need to seek "justice" by avenging those who suffered during the Cultural Revolution.

There is a degree of fluidity among these groups, and there is even greater flexibility in their positions on policy and ideological issues. Leaders, including middle-level cadres, articulate their positions by floating different "code words" and phrases in the media to test the degree of support they can hope to mobilize. At times, the initiatives of one group can be picked up by another group and turned against the initiators.

In sum, the pattern of factions in early 1981 was one in which elements from a minority of Party cadres have unrelentingly initiated actions that threaten the security of the majority. The fact that the rehabilitated cadres are also far older than those of the Cultural Revolution generation further ensures that in time the pendulum will swing so that those now threatened may again gain the upper hand. Or new combinations will emerge to give China a new pattern of factions. The one certain thing is that China's leadership, as it demoted Mao's immediate successor, has not eliminated the role of factions at all levels of the Party.

POLITICAL STABILITY AND FACTIONS

For the last two decades, the most disruptive convolutions in Chinese politics have been associated with factional strife. Even the Chinese themselves will admit today that their national progress has suffered greatly because of the nefarious workings of factions. Moreover, the Chinese proclaim that national disaster will follow if they do not avoid factionalism. Hence, quite understandably, most outsiders who would forecast Chinese developments tend to the view that constructive progress will be endangered by factional strife within the leadership. This is particularly true of those who have convinced themselves that all hope for China rests upon the political fortunes of Deng Xiaoping, as though he were China's Shah.

Our analysis will show that it is nearly inevitable that factionalism will continue in Chinese politics. What is less clear—and indeed goes beyond the reach of this present work—is whether factionalism will in fact threaten either the stability or progress of China. Were it not for the romantic desire to make China into more of a mystery than it is, it would be hard to imagine why anyone should be particularly concerned about the likelihood that one-quarter of mankind will practice the same ordinary forms of "politics" as the other three-quarters of mankind.

Yet the fact that the Chinese pretend to be horrified about the dangers of factionalism is in itself significant for forecasting China's stability. Unquestionably, the Chinese are inclined to decry manifestations of elite conflicts that would pass unnoticed in other societies, particularly those that value diversity and adversary relationships. As the society that bred Confucianism, the Chinese vividly imagine that any breach of consensus will let loose terrifying possibilities. And this hypersensitivity about national unity is shared by the other Confucian societies, Korea and Vietnam. Even the Japanese, who can no longer pretend that factions are not at the heart of their politics, are still easily paralyzed by the thought of having less than a homogeneous public opinion.

Therefore, granting that the Chinese are easily troubled by factional tensions, the question of the prospects for stability still remains. Some

Western observers are concerned about the possibility of a factional backlash if the Four Modernizations should fail. One can dismiss those who have suggested that if Deng should fall he would be replaced by the ideological heirs of the Gang of Four. This uninformed view simply projects onto China a vision of the American two-party system and supposes that the policy failures of one party will set the stage for a shift to the other. The Chinese play for much bloodier stakes, and therefore, before the Gang could return, there would have to be a truly violent conflict that would overshadow the question of whether or not the Four Modernizations had failed.

Indeed, even if the possibility is removed from the American context and placed in a historical Chinese one, it may still be unrealistic because it overstates the liabilities of policy failure in Chinese politics. It should be kept in mind that in the entire history of the PRC there has never been an officially acknowledged failure of any major policy departure while the initiators are in power; criticism surfaces only after the advocates of the policy have fallen from power. Moreover, since there is no source of institutionalized criticism of basic policies (as provided in other societies by the press or opposition politicians), there would be no formal method for establishing that the Four Modernizations had indeed failed.

A more realistic assessment is that developments in particular aspects of the Four Modernizations program will damage the fortunes of some leaders, while other developments will favor other leaders or factions. This may not be saying very much, however, since the Four Modernizations envelop essentially all aspects of Chinese national affairs, especially now that they must be supplemented by the "four fundamental principles": the mass line, the dictatorship of the proletariat, the leadership of the Communist Party, and Marxism–Leninism–Mao Zedong Thought. It is, in fact, hard to envisage any plausible development that would cause any element in the leadership to declare the abandonment of the Four Modernizations or the four principles, for to do so would be tantamount to openly abandoning Communism. (Given the Chinese style of political rhetoric, which we shall be analyzing shortly, it is safe to say that if the Chinese ever abandon Communism, they will do so while claiming that they are supporting it.)

The analysis of plausible developments that could affect China's stability by increasing factional tensions must be directed toward more specific and more concrete trends than the fate of the Four Modernizations. Failure to meet even specific target goals, or the need to "readjust" such goals, will probably not, in itself, have detrimental consequences. One of the findings of our Hong Kong interviews is that the Chinese are far more tolerant than Americans about public officials changing their tune and contradicting themselves: "Conditions change; therefore, of course, officials will have to change what they say." The Chinese, who agree that consistency is the hobgoblin of small minds, find it hard to comprehend why officials might be embarrassed today by statements made yesterday.

To arrive at more specific possibilities, configurative analysis should focus on elements within the elite, institutions and notable individuals, and ask how developments in these spheres might affect factional strife and the stability of Chinese politics. We can only briefly note what such analysis entails by summarizing the situation with respect to the most vulnerable spots in the Chinese leadership.

The Military. Possibly the most uncertain element in Chinese politics today is the PLA leadership, which, since the fall of the Gang of Four, has had to withdraw from its widespread and highly activist role in civilian administration. The PLA, which may be sharply divided, has not received a high priority in the allocation of resources under the Four Modernizations, but, of course, it has tremendous capabilities for disrupting the entire national system. Even before the Sino–Vietnam war made obvious the backwardness of Chinese arms, PLA planners must have recognized that the military's share of China's resources was completely inconsistent with Peking's propaganda pitch about the likelihood of war with the Soviet Union. The universal respect for Marshal Ye Jianying has no doubt kept in check well-known divisions of opinion about Deng's leadership. Also, the general recognition that any surfacing of division within the military would be quickly translated into factional strife among civilian cadres has restrained the leading officers from expressing their dissatisfactions. The situation remains delicate, especially since Deng Xiaoping has done nothing publicly to improve his standing with those elements in the PLA who refused to rally to his support after Zhou Enlai's death and whose inaction thereby ensured his second fall from power. Instead he has sought to command and intimidate by personally taking charge of the Military Affairs Commission. Furthermore, the problem is likely to be long-lasting and unamenable to symbolic solutions, since, aside from the aged Marshal Ye, there is no figure among the Chinese leadership who could rally the support of all elements of the PLA.

As we have already noted, the political cadres in the PLA have remained remarkably loyal to some of Mao's views and hence have not shown great displeasure at the low priority given to military modernization in the Four Modernizations. At the same time, however, their very loyalty, which has made them passive, also caused Deng in early 1980 to dismiss and reappoint commanders at all levels of the PLA. Deng's success in forcing the "resignation" of Politburo member General Chen

Xilian probably did not change the loyalties of the bulk of the PLA cadres who would like a modern and powerful China, but also a China consistent with some of the PLA's traditional values.

Frustrations within the PLA have grown since the Sino–Soviet border clashes of 1969 because even though Chinese political rhetoric has called for urgent preparation for war, Chinese defense expenditures declined *after* the opening to the United States in 1971. In 1968 the defense budget claimed 15.8 percent of China's GNP, but by 1975 it was only 11 percent. Then in the fall of 1980 the defense budget, which at last was beginning to rise, was cut by nearly 16 percent because of the "exceptional expenses of the Vietnam War." These tight limits on defense expenditures, when combined with the steady decline of the political role of the military since the death of Mao, may explain why in 1980 there were frequent references in the Chinese press to the "danger of armies with arms in their hands." Political control of the military has been facilitated by a conscious policy of giving senior officers generous perquisites, largely in the form of luxury housing, use of cars, special shops, and frequent visits to resorts.

Rural Cadres. A second potentially troublesome element is the rural cadres, who play the critical, but often thankless, role of managing China's agriculture. The morale of this key segment of the Party has often been depressed, and at present it cannot be good, because Chairman Hua's tactics in winning over the peasants to the modernization of agriculture have included a campaign against the rural cadres for "corruption" and "repressive harshness." Attacked for their attempts to obtain the few perquisites they have sought, and for being too demanding in forcing communes to meet their quotas, many cadres have become less activist; yet if agricultural production proves to be unsatisfactory, they are certain to be criticized anew. Their capacity for disruption is limited, however, because except for Hua they have no natural ally among the top leaders. Yet should Hua or some other Cultural Revolution cadre decide to champion aggressively the interests of the rural cadres, they might thereby mobilize a considerable factional element. This would be a major destabilizing development because the great potential division in Chinese Communism is that between interior and coast, rural and urban, agriculture and industry.

Indeed, the possibility of this natural division becoming politically sharper should not be minimized. During the first period of Hua's chairmanship and after the rehabilitation of Deng, there was a tacit understanding that Hua should be more associated with agriculture and Deng with industry and science technology. During this initial period, Hua openly supported the rural cadres by stressing the ideal of "learning from Dazhai." Subsequently he was compelled, no doubt by the economic planners at the Center, to shift away from administrative solutions and seek greater agricultural production through the provision of more direct economic incentives for the peasants. By mid-1979, the urban press was openly scornful of the idea of learning from Dazhai. In the meantime, Hua's colleague Ji Dengkui took up the cause of the rural cadres by trying to resist the attempts of Deng and Zhao Ziyang to raise agricultural production and expand market incentives. As we have seen, such a policy directly works against the self-interest of rural cadres whose income and power are tied entirely to collective enterprises.

Although Ji was forced to "resign" at the Fifth Plenum in February 1980, the rural cadres still remain a force within the Party – indeed, its largest civilian component – and it is purely a question of time until we learn either who will succeed in mobilizing them, and for what purpose, or whether they will remain a latent, sullen force, capable of sabotaging policies favoring the private initiative of peasants.

The Educational Establishment. At present the science and technology elites are in a very comfortable position, for they are being honored and not pilloried, but the situation in Chinese education is far from satisfactory. Even at the university level, which is now receiving the greatest attention, there is widespread anxiety over what can be done to make up for the losses of the last two decades. Power and position are now held by a small and aged group of men trained in the West before the 1950s. The younger, and significantly larger, Soviet-trained generation has been pushed to the background, and the training of new teachers is going exceedingly slowly. Thus the potential for disruption is great.

Another potential source of friction within the educational elite involves the large numbers of scholars who suffered during the Cultural Revolution and are now being sent abroad to catch up with world trends in their fields. Many of them are being rewarded for their years of suffering, but many are possibly too old to have creative careers. In time, questions may be asked about how the selection of such privileged people took place, whether they have helped modernization as much as expected, and whether those who did not get sent abroad were unfairly treated. Attention may be attracted to this issue because so many sons of the highest officials have been sent to America for schooling.

Far more serious, however, is the situation in education at the primary- and secondary-school level, where there is great uncertainty about what the curriculum should be. Should the focus be on college preparation when only 3 to 5 percent of the students have any hope of going on to college? What is to happen to all the rest of the young people? Can the schools really be expected to continue trying to support even a curtailed program of sending graduates "down to the country-side?" Middle-school teachers are finding that educational spokesmen at the university level have no sympathy for their problems. The frustrations that exist at all levels of the educational system could easily be transformed into factional alignments that might readily find allies in other sectors of society and thereby seriously destabilize the system.

Propaganda Cadres. Until recently, propaganda and cultural affairs attracted most of the brightest talent in the Party, but now sharp divisions are beginning to form among these concentrations of highly intelligent people. Those responsible for the dissemination of ideological doctrine are confused and demoralized because of the turmoil they have had to go through since the start of the Cultural Revolution. Offices in such places as the Foreign Language Press are filled with people who were persecutors or victims, or both persecutors and victims, during the violence of the Cultural Revolution, and therefore there is little trust, considerable wondering about how scores are to be settled, and a constant interjection of new tensions as purged colleagues are rehabilitated only to find their posts have been filled. The fact that other elements involved in propaganda work and in dealing with the performing arts are now in a state of exuberance at their new freedom only makes more depressing the situation of the once-superior cadres responsible for doctrine. The division here is much the same as that in education, where the few in the most visible, the most prestigious, and the most international aspects of the enterprise are rejoicing, while the great bulk of those involved have intractable daily problems.

Economic Planners. Chinese economic planners welcomed the thrust of the Four Modernizations decreed by their political masters, but as they now seek to staff the implementation of the programs, divisive problems are arising. The Chinese press reveals "debates" between those who would rely upon the market to help make allocations and those who would tighten up the command character of the economy. It would be inappropriate in this overview even to outline the main problems of the Chinese economy. Suffice it to say that while foreigners may believe that China is on the verge of rapid modernization, educated Chinese realize that their country has been trying to modernize ever since the 1911 Revolution and that the problems of modernization have always been profoundly divisive. Now that the program of the Four Modernizations has been taken over from Deng and Hua by the professional economic managers and technical questions and reality itself are replacing the enunciation of wishful goals, the potential for disagreement is obviously greater.

Personal Relations at the Top. Finally, among the potentially most destabilizing sources of intensified factional stress are the relations among the half-dozen men at the pinnacle of the Chinese power hierarchy, the Standing Committee of the Politburo. These are the men who have attracted the most powerful network of followers, as the members of the Central Committee and Provincial Committees all seek to establish their own access to them. Yet there is abundant evidence that until Deng was able in February 1980 to reconstitute the Committee, these six leaders did not have easy relations with each other. Two had been purged and rehabilitated; two others rose rapidly during the time the first two were having troubles, and they undeniably benefited in various ways from the Gang of Four before turning on them; and two have stood aside from the turmoil of the late 1960s and held to the ideals of the loyal but essentially non-political technocratic specialist. The balance among them was clearly delicate, and anything that would alter the position of any pair, including sudden death—which was likely among septuagenarians and octogenarians—would trigger anxieties among their respective networks of cadres. These networks had the potential of reaching nearly every Party member, since the three categories of cadres—the veterans, those who rose during the Cultural Revolution, and those now being rehabilitated—include just about everybody. This delicate situation was slightly stabilized in Deng's favor at the Fifth Plenum of the Eleventh Central Committee, as we shall see.

During the first two years after the death of Mao, the topmost leaders worked for stability by checking their own ambitions and trying to reassure their followers. Hua Guofeng declared humbly that he did not want to be known as "the wise Chairman Hua," since it was apparent that substantial elements in the Party would not spontaneously endorse that characterization. And Deng Xiaoping modestly declared in 1979 that he had no ambitions to rank higher than third in the hierarchy after it became clear that he lacked support in the Politburo for a higher designation. At the same time, however, each of the top leaders sought to protect his followers and promote loyal subordinates.

The potential for disruption, however, persisted as the rehabilitated cadres became more aggressive. The initial attacks on the followers of the Gang of Four were intense but not unduly divisive because veteran cadres and many of those who had benefited from the Cultural Revolution could ally to attack those who were blatantly identified as "Maoists." There were signs in 1981, however, that rehabilitated cadres, possibly seeking revenge, tried to cut further into the ranks of those who rose during the 1960s and early 1970s. The lack of resolution of these problems can be seen from the fact that in spite of the decision of the Third Plenum of the Eleventh Central Committee to terminate the campaigns against Lin Biao and the Gang of Four, there was in fact another round of attacks upon those who failed to recognize that "left" deviation is as dangerous as "right" deviation and those unable to "seek truth from facts," who therefore "take wind as rain and minor aspects as major ones" – all code words used to attack cadres who rose during the Cultural Revolution. Their attack has been countered by the code words of those who would like to normalize relations; this group speaks of the "erroneous tendencies" in the Party of "whipping up great gusts of wind" and of "severing at one blow" by stirring up "all-out movements" and "investigations at all levels."

By the time the Gang of Four were put on trial in December 1980, it appeared that Deng was well on the way to eliminating the influences, especially at the top, of all potential opponents. It was reported that at the November Politburo meeting, at which the decision for the trials was made, Hua Guofeng was compelled to engage in self-criticism, which culminated in his asking to be allowed to "resign" as Chairman. The formal act of giving up the title was delayed through the winter and spring of 1981 because of the postponement of the Sixth Plenum of the Eleventh Central Committee, apparently because Marshall Ye Jianying began to oppose Deng for moving too far from the path that Mao had set for the Party. Ye's authority was enough to check the de-Maoization process and thereby protect somewhat Hua and the Cultural Revolution cadres.

Judging from these observations, it seems likely that the cadres will continue to jockey among themselves, producing cycles of immobilism followed by new outbursts of activity as the victors seek to consolidate their successes.

Looking to the more distant future, it seems likely that as institutionalization increases in China, particularly in terms of more stable administrative ministries and departments, factions will also become more institutionalized. Some of our Hong Kong respondents reported in interviews that the sons and daughters of cadres often tended to take on the factional orientations of their parents. To the extent that this is the case in China, a pattern of political socialization may be emerging that would not be too different from that of other societies in which children tend to identify with their parents' political party. If factionalism could thus become more routinized, it might also cause less anxiety among Chinese and thus be less of a source of instability.

FACTIONS AND FOREIGN AFFAIRS

It is appropriate to end this overview with a few observations about how factions might affect China's foreign policy.

The conventional wisdom about China holds that Peking's foreign policies are closely related to its domestic policies. Therefore, if factions are important for China's domestic politics, they should also have a significant impact upon its foreign policy. But here again there are dangers in overstating the relationship.

At the time of this writing, in mid-1981, no foreign policy issues were central in factional tensions. The consensus about the Four Modernizations seems to apply to foreign policy as well. This does not mean, however, that there is equal enthusiasm in all quarters for the opening to the West; and while a small sector of the urban population may be excited over the introduction of foreign goods, the grip of traditional Chinese xenophobia is still great. (Furthermore, even among those who know the outside world, there are significant divisions that could have profound effects on careers and hence could contribute to factional tensions—for example, older men trained in the West are at present taking over high-status positions from younger, Soviet-trained specialists.) Therefore, it is still possible that factional realignments could alter China's current search for limited but useful contacts with the more industrialized world.

Officials in Washington have taken a different view of the importance of factionalism for China's foreign policy. Since the beginning of the struggle between Deng Xiaoping and Hua Guofeng they have insisted that the former's fortunes are key to improved Sino-American relations and that comfortably harmonious relations will come only when Deng is without factional opposition. The facts, however, do not support such a judgment. On the contrary, some of the crucial advances in mutual understanding between Washington and Peking have coincided with high points in factional tensions, and, more significantly, complications have come on the heels of Deng's domestic triumphs. The official Washington rebuttal that other factors explain such difficulties fails to answer the point because it only confirms the proposition that factional considerations are of secondary importance in foreign policy matters. (No easy explanations exist for Washington's boundless enthusiasm for Deng Xiaoping, which was expressed again by ex-President Jimmy Carter when he met Deng in Peking in August 1981 and exclaimed, "You're a hero in my country. If you had been my running mate, we would have won the election." Walter Mondale's reactions, although unreported, can be imagined.)

Given the Chinese consensus that Western ties would facilitate modernization, the Chinese foreign policy issue that may be more sensitive to factional politics, and hence more speculative, is Peking's relations with Moscow. There is clearly more potential for dissension on this issue than on the policy of seeking technology from the West. To date, all factions in Chinese politics are committed in varying degree to Mao's vision of an evil "revisionist" Soviet Union, but different elements in Chinese society might welcome a relaxation of tensions with the Soviet Union and, furthermore, might view such a development as a way of advancing themselves against others in Chinese domestic politics. This is particularly true now that the Chinese, who have never been sticklers for matching rhetoric with reality, have finally concluded that in light of their Four Modernizations, it is absurd to refer to the Soviets as "revisionists."

Whatever eventually transpires in Sino–Soviet negotiations, Chinese factional politics will be an ingredient. If Deng wishes to push ahead, his colleagues will probably not vigorously oppose him; rather they will insist – as they did when he advocated the "pedagogical war" against Vietnam – that he be personally identified with the move and hence shoulder all the risks. Specific issues in Sino–Soviet relations are not likely to be major issues in factional confrontations. At most, the factions may divide according to what they feel China's basic posture should be toward the rest of the world. So far, the factions have not elevated any particular foreign policy issue to the symbolic plane; on the contrary, since China now tends to be more reactive to the initiatives of others, foreign policy is likely to provide a basis more for consensus than for division. Thus, just as in 1971–1972, when Zhou Enlai sought to use the opening to Washington as a way of containing the struggles between "moderates" and "radicals," the Peking leadership in 1980 used the Soviet intervention in Afghanistan and the visit of Secretary of Defense Harold Brown as domestic consensus-building events.

Factional politics appear to have even less place in relations with other countries. It is true that different Chinese leaders have taken on assignments to treat with specific foreign leaders, but this division of labor does not seem to have any particular significance for those in their networks of followers. Instead, those engaged in calculating relative power appear to attach no significance to who among the leaders is spending how much time meeting with foreign delegations – all of the leaders seem to be uncommonly generous with their time when it comes to such symbolic occasions. The fact that foreign visitors have their prestige rankings for meetings with the different leaders has not made any apparent impression on the Chinese involved; on this score they find it easy to practice "collective leadership."

In sum, therefore, factional politics do not appear likely to be decisive in any particular foreign policy, and hence the rise and fall of individual leaders will not be decisive for any specific bilateral relationship. On the other hand, the flow of factional politics could influence policy orientations toward the outside world. Thus, just as factional politics are more responsive to ideological positions than to specific domestic policies, so in foreign relations factional alignments will influence China's general posture, which in turn may alter particular relationships.

Finally, we must make one general observation about the relationship between changes in the distribution of power and changing impressions about the condition of any polity. Although it goes without saying that dramatic alterations in the structure of power usually produce revolutionary changes in the image a polity projects, what is more impressive is the surprising fact that very modest changes in the power distribution in a political system can produce an entirely different public atmosphere. The variation of a few percentage points in an electorate can, for example, be used to justify the identification of a totally new era in a nation's history. The factional politics that followed the death of Mao produced both a major realignment of power and new departures in China's policy priorities. From now on, however, far more modest shifts in factional power will no doubt create the impression of still further significant changes. The odds thus favor impressions of change, even when little has happened. Hence, the great importance of understanding the dynamics of factional tensions in Chinese politics.

Chapter 2

Consensus, Faction, and Policy

The death of Mao on September 9, 1976, followed by the elevation of the new Chairman, Hua Guofeng, and the incarceration of the
Gang of Four in October, produced a political earthquake in China
severe enough to leave revealing cracks in the wall that had so effectively obscured the workings of the Chinese political process. The brief
glimpses of non-hortatory Chinese politics have since been quickly
obscured by clouds of accusations so extreme as to tax the credulity of all
except whatever remaining true believers China still has. The events of
1976 have also compelled analysts to rethink the essential characteristics of Chinese politics.

While Mao's personality made the inept management of his succession
predictable, the precise kind of politics that would erupt after his death
was less predictable.[1] Clearly we had entered another of those periodic

---

1. Central to Mao's personality was the theme of abandonment: He experienced a form
of abandonment early in his life; he constantly abandoned policy commitments; he assumed
that others would readily abandon their revolutionary faith; and, of course, above all he
abandoned his closest colleagues. Finally, he abandoned *both* the succession arrangements
that Zhou Enlai made before his death and his wife's plans, thereby making it certain that
there would not be continuity after his death. This characteristic of Mao's personality is
analyzed in Lucian W. Pye, *Mao Tse-tung: The Man in the Leader*, Basic Books, New York,
1976.

phases in Chinese Communist political history when it becomes necessary to question the basic workings of the Chinese political system. Analyses of Chinese Communism have always been constructed upon grand generalizations supported by a few tenuous facts. Consequently, any revelations of new evidence instantly send analysts scurrying either for new lofty formulations or ingenious reinterpretations that would preserve the old formulations. The problem, of course, has always been what to make of new facts: Can they be downplayed to preserve our comfortable old perspectives on Chinese politics or should the new be played up so that we can once again thrill at the prospect of a newborn China?

An autumn of revelations in the months immediately following Mao's death left China-watchers from Hong Kong to Washington puzzled as to what to believe about Chinese politics. Reports of attempts to arm the militia in Shanghai and to assassinate the new leader Hua Guofeng in Peking and then the startling news of the arrests of Mrs. Mao and others awakened the world to an underside of Chinese politics that few suspected existed. But in a remarkably short time the outside world absorbed Peking's accounts of events to the point of passively accepting their plausibility. During the Cultural Revolution in the mid-1960s, Red Guard wall posters and publications had also provided a spate of revelations about intra-elite politics in China, which first seemed astounding but which also gradually became accepted as plausible. Similarly, China-watchers were first dumbfounded by the lurid charges that Lin Biao and his co-conspirators three times attempted to assassinate Chairman Mao, but in time these too became a part of the repeated, if not believed, lore. Then the crescendo of attacks on Widow Mao and her three fellow "poisonous weeds" produced a mass of new "facts" that were initially accepted at face value only by awestruck admirers of China; yet the cumulative effect of waves of half-believed propaganda caused even the staunchest professionals to revise their perception of Chinese politics. The effectiveness of mere repetition in changing the implausible into the conventionally acceptable can be seen in the gradual dropping of the label "radicals" and the use of the Chinese expression, the "Gang of Four," by Western analysts—"ultra-rightists" would have been too much.[2]

Less than two years later, in mid-1978, the Chinese leaders again astonished the world by vigorously pushing their grand program of the Four Modernizations, and with no forewarnings hinted that China would be sending tens of thousands of students abroad, forgetting autarky and

2. Apparently even the Chinese found it impossible to believe that the Gang of Four were in fact "ultra-rightists," and therefore in December 1978, the Party took another tack: It declared that they had in fact been "leftists" and ordered the comrades to stop believing that safety lay in always avoiding the right and being on the left.

buying new technologies on credit terms, inspiring labor productivity by material incentives rather than rhetoric, and generally putting aside revolutionary idealism in favor of compound interest.

It was, of course, eminently reasonable that with the passing of Mao, the crushing of the "radicals," and the awkward confrontation between the new Chairman, Hua Guofeng, and champions of the frustrated heir apparent to Zhou Enlai, Deng Xiaoping, analysts of the China scene should believe that a new era had arrived in Chinese politics and all the older interpretations should be forgotten. If the Chinese were ready to present a new face to the world, should the world not respond by forgetting China's preceding follies and pretend that Maoism never existed? Before we jump too quickly to this plausible conclusion, let us pause for a moment to survey the fate of past interpretations of Chinese elite politics, keeping in mind that even as the Chinese are professing to be new converts to rationality in public policies, there is something inherently illogical in their professed reason for conversion: They claim to be mightily concerned over the imminent prospect of war, which they say is certain to erupt because of the aggressive designs of the Soviet Union; yet behind their words they have done pathetically little to improve their own war-making potential.[3] Do they really believe that war is likely? Or are they only trying to entice American support by encouraging the illusion that there is a "China card" to be played? In short, is the current Chinese turn toward more "pragmatic" policies a real change in the nature of Chinese politics or is it only the latest attempt in a long line of Chinese efforts to present to outsiders a make-believe version of their still deeply masked political life?

A BRIEF HISTORY OF MODELS OF THE CHINESE POLITICAL SYSTEM

Students of Chinese Communism will debate the exact number of phases in the history of the movement and the number of consensus views analysts have held about the essential character of Chinese Communist politics. Most, however, would agree that the list should include at least the following models and their variations. Some of these models seek to encompass the entire Chinese political system, while others focus on the decisionmaking process, differences in scope that reflect shifts in the attention of Western analysts in response to changes in China.

3. The relationship between China's protestations about the imminence of world war and their sluggish progress in military modernization is analyzed in Lucian W. Pye, "Dilemma for America in China's Military Modernization," *International Security*, Vol. 3, No. 4, Spring 1979, pp. 3–17.

The first model developed by Western analysts was the Yunnan Round Table model, which held that the Chinese leadership was bonded together by a dedicated consensus – its values were homogeneous, its relations were stable, and it was a band of comrades free of tensions. All those surrounding Mao showed a spirit of camaraderie, and therefore responsibility was diffused and decisionmaking spontaneous.[4] The entire movement in turn reflected this spirit to such a degree that agreement and basic consensus permeated the Party. This model reflected wartime conditions during which the Chinese tradition of blending political and military leadership began. Although they appeared to be emulating Soviet practices by paralleling their military chains of command with a hierarchy of political commissars, the Chinese military commanders were, in fact, from the beginning more skilled in political matters than their Russian counterparts.

The second model, a more sophisticated variant of the first, was most articulately advanced in the work of Franz Schurmann.[5] This model saw the Chinese system as a near-perfect blending of ideology and organization. Indeed, in Schurmann's view, the unity of theory and action, which was Lenin's dream, had become a reality in the Chinese system. Policy "line" and organization "discipline" provided functionally specific bureaucracies of astounding efficiency. The bonds of camaraderie were replaced by those of bureaucracy, best understood, according to Schurmann, by the appealing theories of structural–functionalism.[6]

During this second phase of Chinese Communism, the PLA was intimately involved in civil administration. Indeed, the bureaucratic nature of the system stemmed in part precisely from this critical administrative role of the PLA.

---

4. The politics of the Yunnan period remain strangely obscure in the history of Chinese Communism, largely because all "eyewitness" accounts are so divergent as to suggest that observers could not have been seeing the same thing. None of the reports by members of the American "Dixie Mission" reveals any awareness that the CCP was at the time engaged in an intensive "rectification" campaign – the *Cheng-feng* movement – which was to "Bolshevize" the Party, or that Mao Zedong was proclaiming stern doctrines about literature, the arts, and liberal sentiments. The mood within the Party is best revealed by the translations in Boyd Compton, *Mao's China, Party Reform Documents, 1942–44*, University of Washington Press, Seattle, 1952.

5. Especially in his *Ideology and Organization in Communist China*, University of California Press, Berkeley, 1966.

6. One of the ironies in the politicization of American sociology during the turmoil of the late 1960s is that "structural–functionalism" and its principal theoretician, Talcott Parsons, were vilified as "reactionary," yet one of the most skillful empirical utilizations of the approach was made by Franz Schurmann, who belonged solidly with the radicalized New Left – a fact that suggests that structural–functionalism lacks any inherent ideological bias. (See Stanislav Andreski, *Social Sciences as Sorcery*, Deutsch, London, 1972.)

Then, of course, came the Cultural Revolution and a radically new variety of views about the dynamics of Chinese politics. For a brief time, analysts elaborated a pure Maoist – Revolutionary model in which organization was suddenly "out" and participation was "in." This picture of revolutionary China had considerable life in ideological circles, but it was always slightly suspect in the eyes of professional analysts of the China scene.[7] Stripped of its more romantic trappings, the new version of Chinese politics highlighted certain Mao Zedong predilections, such as "spiritual incentives" being more honorable than "material ones," "rural simplicity" being better than "urban sophistication," "self-sufficiency and self-reliance" being better than "dependency upon foreign technologies," and so on.

The Cultural Revolution and the awareness that the succession struggle had become a dominant factor in Chinese politics produced a fourth, or "generational," model. Who was to follow after the Long March generation? How may generations had there been in the CCP, and how different were their outlooks? The generational model contained the new presumption that change was likely in China and that tensions undoubtedly existed among the leaders.[8]

Thus, by the end of the Cultural Revolution, most analysts had forgotten their earlier consensus models and had adopted various forms of conflict models. Some favored a model that was consistent with the Chinese political self-characterization, which depicted the leadership as divided between "two lines." A variation on this model pictured Chinese politics as essentially "Mao against the others." Armed with these newer models, analysts discovered that they could make more sense of previously unintelligible developments in the pre-Cultural Revolution period.[9]

---

7. For elaborations of the Maoist revolutionary model, see Benjamin Schwartz, "Modernization and the Maoist Vision," in Roderick MacFarquhar (ed.), *China Under Mao*, M.I.T. Press, Cambridge, Mass., 1966; Maurice Meisner, *Mao's China: A History of the People's Republic*, The Free Press, New York, 1977.

8. The earliest analysis of Chinese Communist politics based on the assumptions that generational change would produce systems change was Walt. W. Rostow, *The Prospects of Communist China*, Wiley, New York, 1954; but Doak Barnett has most consistently upheld the view that the passing of the Long March generation will change China. Compare his *China After Mao Tse-tung*, Princeton University Press, Princeton, 1976, and his *Uncertain Passage*, Brookings Institution, Washington, D.C., 1974.

9. Richard Solomon, "Mao's Efforts to Reintegrate the Chinese Polity: Problems of Conflict and Authority in Chinese Social Processes," in A. Doak Barnett (ed.), *Chinese Communist Politics in Action*, University of Washington Press, Seattle, 1968; Philip Bridgham, "Mao's Cultural Revolution: Origin and Development," *China Quarterly*, Vol. 29, January 1967; Edward E. Rice, *Mao's Way*, University of California Press, Berkeley, 1972; Robert A. Scalapino, "The Cultural Revolution and Chinese Foreign Policy," *Current Scene*, Vol. 1, No. 13, August 1, 1968.

These variations of the conflict model were gradually subsumed under various forms of the increasingly popular "factional model." Significantly, much of the impetus for this model came from the study of the Chinese military, and more particularly from William Whitson's suggestion that the Chinese military high command was not a homogeneous group but was divided according to field armies and hence was factionalized.[10] Andrew Nathan probably went the furthest in formalizing the factional model of Chinese Communist politics,[11] to which Tang Tsou responded by cautioning that instead of what he deemed a somewhat pejorative term, "faction," China scholars would be better advised to speak of "informal groups."[12]

Except for a few holdouts espousing the view that the Chinese are really united on all but tactical differences about the best way to modernize, most observers in the immediate post-Mao months recognized the presence of divisions within the Chinese leadership. Uncertainty was evident in judgments about the precise lines of division, the solidity of the combinations and alliances, and the significance of tensions for the future of the Chinese system. In general, however, China specialists in and out of government debated the merits of speaking in terms of "factions," "groupings," "interest clusters," "informal combinations that change according to issues," and other expressions of coalition and conflict. Jurgen Domes, for example, has argued against the indiscriminate application of the term "faction" and has suggested a two-stage approach, in which politics is first dominated by shifting "opinion" and "functional-opinion" groups but there is a general "consensus on procedures," then the consensus on procedures breaks down and only then does a true politics of "factions" prevail.[13]

During the prolonged succession struggle, the Western press adopted

10. William Whitson, *The Chinese High Command*, Praeger, New York, 1973.

11. Andrew J. Nathan, "A Factionalism Model of CCP Politics," *China Quarterly*, No. 53, January/March 1973, pp. 34–66. Nathan's is an elegantly universalistic model that could be used to explain the logic of factional behavior in any setting, time, or culture with no particular reference to Chinese behavior. Nathan has brilliantly analyzed the distinctive Chinese approach to factions in his classic study of the Republican period, *Peking Politics*, University of California Press, Berkeley, 1976.

12. Tang Tsou, "Prolegomenon to the Study of Informal Groups in CCP Politics", *China Quarterly*, No. 65, January 1976, pp. 98–114. Chinese distaste for the word "factions" seems to be limited to discussions of political systems that the Chinese would glorify and does not apply to systems they look down upon. For example, none of the Chinese interviewed in Hong Kong for this study showed the slightest squeamishness about referring to factions in the China they had chosen to leave. Also, I have personally been asked by high Chinese officials which "faction" in which "party" I belonged to, suggesting that it is quite all right to speak about factions in American politics.

13. Jurgen Domes, *The Internal Politics of China, 1949–1972*, C. Hurst & Co., London, 1973, p. 236.

a straightforward version of the factional model and wrote about clashes between "moderates" or "pragmatists" and "radicals" or "ideologues." Sophisticated analysts dismissed this crude division as too simplistic and insensitive to the possibilities for subtle distinctions, but in order to carry on reasonably intelligent discussions they too, needless to say, have had to fall back upon precisely such shorthand terms.

At the same time, numerous scholars, particularly in the pages of the *China Quarterly,* demonstrated the utility of versions of factional models in the immediate post-Mao period.[14] As Western scholars learned more about the dynamics of the Cultural Revolution, especially as seen in the light of the struggle between "moderates" and "radicals" for Mao's authority, the factional model came increasingly into vogue. The result was an increase in the richness of detail,[15] sophistication, and complexity of the theoretical model,[16] and a readiness to examine the play of factions at the local as well as at the national level.[17]

In seeking to describe the orientation of the different factions in the succession struggle at the end of the Mao era, scholars have generally recognized that the Chinese elite was more divided by issues about the proper pacing and the right mix of foreign and traditional elements in China's modernization than it was over clear-cut ideological or even policy issues.[18] A few, most notably Jurgen Domes, have favored identi-

14. Some of the most impressive examples are Jurgen Domes, "The 'Gang of Four' – and Hua Kuo-feng: Analysis of Political Events in 1975–6," *China Quarterly,* No. 71, September 1977, pp. 473–497; Kenneth Lieberthal, "The Foreign Policy Debate in Peking as Seen through Allegorical Articles," *China Quarterly,* No. 71, September 1977, pp. 528–554; Edward E. Rice, "The Second Rise and Fall of Teng Hsiao-p'ing," *China Quarterly,* No. 67, September 1976, pp. 494–500; William Parrish, "Factions in Chinese Military Politics," *China Quarterly,* No. 56, October 1973, pp. 667–679.

15. Probably the most detailed analyses of the inner struggles from the beginning of the Cultural Revolution to Mao's death are the extraordinary work of Byung-joon Ahn, *Chinese Politics and the Cultural Revolution,* University of Washington Press, Seattle, 1976; and Hong Yung Lee, *The Politics of the Cultural Revolution,* University of California Press, Berkeley, 1978.

16. The popularity of complex models is possibly best exemplified by Kuang-sheng Liao, "Linkage Politics in China: International Mobilization and Articulated External Hostility in the Cultural Revolution," *World Politics,* Vol. 28, No. 4, July 1976, pp. 590–610.

17. A graphic account of factional strife among Red Guards was presented by Ken Ling in *The Revenge of Heaven: Journal of a Young Chinese,* G. P. Putnam's Sons, New York, 1972. Evidence of how factions operate in small groups, collected through interviews, was reported by Martin King Whyte, *Small Groups and Political Rituals in China,* University of California Press, Berkeley, 1974, and in studies of particular cities, such as Lynn T. White, III, *Careers in Shanghai,* University of California Press, Berkeley, 1978.

18. See, for example, Andrew Nathan, "Policy Oscillations in the People's Republic of China: A Critique," *China Quarterly,* Vol. 68, December 1976, pp. 721–725; and Kenneth Lieberthal, "The Politics of Modernization in the PRC," *Problems of Communism,* Vol. 27, No. 3, May–June 1978, pp. 11–14.

fying factions according to institutional and career associations.[19] Most, however, have tended to stress differences in predilections about modernization. Kenneth Lieberthal, for example, found it useful to distinguish among "Westernizers" who would aggressively adopt foreign technologies, "Nativists" who wish to protect the cultural and ideological uniqueness of China, and "Eclectics" who would learn from the West but preserve the distinctive qualities of China.[20] Michel Oksenberg developed a more refined typology that included such factions as "radical conservatives," "militant fundamentalists," and "eclectic modernizers."[21]

As the succession struggle became more conspicuous in Mao's last years, the factional model became the standard interpretation of increasingly broader aspects of Chinese public life. Allen S. Whiting found it valuable for understanding Chinese foreign policy.[22] Others applied the model to all manner of domestic developments.[23]

THE POST-MAO SCENE: "PRAGMATIC" BUT "MURKY"

Since the smashing of the Gang of Four in the fall of 1976 and

19. Domes, for example, identified for the period from August 1973 to the purge of the Gang of Four in October 1976 seven major factions in the Chinese power struggle: (1) veteran civilian cadres who remained in office during the Cultural Revolution; (2) rehabilitated cadres who were ousted during the Cultural Revolution and then reinstated along with Deng Xiaoping; (3) the central military machine aligned with Marshal Ye Jianying; (4) regional military leaders led by Chen Xilian; (5) the Cultural Revolution "left" led by Mao's wife, Jiang Qing, (6) the mass organization left represented by the "promoted cadres" of the late 1960s (those who, in Deng's words in 1975, "rose as if by helicopter"); (7) the secret police left led by Hua Guofeng. Domes, "The 'Gang of Four' and Hua Kuo-feng: Analysis of Political Events in 1975-76," *China Quarterly,* Vol. 71, September 1977, pp. 447–478.

20. Kenneth Lieberthal, "The Internal Political Scene," *Problems of Communism,* Vol. 24, No. 3, May–June 1975, p. 7; and his "Modernization and Succession in China," Vol. 2, No. 1, Spring 1979, pp. 53–54. See also, Ting Wang, "Trends in China: Leadership Realignments," *Problems of Communism,* Vol. 26, No. 4, July–August 1977, p. 10.

21. Michel Oksenberg and Steven Goldstein, "The Chinese Political Spectrum," *Problems of Communism,* Vol. 23, No. 2, March–April 1974, p. 2–9.

22. Allen S. Whiting, *Chinese Domestic Politics and Foreign Policy in the 1970s,* Center for Chinese Studies, University of Michigan, Ann Arbor, 1979.

23. See, for example, Monte Ray Bullard, "People's Republic of China Elite Studies: A Review of the Literature," *Asian Survey,* Vol. 19, No. 8, August 1979, pp. 789–800; Galen Fox, "Campaigning for Power in China," *Contemporary China,* Vol. 3, No. 1, Spring 1979; Thomas Fengar (ed.), *China's Quest for Independence: Policy Evolution in the 1970s,* Westview Press, Boulder, Colo., 1980; Harry Harding, Jr., "China After Mao," *Problems of Communism,* Vol. 20, No. 2, March–April 1977; Parris H. Chang, *Power and Policy in China,* 2nd ed., Pennsylvania State University Press, University Park, 1978; and most issues of *Issues and Studies.*

the second resurrection of Deng Xiaoping in the summer of 1977, the Chinese media have projected a contradictory picture of Chinese politics that has confused Western analysts and caused many to say that the post-Mao era remains "murky." On the other hand, the media have earnestly proclaimed that the nation was united in single-minded pursuit of the Four Modernizations, which was taken by many China-watchers to mean that after years of turmoil, Peking was at last about to find the way to the haven of "pragmatism"; that is, solid Chinese good sense was about to rout all the "romantic revolutionary ideologues," and old cadres dedicated to order, progress, and economic growth would finally take full command of China's destiny.

At the same time, the Chinese in unrelieved shrill tones have continued to describe the urgency of keeping up factional struggles throughout the land against not only the remnant followers of the Gang, but also the apparently still lingering believers in the long-disgraced Lin Biao. The lurid, and at times almost hysterical, exposes of the awful things that took place in nearly every organization in China during the heyday of the Gang of Four make it clear that Zhou Enlai and Deng Xiaoping must have had great difficulties in capping the wells of Cultural Revolutionary fervor. Moreover, since the arrest of the Gang of Four, people everywhere in China have been learning amazing facts about not only the "vile Gang of Four" but also their "devious and sneaky henchmen" and their "sinister lieutenants" who, in "concocting wildly anti-Party articles," were "whipping up evil winds" and spreading "poisonous weeds" of "ultra-rightist thought" as they "rabidly opposed the great leader Chairman Mao" and "launched vengeful counterattacks against the esteemed and beloved Premier Zhou." Explaining to the Chinese people that Jiang Qing and her circle were not radicals but ultra-rightists and that for more than a decade the nation's official propaganda organs were elaborating not Marxism–Leninism but a "rampancy of metaphysics" was clearly not easy.

Visitors to China, most of whom are impatient to learn what the new "pragmatic" policies and programs will be, have had to sit through prolonged denunciations of the sins of the Gang of Four and candid confessions that "the last ten years were lost" because of the irrationalities of the "radicals" who had become "ultra-rightists." Officials patiently explain that nearly all the qualities once associated with the Chinese model of development – stress on equality rather than hierarchical authority, rural leveling rather than urban specialization, autarky rather than dependence upon trade, and the supremacy of human willpower over science and technology – were now abominations.[24] When one senior

24. Western scholarship has not been able to keep pace with the changing values in Chinese politics, particularly given the time required for publishing books; and hence,

Chinese official was told that some Americans were quite attracted to features of that radical model, he sucked in his breath, saying he was amazed to learn how far the tentacles of the Gang of Four had reached – and, regaining his composure, he added that such Americans should not denigrate China by speaking about the "bad old days" of the Cultural Revolution but should learn about the "New China" that is to be untainted by the "evil thoughts of the Gang of Four."

Foreign scholars who might also wish to turn over a new leaf and dwell only on China's many technical problems of modernization and development are deterred by the fact that while China may be turning away from much of Maoism, the country has remained true to Mao's most basic dictum: "Keep politics in command." This means that any analysis of China's possible "pragmatic" policies – whether in the military sphere where the Russian threat must be countered or in the civilian economy – that ignores the issues of factional strife and political loyalties will be a castle built on air.

The Chinese press has kept alive the reality of factional difficulty by attacking provincial and local leaders through code names. (The Chinese practice of using code words for people whose names are known to all is a subject we shall be returning to later.) Thus after "sworn followers" and "devious henchmen" had been unearthed in every province, the process continued as dead men were attacked – "that leading theorist" being the deceased Kang Sheng – and finally, most cautiously, unnamed figures at the Center were said to be opponents of national unity.

WITH DENG IN CHARGE, WE'RE AT EASE

As Deng Xiaoping consolidated power and appointed key followers to critical posts, particularly after the meeting of the National People's Congress and the "trial" of the Gang of Four, Western journalists and diplomats developed a new model of Chinese politics. In their view, China was achieving stability under the strong-man rule of Deng, who was supposedly intolerant of ideology but vigorous in championing "moderates" who were universally technocrats, pragmatists, and modernizers. In a sense, a "pragmatic" Deng had come to replace an

---

anachronistically, works appear that extol Maoist values that the Chinese now condemn. In some cases, the lag may stem from the authors' attachments to now discredited practices. See, for example, John G. Gurley, *China's Economy and the Maoist Strategy*, Monthly Review Press, New York, 1978; Al Imfeld, *China as a Model of Development*, Orbis Books, New York, 1978; Godwin Chu, *Radical Change Through Communications in Mao's China*, An East–West Center Book, University Press of Hawaii, Honolulu, 1977.

"ideological" Mao Zedong as the vital force of Chinese politics, and thus much of what happened in China was thought to be understandable in terms of whether events conformed or conflicted with the will of the man who now personified Chinese politics.

For those concerned with foreign affairs, and particularly United States–China relations, this new model of Chinese domestic politics suggested that Deng's political future was critical for the continued improvement of China's relations with the West. Deng's victories became reaffirmation of progress in strengthening United States–China relations, and his setbacks were threats to those relations.

To the extent that scholars have moved to accept this new model of Chinese politics, they have differed from the journalists and diplomats in the degree to which they see Deng as still having substantial opposition within the Party and the government. Scholars are also extremely impressed with the degree to which the Chinese are engaging in experimentation, particularly within their sluggish economy. Most scholars in early 1980 were unsure as to whether Deng would lead China back to a Leninist model of Party domination of State, but guided by technocratic rather than ideological considerations, or whether China was in the process of breaking completely with Marxism – Leninism as it abandoned Maoism. Although it is still too early to say whether Deng will indeed become a dominant strong-man or remain behind the scenes as a new collective leadership is institutionalized, it is obvious that interpretations of the essential characteristics of the Chinese system have become extremely tentative, with much hinging on intuitive judgments about how successful China is likely to be in repairing the damages of the Cultural Revolution and catching up with world standards in all spheres of life.

All of these developments in the post-Mao years seem to suggest that we should set aside all of our earlier concepts about the dynamics of Chinese politics and seek a new model for explaining events in that sequestered land.

SALVAGING PARTS OF
DISCARDED MODELS

Cynics will say that the scramble to construct new models of Chinese elite politics whenever there are dramatic developments in China is a sign that there can be no such thing as a real specialist in Chinese politics and that China-watchers, for all their pretentiousness, are constantly being as surprised by events in that mysterious land as the non-specialist analysts. This criticism is flawed, however, because the new models, while possibly no better than the discarded ones for predicting *future* developments, usually have the extraordinary property of illuminating *past* events.

The fact that each new interpretation of how the Chinese conduct their politics is better for explaining past events as well as current practices generates an impression of progress. Thus, with the advent of the "unity of theory and practice" model of the 1950s it suddenly became apparent that ideology and organization were significant even during the Yunnan Round Table days; the acceptance of the Maoist model with the emergence of the Red Guards caused a revision in thinking about the nature of ideology in the pre-Cultural Revolution period; and, of course, the acceptance of the conflict and factional views about Chinese elite relations since the Cultural Revolution has colored our perception of the entire history of Chinese Communism and made numerous mysterious events of the past intelligible.[25]

We have no desire to introduce a sour note that might deflate sensations of intellectual progress, but knowledge about Chinese Communism might be significantly advanced if we resisted the temptation to discard past models and instead sought to salvage as much as possible from them. The problem is that we tend to exaggerate the significance of current discoveries and thus distort our perceptions of Chinese politics by downplaying the central themes of earlier views. In most cases the real test of actual progress is that of figuring out how the new propositions can fit with the old ones.

For example, with the Maoist model of revolutionary confrontation and the factional models, analysts have tended to disregard the earlier consensual model. Yet a key theme in Chinese politics remains the obligation of everyone, whenever possible, to display adherence to consensus. To ignore the continuing imperative of consensus is to miss a key factor that explains some of the peculiarities of how factional politics works in China. Indeed, the awareness of all actors that they should enthusiastically support a consensus contributes greatly to the exaggerated swings of Chinese factional politics and the political embarrass-

---

25. The influence of contemporary developments on interpretations of earlier phases in the history of Chinese Communism is clearly shown by the differences between recent general accounts of the past and earlier accounts. For example, James Pinckney Harrison, writing in the aftermath of the power struggles of the Cultural Revolution, treats Mao's rise to leadership largely in power terms in *The Long March to Power*, Macmillan, New York, 1972 while Benjamin I. Schwartz's classic study, *Chinese Communism and Rise of Mao Tse-tung*, Harvard University Press, Cambridge, Mass., 1951, written at the outset of the ideological model, treats Mao's success largely in terms of the intellectual polemics of the historical materialist traditions. This development points to the danger that as the ideological standards of Chinese Communism wither, historians may incorrectly belittle the importance ideology once had in the movement.

ment of those who find it awkward to make the proper swing at the right time.

The continued obligation to maintain the appearances of elite solidarity explains why, once a leader is discredited, every organization in every province feels compelled to join in the collective criticism. From April to October 1976, the campaign against Deng Xiaoping required all leaders and organizations throughout the land to join the consensus and revile "that capitalist roader who would reverse correct verdicts"; and, of course, after October 1976, that campaign suddenly stopped and everyone had to display solidarity in denouncing the Gang of Four.

A major source of misunderstanding about Chinese politics may stem from a failure to appreciate the fact that the Chinese conception of consensus is radically different from the Western concept. In the West, consensus tends to be associated with agreement above all about constitutional procedures and the "rules of the game," and to a lesser degree, agreement over immediate goals and values. The Western notion of consensus is consistent with pluralistic contention for power and intense disagreements about the best tactics and strategies for realizing the agreed ultimate ends. In Chinese politics, consensus leaves no room for even tactical disagreements, for the concept is directly linked to notions about authority and the obligation for everyone to conform to the collective will as expressed by the leadership. For the Chinese, consensus means agreement that goes well beyond merely the rules of the game and involves showing deference to established authority.

The combination of adhering to the imperative of consensus politics and engaging in factionalism gives Chinese politics a distinctive characteristic that cannot be appreciated by a simple factional model. We shall examine later the distinctive types of tensions produced by such a combination of political norms, but just to illustrate the point, it may be helpful to consider the awkward problem that Foreign Minister Qiao Guanhua could not surmount during the 1976 shifts of consensus and factional power. The fate of Qiao Guanhua was apparently determined by a variety of factors, including his wife Zhang Hanzhi's ties to the Gang of Four and particularly to Jiang Qing; but one factor that certainly contributed to his downfall was his actions following the death of Zhou Enlai. Qiao felt that he was too closely identified with Zhou Enlai, so when he saw his patron's choice, Deng Xiaoping, losing out to Hua Guofeng at the end of January 1976, he quickly, and apparently enthusiastically, joined the early attacks on Deng, and finally he personally led the Foreign Office chorus, which was trucked through the streets of Peking, denouncing "the unrepentant capitalist roader." By adhering to the principles of consensus politics, he hoped to transform his factional identification. But when the Gang of Four fell and it was time for the leading Foreign Office officials again to be conveyed through the streets shouting out the new slogans of denunciation, Qiao Guanhua did not appear. Two transformations of factional identities in one year were too much, even for one dedicated to the spirit of consensus; the cheerleading for the Foreign Office contingent had to be left to Nancy Tang and Wang Hairong.[26] Had it not been for the continuing obligations of the Yunnan tradition of elite solidarity, it seems likely that the diplomatic skills of Qiao would have enabled him to survive in a purely factional form of politics. (The same tradition two years later caused Nancy Tang and Wang Hairong to be removed from their conspicuous posts in the Foreign Office, demotions that cannot be explained by those who either deny the existence of factions or assume that policy issues are all that can divide Chinese leaders, since Tang had a special interest in the opening to the United States and it was Wang who laughingly responded to Zbigniew Brzezinski's challenge that the last to the top of the Great Wall would have to "take on the Polar Bear.")

The explosion of the Cultural Revolution appears to have shattered the ideology/organization-based model of the Chinese political system. Since then, those who seek to make politics meaningful by applying the traditional ideological continuum of "left" and "right" must admit to considerable confusion. Many would say that coherent ideology is indeed dead in China. What is one to make of the fact that Mrs. Mao and her Shanghai colleagues, who were so long known as the "ultra-leftists" and the "radicals" of Chinese politics should, after their incarceration, be denounced as "ultra-rightists," but then two years later be resurrected as "leftists." Analysts who are wont to rely upon ideological calibrators must be mystified that the language used to denounce the Gang of Four in time became indistinguishable from that used to vilify Deng Xiaoping when he was the most popular target for abuse in the PRC, even though he was obviously of quite a different ideological persuasion. What happened to the Gang of Four had earlier happened to Lin Biao, who while in power was a certifiable "leftist" but once in disgrace was discovered to have been an "ultra-rightist," and then an "ultra-leftist."

It is true that in traditional Leninism, "left deviation" and "right deviation" were seen as opposite sides of the same coin; but what the Chinese did for two years after Mao's death was to make "right deviation" both sides of the coin. The reason, of course, was that everyone was terrified of the danger of "revisionism," a disease of the "right," and hence the place of safety and symbolic honor became the "left." Therefore, even as the leadership carried the country to the right, it was necessary for cadres to pretend until 1978 that there was nobody to their left. Finally,

26. Georges Biannic, AFP, Peking, November 6, 1976.

reality was recognized, and almost overnight all sins were identified as "leftist," and thereafter it was safer to be of the right.

Yet this strange tilting that made all crimes turn out to be the work of, first, only "rightists" and then only "leftists" represents the continuing, but modified role of ideology in Chinese public life. The ideological model did distinguish between ideology as applied to "Party line" (i.e., public policy) and as applied to individual conduct and cadre discipline. Now it seems that whereas the former type of ideology has been seriously eroded by recent events, the latter concept is still a factor in Chinese political behavior.[27]

We can see this continuing role of ideology in the oddly indiscriminate but essentially trivializing character of the charges hurled against the Four. Jiang Qing was charged with the bloodcurdling act of attempting to assassinate Chairman Hua and also of helping to bring on the death of the now officially "beloved" Zhou Enlai. Yet the massive propaganda organs of the regime provide few comments and fewer details about these capital offenses; rather, they dwelt endlessly on a host of petty personal failings – she refused to interrupt her poker game to visit her husband's death bed; she secretly watched the movie "Sound of Music" and a Kung Fu film smuggled in from Hong Kong; and on visiting a rest spa, she insisted on quiet to the point that cars as far as two and a half kilometers away had to be pushed by servants so that their motors would not have to be turned on.

The habit of setting aside the serious and harping on the trivial is not new to Chinese politics. The same things occurred after Lin Biao was accused of plotting a "counterrevolutionary coup d'etat" and of making three attempts to kill Chairman Mao Zedong; but these capital offenses were played down, and instead the masses were expected to be horrified to learn that he kept a Confucian quotation on the wall at the head of his bed. And, of course, when Liu Shaoqi and Deng Xiaoping were charged during the Cultural Revolution with practically extinguishing Communism in China by their "revisionist" proclivities, the one was earnestly accused of liking fine foods and the other of compulsive bridge playing.

The point is that a form of ideology remains that significantly modifies

---

27. It would, however, be premature to write about the end of ideology even as a guide for policy in China, for there are signs that the decision to establish Party schools at all levels and, more importantly, the creation by the Central Committee in mid-January 1979 of a Discipline Inspection Commission are likely to cause intra-elite disputes to be cast in ideological forms. Defenders of Chairman Hua Guofeng have, for example, been calling for a more complete appreciation of Marxism and charging that the "crimes" of Lin Biao and the Gang were that they sought to debase Mao's system of thought into mere "utilitarian" slogans that were "propagating pragmatism." See Shen Taosheng, "Lin Biao's Anti-Marxist 30-Word Principle," *Beijing Review*, No. 5, February 2, 1979, pp. 16–19.

the factional nature of current Chinese politics. Political figures are exceedingly vulnerable because they can be brought to task for personal conduct that is inconsistent with Party ideals for cadre behavior. The combination of factional strife, the obligation for consensus, and ideologically correct behavior means that everyone must store away memories of the inappropriate private acts of others to be recalled as damaging evidence in possible later factional confrontations.

Similarly, the discovery of the importance of factions should not cause analysts to ignore the continuing importance of organizational issues, because factions tend to be based in part upon organizational identification. Indeed, a first step in distinguishing factions is the investigation of both the internal conflicts of particular institutions and the clashes between organizations. The Chinese practice of freezing cadres and technicians into particular career lines intensifies the potential for intra-institutional conflicts. In government and administrative offices, people have lifetime commitments to particular activities, and so it is in the various industries.[28]

According to the earlier model of Chinese mastery of organizational principles, it was assumed that the blending of ideology and practical considerations in a disciplined organizational context ensured efficient and smooth performance. But Schurmann and others overlooked the fact that such arrangements could also produce inter- and intra-organizational tensions of a high order. Therefore, instead of abandoning the model that emphasizes the strong organizational basis of Party discipline we can greatly increase our understanding of factional politics by carefully noting the precise points at which stress might appear according to the insights of organizational theories. The only change called for is a skeptical approach to the earlier presumption that the Chinese Communists had discovered how to use ideology to integrate their total system. Analysts should concentrate instead on where the gaps in organizational loyalties are most likely to exist – between "localities" and the Center, between provinces, between the PLA and the militia, between the field armies, and the like.[29]

In addition to preserving elements of the organizational model, we

28. Whereas William Whitson first observed that Chinese army officers were not transferred about among the field armies as would be expected in a national army, it was A. Doak Barnett who first described in detail the fact that all Chinese who get ahead have to stay within the same "system," or *hsi-t'ung*, in which they began their careers (*Cadres, Bureaucracy, and Political Power in Communist China*, Columbia University Press, New York, 1967). The fact that one's entire future is bounded by one's "system" means that personal interactions with the same people become extremely important, memories do not easily fade, and feuds and factions linger on.

29. The limits of the institutional or organizational bases for factions will be discussed in Chapter 4.

should also keep in mind some of the things we once learned from the generational model. The very rigidity of Chinese promotional practices and the lack of flexibility for lateral mobility limits the strength of factions built solely out of institutional or professional loyalties because of the sharp cross-cutting tendencies caused by generational identification. Generational loyalties, which began with the Long March comrades and were successively reinforced right through the Cultural Revolution activist generation, have at each stage tempered institutional loyalties.[30]

Indeed, precisely because promotions have been so slow, inter-generational conflicts have been exceptionally intense within most institutions. The Chinese have yet to discover a method for bringing new blood to leadership roles without creating jealousies and even greater inter-generational tensions. Certainly there are tensions throughout the country as cadres in nearly every organization, commune, factory, revolutionary committee, and government bureau who pushed themselves ahead during the Cultural Revolution are now being eyed with suspicion by those older "veteran cadres" who have been rehabilitated and now are on guard against any further upstart moves. Indeed, one of the vilified Gang of Four, Wang Hongwen, was referred to as a "helicopter" because he rose directly to the top without any gradual climb, but there are many others who have advanced ahead of their generation and thus are targets of both their elders and their peers.

Since the smashing of the Gang of Four, the Chinese press has, with the exaggerations of exuberance, brought to light innumerable examples of how the Chinese in the early 1970s, behind the pretensions of participatory democracy and anti-hierarchical egalitarianism, were playing vicious power games, with winners showing no mercy toward losers. The stakes were high even in ordinary factories – for example, in the diesel engine plant in the town of Weifang, where the Gang of Four's "confidant in Shandong" engaged in "reversing the relationship between enemies and friends, obstinately conniving with evil persons and ruthlessly attacking and persecuting cadres, staff and workers."[31] Apparently, during the Cultural Revolution the former chief of the Weifang diesel engine plant "actively followed" the bourgeois statesman of Shandong and "hired" himself out to the Gang's "confidant in Shandong," and in so doing "he did a lot of evil things."[32] In 1967, he allegedly recruited others to form a "so-called secret police group and information network," and he resorted to such "improper methods" as "creating

30. The relationship of generations and factions will be examined in Chapter 4.
31. "Shantung Plant Handles Case of Trumped-up Charges," Tsinan, Shantung Provincial Radio, Foreign Broadcast Information Service, *Daily Report – People's Republic of China,* June 16, 1978, p. G5.
32. Ibid.

something out of nothing," "shifting the blame to others," and "keeping a close watch over others." These representatives of the Gang "unreasonably decreed that two persons talking together were 'establishing sinister ties', and three persons together were 'holding sinister meetings'." They further "blacklisted" 256 people on "fake charges" of forming a "knives group" and secretly "sharpening knives" at night and "planning to kill somebody." "In June 1968 they labeled 308 staff and workers of the plant as members of a 'counterrevolutionary clique reversing verdicts', a 'knife group' and an 'explosion group'," of which 71 were Party members, 58 were CYL members, 81 were intellectuals, and 42 were cadres.[33] (A common Chinese practice, when striving for verisimilitude, is to intersperse specific numbers in the lurid prose of moral indignation.) In recounting the events of a decade earlier, the report makes it clear that the shoe is now on the other foot and "that confidant in Shandong" and his "gang" are at last under righteous attack. Even if we discount to some degree the possibility of exaggeration in such accounts of political conflicts, it is still important to recall that they do provide examples of how Chinese politics was in fact far more vicious in the early 1970s than we were aware of.[34] The memories of intensely physical "struggles" during the Cultural Revolution have thus continued on and shaped the lines of submerged conflict in the post-Cultural Revolution period, so that while Western analysts may be inclined to put aside past periods, it is clear that the Chinese live with them.

A COMPOSITE MODEL

When we combine the past and present models of politics in the PRC, it becomes apparent that there are two dominant yet conflicting themes in every phase in the development of Chinese Communism. The first is the supreme importance of consensus, conformity, and agreement and the need to deny conflict and unresolved disagreement. The second, however, is that beneath the surface conformity there is tension,

33. Ibid, p. G6.

34. In the last few years, since China began welcoming foreign delegations to its factories, schools, and tourist sights, many Americans have undoubtedly unknowingly witnessed scenes of masked emotions and suppressed internecine hatred. We now know, for example, that when China's greatest pianist, Lin Shih-kang, met Americans at the time the Philadelphia Orchestra visited China, he had just been brought out of prison, where he had been for ten years, and he was promptly put back for another year after the Americans left. Many American scholars have had the troubling experience of revisiting Chinese campuses and discovering that during their prior visit, when the Gang of Four were still in charge, they had been hoodwinked as to the actual conditions.

feuding, and factional conflict. Although Chinese politics has historically vacillated between elite solidarity and factional struggle, the two tendencies have always been present and the most significant characteristic of Chinese politics has been the ceaseless tension between them. This tension seems to be basic to Chinese culture, which has traditionally demanded both conformity and self-assertion, both humble self-effacement (or self-sacrifice) and constant striving to be exceptional, distinguished, and competitively superior.

Politically, the cultural need for conformity has produced a deep craving for order and propriety and also a profound fear of disorder, or *luan*.[35] The general Chinese expectation is that life is better when agreement is widespread and non-conformity has been rectified. Even the Maoists, who extolled the merits of conflict and struggle, expected that the outcome of such tensions would be a new conformity, and they never accepted as a viable alternative the idea of merely agreeing to disagree. For most Chinese, the imperatives of political order and of social life in general require widespread conformity, and this in turn requires denial of self-interest. Ideally, the collectivity will so take care of all of its members that no one will ever need to assert his individual rights.[36]

Yet at the same time, individual Chinese—especially when experiencing anxiety—are predictably inclined to do something, to act to remove the source of trouble or at least to reduce its consequences. Action usually means striving to manipulate social relations, which for the Chinese are not abstractions but very concrete personal ties and associations that are palpably measurable. One tries to share one's innocence of any wrongdoing, place blame elsewhere, and generally make others aware of one's misfortunes.[37] Most Chinese do not believe that troubles will go away if one ignores them or pretends that they do not exist.

This Chinese response to tensions is in distinct contrast with other cultures; for example, in Malaysia the fundamental ethnic clash between Malays and Chinese seems to be exaggerated by a lack of fit in the ways in which the two communities typically deal with tensions and anxieties. William Parker hypothesizes that the Chinese tend to employ defense

35. For the classic statement of the problem of *luan* in Chinese political culture, see Richard H. Solomon, *Mao's Revolution and the Chinese Political Culture*, University of California Press, Berkeley, 1971.

36. For survey evidence of the Chinese propensity for conformity and group orientation, see Richard W. Wilson, *Learning to be Chinese: The Political Socialization of Children in Taiwan*, M.I.T. Press, Cambridge, Mass., 1970.

37. Two themes have dominated Chinese Communist propaganda for the last twenty years: bewailment over mistreatment by "landlords," "imperialists," "social imperialists," "Kuomintang," "capitalist roaders," "Gang of Four," etc., and the bliss that comes from being spared all mistreatment, that is, the happiness "after liberation," "after the Gang of Four," "after . . . ." The two themes are, of course, the opposite sides of the same coin.

mechanisms of a "sensitizing" character, such as intellectualization, obsessive behavior, and ruminative worrying, while the Malays tend toward "repression" mechanisms, involving the avoidance of confrontation, denial, and the repression of all responses.[38] Thus the Chinese tend to vocalize their anxieties, dwell on worst-case scenarios, and seek sympathy – if not pity – from all possible sources, while the Malays refuse to respond to criticisms, pretend that there is no cause for tension, and generally hold in their feelings until they explode. Parker has found that Chinese students in responding to T.A.T.s tend to stress the importance of gaining sympathy and of "making a scene," while Malay students stress the advantages of withdrawal, isolation and papering over situations.

This means that when individual Chinese feel tensions and anxieties they tend to act in ways that can threaten the social ideal of a tranquil, conformist social order. In particular, because the Chinese often feel a strong compulsion to verbalize their anxieties, it is generally accepted that those who feel that they have suffered undue hardships or injustices have license to tell their woes and to seek relief. The strongest emotions Chinese are permitted to show in public – indeed, almost the only emotions permitted – are those associated with being mistreated. The presumption is that such demonstrations will both shame those causing the agonies and mobilize allies among those who are sympathetic. Personal misfortunes thus tend quickly to become public matters.

The combinations of these two cultural traits – the craving for conformity as a means to avoid social tensions, and the need to articulate grievances to reduce personal tensions – create a basic conflict within Chinese political life. At the public level, it is universally expected that orderliness should always prevail and therefore all forms of social pressure to bring individuals into line are legitimate; yet at the personal level, people are quick to voice their anxieties, and thus in managing their tensions, they tend to act in ways that threaten the collective order. In particular, they are inclined to seek security in highly particularistic relations. Although the Chinese are taught from childhood to guard against acting out emotions and they are generally skilled in separating actions and sentiment, they are not at all inclined to remain passive in response to perceived mistreatment; rather, they feel compelled to tell someone about their pain, to do something either against someone else or against themselves.[39]

38. William Parker, "Culture in Stress: The Malaysian Crisis of 1969 and Its Cultural Roots," Ph.D. dissertation, Department of Political Science, Massachusetts Institute of Technology, 1979.

39. For observations on Chinese modes of expressing aggression against others and/or the self, see Nathan Leites, "On Violence in China," in Elizabeth Marvick (ed.), *Psychopolitical Analysis*, John Wiley and Sons, New York, 1977, pp. 213–246.

Chinese culture thus generates a pervasive tension between outward pretenses of conformity and socially disruptive private actions. Historically, there were certain standardized ways of expressing tensions without disrupting the social order: Aggrieved wives could go out into the street and publicly proclaim their husbands' failings; individual citizens could stand before the gates of the magistrate's *yamen* and pour out all their misfortunes at the top of their lungs; and students could post on school walls their accounts of mistreatment by their teachers. The wall poster, filled with personal complaints, is more than two hundred years old in China. And, of course, the Chinese Communists have institutionalized the practice of describing in public how in the bad "old days" they had to "eat bitterness" and suffer endlessly. Now, however, the objects of complaint have been updated, as everyone in the country is expected to criticize unrelentingly the Gang of Four and their followers. This means that everyone must publicly pour out their grievances and give voice to any mistreatment, thereby keeping alive the memories of factional conflicts and possibly stimulating new antagonisms, which may in turn threaten the desired anti-Gang consensus.

Thus, although these institutionalized complaints have been largely cathartic in nature—ends in themselves rather than the means to other ends—they also serve to keep alive issues and lines of division within the society. More importantly, when the Chinese do feel anxieties based on real causes for alarm, they tend to act in ways that are conducive to the formation of factions and that threaten the ideals of conformity.

Such behavior need not, and usually does not, directly challenge the prevailing social ideals; on the contrary, compulsive behavior in response to anxieties usually takes the form of protesting that one has been adhering to the ideals of his proper role, and that injustice comes from the fact that in spite of his exemplary behavior, he has suffered. Rebellion based on greivance over mistreatment of the innocent is rebellion of limited reach, not of revolutionary transformation. Collective ideals have not been challenged but have actually been reinforced by the complaint that an injustice has been done in terms of the conformist ideals. In pre-Communist China, the attitude toward factions was usually coupled with the criticism that Confucian norms were being violated—even when those complaining would have been happier with Taoist or other norms. Similarly, in Communist China, the complaints that become the building blocks of factions are cast in Maoist terms, even when the protagonists may have doubts about Maoist ideals.

Under the new regime of Deng Xiaoping and Hua Guofeng, the tension between consensus and faction has been intensified as the new leaders seek simultaneously to strengthen legitimacy and to eliminate all who might be loyal to the Maoist factions of the past. Two years after the smashing of the Gang of Four, the Chinese press and radio continued to employ far more revolutionary rhetoric than might be expected of "pragmatic" rulers. This was because the need to maintain consensus – that is, legitimacy – precluded unduly sharp breaks with the past. The danger, of course, was that once again, as has so often happened in Chinese history, public discourse would increasingly diverge from actual practice, and the realities of behavior would no longer be the basis for legitimacy.

The ascendancy of Vice-Chairman Deng Xiaoping and the appointment of Zhao Ziyang to replace Hua as premier did not change the problem of rhetoric and practice; it only established a new version of the consensus. Instead of a revolutionary rhetoric obscuring essentially pragmatic policies as in the late 1970s, the change was to a rhetoric of innovations and praise of the market mechanism while bureaucratic planning continued to prevail. Behind the words about experimentation there continued to be obstructionism by skilled bureaucrats interested in protecting their powers and prerogatives.

It is still too early to judge how far the new regime will permit ritual rhetoric to be out of phase with policy initiatives. There are many reasons to believe that the regime can tolerate a considerable gap between the two because Chinese culture has, for reasons we shall explore later, found it comfortable to maintain distance between words and actions, and people are trained to observe only whether their rulers are using the right ritual words and not to ask whether the emperor is wearing any clothes.[40]

On the other hand, the experience of more than two decades of violent vacillation in the Party line, encouraged at times by ambivalences in Chairman Mao's personality, has produced a degree of skepticism, if not

---

40. Western observers of China have considerably more difficulty in coping with the Chinese practice of separating reality from rhetoric, and they apparently attach great value to the latter. Westerners often seem to suspend disbelief when dealing with China and thus do not recognize Chinese rhetoric for what it is, namely, that "the emperor wears no clothes." For example, one segment of Western observers during the height of the "Maoist phase" went to great lengths to "prove" that apparently foolish economic policies really "made sense." Of course, since the fall of the Gang of Four, the Chinese themselves have made it clear that those policies were indeed foolish and "ten years were lost." At present, a different segment of Western observers is treating equally uncritically the Chinese statements of what they intend to accomplish with the Four Modernizations. The problem is in part the traditional mystique that encourages Westerners to look to China for the fulfillment of their wishes and fantasies. A sobering exercise would be to compare the pre-1976 statements of Americans about the almost magical accomplishments of the Chinese in various fields (particularly institutions) with what the Chinese, since the fall of the Gang of Four, say about the same subjects. Such an enterprise would reaffirm that foolish people will in time appear ridiculous, and it would remind us that the Chinese always maintain a gap between rhetoric and reality and attach importance to the former without necessarily expecting that it need have any relationship to the latter.

cynicism, that is new to revolutionary China. What seems to be happening is that consensus now has to be formed at a level slightly removed from the dominant Party line but still not consistent with actual practices. Thus somewhere in the gap between words and actions is the realm of consensus, which is still believed to be absolutely essential. This means that the test of whether consensus is being strengthened or weakened will remain uncertain, and hence fears of incipient factionalism will persist. As the country's policies become more "pragmatic," there will in fact be substantial room for honest disagreements and conflicting judgments as to what should be done, a situation that will threaten agreement and favor factions.

The gaps between words and actions mean that it is relatively easy to maintain a veneer of consensus even while acting according to the realities of cliques and factions.[41] Yet the need to preserve a symbolic veneer has profound consequences for the dynamics of Chinese politics; some of those consequences we can briefly identify here, but most will have to await deeper analysis.

First the obligation of respecting the pretense of consensus requires that public discussions of policy matters be elliptical, employing code words without straightforward identification of people and positions. At the same time, informal communication among cadres has to be even more circumspect than public statements because everyone is expected to be alert in identifying any hint of secrets and any behavior that might be taken as a sign of potential cliques. It is dangerous for officials to try to change policies by seeking confidential channels of communications to gain potential allies. The only safe approach is to try to hint cryptically at the direction of new policy through the mass media to make it seem to be part of the consensus and hope that other officials will pick it up and demonstrate their sympathy by repeating the new code words.[42]

Second, the veneer of consensus effectively operates to impede initiatives from below. Change in formal policy tends to take the form of grand pronouncements by the top leaders, with almost no regard for the day-to-day operations of government. Once such dictums are issued, lesser officials must scurry about to try to implement them by figuring out how they can be administratively operationalized. The obligation of maintaining the consensus means that the bureaucracy does not push

41. For a sophisticated analysis of the Chinese mode of handling "cognitive dissonance," see Paul J. Hiniker, *Revolutionary Ideology and Chinese Reality*, Sage Publications, Beverly Hills, 1977.

42. The extent to which the Chinese political process is geared to responding to commands from above rather than pressures from below is examined in such locally oriented policy studies as Lynn T. White, III, *Careers in Shanghai*, University of California Press, Berkeley, 1978.

demands for decisions and policy changes to the top.[43] The situation is not just that minority views can rarely surface, although this is certainly the case, but also any faction can readily veto activist policies sought by others.

Third, the rule of consensus, even as ritual, tends to limit the scope and size of factions. Because the mass media can tolerate only a small range of opinions, factions have to be built closer to the networks of acquaintanceships. This places significant limits on the numbers of their active supporters and further pushes faction formation into the more clandestine realms of social and political life.

These rules of consensus, when combined with the Chinese belief in the need to advance one's interests through particularistic relationships, contribute to the very acute Chinese need to be alert and shrewd in dealing with social and political situations. The knowledge that beneath the layer of consensus there must be constant personal calculation and planning reinforces the strong Chinese necessity to mask one's own actions while trying to unmask the private intentions of others. Hence the extraordinary emphasis in Chinese culture, in both social and political relationships, for designing and executing ploys, stratagems, and game-playing tactics—many of which, in part because of the rules of consensus, rely upon deception because of the assumed inevitable gap between appearances and reality.

The anthropologist Chien Chiao has argued that "social and political strategies form a highly enduring tradition in Chinese culture," and that both quantitatively and qualitatively the Chinese use of social stratagem exceeds the American. He has identified some two dozen categories of Chinese strategies. Some of his classic stratagems include: "Besiege Wei in order to save Zhao" (save one party by attacking another); "Loot the house while it's on fire" (take advantage of chaos for private gain); "Watch the fire from across the river" (allow others to destroy themselves from a safe vantage point—a version of "Watch the tigers fight from the mountain top"); "Befriend distant states while attacking the nearby"; "Put Zhang's hat on Li's head" (attribute something to the wrong person in order to generally benefit); "Avoid the important and dwell on the trivial" (keep silent about major mistakes and confess to minor ones); "Kill the chicken to frighten the monkey" (punish the weak in order to warn others); "Point at the mulberry and abuse the locust" (point at one while abusing another); "Take away the ladder after climbing into the chamber" (don't give those behind you a chance); and "Drop

43. For a fascinating first-hand account of how a leading political figure introduced a policy debate in the field of education through cryptic signals, see David S. Zweig, "The Peita Debate on Education and the Fall of Teng Hsiao-p'ing," *China Quarterly*, No. 73, March 1978, pp. 140–159.

stones on someone who has fallen into the well."

On the basis of his collection of Chinese strategies, Chien Chiao has "drawn a sketch of a fine Chinese strategist [in social relations]:

> He waits patiently for the right opportunity with full alert, constant observation and investigation of the situation. When he moves, his actions tend to be deceitful and indirect, and often he tries to achieve his goal by making use of a third party. He may exaggerate or fabricate occasionally, but always feigns. He does his best to stop his opponent's advance. He may allure, prod and warn his opponent, but unless it is absolutely necessary, he will not have a real direct confrontation with him. If he has to, he will move fast and try to quickly put his opponent under control. He is always ready to abandon or withdraw, for that is only a step for coming back."[44]

VIEWS OF THE RESPONDENTS

The testimony of our interview respondents further confirms the importance of consensus and conformity in the dynamics of Chinese politics. Most telling is the finding that 86.4 percent of the respondents agreed with the statement, "Conflicts among leaders are bad for the common people." When asked how they could reconcile opposition to intra-elite conflicts with their pleasure over the fall of the Gang of Four, most gave answers that indicated that in spite of the benefits from that particular event, their view was still that effective and good leaders should be able to work out their difficulties without upsetting the consensus. Their explanations of why conflicts among leaders are bad reveal much about the meaning of consensus in Chinese political culture:

- A former technician in the Geological Bureau said, "When leaders are in conflict with each other they have no time or energy to give to the problems of the common people. Only when there is harmony at the top will the lesser official feel the need to implement policies, and the common people need to have policies implemented. When the leaders fight with each other the lesser officials will take the time out just to look after their own affairs."
- The daughter of an economics professor who was sent to the countryside after high school said, "When conflicts among leaders take place, everything becomes confused and nobody can control the situation he is in. It is important to have consensus because other-

44. Chien Chiao, "Chinese Strategic Behaviors: A Preliminary List," in *Proceedings of the International Conference on Sinology*, Taipei, August 15–17, 1980, Academia Sinica, Taipei, 1981.

wise everything is unpredictable. When there is a great deal of uncertainty everyone must look after his own affairs and the common people get left out."

- A young man who swam out to Hong Kong and hopes to join a brother in Los Angeles said, "When leaders are in conflict with each other, politics get very confused and nobody knows what they should be doing. Good leadership means that everybody wants to work together. When Mao worked well with the Central Committee all of China benefited; when Mao fought with the others we all suffered."

Our respondents also reported that in their own situations, far from the levels of leadership, conformity and consensus were also expected and necessary, and that this need resulted in a substantial gap between what people said and what they believed. The vast majority, for example, believed that individuals are quite capable of making up their own minds on most issues, but that an observer would not know this because most people also feel the need to follow majority opinion.

The agreement by 97.7 percent of the interviewees that "most people can make their own decisions, uninfluenced by public opinion," might have reflected acceptance of Maoist ideals of self-reliance were it not for the fact that there were no differences between the expressed views of the younger former Red Guards and those of the older respondents. The fact that this response indicated their belief in human potential and not the way people actually behave in China was revealed by their answers to several other questions. For example, only 29.5 percent agreed that "the average person will stick to his opinion if he thinks he is right, even if others disagree." (The former Red Guards and "sent down" youths were significantly more cynical, with 22 percent agreeing, compared with 45.5 percent of the older respondents, a chi square of .807.) When the questions were given a slight political overtone or were cast as responses in a group context, the respondents' belief in conformity became even stronger: 95.5 percent agreed that "nowadays people won't make a move until they find out what other people think." Only 11.4 percent believed that "most people will speak out for what they believe in," and 88.6 percent agreed that "the average person will rarely express his opinion in a group when he sees others disagree with him." At the same time, there was overwhelming appreciation that overt conforming did not imply private agreement, as 93.2 percent agreed that "most people will change the opinion they express as a result of an onslaught of criticism, even though they really don't change the way they feel."

The views expressed in these answers might seem to be exactly what would be expected of people long exposed to the ideological conformity of the PRC. What is surprising, however, is that the respondents believe that such conformity is good in a society and not that it is the product of repressive authority:

- A former cook on a state farm said, "It is not just that people know they can get into trouble by saying the wrong thing, but everything goes along much better when there are no open disagreements. Why should I say anything when I know it will only cause controversy? A minority disagreeing only takes up everyone's time and nothing is accomplished."
- A former rubber tapper on a state farm on Hainan Island said, "You never knew how many people might agree or disagree with your own thoughts, so you always held back and only disagreed with the leaders of your own small group *(xiaozu)* when you were sure that you might be protected by higher leaders. This is one way that factions get formed."

What considerations would lead people to violate the consensus? The majority said that it was impossible to specify particular bases for speaking out, and that whenever it happened it was for some unexplainable personal reason, such as an explosion of frustration or simply an act of folly. About one-fourth of the respondents felt that it could happen only when one felt that he could be protected from above.

Very significantly, nearly one-third suggested that people broke the consensus most often because of a sense of personal mistreatment and injustice. On a related question in which the issue of censure for violating the consensus was not prominent, 81 percent agreed that "most people exaggerate their troubles in order to get sympathy," a finding that supports our basic hypothesis that Chinese do seek attention for their troubles and this sets the stage for the search for allies, and the formation of factions.

THE CROSS-PRESSURES OF FACTIONS

A second major point to be salvaged from current models of Chinese elite politics is the fact that there are several bases for factional identifications – institutional, geographic, and generational. This situation should produce cross-cutting pressures that, according to the conventional wisdom of political science, should prevent the polarization of conflicts and encourage political stability.[45] The usual reasoning is that if

45. For a general discussion of cross-pressure theories see Sidney Verba, "Organizational Membership and Democratic Consensus," *Journal of Politics,* Vol. XXVII, August 1965, pp. 467–497; also, Bernard C. Hennessy, *Public Opinion,* Wadsworth Publishing Co., Belmont, Calif., 1965.

people feel that they have alternative sources of group identification, and they are exposed to different partisan views, they are likely to modify their behavior and seek accommodation on all sides.

In the case of Chinese culture, however, cross-pressure situations tend to exacerbate personal tensions and thus cause greater polarization and conflicts. Instead of allowing an individual to feel that he has more options and that he can share his concerns and values with a variety of interests, such cross-pressures appear to be threatening to the Chinese. Much of Chinese conduct is geared to reading social cues and assuming that for any situation there is a correct response that will ensure one's well-being – in short, the Chinese people tend to be situation-oriented, and hence they feel comfortable in unambiguous situations and threatened when confronted with conflicting cues.[46] The Chinese response to their feelings of anxiety over too fluid a situation is, of course, their craving for order and their fear of *luan*.[47]

This hypersensitivity to the potential awkwardness of cross-pressure situations (the assumption is that only "shameless" people rejoice over exploiting multiple options for group identification) leads the Chinese to fear national disaster whenever power becomes slightly diffused and authority figures begin to contend with each other. To admit that "factions" might even exist is to suggest an unhealthy and dangerous situation.

Therefore, faced with cross-pressure choices, the Chinese tend to react quickly and often in an extreme way. They usually try to deny their feelings of tension either by withdrawal or by unambiguous commitment to a particular group. Under the rules of Communist politics it can be exceedingly difficult to practice the generally preferred alternative of keeping one's views to oneself; privateness is not encouraged and may even be impossible. Yet the alternative of commitment to a group produces serious strains in the system, for it means that people tend to polarize conflict situations and to exaggerate the degrees of differences. As polarization takes place, those who would opt for withdrawal suddenly find that they have a viable choice: They can strive to become "middlemen" who can bring together the contending sides. But in time, middlemen usually become poles themselves and thus contribute to the increasing fractionalization of the situation.

This process is usually accompanied by protestations and proclamations of innocence, for precisely the same reasons that Chinese tend to

---

46. *Culture and Personality*, Columbia University Press, New York, 1948, Chap. X; Francis L. K. Hsu, *Americans and Chinese: Two Ways of Life*, Henry Schuman, New York. 1953.

47. Solomon, op. cit.

vocalize their misfortunes when experiencing tension. When someone decides that he has no choice because the cross-pressures are too great and he must ally himself with a particular group, he is likely to want to make clear to all where he stands and that he is not associated with others with whom he might have allied. Precisely because of his discomfort with an ambiguous objective situation, he feels compelled to make his position appear unambiguous to others.

All of this is to say that the Chinese generally feel that there is something sinister in a relationship in which people agree with each other on some matters, but disagree on others. Qualified loyalties and partial commitments of friendship are to be distrusted, and someone who is not prepared to make a complete covenant or alliance is in the end unreliable. Thus, when faced with the cross-pressures that inevitably arise because today's factional associations can be based on institutional ties, generational categories, regional associations, policy interest, or ideological preferences, the Chinese way is to seek a more vivid and coherent reading of power relations than is possible. They tend to act in a manner that accentuates the legitimacy of whatever decision they feel that they "had no choice but to make."

To a striking degree, our survey respondents confirmed the belief that it is impossible to communicate accurately about human troubles and consensus, because people both inflate their own problems and discount those of others. For example, 81 percent agreed that "most people exaggerate their troubles in order to get sympathy" – a practice that Parker's theory about Chinese handling of tensions would predict – and 82 percent said that "people pretend to care more about one another than they really do." (The comparable figures for American samples on these two questions are 22 percent and 18 percent, respectively.) In light of these views, it is not surprising that 56 percent of the Chinese interviewees disagreed that "the typical person is sincerely concerned about the problems of others." In contrast, 82 percent of the Americans sampled agreed with the statement. The explanations that were given for these views are not surprising, but they do reveal how little faith the Chinese have in manifestations of "sincerity," which was once a traditional Chinese value.

- A young woman who had suffered the shock of being sent from a relatively good middle school to an exceedingly poor small brigade said, "People everywhere want to tell you how they have misfortunes but you don't know how true their words are, and therefore you must pretend to feel sorry for them, but you can't really. Just because people act as though they want to be friends with you, you have to be very careful and only make friendships with those you trust. Once you have some really reliable friends you can ignore most people."

One important source of anxiety experienced by most of our respondents was their surprising ambivalence over whether people are predictable. On the one hand, they displayed the traditional Chinese confidence that they had great skill in reading situations and judging probable behavior; on the other hand, they confessed that people were generally able to mask their real motives. The vast majority, for example, gave what appeared to be inconsistent answers to two supposedly contradictory statements: 68 percent agreed that "people are unpredictable in how they'll act from one situation to another," while 70 percent agreed that "if I can see how a person reacts to one situation, I have a good idea of how he will react to other situations." When asked how they explained these apparently contradictory answers, they provided some revealing justifications:

- "People's actions in daily life are very predictable; but in politics people can be very unpredictable."
- "It is easy to figure out what a person's real interests are, even in political matters; but it is impossible to know what his real political views are, and he can surprise you."
- "In general, people can be said to be unpredictable because you don't even know their real attitudes, but if you know the specific circumstances a person finds himself in, you can usually guess what he will do."

The source of their ambiguity, and hence of their anxieties when judging other people, appears to be an awareness that the degree of politicization of life in China has made people increasingly prone to cover up their true thoughts and feelings. The experiences of the last decades appear to have taught many Chinese that intelligent people are not likely to reveal very much about themselves. They therefore are apt to rein in their natural tendency to pretend wisdom about the ways of others. Even though nearly 60 percent showed traditional Chinese confidence in their ability to judge others by denying the statement, "I find that my first impressions of people are frequently wrong," only 35 percent agreed with the statement, "I think I get a good idea of a person's basic nature after a brief conversation with him."

These responses point to the likelihood that our respondents have little trust in other people, a hypothesis readily confirmed by Table 2–1, which reveals the difference between Chinese and American feelings about "trust."

Table 2-1. Chinese and American Attitudes Toward Trust in People

Survey Question and Response	Chinese Respondents (percent)	American Respondents[a]	
		1964 (percent)	1968 (percent)
1. Generally speaking, would you say that most people can be trusted or that you can't be too careful in dealing with people?			
Most people can be trusted	12.2	54	54
Can't be too careful	87.8	46	44
2. Would you say that most of the time, people try to be helpful, or that they are mostly just looking out for themselves?			
Try to be helpful	16.3	57	60
Look out for themselves	87.7	43	40
3. Do you think that most people would try to take advantage of you if they got the chance, or would they try to be fair?			
Take advantage	64.3	30	31
Try to be fair	35.7	70	69

Source: University of Michigan Survey Research Center. *The 1964 Election Study,* University of Michigan, Ann Arbor, 1971.

[a]National samples from the 1964 and 1968 election study.

The figures confirm what one would expect: People who have experienced the traumas of life in Communist China and especially the threats of mutual criticism meetings and struggle sessions are certainly likely to have less trust of others than citizens of an open society. During the interviews, the Hong Kong refugee respondents communicated in numerous ways their belief in the dangers and even more the follies of being too trusting of others. Several recounted, with laughter, the foolishness of people they knew who had naively trusted their teachers, co-workers, or immediate superiors and then suffered severe consequences.

The quality of this "distrust," however, seems to be more that of the worldly wise and politically sophisticated than that of people who have deep suspicions about human relations and are therefore psychologically incapable of having close family bonds. "Distrust" was the shield these people used toward the outside world, behind which they in fact sought out, in a semi-conspiratorial spirit, the security of real trust. Therefore all things "political" should be treated with distrust, while any relationship that could be truly private could be infused with an extraordinary degree of trust – much like the attitude of some post-Vietnam, post-Watergate Americans.

When asked if they thought Deng Xiaoping was likely to reverse directions and tighten controls, they generally responded by saying that one could never foresee what might happen in politics, and hence they thought it entirely understandable that the relaxation of controls in China had produced the highest rate of outflowing of refugees into Hong Kong in recent years. People would just be foolish, in their view, not to take advantage of these opportunities; and as far as they were concerned, Peking would have to maintain its current policies for a very, very long time before they would be prepared to concede that things in China had changed enough to make it wise to trust anyone with power there.[48]

Yet the respondents repeatedly cited situations in their personal relationships in which they risked a great deal in trusting others. It appears that the more politically dangerous their world was, the more they sought out the security of a few very trusting relationships. Most often these involved classmates, children of family friends, and, of course, family members. All of those who swam across the bay into Hong Kong had to establish first a bond of trust with the other escapees, since none of them had been bold enough to attempt a solo escape.

The behavior of our respondents confirms this general observation about Chinese culture: The greater the manifest uncertainties in political life, the greater the sense of general distrust and the greater the search for more private and intimate association – that is to say, the greater the tendency to form factions.

TWO INTO ONE

If we now combine our two central hypotheses about Chinese political behavior under conditions of factional tension, it becomes immediately apparent that we are working toward a model that has built

48. The spectacular increase in the number of both illegal and legal immigrants to Hong Kong in 1978–1979 clearly suggests that both groups felt the opportunity for leaving should be grasped even though the regime was changing in a somewhat more positive direction. At the same time, there is a significant difference between them: The illegal immigrants feel that they have burned their bridges in China, and therefore they are more open in their criticism and their willingness to talk with foreign scholars, while the legal immigrants still have the option of returning to China and hence are more reticent in talking about their experiences.

into it some profound contradictions: The absolute need for consensus alongside the tremendous pressures for vocalizing innocence, moving toward more exaggerated and polarized positions, and distrusting any agreement to disagree. The paradox of Chinese politics is that the Chinese are quick to proclaim consensus and simultaneously to act so as to exaggerate polarizations. What this means is that the validity of consensus is deceptive: The surface can present an appearance of unanimity, with not a discordant voice, once the ritual language is established, but beneath the surface, tensions contribute to factionalization, which requires some degree of vocalization and usually leads toward polarization.

This inherent contradiction has characterized nearly every period in the history of Chinese Communism, except, of course, during the Cultural Revolution. It was present at the time of the first united front with the Kuomintang (and even more so during the second united front). From Yunnan through the explosions of the Cultural Revolution, there was a continual redefining of consensus and a realigning of power relationships. After the Cultural Revolution a new consensus was proclaimed, but the factional struggles beneath the surface only intensified. The crushing of the Gang of Four produced one more new consensus, but the principal actors quickly began to align themselves around the three poles—Chairman Hua Guofeng and Vice-Chairmen Deng Xiaoping and Ye Jianying—as they sought to figure out how old scores should be settled.

THE STRUCTURAL BASES OF THE COMPOSITE MODEL

Thus far we have been stressing the cultural factors that have critically shaped this composite model of Chinese elite politics. Before proceeding with more detailed propositions about Chinese political behavior according to the model, it is appropriate to note that there are also some fundamental structural considerations that govern Chinese politics and that reinforce the tendencies we have identified.

The most obvious structural considerations are the Chinese commitment to a Marxist–Leninist system of Party rule and all that is associated with an elitist party system and democratic–centralism. The traditional Chinese stress on the importance of ideology and the need for hierarchy is thus reinforced by the requirements of Marxism–Leninism.

Since it is not easy to forget that China has this commitment to a Leninist form of politics, we do not need to dwell long on the structural implications of this fact. But it is easier to overlook the fundamental fact that China is a "developing country," and its politics are also affected by problems associated with the developmental process.

Although it is not frequently noted, Chinese political behavior is strikingly typical of certain forms of developing systems. To demonstrate this point and to highlight significant features that are likely to become even more pronounced as China experiences more development, it is useful to view Chinese politics from the perspective of J. P. Nettl's theories about the two basic categories of political mobilization into which all societies moving away from traditional forms can be fitted. Nettl distinguishes between "elitist" systems, in which authority is associated with particular individuals or a ruling class, hierarchy is accepted, and politics is supreme, as in China, and "constitutional" systems, in which authority is legalistically defined and proscribed, institutions and not individuals have powers and responsibilities, and authority can be divided and balanced or checked, as in the United States.[49]

Generally, Nettl's "elitist" systems are closer to the "traditional" state, for they include many "traditional" features. Yet the point is that as they experience political mobilization, developing systems can either accentuate the "elitist" characteristics, as did Britain, Japan, and other now-developed societies, or they can move at an early stage in a "constitutionalist" direction, as did the United States, Scandinavia, and Switzerland, among others.

Before spelling out Nettl's dichotomous scheme, we must concede that his term "elitist" is not an entirely happy one when applied to the PRC, because of the present regime's ideological stress on equality and on the appearances of egalitarianism. Yet, the concept is correct in that in China (as in most "traditional" systems) elite politics are played out behind the scenes, the public is not well informed about how power is divided among the mighty, and those with power are not exposed to rigorous public criticism. With this point in mind, we shall summarize Nettl's dichotomization of systems, with some modifications to serve our purposes.

In elitest systems, authority – and indeed the entire political process – is assumed to adhere to informal practices and operate in a latent manner. Everyone accepts the idea that the leaders must work out their problems in private and that there should be a minimum of constraints on the "wisdom" and the "moral virtue" of the leaders. Today the workings of the Center in Chinese politics are as far removed from sight as are the decisionmaking processes of any council of elders in a "tradi-

---

49. J. P. Nettl, *Political Mobilization: A Sociological Analysis of Methods and Concepts,* Basic Books, New York, 1967.

tional" system of authority. It is taken for granted that one's betters are making the right decisions, and one only waits for the opportunity to display one's own virtues by supporting those decisions without question. In contrast, a constitutional system embodies a presumption that administrative and political processes are to some degree distinctive and somewhat separated. Above all, authority is perceived as being vested in very specific institutions, and power is associated with offices and posts. In elitist systems, political institutions are not particularly important in themselves; instead, importance is attached to the status of figures and personages. The authority of any political communication is determined by the political status of the source, not its legal role.

In elitist systems, there is little differentiation between the political sphere and the spheres of social and personal relations.[50] On the other hand, in constitutional systems, there is clear "boundary maintenance" between the political system and the social system,[51] and leaders tend to move into political roles from associations and groupings that are important as autonomous subsystems. Once in political roles, such leaders usually tend to defend the autonomy of subsystem institutions. In constitutional systems, movement from autonomous subsystems into the political system tends to be easy, but inside the political system there is a high degree of specificity of role; in contrast, in elite systems, there is little systems autonomy and very little movement from whatever subsytems may exist, and those who gain political roles have very little specificity in their decisionmaking capacities.

Institutions in elite systems tend to be highly expendable in the preservation of the elite status; in constitutional systems, leaders are expendable in order to strengthen or preserve institutions. Leaders in elite systems tend to "capture" institutions and then transform them for their own purposes. Institutional change is easy; the numbers of ministries in China, for example, can be increased or decreased with little or no reaction, even from their "clients," to say nothing of the public. Constitutional systems have elaborate and formalized ways of changing institutions, designed to inhibit the whims of leaders.

For our purpose, the most important differences between these two types of systems are their structural constraints, which produce completely different modes of behavior when leaders are faced with tensions and must resolve conflicts. In essence, authority in elitist systems rests upon a myth of legitimacy that holds that the right to rule is related to

50. Lucian W. Pye, *Politics, Personality and Nation Building*, Yale University Press, New Haven, Conn., 1968, p. 16.

51. For the concept of boundary maintenance, see Gabriel A. Almond and James Coleman, *The Politics of the Developing Areas*, Princeton University Press, Princeton, N.J., 1960, pp. 7ff.

the moral superiority of the rulers. Therefore, it is "normal" for leaders to be united, and conflicts within the circle of leaders are exceedingly dangerous for the entire system. Finally, the people should want to agree with their morally superior rulers' wishes, and hence it is emphasized that all should work to uphold *consensus*. In contrast, conflict is accepted as normal in constitutional systems, which begin with the premise that authority should be divided according to checks and balances. Ultimately, the maintenance of order in such systems depends not upon shared values but upon adherence to the rules of the game for the playing out of conflicts.

Because of the importance of consensus for conflict resolution in elitist systems, authoritative decisions tend to be dramatized for the purposes of mobilization; however, the rationale for the decisions is obscured rather than explained, since efforts to define the situation might only weaken consensus. (In constitutional systems, the justification or decisions depends largely upon skill in explaining circumstances, which means that even the most clearly "constitutionalist" of them may tend toward slightly elitist practices in the conduct of foreign affairs, where all systems must rely at times upon secrecy.)

Related to the need to dramatize decisions is the tendency in elitist systems for leaders to seek any major changes by doing away with institutions. Nettl's theoretical observation of this structural characteristic could be taken as a remarkable "prediction" of Mao Zedong's readiness to mount the Cultural Revolution and his appreciation of the expendability of the Party organization. We can push the analysis even further and note that Nettl's theory of mobilization explains Mao's well-known distrust of bureaucratization as being completely normal in elitist systems and thus there is no need to make Mao into a "revolutionary romantic." In elitist systems, leaders do not want mobilization to take the form of greater institutionalization because their emphasis is upon loyalty to the elite's values.

The significance of these observations is that they should alert us to the probability that even with the passing of the "romantic revolutionary," Mao Zedong, Chinese leaders will continue to emphasize consensus rather than institutionalization, and decisionmaking will continue to respond to the informal relations among the elite rather than to bureaucratic procedures.

We can see how Mao's effort to mobilize the Chinese system for the purposes of modernization involved a basic contradiction, or rather an inherent flaw: Mao was prepared to move away from the elitist system in order to teach the Chinese to accept conflict and not overvalue consensus, but only to a limited degree, because he continued to cling to the system's inherent distrust of institutionalization. It is probably impossible to have an open acceptance of conflict in a political system whose institutions of authority are weak and lack autonomous integrity. Mao's encouragement of inter-elite conflict only served to weaken authority, and his enthusiasm for dispensing with basic governmental institutions made him conform to standard leadership practices of elitist systems striving to mobilize. In short, Mao's behavior was largely consistent with what should be expected in an elitist type of polity, and where it was inconsistent, it was self-defeating because it violated the basic structural imperatives of the system.

We may now return to our composite model of Chinese politics, assured that its basic features reflect not simply cultural tendencies but also profound qualities of the mobilization process of elitist systems. We shall next advance a series of hypotheses about Chinese political behavior that, if valid, will further refine this initial composite model and provide a basis for understanding of factional tensions in the post-Mao era.

It should be noted that hypotheses inevitably do overlap to some degree and that at times we examine certain aspects of behavior from different perspectives. Although this means that we risk repetition, it has the virtue of highlighting core matters: Any ground that is crossed and recrossed is important territory.

We shall begin with structural or objectively defined matters and proceed toward the psychological and cultural. For each of the propositions, we shall cite illustrative examples from China's recent politics, testimony about Chinese culture and political practices of scholars, and interview data gathered in our survey of Chinese people who have lived in the PRC. These informants were administered a questionnaire that contained questions that have also been widely used for measuring attitudes among Americans. Thus we are able to make some explicit comparisons between Chinese and American attitudes.

Chapter 3

The Suppression of Bureaucratic Interests

Our first hypothesis is that in Chinese politics, cultural and structural factors conspire to suppress the manifestation of institutional interests, and hence it is generally inappropriate to apply the "bureaucratic politics" model to Chinese politics.

In most political systems it is assumed that departments, ministries, agencies, and other formal organizations have their own institutional interests, and that there will inevitably be clashes among these interests. Sometimes the conflicts involve broad and fundamental issues, such as agriculture versus industry, or light versus heavy industry; at other times, the conflicts are quite narrow and revolve around the allocation of resources or questions of authority and jurisdiction. Such conflicts lie at the heart of most governmental processes, and described as bureaucratic politics, they are taken as a normal fact of life in most countries.

Not so in China. The very admission of the normality of such conflicts would be an acknowledgment that consensus is impossible or at least unlikely. Indeed, precisely because any factions based upon institutional or organizational considerations would be objective and logical challenges to the ideal of consensus, the Chinese go to great lengths to prevent the emergence of such bureaucratic interests. Governmental institutions are supposed to fit together as cogs, and no leader should assert his special interests over the collective interests.

Mao Zedong, of course, did legitimize what he called "non-antagonistic contradictions," but these were of a more general nature, largely between the people and the Party, and they did not involve clashes between parts of the government that in theory should work smoothly together. The Marxist–Leninist doctrines of the unity of theory and practice and of the correctness of Party line have also contributed to the conviction that institutionally based conflicts are abominations that threaten the integrity of the regime.

Although Mao Zedong's assertion that the history of Chinese Communism can be encapsulated in his theory of the struggle between "two lines" is an admission that intra-elite conflicts are possible, it is significant that all of the struggles between the "two lines" have been officially described as manifestations of personal ideological failings, and never has there been a hint that clashes over the correct line might arise out of the logic of different institutional interests. While Western students of Chinese Communism saw as completely "natural" the early 1930s conflict between a rural, guerrilla-based Mao Zedong and an urban, Shanghai-based Party leadership, the Chinese themselves have always described the difficulties as stemming from the moral character and the ideological failings of those involved.[1] The "ten great line struggles" that Mao spoke of and the two additional struggles involving the purges of Lin Biao and the Gang of Four, which the current leadership identifies, all presumably represent the failings of individuals, never the logic of institutional conflicts. The Chinese refuse to entertain the notion that their intra-Party disagreements might have resulted from such leaders as Liu Shaoqi, Peng Dehuai, or Lin Biao responding to the interests and the perspectives of the institutions with which they were most closely identified.[2]

Significantly, in imperial China, although political life was structured

---

1. Aside from its manifestly thoroughgoing scholarship, Benjamin Schwartz's *Chinese Communism and the Rise of Mao Tse-tung*, (Harvard University Press, Cambridge, Mass., 1951) became an acknowledged classic largely because it rejected the normal Western assumption that the early intra-Party clashes were primarily the product of differing policy interests, without at the same time accepting the assumption about the importance of private motives. Schwartz found middle ground by stressing the importance of ideology, which by its nature is well designed to mask both institutional interests and personal predilections.

2. Lowell Dittmer has shown the Party "struggles" involving deviations from the one "correct" Party line generally reflect the Chinese notion that the conflicts were rooted in personal and not structural faults, although he does cite some evidence that the opposite was in fact the case in several instances. (Lowell Dittmer, " 'Line Struggle' in Theory and Practice," *China Quarterly*, No. 72, December 1977, pp. 675–712. For the traditional Chinese view, see Michael Loewe, *Imperial China: The Historical Background to the Modern Age*, Praeger, New York, 1966.)

around a centralized bureaucracy that was divided into ministries or boards, factional politics rarely reflected institutional interests. The Chinese have historically been extremely sensitive to the dangers of officials becoming contentious, because of the need to represent their bureaucratic interests. The principal defense employed in traditional China was that of preventing specialization. In the earliest period, the highest officials around the emperor did not represent functional boards and hence particular interests, but were rather designated in entirely meaningless symbolic ways, such as according to the points of the compass. (To a curious extent, some of the members of the current Chinese Politburo are equally free-floating and have no specialized responsibilities.) Later, as the six ministries or boards became more formally institutionalized, the Chinese continued to protect themselves against bureaucratic politics by ensuring that officials did not develop institutional loyalties that would drive them to excessive zeal in championing the interests of any department. The tradition of "gentlemanly power" among mandarins required that officials never become too interested for too long a time in the technical problems of any ministry.[3] By conscious design, enthusiastic advocates of any upsetting policies in any particular ministry could expect to be reassigned so as to have to work against the very programs they had just initiated. A high official in, say, the Ministry of War could be certain that if he pushed too hard for greater allocations to the military he would shortly be transferred to the Ministry of Finance, where he would be expected to advance with equal enthusiasm all the arguments against his previous pleas for more funds for the Ministry of War.

To a startling degree, cadres who reach high positions in the PRC today also tend to have careers that have forced them to periodically alter their enthusiasms for specialized institutional interests.[4] Deng Xiaoping's career has been divided between managing Party affairs and working within the State Council; Hua Guofeng rose out of rural agricultural work and service in the domain of public security; and lesser figures who have

3. In a subtle and insightful comparative analysis, Rupert Wilkinson has shown that the British concepts of admirable leadership, rooted in the public school tradition, were very close to the Chinese ideals of the amateur as ruler. See (*Gentlemanly Power*, Oxford University Press, London, 1964). For a vivid statement of the Chinese abhorrence of specialization, see Joseph R. Levinson, "The Amateur Ideal," in John K. Fairbank (ed.), *Chinese Thought and Institutions*, University of Chicago Press, Chicago, 1957.

4. One of the difficulties in applying the bureaucratic politics "model" for uncovering the secrets of Chinese politics is that the model is not a "theory" with predictive powers. It is thus not possible to take limited data and arrive at "predictions" or "explanations" that go beyond those data. The model's usefulness lies precisely in the opposite direction: It is a very helpful heuristic device for organizing and giving coherence to large quantities of descriptive data.

stayed in the same place or even within the same organization will usually have had a variety of duties over the years. The "ladder of success" in Communist China, as in imperial China, thus involves constant reassignments of cadres from place to place and from task to task.

It is only the exceptional few who have had the chance to move about, since most cadres find that their careers are sharply circumscribed. Anyone assigned to a "system" is expected to devote his entire life to it. Almost without exception, the highest rungs of leadership have been reserved for those who have been fortunate enough to avoid undue specialization and have consequently established a wider network of acquaintances. Yet, the diversity of the responsibilities over the years of even such leaders as Deng and Hua may be illusory, since their official postings (read as *"Who's Who"* listings) can suggest a rich variety of experiences, while in fact their actual work has been rather narrowly concentrated in terms of "Party work." Their official titles have generally been merely formalistic designations that mask their primary responsibilities in managing Party problems.

Those who have stayed in a particular field have had to learn to restrain their advocacy demands, since the secret of success is almost inevitably in not antagonizing political masters and always adapting specialized interests to the current policy directions of the top leadership. While it may seem unfair to cite individual cases, it is clearly appropriate because it makes obvious our general point that specialized institutional interest should never be too vigorously championed. A model of restraint in defending institutional or bureaucratic interests is Zhou Peiyuan, a leading educator and science statesman of Communist China. During the 1950s, Zhou vigorously championed close collaboration with Soviet scientists; then in the 1960s he was at the forefront of those who proclaimed that China could be scientifically self-sufficient; throughout the Cultural Revolution period he denounced elitist education and praised peasant and worker wisdom; in the early 1970s he told foreign visitors that all was well with Chinese higher education even while the Gang of Four dominated the cultural scene; and now with the smashing of the Gang and the Politburo decision that "science and technology" should be one of the keys to the Four Modernizations he enthusiastically proclaims that Chinese education, and especially scientific work, is at last free to go ahead unhampered by previous impediments. The point is not that Zhou has had to trim his sails for every change in the political winds or that he should be thought of as an unprincipled man, but rather that he has not at any stage been able to champion effectively the particular institutional interest for which he has been the leading figure in the country. If Zhou Peiyuan could not push the interests of education and science from his power base, then clearly no one else has been in a position to advance those special interests either.

In Chinese politics, policy issues have long been relegated to second place behind questions about legitimacy and propriety. Whether it was mandarins seeking to rule an extensive empire or cadres today straining to govern a billion people, the first priority in China has always been the need to uphold correct conduct so as to ensure the maintenance of social order. Both mandarin and cadre discovered from experience that their first concern always had to be adherence to their respective norms of propriety, which in the Chinese spirit of consensus always included the rule that everyone else should also conform. Historically, Chinese bureaucracies have been wondrous institutions for providing the necessary inertia for governmental durability. By being impervious to the costs of stalling actions and of obstructing policy initiatives until the illusion of consensus has been realized, and by being hypersensitive to the psychic rewards of condescension toward the lesser kinds, Chinese bureaucrats, both of long ago and of today, have proven that the continuity of regimes resides more in being than in doing.[5] Rather than chase the will-of-the-wisp of accomplishments, they have valued the universal instinct of deference for the exemplar of a culture's ideals, even if the ideals are only of the moment – the "model" worker, peasant, cadre, or leader, or the quintessential Confucian scholar-mandarin. (Hence the almost irresistible Chinese proclivity for the cult of personality.)

There is even a deeper reason why the politics of Chinese Communism has made it imperative to discount the importance of policy questions as compared with their significance in non-Communist society. One of the great, and generally unrecognized, advantages of non-Marxian political systems is that they accept as self-evident, and hence beyond all questioning, an inherent bifurcation between the constitutional norms of system legitimacy and the norms appropriate for partisan policy evaluation. In Communist systems, and most definitely the Chinese system, the legitimacy of the entire regime rests upon the professed claim of being in tune with history, or being in control of the "good" present as against the "bad" past, and of being able to provide a better future. Hence, in theory, legitimacy is linked to policy performance, and therefore, paradoxically, every effort must be made to treat policy as mere rhetoric, as a part of a captivating make-believe, and not allow it to become too exposed to rigorous scrutiny. (Note how carefully the Chinese mask from themselves all the critical evidence necessary to evaluate systematically

---

5. For an exceptionally illuminating explanation of why concerns for proper conduct and form had to take precedence over substantive issues in Imperial China, see Ray Huang, *1587: A Year of No Significance*, Yale University Press, New Haven, Conn. 1981.

the policy performance of the regime.) Precisely because the legitimacy of the system is in theory so intimately tied to policy accomplishments, it is imperative that too much not be made over any particular policy. Consequently, the stage is set to make discussions of policy a highly symbolic matter. All of this also explains why Communist regimes are commonly beset with problems of cynicism, for they must pay a high price for making their basis of legitimacy the hubris claim of being able to command the future.

This first hypothesis directly challenges a major school of thought about how Chinese politics can best be analyzed. Many political scientists have hoped that the screen surrounding Chinese politics could be punctured by applying the concepts of "bureaucratic politics" that have been developed to explain American and European governmental behavior. Their argument has been that Chinese leaders are probably motivated by the manifest interest of whatever institutional associations they have. We are asserting that, on the contrary, any attempt to explain Chinese politics according to the logic of bureaucratic politics rests upon questionable assumptions. Cultural sensitivity about the dangers of direct confrontations, along with their anxieties about explicit disagreements, has made the Chinese hypersensitive to conflicting bureaucratic or institutionalized interests. There is, therefore, less tendency in Chinese politics than in most systems for bureaucratic interests to become the pivotal points of political conflicts and alliances.

Graham Allison's *Essence of Decision* popularized the idea that much of American governmental decisionmaking can be explained by the bureaucratic politics concept. It has also had an understandable influence upon China analysts and has caused them to assume – unfortunately, with little empirical evidence – that the Chinese must also act in response to whatever bureaucratic interests are implied in their official roles. Several scholars have explored such bureaucratic interest group pressures in different fields of Chinese government, but with the exception of David M. Lampton's work on the Chinese medical profession, the interpretations have generally consisted of tenuous arguments.[6] The Chinese have been remarkably successful in muting bureaucratic interests; but this is not to say that career experiences in both Party and state bureaucracies may not be very important in determining the personal relationships that can be so important in forming factions.[7]

6. David M. Lampton, *The Politics of Medicine in China*, Westview Press, Boulder, Colo., 1977.

7. Although Paul Wong's *China's Higher Leadership in the Socialist Transition* (The Free Press, New York, 1976) purports to be an application of the concept of "bureaucratic politics," it is in fact a very sophisticated and ingenious quantitative analysis of career pat-

The key structural or organizational reason for the muting of bureaucratic interests in Chinese politics is that Chinese procedures prohibit communication among subordinates in different ministries or departments. All inter-ministry or inter-department coordination must take place at the very top. Thus, instead of the constant flow of telephone calls and meetings among subordinates that takes place in most bureaucratic systems, Chinese subordinates only communicate up or down in their own ministry. The responsibility for coordinating policy and settling organizational conflicts is reserved for those at the Center. Junior officials are denied the possibility of seeking allies in other ministries or departments and are not able to impress their superiors with having outnegotiated competitors in other hierarchies. Superiors do not expect their subordinates to test out the positions of other ministries or even to explore ahead of time the views of potentially contending power centers.

We have solid evidence about the lack of inter-departmental communications from the testimony of numerous foreign businessmen who, much to their amazement, have had Chinese in one ministry ask them about the views and positions of Chinese in another ministry. The Chinese have explained their need to ask Americans to serve as middlemen on the grounds that it is improper for them to contact directly people in another chain of command.

By precluding such lower-level inter-ministry communications, the Chinese have been able to stifle both organizational politics and bureaucratic politics. (By "organizational politics" we mean the power conflicts that can flow from clashes in the institutional interests of different organizations with their separate goals and responsibilities; by "bureaucratic politics" we imply the much more personal "games" in which individuals strive to advance their own interests by playing off superiors and subordinates not only in their particular chains of command but also in other hierarchies.)

Thus the flow of policy-oriented demands can only move directly upward within separate encased hierarchies, an organizational arrange-

---

terns that belongs essentially to the great traditions of studying Chinese elites. In any hierarchical polity, be it traditional or Communist, men will have careers that take some to the top, throw others out in the process, and leave most at lower levels of attainment; and of course people will come from different parts of the country, from different schools, and they will have different networks of friendships – facts that are very important for understanding life within such bureaucratic structures but that do not constitute what is known as the "bureaucratic politics model" in contemporary political science. Wong's approach is a significant advance in quantitative techniques for the analysis of essentially the same questions as those addressed in such traditional Sinological works as *The Eminent Chinese of the Ch'ing Period* and *The Ming Biographical Dictionary*.

ment that from time to time contributes to the impression that the Chinese are about to surge ahead on all fronts—with no sense of priorities—as each ministry or organization seeks in its own way to carry out the general policies of the day. Only when all the separate bureaucracies have made their "commitments" or their "demands" and these have been passed up to the State Council or the Politburo are there any dampening effects from the ultimate imperative that resources are scarce and priorities must be set. Instead of the complex game of governmental politics in which almost no one is too humble to seek allies elsewhere or to strive for recognition by winning inter-agency battles over substantively trivial issues, the Chinese system permits subordinates only to push whatever policy initiatives they have toward the top of their own ministries.

When such initiatives do reach the top, they cannot become the stuff of open, bureaucratically based politics because of a peculiar lack of congruence at the pinnacle: For reasons that have never been explicated but seem to be ingeniously clever—given the Chinese commitment to repress all policy conflicts—the Chinese have more ministries than vice-premiers. (As of early 1981 there were 53 ministries and commissions and only 13 vice-premiers.) Thus individual vice-premiers have to take responsibility for several related ministries, resolving in their own way any potential conflicts.

The result of this arrangement is that the vice-premiers seek to suppress excessive enthusiasm for particular bureaucratic policies. Furthermore, their advocacy of particular policies is dampened by their understandable desire to prove themselves to be the loyal champions of the collective interest of the Center rather than pesky advocates of special interests (that is, selfish individualists).

Inescapably, the vice-premiers do tend to assume responsibility for different policy domains—for example, Fang I presently dominates decisions in the fields of science, education, and the procurement of technology, while Chen Yun presides over economic policies—but how much individual authority each has, or how tradeoffs are made in the State Council, are mysteries to all except those directly involved. Nevertheless, we can be confident that however the decisions are made, they represent processes of compromise among the highest authorities rather than victories in bureaucratic power struggles. (We know this not only because the struggles did not begin at the lower levels but also because the numbers of vice-premiers do not increase or decrease in direct proportion to the numbers of ministries; rather, the growth in the numbers of vice-premiers is a measurement of the number and power of the factions that must be recognized at the top.) Thus, before the current expansion to 18 to include champions of the Cultural Revolution or the "whatever faction," the "veteran cadres," and the rehabilitated cadres of both the "restoration" and the "practice" factions, the largest number of vice-premiers was 16 (the number in 1965 when Mao's and Liu's followers were competitively seeking greater status). The result is a tendency toward a muted process of policy accommodation in which high officials support their policy concerns implicitly rather than explicitly.

Thus it is not surprising that Western analysts, in spite of their natural bias to suspect "bureaucratic" tensions and factions, have found it surprisingly hard to identify persistent institutional clashes in Chinese politics. Jurgen Domes, for example, in speculating about possible "groupings" under Chairman Hua, identifies seven possible bases for factional developments, but none involves specific inter-institutional or inter-organizational conflicts.[8] In the friendly debate between Andrew J. Nathan and Edwin A. Winckler over whether or not it is appropriate to characterize the Chinese political system as constantly involved in policy "oscillations," neither argues that vacillations might come about because of shifts in the relative power of contending institutions, and hence different bureaucratic interests. Both see only leaders with little regard to their organizational interests seeking policy solutions through a process of "learning" and "contending."[9]

Given the casualness with which the Chinese establish or do away with whole ministries (often by merely merging them together) and the ease with which entire organizations are reorganized, civilian cadres are not likely to develop strong institutional identifications. And as we have already noted, the rather diffuse concept of the Center helps to blur institutionalized conflicts. Since the PLA is probably the most solidly institutionalized organization in the country – even more so than the Party, after its travails of the Cultural Revolution – it is not surprising that the first symptoms of factional conflicts based on clashes between "institutions" have been noticed in relations among the Field Armies. Whether one accepts the Whitson[10] thesis that the Field Armies have been the bases for firm factions or William Parrish's[11] more modest

8. He, of course, identifies several "institutions" as providing the basis for a power grouping – the central military machine, the regional military leaders, and the secret police – but he does not identify any specific inter-institutional conflicts of interest. (Jurgen Domes, " 'The Gang of Four' – and Hua Kuo-feng," *China Quarterly*, No. 71, September 1977, pp. 477–478.)

9. Andrew J. Nathan, "Policy Oscillations in the People's Republic of China: A Critique," *China Quarterly*, No. 68, December 1976, pp. 720–733; and Edwin A. Winckler, "Policy Oscillations in the People's Republic of China: A Reply," *China Quarterly*, No. 68, December 1976, pp. 734–750.

10. William W. Whitson, *The Chinese High Command*, Praeger, New York, 1973.

11. William L. Parrish, "Factions in Chinese Military Politics," *China Quarterly*, No. 67, September 1976, pp. 494–500.

thesis that the bonds among officers are probably no more intense than those in limited forms of bureaucratic politics, it still seems true that army politics have produced the clearest example of legitimate inter-institutional conflicts; at the same time, this is only an incipient development, since significant clashes of interests have not broken out between the PLA and other institutions.

Yet, significantly, the Chinese military provides the most support for our basic propositions: By any logic of bureaucratic politics or of institutional interests, the Chinese Air Force should have been solidly in the camp of the "moderates" during the succession crisis near the end of Mao Zedong's life, yet, defying all such reason, the Air Force was a stronghold of the "radicals." The assumption that leaders are motivated by their institutional interests would suggest that the Air Force should have sided with those who stress the importance of technology and modern weapons – indeed, it is somewhat absurd for Air Force officers to preach willpower over machines and to extol peasant guerrillas. Yet historically the Air Force was the strongest center of radical Maoist power in the Chinese military.

How are we to account for the fact that the Chinese have been so successful in suppressing institutional interests, thus compelling factional coalitions to polarize around other considerations? The answer lies partly in the stage of structural development of the Chinese polity and partly in aspects of Chinese political culture.

A BUREAUCRATIC POLITY, BUT NOT BUREAUCRATIC POLITICS

Instead of having bureaucratic politics that involve the clashes of functionally specific interests, the Chinese political system remains a "bureaucratic polity," that is, a political system in which power and participation are limited to a small, hierarchically organized elite of officials whose attitudes, values, and personal relationships shape all decisions.[12] In a bureaucratic polity, the decisionmakers do not have to respond to pressures from the society at large, and no interests outside of the state (or single-party) hierarchy are allowed.

In this sense, the Chinese system, in spite of its "revolutionary" and

12. For a general discussion of the concept of a "bureaucratic polity," see Karl D. Jackson, "Bureaucratic Polity," in Karl D. Jackson and Lucian W. Pye (eds.), *Political Power and Communications in Indonesia*, University of California Press, Berkeley, 1978, pp. 3–22; Fred Riggs, *Thailand: The Modernization of a Bureaucratic Polity*, Cornell University Press, Ithaca, N.Y., 1966, pp. 310–396; Samuel P. Huntington, *Political Order in Changing Societies*, Yale University Press, New Haven, Conn., 1968, pp. 78–92.

"mobilization" aspects, still remains close to a traditional polity with its ruling elite. Viewed in such developmental terms, political evolution may be thought of as having three general stages:

1. In the first stage, a more or less unified elite makes all decisions and in particular reserves to itself the prerogatives of deciding what is best for the "people" or the "masses." When the elite is well organized, hierarchically structured, and commands the organs of a state, a bureaucratic polity exists. This stage covers most traditional systems and also those transitional systems in which the elite is either (a) more modernized than the masses and thus attempting to transform a "traditional" population into its own image or (b) more conservative than the general population and thus striving to retard development. In either case, the elite is engaged in its own political life, and the masses are not effective, autonomous participants.

2. The second stage finds the elite divided to some extent as institutionalization has progressed to the point where different leaders have different bureaucratic interests. At this stage, much of politics revolves around inter-elite conflicts. Some departments, such as ministries, are more committed to "rational" programs, while others are clinging to more ideological interests. A bureaucratic polity may begin to engage in bureaucratic politics, as a diffuse elite becomes increasingly institutionalized along functionally specific lines.

3. In the third phase, politics moves out into the general population, and the divisions and conflicts arise out of the clashes of interest within the general society or economy. At this stage, the function of government is mainly to respond to demands from the people or to "manage" conflicts so as to reduce tensions and protect the "general interest."

China today is still at the first stage, but there are signs from time to time that some elements of society are ready to move to the second stage, and there are even moments when wall-poster rhetoric might suggest hints of the third. Evidence that the Chinese leadership, both Hua Guofeng and Mao Zedong, sensed that China might be in the process of moving from stage one to stage two can be seen in Mao's speech on "The Ten Great Relationships," which he gave in 1956 when the Chinese system seemed on the verge of becoming stably institutionalized and which Chairman Hua republished in 1976 when he hoped to institutionalize a more bureaucratic system of rule. Significantly, of the ten major problems Mao foresaw for his government, four had the potential of becoming inter-organizational but all were treated as decisionmaking problems for a consensus-defending elite. For example, Mao identified the problems of "the relationship between heavy industry on the one hand and light industry on the other" and "the relationship between economic construction and defense construction," problems that certainly could become the clash of separate bureaucratic interests but which he treats as command-decision problems. Yet he must have sensed the potential for inter-institutional conflicts, because he adopted the placating formula of arguing that the way to favor one set of interests was to focus on the competing one – that is, if the Party's objective is to develop heavy industry, then it should stress light industry and agriculture; if the objective is to construct a strong national defense, then it should emphasize the civilian economy. We can see in Mao's methods an early attempt to ward off inter-institutional conflicts, an objective that he later attacked with the much more draconian measures of the Cultural Revolution and his total assault on all forms of institutionalization.

Indeed, most interpretations of Chinese Communist politics in recent years recognize that there has been an enduring tension between, on the one hand, tendencies toward institutionalization – that is, advancement to stage two – and on the other hand, a craving to operate without formal structures – that is, a clinging to stage one. The conventional interpretation of Chinese politics in the late 1960s perceives Mao Zedong as personally having strong antipathies for any form of institutionalized rule. However, there was considerable confusion and misunderstanding about why Mao opposed "bureaucratization." Many admirers of Mao believed that his anti-bureaucratic sentiments were a manifestation of a populist faith in the people and a call for more popular participation; these people failed to appreciate that his principal concern was with the "dangers" inherent in the institutionalization of governmental administration, which tend to produce inter-elite conflicts, clashes of interests, and loyalties that are not focused solely on the paramount leader.

In China, hostility toward bureaucratization long preceded Mao Zedong and was indeed basic to imperial Chinese politics. Emperors constantly had to guard against their ministers' advocating special bureaucratic interests. In most traditional systems, rulers have sought to claim direct linkage with their subjects whenever they felt their ministers were unduly pressing upon them the claims of their particular interests. Thus Mao Zedong's way of suppressing the potential danger of factions forming out of institutional interests was to challenge the basic concepts of a functionally divided government and to appeal to the traditional ideal of a unified leadership working in close contact with the common people. The other, more "pragmatic" Communist leaders, such as

Liu Shaoqi, Deng Xiaoping, and even Hua Guofeng, have followed a somewhat different strategy to achieve the same goal of suppressing functionally specific institutionalized interests. These leaders have relied more upon the Communist ideal of the "correct Party line" providing the unity necessary for overcoming any bureaucratic-politics tendencies. Before the Cultural Revolution, Liu Shaoqi fought against inter-agency and inter-institutional conflicts by stressing the personal and professional qualities of the perfect Party cadre, and today both Deng Xiaoping and Hua Guofeng are calling for "all-around support" for the presumably harmonious goals of the Four Modernizations.

Granting that Chinese leadership has been remarkably successful in repressing institutionally based interests and factions, is it reasonable to assume that as Communist rule becomes more institutionalized in the post-Mao era, there will be no rise in bureaucratic politics? Is China not likely to move increasingly into stage two and eventually lose more and more the characteristics associated with stage one?

No doubt there are pressures toward bureaucratic politics and the end of a homogeneous bureaucratic polity. But there are also counter-pressures. There is nothing historically inevitable about the three stages we have outlined. Indeed, in some countries the trend has been in the opposite direction, with increased modernization reducing some forms of inter-elite tensions. Some people, for example, would argue that in France the process of modernization has alleviated many tensions and produced greater harmony within the ranks of government.

Progress toward modernization in China will no doubt cause increased specialization and will hence strengthen professional interests. Yet at present the pervasive power of a fused and unstructured Center seems to be more than adequate to inhibit bureaucratic interests. Moreover, there are strong cultural predispositions, which we shall turn to next, that also constitute obstacles for transforming a bureaucratic polity into a system of bureaucratic politics.

AVOIDING CONFLICT BY KNOWING
WHERE CONTROL LIES

There was no way to design questions for our Hong Kong respondents that would test directly this first proposition, which is at the level of macro-analysis. We therefore have the micro-analysis problem of determining what attitudes and values would have to exist to make the system perform as suggested by the proposition, and what values and attitudes would call for different systemic behavior.

As we have already noted, there has been widespread recognition that much of Chinese behavior is situation-oriented, and therefore the Chinese are inclined to act according to the "logic of the situation" as they see it.[13] Sometimes this behavior is seen as a form of fatalism, of having to accept things as they are and go with the tide.[14] At other times this propensity is seen as a mark of realism and practicality.[15]

The very vividness with which the Chinese perceive circumstances and their need to act according to the dictates of the situation as they perceive it might suggest that they would be very responsive to the "logic" of organizational interests. Should we not expect that the Chinese, contrary to our first proposition, would tend to act according to their organizational interests and expect others to do the same? Why is it then that factions do not more readily adhere to institutional interests?

The answer, as our sample demonstrates, seems to lie in some of the secondary characteristics associated with the psychological trait of perceiving the locus of control over events in one's life as lying outside of the self. In recent years several psychologists, led by Julian Rotter, have found that it is possible to distinguish between people who think of that locus as being either internal or external to themselves.[16] The response to a series of questions on this "locus of control scale" showed, not sur-

13. Francis L. K. Hsu, *Under the Ancestors' Shadow*, Columbia University Press, New York, 1948; Francis L. K. Hsu, *Class, Caste and Club*, Van Nostrand, Princeton, N.J., 1963.

14. Robert S. Elegant, *The Center of the World: Communism and the Mind of China*, Methuen, London, 1963.

15. Richard W. Wilson, *Learning to be Chinese*, M.I.T. Press, Cambridge, Mass., 1970.

16. The concepts of internal and external locus of control were first expanded upon in Julian B. Rotter, "Generalized Expectations for Internal Versus External Control of Reinforcement," *Psychological Monographs*, Vol. 80, No. 1, 1966, pp. 1–28. The concepts were further refined by Hanna Levenson, "Activism and Powerful Others: Distinctions Within the Concept of Internal-External Control," *Journal of Personality Assessment*, Vol. 38, 1974, pp. 377–383.

As initially defined, the concept of "internal/external" locus of control related to the perceived source of reinforcement, reward, or gratification for behavior. Thus when reinforcement is perceived as not being entirely contingent upon one's own actions but as the working of luck, chance, or fate, the individual can be said to believe in *external* control. If, on the other hand, events are seen as contingent upon his own behavior, he can be said to believe in *internal* control.

Further work on these concepts made it apparent that each category had to be subdivided. One type of external control would indeed suggest that the individual is controlled by fate or chance, while another could have an entirely realistic appreciation of the existence of "powerful others" who could influence one's fate but whom one might also be able to influence to one's advantage. Similarly, there are "internals" who have a realistic sense of self-confidence and are prepared to take calculated risks, and others who act out of mindless hubris. Unfortunately, the questions used for the basic scale do not distinguish between the "passive" and the "active" externals and the internals who do or do not have a strong sense of the reality principle. In our work, however, we shall try to make these distinctions through correlations with responses to questions not included in the scale.

prisingly, that, compared with American samples, our Chinese respondents tend to be very strongly "externals."

This finding *both* confirms that the Chinese tend to be "situation-oriented" and points to certain other tendencies that help explain the paradox of why they are not also oriented to the interests of the particular organizations with which they are identified. These secondary tendencies include a strong sense of dependency upon authority, so that they are not likely to spontaneously support institutional interests; rather they respond more to leadership directives – which tend to warn of the danger of championing institutional interests. Spontaneity in advocating the self-interest of institutions is further inhibited by the fact that "externals" tend to have less sense of efficacy than do "internals," and they generally assume that there is likely to be some form of intervention between intentions and outcomes of actions.

In short, "externals" are more sensitive to authority – and the logic of the situation as defined by lines of authority – than they are to institutional interests – and the logic of the situation as defined by specialization.

Among the specific questions designed to measure "locus of control," our respondents were asked to choose between:

(a) "In the long run people get the respect they deserve in this world," and
(b) "Unfortunately, an individual's worth often passes unrecognized no matter how hard he tries."

The contrast between their "yes" responses and those of American businessmen and Air Force officers[17] is shown below:

	Response a	*Response b*
Hong Kong respondents	40%	60%
American businessmen	70.4%	29.6%
American Air Force Officers	62%	38%

The differences suggest that the Chinese are not only more "external," but they also see the world as less fair and see hard work as less likely to be rewarded, which is consistent with our previous analysis.

In being forced to choose between "Without the right breaks, one can-

17. David Rothberg, "Insecurity and Success in Organizational Life: The Psychodynamics of Leaders and Managers," Ph.D. dissertation, Department of Political Science, M.I.T., 1978.

not be an effective leader" and "Capable people who fail to become leaders have not taken advantage of their opportunities," the Chinese respondents demonstrated not only a greater belief in luck than the Americans, but also less willingness to blame themselves for failures to get ahead. Hence they have a greater belief in the legitimacy of complaining to others about one's misfortunes. Significantly, the experience of being a Red Guard during the Cultural Revolution and/or being sent down to the countryside seems to have increased the feeling that one's worth could go unrecognized (gamma = .72), but it also increased the feeling that capable people who don't get ahead have not taken advantage of their opportunities (gamma = -.375). That is to say, these traumatic experiences appear to have made young Chinese more cynical about justice in the world and more sensitive to the payoffs of aggressive, opportunistic behavior.

The most dramatic difference between Chinese and American samples was in their choice between "When I make plans, I am almost certain that I can make them work" (chosen by 97.1 percent of the businessmen and 93 percent of the military officers) and "It is not always wise to plan too far ahead because many things turn out to be a matter of good or bad fortune anyhow" (favored by only 2.9 percent and 7 percent of the two samples of Americans). Only 50 percent of our respondents were optimistic about their ability to carry out plans – even though all of them had clearly been successful in executing such a major plan as to leave China either legally or illegally.

This question, combined with others we shall come to shortly, indicates the extent to which the Chinese may have a weak sense of efficacy, are inclined to feel that they are victims of circumstance, are comfortable in dependency relationships, and feel little need to look far ahead. These characteristics, which are associated with a sense that control of events is largely external to oneself, do go beyond the general themes of this chapter on the dynamics of the Chinese political system; yet it may be appropriate to explore some additional dimensions that arise from their responses to locus-of-control questions.

It is fair to ask whether our respondents' experiences with an all-powerful system of authority in China may not have made them appear to be more sensitive to the limits of their own range of choices for action than might otherwise have been the case. This would certainly seem to be true with respect to some of the questions on the scale; but at the same time, the contrary would hold on other questions and thus the overall influence might in fact be neutralized. For example, in choosing between "It is impossible for me to understand what politicians are up to" (an "external" response) and "Societies generally get the quality of government they desire" (an "internal" response), 88.7 percent of our respondents chose the first statement (compared to only 16.9 percent of businessmen and 9.6 percent of the military). Here, however, the fact that the Chinese political system is indeed shrouded in secrecy may have strongly biased the responses in favor of the "external" choice.

On the other hand, political experiences probably made our respondents appear to be far less "external" in their choices between (1) "There are certain people who are just no good" (the "external" answer) and (2) "There is some good in everybody" (the "internal" answer). On this question the Chinese responses were practically identical with those of the Americans, 86 percent saying that "All have some good in them," as did 83.1 percent of the businessmen and 81.7 percent of the military. Those who had lived in China had apparently learned that "good" people often get criticized, that those whom the regime have classified as "bad elements" are not necessarily bad, and that some of their immediate leaders were good people even though they were working for what the respondents considered to be a bad system.

THE EFFECTS OF IDEOLOGY ON CULTURE

Carrying our analysis of internal–external locus of control even further, we arrive at significant evidence of some of the effects of Communism on traditional Chinese culture. A key objective of the Communist leaders in changing Chinese culture has been to reduce the degree to which the Chinese people have been "passive externals" and to make them into "internals," even of the mindless hubris type.

Our sample would suggest that the regime has been quite successful in producing more "internals," yet paradoxically the result has been to produce greater disillusionment and pessimism.

We arrive at this conclusion by first dividing our sample between young and old: that is, between those largely socialized under Communism and those who knew the previous society. The result shows some striking differences. First, the younger generation is more inclined to believe that they have control over their lives. Although a majority of both believe in external locus of control, a higher proportion of the young gave internal answers. One might therefore assume that exposure to constant stress and "self-reliance" has had some influence on the younger Chinese.

Second, the young were less inclined than the old to believe in luck and chance (93 percent of the old and only 58 percent of the young agreed with the statement, "Most of the unhappy things in people's lives are due to bad luck"). Third, the young were somewhat less impressed with the role that powerful people can play in one's life (73 percent of the old and

66 percent of the young agreed with the statement, "The most important thing in getting ahead is being on good terms with the right people").

Yet, in spite of these general indications of greater sense of personal control over their destinies and a greater feeling of self-reliance, all consistent with the objectives of Communist socialization, we find that the young, paradoxically, have far less confidence than the old that their efforts will be rewarded and that if they try hard enough they will be able to realize their goals. We see this in the fact that only 10 percent of the young, as compared with 80 percent of the old, agree that "If people try hard enough they will usually reach the goals of their lives."

How are we to explain this apparent contradiction? Why should those who have a greater sense of self-reliance and are less fatalistic turn out to be the most pessimistic about their own lives? If we distinguish between those among the young who had Red Guard experience and those who did not, we find hints of a plausible answer: The ex-Red Guards are, like others in their age cohort, more "internal" than the older generation, but they are more pessimistic than the non-Red Guard young about reaching their goals in life. That is to say, the ex-Red Guards were taught to believe in "internal" values, but they were also the most disappointed and hence the most cynical.

All of this suggests that in the larger scheme of Mao's attack upon traditional Chinese values, the regime had some successes, but those very successes have also made the Chinese more vulnerable to cynicism. By making young Chinese believe that they should be able to have a greater influence over developments in their lives but then creating great disappointments, the Chinese political system may have more than cancelled out its achievements in molding attitudes. Chinese with more traditional attitudes clearly find it easier to accept the ups and downs and the vacillations inherent in the modernization process. And it must be remembered that most of our sample still had those traditional orientations, insofar as they believed in an external locus of control.

Let us now return to the theme of the Chinese ability to repress interinstitutional conflicts by way of a few conclusions relevant for analysts seeking to forecast Chinese factional politics.

IMPLICATIONS FOR FORECASTING

The most obvious implication of our first proposition about Chinese factional politics is that analysts must be on their guard against assuming that inter-agency struggles are likely to bulk as large in Chinese factional politics as they do in the governmental politics of most societies. It cannot be assumed that leaders of particular ministries or departments will vigorously champion the logical or functional interests of their organizations.

Similarly, leaders who have been long associated with each other in particular organizations may later function together in a faction, but this does not mean that they will necessarily be advocates of their former common organization's interests. Career specialization may cause individuals to be especially knowledgeable or sensitive to particular problems, such as agriculture, propaganda, or education, but those who have been able to rise to the top are unlikely to be wedded to the interests of their former organizations. The fact that it may seem useful to identify individuals according to career specialization should not be taken to mean that common identifications imply a common factional orientation. Other factors, which we shall discuss later, and which include personal ties, are likely to be far more important in orienting factional cleavages.

Ever since the fall of the Gang of Four, and in spite of national defense being one of the Four Modernizations, it has not been easy for representatives of the military to press openly for greater military appropriations. Any spokesman so bold as to do so would be politically compromised and seen as a dangerous, selfish figure, capable of creating factional interests that might damage the unity of the leadership. Consequently, the case for modernizing the military has to be left largely to those who would seem to have no personal interest in the policies being advocated.

Although it would seem that the Chinese military should have had an easy time in getting larger allocations of the nation's resources, national defense has not been receiving higher priorities, for many reasons. Surprisingly, the situation has not changed even after the poor showing of Chinese arms in the 1979 border war with Vietnam. First, while inhibited in advancing their own interests, the military has not had many strong national allies to argue their needs, because many of the old, technologically oriented cadres still distrust the military for the administrative roles the PLA assumed at the end of the Cultural Revolution. PLA officers who were assigned to all kinds of "revolutionary committees" more often than not appeared to be managing affairs that rightfully should have been under the unfettered control of "old cadres." The fact that the military was seen as being reluctant to give up political and administrative power created further suspicions among many technocratically oriented cadres who might otherwise have been natural allies of the PLA. In the fall of 1975, many PLA commanders considered Deng Xiaoping himself to be an enemy because he sought to cut back military manpower and the PLA's political influence. Therefore, after Zhou Enlai's death in 1976, many of the key commanders sat on their hands and allowed Deng to be purged. Although Deng and the cadres being rehabilitated after his restoration are thought of as realists and technocrats, they have had little incentive to help the military out of its dilemma of being unable to openly advocate its interests.

The need to mask the interests that are being advanced means that it is often difficult to judge the precise dimensions of what is being called for. Little hints of what is wished for may be the most that partisans feel is prudent to publicize; or under different conditions, modest programs can be packaged in grandiose rhetoric, if that is the legitimized rhetoric of the day. The expansive rhetoric of the Four Modernizations masks what the Chinese will actually be doing in most of the four areas. The weakness of institutional interests can be seen in the ease with which advocates of particular grand schemes under the Four Modernizations have been willing to accept retrenchment and cutbacks of their interests.

Chapter 4

Deference for Generational Differences

Our second hypothesis is that generational differences are more easily articulated and tolerated than institutional differences, but they are difficult to organize for political objectives.

In contrast to their suppression of institutional differences, the Chinese highlight generational differences, openly acknowledging the reality of age and freely speaking of old and young cadres, of the Long March veterans, the Yunnan generation, the Civil War cadres, and on down to the Red Guard and the young cadres of the post-Cultural Revolution period.

The Chinese find it both more difficult and less necessary to deny that age and experience can divide people than to deny that institutional identifications might do the same. The Chinese have, of course, always been extremely age-conscious, appreciating the importance of seniority and the propriety of respecting elders, whether they be ancestors or old cadres who fought the revolution. It is also noteworthy that the Chinese in modern times have always made much over their bonds with classmates and schoolmates.

When the Chinese admit to factional tensions that involve more than just discredited leaders, they speak almost without exception of inter-generational and not inter-institutional conflicts. For example, the Gang of Four is denounced for opposing veteran cadres and favoring young ones.[1] There is a tacit assumption that generations will differ – older generations are said to have more wisdom, younger generations more enthusiasm, and middle-aged generations more skills. Some generations are, of course, seen as more worthy, more honorable, and more tested, while others have yet to prove themselves. Yet, aside from these self-evident distinctions, little is said that would explain the presumed nature of generational differences or the perception that some differences are more legitimate than others.

Whereas there are clearly recognizable generational differences, there is no manifest way in which generational *similarities* can be transformed into effective political power. People of the same generation presumably have an affinity for each other, but it is not clear why they should coalesce for common political objectives or form a coherent political grouping. Above all, there is little linkage in Chinese politics between specific generations and particular policy goals.

As potential power constellations, members of the same generation can perform in negative ways, blocking policies and seeking to protect the interests of their members, even seeking to rehabilitate those who have been discredited. Generation thus provides far more basis for status, respect, and perquisites than for manipulatory power. Generational factions tend to become status groupings, concerned with career well-being, and aside from this there is little rational linkage between policy alternatives and age-based factions.

Generations can also be the targets of attack. The indictment of the Gang of Four frequently charged that they were opposed to the "veteran cadres" and excessively favored "young cadres." For example, in criticizing the film *Counterattack* as "a big poisonous weed carefully concocted by the Gang of Four," Yang Zhijie and Zhu Ping wrote in the *People's Daily* that the Gang developed the theory that "old means seniority," and "in the eyes of the Gang of Four, all old cadres stand for revisionism: the older they are, the more revisionist they will become." Furthermore, the Gang of Four and "its confidants labeled the old revolutionaries as 'democrats' and described the process of transforming them 'from democrats to capitalist roaders' as 'an inexorable law'."[2]

Thus an age cohort in China can be the object of either praise or vilification, which means that "generation" has a strong symbolic dimension and that it is more a passive than an active factor in mobilizing for political action. Individuals, finding that they are symbolically

1. See, for example, "How the 'Gang of Four' Used Shanghai as a Base to Usurp Party and State Power," *Peking Review*, No. 6, February 4, 1977.

2. "The End of a Counterrevolutionary Rhapsody," *People's Daily*, January 12, 1977, Foreign Broadcast Information Service, *Daily Report – People's Republic of China*, January 1977.

characterized according to the honors or the liabilities of their age group, feel the necessity for collective action; but until there has been some generally recognized characterization, it is impossible for a leader to actively mobilize people simply because they are of the same generation. Generational considerations thus can contribute strongly to factional divisions, but they are not usually sufficient in themselves to create factions.

Chinese sensitivity to the potential for age grouping as the basis of political bonds tends to raise the level of suspicion in Chinese politics. Although they are aware that they cannot easily exploit generations to initiate actions on their own behalf, individual leaders are prone to suspect that others may have latent associations to which they are not parties.

Furthermore, the need to defer to elders as a matter of respect may also complicate power considerations. The distinction between status and power is not as vivid in China as it is in the West, which means that status relationships can often be turned into power. Yet at other times deference is treated as a mere formality and is not permitted to influence substantive considerations. Thus, in some situations, nobody can be quite sure whether a younger official who shows respect to his elders will in fact feel bound in any way by their wishes.

All of these considerations are further complicated at the present time in Chinese politics because of the peculiar "generational conversion" that took place in the struggle for succession after Mao's death. Chairman Mao, in bypassing the remnants of the Long March and the Yunnan generation in favor of Hua Guofeng, who was of the anti-Japanese war generation, initiated the "conversion," and it was compounded with the demise of the Gang of Four, when the whole Cultural Revolution generation became suspect and the formerly discredited cadres were rehabilitated. Because the Chinese believe that age is a major factor in human affairs, these shifts in political fortunes cannot be passed off as mere alterations in policy but must have lingering and potentially backfiring consequences.[3]

With current shifting of political generations, those who once had positions of power have been discredited and are now uncertain as to whether they have a political future, while those who have been rehabilitated are both aged and uncertain about whom they should pass their power on to. In several respects, the Cultural Revolution generation is a "lost generation"—it is damned for having moved ahead so fast

3. For an excellent analysis of current generational relationships in China, see Michael Yahuda, "Political Generations in China," *China Quarterly*, No. 80, December 1979, pp. 793–805.

during the upheavals, and it may remain damned for retaining positions of responsibility. It is also a lost generation because of its inadequate education and its lack of disciplined professional training.

As we shall see, given the nature of revenge in Chinese political culture, the shifts in power among well-defined generations leave the system in a potentially explosive state. In every office and bureau, carrying out the implications of the smashing of the Gang of Four has produced such major short-run concerns about who should have power that little attention can be given to what will happen when nature has its ultimate say about the inordinately old generation in power.

These problems of generational conversion were dramatized at the Politburo level in the post-Gang of Four period. For nearly two years, the five-member Standing Committee faced the extraordinarily awkward situation of Chairman Hua and his ally General Wang Dongxing being some twenty years younger than the other three members. Thus the formal superior was in fact a generation the junior and should have, according to the conventions of status, deferred to his elders. Furthermore, Hua Guofeng could not escape from his identification with those of his generation who profited politically from the Cultural Revolution and from the acts of an aged Mao Zedong who in advancing him also sought to destroy Deng Xiaoping and push ahead the Gang of Four. Consequently, no matter how much Deng professed that he was comfortable with Hua as chairman, most Chinese harbored the correct suspicion that it was not a smooth relationship.

In Chinese organizations, whether institutions or family businesses, the elders (grandfathers) have the prerogative of voicing their opinions and proclaiming how affairs should be managed, and the juniors in charge must treat such opinions respectfully but act on their own responsibility. Hua, acting as a normal Chinese, would be expected to solicit the opinions not only of Deng but also of Ye Jianying and Li Xiannian; then, he must appear to defer to his elders' opinions but in the end make correct decisions. Similarly, Deng Xiaoping would be expected to show deference to Ye Jianying, who is his senior in Party ranking, but Deng too must appear to maintain his independent judgment.

These rules about status and age, and especially the tension in Chinese culture about the prerogatives of seniority, were quite central to much of the maneuvering that brought about the downfall of Hua Guofeng and the triumph of Deng Xiaoping's group in 1981. During the years when Hua was still the ranking Party leader, Deng could get away with cavalierly asserting arbitrary demands that, because of his age, could be ambiguously interpreted. Was he only acting as a meddling "grandfather" to whom deference was due but not necessarily full obedience? Or was he in fact aggressively challenging the actual power of his younger "superior"? Frequently it was the latter in the guise of the former, and consequently Hua was inhibited from open retaliation. It was thus easy for the older person to make telling power moves in an offhand manner, while the younger man was shackled by cultural constraints. (Deng's advantages from craftily exploiting his age must have been especially galling for Hua because even as Deng was cashing in on the deference owed him for his age he was publicly calling for older officials to step aside to allow younger cadres to move ahead.) Near the end, however, the shoe was briefly on the other foot, in that during the winter and spring of 1980–81 the supreme elder, Ye Jianying, succeeded in using excuses about his age problems to postpone for nearly six months the plenum session designed to accept Hua's "resignation."

FOUR THEORIES OF GENERATIONS

Before we go further into the cultural dimensions of how generations can both divide and unite Chinese, it is useful to review briefly the general concepts and theories of generations in political analysis.

Four theories have been advanced about the role of generations in politics.[4] First, there is the Experiential Theory, which holds that a political experience may permanently mark a group and leave it with a distinctive socialization experience. This theory points to the lingering effects of such dramatic collective experiences as the Depression and the New Deal or the Vietnam War in the United States; World War I and the rise of Hitler in Europe; and the pre-war, wartime, and Occupation periods in Japanese society. In the case of China, this theory is vividly supported by the widespread acknowledgment of, first, the Long March generation, then the Japanese War generation, the Civil War generation, the post-Liberation generation, and finally the Cultural Revolution generation – each being defined by the period of entry into the CCP.[5]

The second theory of generations is the Maturational or Life Cycle Theory, which suggests that people at different stages of their lives will

4. What follows is a modification of concepts advanced, particularly by Samuel P. Huntington, in sessions of the Joint Seminar on Political Development, the report of which appears in Richard J. Samuels (ed.), *Political Generations and Political Development*, Lexington Books, Lexington, Mass., 1977.

5. The concept of "political generation" based on a shared experience was first defined by Karl Mannheim, *Essays in the Sociology of Knowledge* (Routledge and Kegan Paul, London, 1938), and was later greatly expanded by Sigmund Neumann, *Permanent Revolution: Totalitarianism in the Age of International Civil War* (2nd ed., Praeger, New York, 1965). See also Marvin Rentala, "Political Generation," *International Encyclopedia of the Social Sciences*, The Macmillan Co., New York, 1968; and William Quandt, *Revolution and Political Leadership: Algeria 1954–68*, M.I.T. Press, Cambridge, Mass., 1969.

have different political attitudes, and that each generation ultimately goes through much the same transition as its predecessors. Rebellious and radical youths in time become moderates and even conservatives. People of the same age cohort may think alike, but they will also change, and thus in spite of differences there is much continuity in society as a whole.[6] In China, as in most cultures, this theory of generations assumes that youth is the time for idealism and that with aging comes pragmatism and greater impatience about performance. The relative power of each generation at any time will thus set the tone of politics for the country.

In China the Maturational Theory illuminates additional dimensions of tension, particularly the tension that existed during and after the Cultural Revolution. Mao's decision to mobilize youth and to give the Red Guards the exhilaration of knowing power altered the progression of the generations, and for a time it did add an extraordinarily youthful flavor to Chinese politics. After the Cultural Revolution, and more dramatically after Mao's death and the crushing of the Gang of Four, the youthful generation was demoted and the older generation was restored to power, with many scores to settle. Thus, the experiential considerations were combined with a distortion of maturational developments to produce an exaggerated swing from idealism to disillusionment and resentment. The long-run effects of these generational reversals may be to reduce the significance of maturational factors in Chinese politics, since Chinese youth of the post-Cultural Revolution generation seem to have learned from the experiences of their older brothers and sisters and thus have contained their inclinations for idealism. There is evidence that young Chinese are cynical beyond their years, and hence there may be a smoothing out of generational differences.

The third theory of generations is the Adversary or Clash Theory, which is as old as Plato and was given dynamic dimensions in Freud's concept of the Oedipus complex. In contrast to the Experiential Theory, which permits each generation its unique qualities that may only incidentally be in conflict with those of another generation, or the Maturational Theory, which allows each generation to look with bemusement to the next for reviving memories of its own earlier years, the Adversary Theory postulates that each generation seeks to define itself by clashing

6. On the concept of "generation" as a phase of age cohort changes, see such studies as Paul Abramson, "Generational Change and the Decline of Party Identification in America: 1952–1974," *American Political Science Review*, Vol. 70, No. 2, June 1976, pp. 469–478; S. N. Eisenstadt, *From Generation to Generation: Age Groups and Social Structure*, Free Press, Glencoe, Illinois, 1956; and N. D. Glenn and R. Hefner, "Further Evidence on Aging and Party Identification," *Public Opinion Quarterly*, Vol. 36, No. 1, Spring 1971, pp. 21–47.

with another generation. The conflict must invoke more than just life-cycle differences – liberal periods are thus "naturally" followed by conservative phases, and activists are scorned as old-fashioned and lacking in "consciousness" by detached successors. (As Plato first observed, it is entirely normal for liberal parents to have radical children, since that is only a difference of degree in views, but it is really damaging for liberal parents to have conservative children – that is a truly adversary generational relationship.)[7]

Historically, much of the tension in Chinese society associated with age difference has fitted the theory of adversary generations. The early process of modernization set progressive (and better educated) younger generations against conservative, Confucian older ones. Indeed, much of the story of modernization in China took precisely the form of each succeeding generation feeling ashamed of its elders and trying to oppose all that they represented. This was certainly true of the dynamic generations of Chinese students from the May Fourth Movement through the fall of the Kuomintang. What is striking, however, is that since the establishment of the PRC, each generation has been, on the manifest level, increasingly conformist. Nevertheless, at a more latent level, younger cadres have been basically frustrated about advancement prospects because of the tenacious hold of the older generations on offices.

Finally, the fourth theory, that of Succession to Leadership, states that generational conflicts are most sharply delineated when one age group holds on to ultimate power and the others are forced to queue up for their turn at power. This is the most common generational problem in traditional societies, where leadership is supposed to be based on wisdom and wisdom is associated with age. This is also the Chinese Communist concept of the proper sequence for acquiring power.

Paradoxically, while the Chinese Communists have official justifications for the importance of including youth in leadership roles, they have no doctrines that explicitly favor seniority; yet in practice, the Chinese adhere unquestioningly to the doctrine of seniority – to the point of having produced under Mao a gerontocracy.[8] Although the Chinese are acquainted with the idea of older leaders getting the honors while younger

7. See, for example, Lewis S. Feuer, "Generations and the Theory of Revolution," *Survey*, Vol. 18, No. 3, Summer 1972, pp. 161–188; Robert E. Lane, "Fathers and Sons: Foundation of Political Beliefs," *American Political Science Review*, Vol. 24, No. 4, August 1959, pp. 502–511; M. P. Sinha and K. P. Gangrade, *Inter-Generational Conflict in India* Nachiketa Publications, Bombay, 1971.

8. On the effects of gerontocracy on Chinese political development, see Lucian W. Pye, "Generational Politics in a Gerontocracy: The Chinese Succession Problem," *Current Scene*, Vol. XIV, No. 7, July 1976; and "Generations in Chinese Politics," in Samuels (ed.), op. cit.

followers do the work, they seem to have problems with delegating responsibility; and therefore, quite unlike the Japanese, they cannot smooth over the succession process. Furthermore, when it comes to the holding of power, the Chinese are impervious to the concept of retirement. As a result, succession questions in Chinese politics have a heavy mortality dimension; to look ahead requires thinking about the death of one's superior and not about impersonally set periods of tenure.

To varying degrees, all four of these theories shed light on the characteristics of the generational problem in Chinese politics. It is important to understand that while we are predisposed to think of the Chinese Communists as having come to power as a revolutionary wave, the fact is that their leadership has generally consisted of neat and orderly layers of generations. Cadres of the same cohorts have proceeded in lock-step careers and without the confusion and mixing up of ages and experiences that are expected in a revolutionary upheaval.

The fact that generational considerations are given so much sympathetic attention testifies to the degree to which China has a managed revolution. Opportunity has been directly associated with promotion in a hierarchy in which extraordinary weight is given to seniority.

It was, of course, this orderly sense of status by generational seniority that provided the basis for a gerontocracy. Not only was government under the elderly Mao Zedong conducted in the style associated with gerontocracy – decisions by an inner council of elders, much use of moral justification, repeated harping on the failures of youth to live up to past standards, fear that the future will be dark, constant reflection on the virtues of a heroic past, and so on – equally significant have been the efforts of Hua Guofeng to seek legitimacy according to the norms of gerontocracy: the early attempt to identify the new supreme leader as "the wise Chairman Hua Guofeng," the use of large conference gatherings at which elderly officials harangued and preached to massed and mute lesser officials, and the belief that the new leader could provide inspiration by merely visiting factories and schools.[9]

It is somewhat incongruous – indeed, some might say ludicrous – that a system that proudly conceives of itself as revolutionary has been largely governed by men in their seventies and eighties. (Plato, of course, be-

9. Part of the buildup of the Hua Guofeng image consisted of widespread reporting on his inspection tours. Typical was the report of his visit to the Northeast: "Chairman Hua inspected the Sungling and Hsingyang machine building plants which the great leader Chairman Mao inspected in 1958. The visit of Chairman Hua, the worthy successor of Chairman Mao, gave inspiration to the workers ... Chairman Hua carefully listened to the introduction of every project . . ... He looked with keen interest at the new products ... asked about their performance . . .." Foreign Broadcast Information Service, *Daily Report – People's Republic of China*, May 6, 1977, p. E4.

lieved that government should be the domain of old men because he thought they would have greater wisdom, a more refined sense of justice, and not enough energy to commit acts of folly. But he could not have been expected to imagine the implausible things the elderly Mao dreamed up, such as his Great Leap and Cultural Revolution.) The problem of aged leadership is almost certain to become more acute as China modernizes. First, with the need for more advanced technology, the Chinese will have to give responsibility to better-trained people who will also be younger; and second, as government becomes more a problem of management, leaders will have to have more energy. Rulers can be elderly and even withdrawn figures, but executives must be dynamic people with the energy necessary to cope with a multitude of problems and the ability to make quick but not capricious decisions.

Jurgen Domes has demonstrated that the fall of the Gang of Four produced a dramatic rise in the age of the Chinese leadership, as old cadres were rehabilitated and younger ones dismissed. His figures reveal that during the period from October 1976 to June 1977 the average age of the purgees from the Central Committee was 53.2 years, while the reappointees averaged 63.7 years; none of the new appointees was under 50 years old, while 75 percent were over 60; and all new appointees had joined the Party before 1949. In contrast, 60 percent of the purgees had joined after "Liberation," and 50 percent were under 60 years of age.[10] These figures suggest a built-in ominous situation, since the victory of Deng and Hua has left China with an even older leadership than it had under Mao; and most serious of all, the next generation, which has already tasted a bit of power, has now been pushed aside as a suspect group.

The same situation exists in most Chinese institutions, as younger cadres who came into the Party during the Cultural Revolution have been removed in favor of older cadres, and the older group must cling to power well into their old age as they compete with those whom they have just purged. This generational antagonism explains why the campaign against the followers of the Gang of Four has lasted for so long and has been so bitter.

Thus in the post-Mao era, the traditional importance of generational considerations in the formation of factions has been accentuated and the mere age of a person may, to an inordinate degree, be taken as prima facie evidence of his political proclivities. Older men in the hierarchy are automatically declared to be "old cadres," who are thus classified as opposed to both the Cultural Revolutionists and the impulsive pragmatism of Deng Xiaoping. Anyone younger is suspected of having been at one

---

10. Jurgen Domes, "The 'Gang of Four' – and Hua Kuo-feng," op. cit.

time a follower of the Gang of Four. If it is true, as rumored, that Hua Guofeng had to confess before the Politburo that he had once been a "helicopter" – that is, he rose straight up during the Cultural Revolution – then old cadres will probably believe that they should withhold trust in him, while the younger Party leaders will see him as more their man than Deng is. Hence, the widespread rumors in China about Hua's self-criticism may prove to be helpful to him rather than damaging – particularly if the countless lower- and middle-level cadres in China decide to employ the quiet methods known to bureaucrats throughout the world to even the score against Deng for having set back their careers.

In a strange fashion, the post-Mao political structure has gotten itself into the same peculiar inversion of generations as was the case in the last days of Mao's reign: An older generation is holding onto power in a manner that alienates the inevitably succeeding generation. Clearly, a major source of tension in both situations has been the strong Chinese propensity to assume that generational differences naturally make for different factional clusterings.

Faced with this situation in which he must distrust his immediately younger generation as his successors, Deng Xiaoping has sought to employ, but not in such an extreme form, the tactic used by Mao Zedong. When faced with a similar situation, he sought to pass over his immediate successor generation and strike an alliance with China's youth, thereby causing the Cultural Revolution. In a much more restrained fashion, Deng has repeatedly called for older cadres to step aside and for the rapid promotions of younger leaders. By his characterization of "old" and "young," he has made it clear that he would like men of Hua's generation, who are only in their early sixties, to yield to a completely fresh generation who will be "more knowledgeable and specialized."[11]

A PARADOX ABOUT AMBIGUITY AND ANXIETY IN CHINESE CULTURE

There seems to be a contradiction between the Chinese reactions to institutional and generational conflicts and our earlier observation that in Chinese culture uncertainty produces anxiety. Institutional

11. Deng Xiaoping has had to delicately advance his call for younger cadres for fear of violating the Chinese taboo against openly recruiting a personal following of aspiring young Party members. He has thus, first, linked his appeal for more youthful cadres with a need for greater skills and specializations, and, second, endorsed the slogan "In first, out afterwards," which means that new recruits should be brought in first before the older cadres need to retire. See "Deng Xiaoping's Important Speech at the Central Work Conference of December 25, 1980," *Ming Pao*, Hong Kong, May 3, 1981, p. 9.

conflicts are inherently more straightforward, while generational differences may be uncertain, and hence it might be assumed that the Chinese would be more uncomfortable over generational conflicts than institutional ones. Yet historically it has been the other way around.

Unquestionably, Chinese culture values clarity of relationships and abhors ambiguity. Purposeful obfuscation is therefore legitimate if the object is to establish or preserve the smoothness of a relationship; thus what is often taken as deviousness is instead a readiness to shade the truth in the hope of bettering personal ties and of strengthening the impression of unqualified friendship. ("I am so anxious that nothing should complicate our relationship that I am prepared to tell any necessary lies.") In this sense, the indirect graciousness and crude bluntness between which the Chinese vacillate are merely parallel responses to an underlying craving for certainty and predictability in human affairs. Above all, however, political leaders wish to appear to be fully in command, sure of what they want and confident of how they should be acting.

Therefore, it seems paradoxical that the Chinese are happier with generational differences, which are imprecise, inherently unpredictable, and basically vague, than they are with institutional clashes, which are unequivocally clear-cut and organized around contending power constellations that are committed to precise but usually different objectives. The explanation of this paradox lies at several levels.

First, the Chinese take status considerations very, very seriously. Their instinct is that people should defer interests, particularly their own, in favor of status calculations. Current visitors to China are often impressed with how automatically the Chinese suppress their private interests and state that they "only want to serve the people." Yet in traditional China as well, it would have been inconceivable for even the most rapacious Chinese to admit to personal ambition rather than to merely serving some larger collectivity, such as his family. (In American culture, where individualism is so valued, to say that one is doing something because it is "the wish of his family" is to imply that otherwise he would do something else; in traditional Chinese culture, the only way a person could say what he wanted was to attribute the desire to his family.) Almost in compensation for this profound inhibition in expressing personal interests, Chinese culture has long legitimized people's rights to claim their proper status considerations. Superiors should accept their rights, and older people unabashedly acknowledge the deference of youth.

In order to be admitted to participation in Chinese politics, one must prove an ability to discriminate relative status positions with great precision. Generation groups provide an easy measure, but among organizations and institutions status ranking is more complex and ambiguous.

Second, the Chinese are extremely wary of inter-institutional clashes, since the very vividness of policy differences can lead to confusion as to what the ultimate outcome will be. Thus, while the policies of different parts of government can be clear-cut, the consequences of disagreements can produce the highest forms of uncertainty and great dangers for those caught in such conflicts. On the other hand, while generational differences involve more obscure issues, they have the virtue of being a part of the natural order of life. If those involved are moderately considerate and show minimal respect for each other, they should have no problems with generational differences. If, on the other hand, they choose to be correct according to the formal responsibilities of their offices, they cannot compromise differences without risking the appearances of corruption.

At a third level, the clashes inherent in organizational differences – such as between the army and the militia, or between export industries and those oriented toward interior development – go far beyond providing clear-cut definitions of the situation and spill over into what the Chinese would consider to be aggressive adversary relationships, which are always very threatening. Generational differences, which are inherently vague on policy and power, provide the basis for more manageable disagreements.

In short, this paradox illustrates that Chinese behavior operates within a rather restricted range: There is a need to avoid ambiguity and a highly fluid context, but at the same time, too sharply defined situations can become threateningly aggressive. Stated the other way around, the Chinese do want clearly defined situations, but there must be no hint of conflict or aggressiveness. Subtlety is valued because it smooths off the edges of aggressiveness, cushions collisions, and allows for the tingling ecstasy of masked hostility.

For purposes of forecasting factional developments in Chinese politics, we thus have the conclusion that (1) the Chinese are very fearful of institutionally based conflicts, which could result in clashes that could be exceedingly damaging to the system, and hence they will go to great lengths to suppress, but not always with success, factions aligned according to organizational or bureaucratic interests; and (2) the Chinese are more tolerant of generational differences, which they believe cannot be suppressed, and hence generation becomes a ready basis for factional alignments and a more common cause of difficulty. Western observers must thus restrain their natural inclination to attach importance to bureaucratic interests and become more sensitive to the potential significance of differences in age and experience.

This requirement seriously complicates the analysis of Chinese politics because alliances of bureaucratic interests generally appear to be more manifest and "objective," conforming to the logic of circumstances, while generational ties (and antagonisms) are latent and particularistic, depending very much upon idiosyncratic experiences. Thus, analysis must be more inductive than deductive.

Nevertheless, based on what we have been able to learn about Chinese attitudes, some general guides to the probable character of generational differences can be discerned. To note these, we return to our sample of Hong Kong interviewees.

EXPERIENCE CHANGES MATURATION

We noted in Chapter 3 that the young Chinese who had gone through the experience of the Cultural Revolution and who had been sent down to the countryside differ in some important respects from older Chinese. When we examine these data and other responses in our questionnaire more thoroughly, we find at the most general level that those who have been socialized under Communism differ from the older generation on some dimensions but, significantly, not on others. More importantly, the differences seem to cancel each other out, so that the end products are barely distinguishable. The current generation of young Chinese have followed different paths, but they seem to have arrived at much the same attitudinal position as their elders—and they have arrived there at an earlier age. Or at least their attitudes seem to make them old beyond their years.

Indeed, our evidence, along with other relevant evidence,[12] seems to suggest that in spite of the manifest differences in their initial experiences with politics, the current young generation of Chinese feel that they are remarkably close to their parents in their political attitudes. The Confucian doctrine of filial piety may be officially dead in China, but the acceptance of parental views lives on as everyone copes as best he can with the dictates of an unpredictable state and Party.

The fact that the younger generation feels itself to be closer to its parents, family, and peers than to its political superiors can be seen in responses to the question, "Generally speaking, would you say your political views were similar to those of (a) your parents, (b) your brothers

12. David Raddock's in-depth interviews with former Red Guards provide substantial support for the view that the current generation of young Chinese feels closer to their parents than did earlier generations. More specifically, he found that the traditional hierarchical authority relationship of fathers and sons is becoming a more horizontal one. (See David Raddock, *Political Behavior of Adolescents in China: The Cultural Revolution in Kwangchan,* University of Arizona Press, Tucson, 1977.)

and sisters, (c) your friends, (d) your direct superior at work, (e) your local political authority, (f) the national leaders, (g) others?" Interviewees were asked to graduate their responses according to five degrees of similarity: (1) least similar, (2) next to least similar, (3) mid-similar, (4) next most similar, and (5) most similar.

Very significantly, 54.5 percent of the older generation said that their parents' views were the "least similar" to their own, while 50 percent of the young generation said that their parents' views were the "most" or the "next most" similar to their views. Of the older generation, 54.6 percent said that their brothers' and sisters' views were the "least" or the "next least" similar, while 66.7 percent of the younger generation ranked their siblings' views as being the "most" or the "next most" similar to their own (chi square = 2.16; significance = .54; gamma = .25.)

The fact that so many of our respondents claimed that they shared their parents' political views led to the natural question of whether the Party may not be right in believing that class backgrounds are decisive in determining political views. The CCP has often been criticized for stigmatizing individuals with the class identification of their parents or even their grandparents. When explicitly asked whether their responses to the questionnaire might not justify the Party's belief in the hereditary nature of political views, most respondents either agreed sheepishly or shrugged their shoulders and said such coincidence of attitudes was only natural. Rather surprisingly, only a small minority of those with what the Party calls "bad class background" showed any resentment of the fact that the curse of their father or grandfather had been automatically passed on to them. The majority did, however, claim that there was a significant distinction between their perception of the relationship of parents' and offsprings' views and that of the Party.

A young girl, for example, who came from a reasonably cultured family – the father had been a teacher and the mother an administrative secretary at a school – said, "The Communists believe that class background decides everything, and they do not understand that in a family there are many levels of relationship which are much more important than just class interests. I think that they really understand that family relations are very important but they cannot admit it, and therefore they have to say that it is class when in fact it is family [that is decisive]." Similarly, a much older respondent, a former PLA officer who had left home at 15 but still felt close to his father, declared with some passion, "The Communists only understand crude political views; my father and I think alike in much more intelligent and complex ways than their foolish Marxist class categories."

The Party has, of course, sought to counter what it perceives as the enduring hereditary nature of political opinions with policies designed to revolutionize in particular the younger generation. Yet, ironically, the most notable of these policies – sending educated youth to the countryside – has actually worked to unite parents and children. The mere experience of being sent down to the countryside appears to have strengthened family bonds between generations, because the young know that they have the concerned and sympathetic support of their parents, who are equally distressed over the prospects of a lifetime of rural existence.

Beyond sentiment, however, there are also objective reasons for the tendency of sent-down youth to identify with their parents, the most important being that a surprisingly large number need money from home to support themselves on communes. The sent-down youth do not have the added income that rural people get from working their "private plots," and hence they must exist solely on what they can earn through "work points," which is generally not enough to cover even basic necessities. As Thomas Bernstein has documented, the Chinese authorities have long been aware of this problem – indeed, Chairman Mao, on receiving a letter from a distraught father who was worried over who would help support his resettled son after his death, sent the father 300 yuan and promised that something would be done. Some remedial allowances were established but these seem to be still inadequate.[13] This problem caused most of the sent-down youths in our sample to try very hard either to be assigned to state farms, where they could count on an adequate living wage, or to become teachers or other salaried workers in the commune. Such assignments, however, usually put them directly into unpleasant competition with rural youths, who naturally wanted the same jobs.

This situation has completely reversed the traditional Chinese pattern of family remittances. In the past, it was the sons who left the countryside, went to the cities, and then sent back to their parents a share of their earnings. Now the urban-based parents must send funds to relocated rural offspring. The sense of prolonged dependency of the offspring is further heightened by the awareness that any prospect of leaving the countryside must generally involve parental assistance. Whether through routine legal leaves or illegally drifting back permanently to the cities, our respondents unhesitatingly returned to their homes, expecting their parents to look after them, even though they took personal risks to do so.

It is noteworthy that, according to the findings of Deborah Davis-Freeman, the housing shortage in China has increased the dependency

13. Thomas P. Bernstein, *Up to the Mountains and Down to the Villages*, Yale University Press, New Haven, Conn., 1977, pp. 82, 152–153.

of both rural and urban youth upon their parents to the point even of strengthening parental control over marriage decisions.[14] Since young people have to depend upon their parents for housing even after marriage, and since the puritanical morality of the regime makes socializing between the sexes difficult, parental influences easily become decisive in the critical areas of house and spouse.

Although young Chinese may feel that their beliefs are close to those of their parents, this does not mean that there are no differences in generational outlook. As we noted at the end of Chapter 3, our younger respondents, reflecting, no doubt, their exposure to the rhetoric of self-reliance, were somewhat more "internal" than their elders, who exhibited the more traditional Chinese situation-oriented approach and were thus more inclined to believe in external loci of control. Clearly, the former Red Guards had been taught to speak out as though they believed that they were martyrs. Yet, this "internal" attitude was contradicted by the very low sense of efficacy of the young who had suffered from being sent down to the countryside.

If we examine further this difference in generational attitude, we get a hint as to how older, and presumably more traditionally socialized, Chinese have been able to reconcile the seemingly contradictory attitudes of strong belief in the powers of chance or fate along with a strong sense of "efficacy." Using the relevant items from Rotter's I–E scale, we find that there is no significant difference between the generations in terms of belief in the importance of "powerful others" (chi square = .0081, p = .95)[15] All generations of Chinese appear to be "externals" when it comes to acknowledging that powerful people can affect one's life, but there is a significant difference when the external force is defined as "chance or fate."[16] The sense of efficacy of the older generation thus stems not just from a feeling of confidence in their ability to manipulate more powerful individuals, but even more from a remarkable sense of confidence about how "chance" or "fate" might affect them. In

14. Deborah Davis-Freeman, "Aging in the People's Republic of China," Ph.D. dissertation, Department of Sociology, Boston University, 1978.

15. For those unfamiliar with statistics, "chi square" indicates the extent of deviation from a random distribution in which 0 represents complete randomness; therefore, the *larger* the number, the greater the systematic relationship. In contrast, p indicates the percentage of times the null hypothesis would have been true at that level of chi square; thus, the *lower* the number, the greater the degree of association. According to convention, only when p is below .05 is the degree of association considered to be significant.

16. Because of cultural considerations, it was necessary to focus on eight items in the I–E scale (J. B. Rotter, "Generalized Expectancies for Internal vs. External Control of Reinforcement," *Psychological Monographs,* Vol. 80, 1966). I am indebted to Lu-tao Sophia Wang for noting this difference with respect to "powerful others" and "chance" and for her analysis of the Chinese concept of fate which follows.

Chinese culture, "fate" and "human effort" are not necessarily in conflict—rather, there is a tension between the two that demands that the individual both respect the force of the inevitable and strive to influence his fate. This is not dissimilar to Max Weber's interpretation of how a Calvinistic belief in predestination was consistent with—and indeed was a psychological motive force for—aggressive entrepreneurial strivings.

In the Confucian scheme, the basis of world order was the Will of Heaven (*tian*), which as the ultimate governing force in the universe was also responsive to man's behavior and more particularly to the conduct of sovereign authority and to the correctness of governmental behavior. At the more immediate, personal level, the Chinese recognized the importance of "fate," or *ming*, which quite significantly was seen as being of two distinct types: *daming* or "major fate," essentially a version of predestination, and *pienming* or "contingent or influenceable fate," which is responsive to individual conduct.[17] These concepts gave to the Chinese a strong sense of realism as they confronted the fortunes of life and balanced the payoffs of their own efforts with an acceptance that some things lie beyond human comprehension and influence. One could always perceive one's good or bad fortune as being dependent in varying degrees upon both oneself and a larger fate. Chance or predestination might at any moment be good or bad, and one's efforts might or might not under different circumstances prove decisive.

This blend of concepts about fate and human effort encouraged initiative while reducing feelings of guilt about misfortune. Various folk sayings explain the need to exert effort while accepting fate: "Exert the utmost of human abilities, and then resign the rest to the decree of Heaven (*jin renshi yi ting tianming*)," and "It is up to man to plan things, but it is up to Heaven to decide their success (*Mou shi zai ren cheng shi zai tian*)." Fate or chance was not always seen as the enemy, for they could at times smile on one's efforts. Indeed, one of the worst tragedies many Chinese could contemplate was that of not acting when one's fate was favorable—hence the need to test one's luck regularly by gambling. From the evidence of our respondents, it seems that younger Chinese have lost the sense of balance between fate and will; and, left only with an exaggerated notion of what one should be able to accomplish by effort, they have inevitably arrived at a more cynical view of the world.

This cynicism can be seen in several areas of their beliefs, perhaps most significantly in their greater tolerance for ambiguity and their greater lack of "faith in people."

17. See Hsu Cho-yun, "The Concept of Predetermination and Fate in Han," *Early China*, Vol. 1, 1975, pp. 51–56.

Of all the concepts from social psychology that we incorporated in our questionnaire, tolerance for ambiguity appears to travel the least well across cultures to the Chinese. The concept, as it was originally conceived by Adorno and his group,[18] and more particularly as elaborated by Else Frenkel-Brunswick,[19] was seen as a measure of the quality of rigidity of mind associated with authoritarianism; thus, the more tolerance for ambiguity, the greater the liberalism. Yet it seems that the questions used to scale tolerance of ambiguity also measure another, and presumably quite different, psychological concept, that of "cognitive dissonance." Consequently, what may appear among Chinese to be a high level of tolerance for ambiguity may in fact represent the well-established Chinese trait of being relatively immune to the tensions Westerners feel when confronted with contradictions between belief and perception. Just as the Chinese have traditionally felt comfortable practicing different religions, believing in different versions of salvation and the hereafter, and not believing it necessary to put all one's faith in any particular set of doctrines, so they seem to find it easy to tolerate contradictory political and secular views.[20] In our later discussion of Chinese attitudes of dependency we question whether it is appropriate to picture older respondents as having "authoritarian personalities" even when they indicate some degree of intolerance of ambiguity, but here we wish only to observe that the Red Guard generation was significantly more tolerant of ambiguity than the older generations (chi square = 21.05, p = .001). Viewed more closely, however, much of the tolerance seems to take the form of "it doesn't matter very much." Exposed as they were to dramatic reversals of interpretations of political right and wrong, they tend now to be tentative and skeptical about much of life; many declared that it was quite impossible to understand the irrationalities of politics. (When asked to choose between the statements "Most of the time I can't understand why politicians behave the way they do" and "In the long run people are responsible for bad government on a national as well as on a local level,"[21] 69.6 percent of those who said they could not understand politicians were of the younger generation, and on-

18. T. W. Adorno, et al., *The Authorization Personality*, Harper, New York, 1949.

19. E. Frenkel-Brunswick, "Intolerance of Ambiguity as an Emotional and Perceptual Personality Variable," *Journal of Personality*, Vol. 18, 1949, pp. 108–143.

20. For empirical tests that reveal that remarkable Chinese capacity to live easily with contradictions, see Paul Hiniker, "Chinese Reactions to Forced Compliance: Dissonance Reduction and National Character," *Journal of Social Psychology*, Vol. 77, 1969, pp. 157–176.

21. This question clearly was at the outer limits of the items in the I–E scale that could be used with Chinese respondents, given the authoritarian character of the Chinese political system. It was not, however, discarded, because a surprisingly high number (16.3 percent) did select response b.

ly 30.4 percent were of the older.) Thus, even though the young were better educated, they frequently adopted the quite un-Chinese approach of admitting to knowing less about political affairs than they actually knew.[22]

Based on the Rosenberg scale[23] for measuring "faith in people," this cynicism of the former Red Guards left them precociously distrustful of others. Of all of our respondents, only 12 percent believed that "most people can be trusted," which compares with 55 percent of the Americans, 49 percent of the British, 30 percent of the Mexicans, and 19 percent of the Germans – only the Italians, at 7 percent, are more distrustful.[24] In general, the younger generation was slightly, but not significantly, more distrustful than the older. (The only noteworthy difference was that 45 percent of the older generation believed that most people "try to be fair," while only 31 percent of the younger generation had that much faith in others (gamma = .29).)[25]

IMPLICATIONS FOR FORECASTING

It is clear that the Chinese do think in generational terms, that they feel more comfortable with their peers, and that the events of modern Chinese history have produced some significant differences in the attitudes of the generations. Furthermore, the post-Mao power struggles have created an awkward situation in which a discredited younger generation has been demoted but in time will certainly have another chance at power. There is thus implanted in Chinese politics a generational time bomb of uncertain explosive potential. The evidence is also very strong that the younger Chinese have reacted with bitter cynicism toward their experiences with politics and hence are not likely again to make strong ideological commitments.[26]

22. For a discussion of the Chinese trait of pretending to greater political knowledge and fearing to show ignorance, see Lucian W. Pye, *Guerrilla Communism in Malaya*, Princeton University Press, Princeton, N.J., 1956, Chap. 7.

23. Morris Rosenberg, "Misanthropy and Political Ideology," *American Sociological Review*, Vol. XXI, 1956, pp. 690–695.

24. Gabriel A. Almond and Sidney Verba, *The Civic Culture*, Princeton University Press, Princeton, N.J., 1963, p. 267.

25. Again, for the statistically uninitiated, the value of a gamma goes from 0 to 1; the higher the figure, the greater the degree of association.

26. An important qualification to this generalization is that the younger generation of Chinese, cynical about ideology as they are, did receive extensive training in ideological rhetoric; hence they may, at some time in the future, decide, albeit for cynical reasons, that the value of ideology should be elevated so as to give them a profit on their marginal advantage.

Balanced against these considerations about generational conflicts is the fact that age differences do not provide a solid basis for organizing political power. Except for such events as the Cultural Revolution, policy differences cut across the generations, and there seems to be little potential for mobilizing particular age groups for political action. It is significant, for example, that Deborah Davis-Freeman has found that "senior citizens," who are now rapidly increasing in number, do not think of themselves as belonging to distinctive segments of society with special interests that could be collectively pursued.[27] Rather, older Chinese still identify across generational lines with their children, preserving the cellular structure of a family-oriented society, which inhibits the old in acting as a common force.

In sum, therefore, while factions are not likely to be organized in terms of generations, generational considerations can influence the performance of otherwise organized factions. Significant differences in age can, for example, make it difficult for particular individuals to work together. Chairman Hua Guofeng must have found it hard to be at ease with Deng Xiaoping and Ye Jianying, who were more than twenty years his senior; and there is little wonder that Wang Dongxing felt "vulnerable" on the Standing Committee of the Politburo, since he was thirty years younger than the most formidable figures.

With these considerations in mind, we can now examine another factor that has traditionally been important in the forming of factions in Chinese politics: geography and identification based on place of family origin.

27. Davis-Freeman, op. cit.

Chapter 5

The Partisan Value but Policy Irrelevance of Geography

Next to generation, the Chinese accept geography as the most "natural" basis for factional alignments, yet in Chinese politics geography provides little guide to policy preferences.

Among Chinese it is universally assumed that people from the same locality – be it county, town, or province – have a natural affinity for each other; and therefore, wherever they may be they will automatically seek each other out, stick together, provide mutual support, and to some degree ally themselves against others. These sentiments of affinity derived from common territorial identities are believed to be expressions of passions, natural yearnings that only the most self-disciplined and almost saintlike individuals can repress. It is therefore not surprising that most Chinese also tend to suspect that any clustering of people from the same place in any institution is proof that a cabal or faction exists.

Most Chinese, immodestly, believe that they personally are less propelled by the urge than others – or at least that they have been less able than others to benefit from this visceral dimension of man. But they are not inclined to find comfort in the purity they possess for not having such automatic support; they only seem to be suspicious that others are receiving such help.

Recognition of the clique-forming potential of geography was codified in the imperial Chinese regulations about the posting of officials, that is, no one should be subjected to the impossible temptations of being assigned to his own district, and the entourages of all high officials should consist of men from diverse places (the latter required by propriety, if not legality). Needless to say, the exposure of China to the modern world has heightened Chinese disgust at geographical favoritism to the point that there is now an official prohibition of such practices. But suspicion lingers on, and whenever the crimes of a disgraced official are catalogued, it is customary to suggest that he indulged in geographical favoritism.

In spite of this intense belief in geographical affinity, however, the Chinese have almost totally repressed geographical interests in the making of public policy. Neither in the past nor at present have the Chinese allowed the economic or other special interests peculiar to different parts of the country to become the legitimate subject of explicit political competition. Thus, knowledge of factions among officials based on provincial identities provides little guidance as to the policy preferences of the different groups.

It is rarely noted but truly astonishing that despite their long history of political intervention in economic matters, the Chinese still have not developed a political economy in which regional interests are openly acknowledged. It is true that officials have historically followed the rather primitive objective of trying to limit extractions from their favored area while seeking greater allocations for it; but they have not sought to change public policy in more substantive and imaginative ways in order to favor one region over another. Under Communism it has, of course, been even more improper to show concern for anything but the collective interest of the nation. Indeed, if anything, leaders in the different regions and provinces have vied with each other to sacrifice the interests of their own areas in favor of the country as a whole.

Thus, in terms of geography and politics, the Chinese have created a paradox of exaggeration in contradictory directions. Chinese culture has been extremely sensitive to the potential affinities of people from the same geographical area, yet the Chinese have denied probably more completely than any other society the fact that geography can produce quite different priorities for governmental policies. This paradox is testimony to the extraordinary degree to which the Chinese have elevated ideology and debased economics. The Chinese have long recognized the instinct of men to identify with their own territory, and they therefore deny any moral virtues to geographical interests to such an extreme degree that they cannot admit the legitimacy of the self-interest of one place over another.

There are many reasons for China's historical failure to develop a vigorous economic system, and there are equally many reasons for its erratic economic development since the establishment of the PRC. Among the most important reasons for both failures is the Chinese compulsion, associated with their need for moralistic ideological systems, to deny that economic thought must begin with concrete factors defined by geographical realities. To declare that the only possible interests are the interests of the whole, without any recognition of the effects of such generalized definitions on the relative costs and benefits of each of the parts, is to place idealistic ideology, whether Confucian or Maoist, above economics – either pragmatic private calculations or collectivist planned decisions.

In other societies, whenever geography contributes to significant regional variations, it is universally understood that different policies will favor some areas over others; hence, officials identified with a particular region can be expected to champion their preferred policies. Americans do not need even high-school history courses to appreciate the traditional clashes between an industrialized East, a plantation South, and a freeholding agrarian West. Election eve news commentators feel it is an insult to the intelligence of their listeners to explain why the rural returns are likely to differ from those from the cities. Similarly, in nearly every country, from the United Kingdom to Japan in the industrial world and from India to Latin America in the developing world, it is taken as self-evident that geographical differences contribute to economic differences, which in turn will certainly be the source of political contention.

In these societies, the political question quickly becomes, Which combination of geographical interests will prevail and produce what mix of public policies? It is widely presumed that representatives of particular regions should advocate policies that favor their constituencies. Failure to do so would be seen as odd, a sign of either incompetence or ambition to represent a larger constituency. Finally, leaders are not expected to form alliances only with those from their own region; they are expected to join with outsiders in order to expand their influence.

Chinese political behavior is exactly the opposite. In spite of, or rather precisely because of, the Chinese belief in the potential of geography to nurture cliques, leaders may not properly advocate the economic interests of their regions. Indeed, no one would think it odd for them to advance policies detrimental to their own region if they could pretend that the policies had ideological or moral merit.

As a dramatic example of this mode of thinking, the Chinese did not think it particularly perverse that the extreme advocates of populist egalitarianism should be the leaders whose power base was Shanghai, the most industrialized, technologically sophisticated, and cosmopolitan city in the entire country. Thus, although Shanghai was the base of the

Gang of Four, the city had no economic, cultural, or other interests that were advanced by their radical policies. On the contrary, it suffered from their policies. Indeed, if there were any connection between geography and policy choices in Chinese politics, Shanghai's leaders should have ardently opposed rather than championed the policy of sending its skilled workers and the best-educated of its youth to other parts of the country. A Shanghai leadership sensitive to the real interests of the largest urban center in the country (and thereby adhering to the rules of politics elsewhere in the world) would have tried to exploit Shanghai's marginal advantages as China's most advanced industrial base.[1] The national policy of seeking to reduce inequalities among the provinces held back Shanghai's rate of growth and prevented its citizens from achieving a higher standard of living. Yet as long as the Gang of Four had Shanghai as their power base they worked vigorously against urban interests; and nobody in China thought it to be strange. Even after their fall, when the Four were being denounced for every imaginable crime, the one charge that was never made against them was that they had not represented the interests of their own power base. Elsewhere such negligence would be seen as corrupt behavior. Imagine what would be said if New York City's leaders were to devote all their energies to the well-being of the rural people of the Ozarks and Appalachia at the expense of the interests of New Yorkers!

Although the Shanghai-based "radicals" are an extreme example, they were not exceptional in their use of territory as a factional base without regard to policy. In the spring of 1977, for example, when the second rehabilitation of Deng Xiaoping was initiating the new factional conflict between him and Chairman Hua, there was a tendency for supporters of each man to exploit regional prejudices, identifying Deng with South China and Hua with the North. At the time, a wall poster appeared at the Peking Agricultural College entitled "A Comment on the North–South Confrontation." It denounced Wei Guoqing, the first political commissar of the Canton Military Region, and Xu Shiyou, the commander of the Canton Military Region for insisting on the reemergence of Deng as "Premier" and thereby seeking to advance the South over the North. In response, a *dazibao* was posted at the Canton Medical College that described Hua Guofeng, Ye Jianying, Li Xiannian, and Wang Dongxing as the "new Gang of Four" for fearing the restora-

---

1. David S. G. Goodman, puzzling over why Shanghai should have been the base for the "radicals," arrived at an explanation that reflects Western political concepts more than Chinese practices: He suggests that since Shanghai is the most sophisticated of China's cities, its citizens might tend to be "radical-chic" in their outlook. (See "The Shanghai Connection: Shanghai in National Politics During the 1970's," in Christopher Howe (ed.), *The Development of Shanghai Since 1949*, Cambridge University Press, Cambridge, 1979.)

tion of Deng.[2] Significantly for our thesis, Chinese speculations at the time saw no connection between the two men's positions on issues and the regions associated with them; the Chinese believed it to be entirely natural for each to have a geographical power base.

The policy irrelevance of geography is even more astonishing when it is remembered that the careers of cadres are usually tied to particular activities in particular places. The Party's personnel policies produce clusters of cadres who have long served together in the same place. Furthermore, the CCP has always had a disproportionate number of members from those provinces in which it had its longest history, but its policies have not been biased in favor of those particular provinces.

What this has meant in practice is that relations among the leadership have reflected what would appear to be favoritism according to region in terms of promotions and leadership clusters, but not in policy emphasis. Jurgen Domes has calculated the changing patterns of disproportionately sized provinces in the Party's history: Hunan, Hubei, Sichuan, Jiangxi, and Shanxi, which contain 29.6 percent of the Chinese population, were represented by 63.7 percent of the members of the Eighth Central Committee, 58.9 percent of the Ninth, 52.0 percent of the Tenth, and 54.6 percent of the Eleventh.[3] Hunan (Mao Zedong's home province), with only 5.6 percent of the total population, had the highest percentage of members, an extraordinary 23.3 percent of the Eighth Central Committee, declining to 17.7 percent of the Tenth. This distribution of *senior* cadres no doubt facilitated the election of Hua Guofeng, who had long served in Hunan, to the Chairmanship.[4] Furthermore, when Deng Xiaoping appeared to be pushing his challenge to Hua's leadership in the spring of 1979, it was the Hunan leadership that solidly backed Hua and turned back the Deng threat.[5] But in spite of the manifest importance of Hunan in the ranks of the leadership, there are no governmental policies that reflect the distinctive interests of that province; at best, there may be only the traditional Chinese practice of officials being slightly more generous in implementing standard national policies in their own districts and provinces.

It might be argued that the irrelevance of geography in Chinese policymaking reflects the unity of the regime and a commitment to the

2. Foreign Broadcast Information Service, *Daily Report–People's Republic of China*, May 23, 1977, pp. E1–E2.

3. Jurgen Domes, *China After the Cultural Revolution*, University of California Press, Berkeley, 1977, p. 191.

4. Michel Oksenberg and Sai-cheung Yeung, "Hua Kuo-feng's Pre-Cultural Revolution Hunan Years, 1949–66: The Making of a Political Generalist," *China Quarterly*, No. 69, March 1977, pp. 3–53.

5. Jay Mathews, *Washington Post*, April 11, 1979.

larger national interest rather than to parochial interests. This argument cannot withstand scrutiny, because geographical distinction has historically produced no policy differences, even when China manifestly lacked any sense of national unity, as during the warlord period. Although the warlord alliances were often formed explicitly along geographical lines and it was assumed that certain territorial alliances were natural ones, the goals of these ties were never distinctive geographical interests. The two principal groupings were, for example, the Chihli and the Anhui factions, one consisting of the northern warlords and the other of the central and eastern ones; but no perceptible policy differences between them could be traced to the economic or social interests of their respective regions. The warlords were equally dedicated to maximizing their power and resources while striving to extract as much as possible from their spheres, and all dreamed of gaining access to ever-richer domains. They shared the objective of capturing the capital, Peking, not to enforce policies that would favor their regions, but to dip into the national treasury, which, even if empty, might always be replenished by foreign loans from international bankers who had their own reasons for wanting to "help" China.[6]

The Chinese have found it easy to ignore regional economic interests in the shaping of their national policies partly because they tend to treat regional and provincial differences as personal and even idiosyncratic matters, not as manifestations of varying economic or material concerns. There are long-standing stereotypes of the personal characteristics of people from the different provinces, most of which are uncomplimentary. For example, Emperor Kangxi once wrote, "Sometimes I have stated that the people of a certain province have certain bad characteristics – thus the men of Fukien are turbulent and love acts of daring – even their scholars use shield and sword; while the people of Shensi are tough and cruel; they love feuding and killing, their practices are truly repugnant. Shantung men are stubborn in a bad way; they always have to be first, they nurse their hatred, they seem to value life lightly, and a lot of them become robbers . . . whereas the people of Shansi are so stingy that they won't even care for the aged in their own families; if a stranger comes to them they won't give him a meal, but they'll encourage him to drink and gamble and lead him into wild expenditures. And since the Kiangsu people are both prosperous and immoral – there's no need to blow their feathers to look for fault – I was not surprised to learn that the 'rich merchants' I had heard about in Kiangsu were mostly from Shansi."[7]

6. Lucian W. Pye, *Warlord Politics*, Praeger, New York, 1971, Chap. 9.
7. Translated in Jonathan D. Spense, *Emperor of China; Self-Portrait of K'ang-hsi*, Penguin Books, New York, 1974, pp. 49–50.

Blind to all provincial differences between the rice-growing South and the wheat culture of the North, between the densely populated and highly urbanized East and South coast and the more thinly populated interior regions, especially of the North and West, Chinese politics has operated as though the country were economically homogeneous. As a careful student of Chinese regionalism had to conclude after a detailed examination, "If regionalism was always present in traditional China, it was usually unimportant in political terms . . . . To the extent that it existed, it provided a potential retreat, a fall-back position."[8]

As the Chinese increasingly came to stress the potential dangers of nepotism and particularistic loyalties, it became harder and harder for leaders to openly champion the interests of different regions. As China modernized, its leaders may have found it increasingly difficult to deny regional differences; but, unable to establish the legitimacy of such competition of interest, they inevitably were seen as being corrupt. To some degree, the Nationalist rule was compromised by the conflicting demands of coastal industrialists and interior landlords.

Indeed, the very possibility that the factions within the Kuomintang reflected the growth of regional interests made the Communists even more determined to prevent the same "corrupt" practices from developing under their rule. The extreme commitment of the regime to the idea of equal development of all provinces, through 1978, cannot be explained solely in terms of opposition to inequities. By carrying the ideal of equality to the point of denying the relevance of marginal utility and believing that every province could become self-sufficient, the leadership must have been in some measure manifesting the traditional Chinese belief that geography should be irrelevant in public policy.[9]

The current program of the Four Modernizations involves a complete reversal of the previous emphasis upon equality, and therefore legitimacy will be increasingly given to regional differences; and, to the degree that the modernization policies are successful, the need to acknowledge the significance of geographical differences in national

8. Diana Lary, *Region and Nation: The Kwangsi Clique in Chinese Politics 1925–1937*, Cambridge University Press, Cambridge, 1974.

9. Western economists have debated both the success and the wisdom of the Chinese efforts to establish provincial equality and self-sufficiency. (As late as 1974, Chinese officials asserted that their goal was for every province to produce its own automobiles, such an absurdly romantic notion as to suggest that the whole program of provincial autarky might have had a very large dose of propaganda in it. A presumption that such an idea would have any appeal to rational minds makes sense only in the light of the inordinate Chinese opposition to the legitimacy of geographical special interests.) The most detailed analysis of Chinese policies for provincial equality is that by Nicholas R. Lardy, "Regional Growth and Income Distribution, The Chinese Experience," Economic Growth Center, Yale University Discussion Paper 140, October 1975.

policies will become more intense. Many observers have forecast that the Chinese system will have to confront increasing internal strains resulting from the changes associated with modernization, but few have suggested that such strains may arise from greater conflicts in regional interests.

This possibility is relevant not only for understanding Chinese developments but also for better appreciating theories of political development and modernization. The standard notion has been that parochial geographical interests tend to prevail in traditional societies and that with the process of modernization regional differences decline and national sentiments replace local interests.[10] The Chinese experience seems to suggest that while parochial loyalties may indeed be very strong in a traditional society, only after significant economic development will geographical interests assert themselves into the domain of public policy.

VIEWS OF THE RESPONDENTS

Our Hong Kong respondents were explicitly asked how important the influence of being co-provincials was in the formation of factions, and those who saw some importance in this factor were asked to explain how they believed such sentiments operated in elite politics. We also compared the answers of the Guangdong respondents with those from other provinces to determine the influence of geography on their attitudes.

In general, the samples indicated that being co-provincials had little effect in the creation of factions. None saw it as the "most important" factor, while 47.7 percent said it was the "least important"; 20.5 percent thought it "next to least important," 25 percent "mid-important," and only 6.8 percent "next to the most important."

When asked to explain their answers, those who discounted the importance of territorial affinity generally indicated that they saw China's national leadership as a distinct elite for whom place of origin had lost significance in comparison with their personal relationships with each other. For many, if not most, the national leadership was a "they" who lacked the attributes of ordinary people, including family backgrounds. Most respondents could not identify the place of origin of Politburo members; they saw them only as leaders who ruled the country.

Those who did acknowledge that sentiments of place had some sig-

10. See the works of Karl W. Deutsch, particularly *Nationalism and Social Communication*, M.I.T. Press and John Wiley, New York, 1953.

nificance suggested various explanations. Most emphasized language and customs:

- An older worker said, "I know that people are more at ease when they are surrounded by people who speak the same dialect and have the same customs. So it is natural for people to want to join together with others from the same province."
- A former soldier said, "You have to be careful about people from other places because they will feel that it is all right to take advantage of you. If there is too much difference in customs and in the way people think, they will always end up fighting each other."

For a very few, regional differences within China were almost as great as national cultural differences:

- An Overseas Chinese stated, "I soon learned that I was different from others even though I was strongly nationalistic – that was why I came back to China. But the difference was not just between those of us who had been Overseas Chinese and those who grew up in China, but as I traveled about I discovered that people from different places in China had very different outlooks and often did not trust each other."

Finally, a great many related the fact of being from the same place to other personal considerations that would reinforce compatibility.

- The daughter of a school teacher said, "People from the same province will have a lot of things they can talk about together; they can compare descriptions of the same places they have been; they can ask each other whether they remember this or that town or sightseeing place; and then maybe even they will find out that they know people in common. If this happens they will immediately become friends. So, of course, they will work together in politics, just as they would work together in anything else."

IMPLICATIONS FOR FORECASTING

The self-evident conclusion for purposes of forecasting is that groupings based on place of origin or of long service must be taken as indicators of the mutual attractions associated with clique formation, but the peculiarities of the geographical base should not be taken as guides to policy preferences. Deng Xiaoping's association with South China leaders and his ties with the Second Field Army and with Sichuan province do help to define his circle of allies and supporters, but they do not place any restraints or imperatives on his policies. Hua Guofeng's links to Shanxi and Hunan point only to the limited range of his experiences. To the degree that Deng has been identified with policies favoring science and technology, and Hua with those favoring agriculture, the explanations lie in how they have played their hands in intra-elite power maneuverings: Deng and his followers have had a greater opportunity to assert commanding roles in the more dramatic and hence more politically attractive domain of science and technology, while Hua was left with the more intractable, but ultimately critical, area of agriculture.

A less obvious but more fundamental conclusion is that this lack of linkage between geography and policy preferences points to the inordinately wide gap between power and policy in China. The processes by which any power grouping is aggregated and made into a significant force do not contain the inherent accumulation of policy commitment that exists in most political systems that share a fundamental presumption that power should be intimately related to alternative policy programs because people seek power in order to advance their preferred values.

The values the Chinese tend to idealize for politics are generally quite abstract and heavily moralistic and hence are not readily advanced by power. In the politics of both Communist and Confucian China, the power required for governance is supposed to be primarily dedicated to uplifting the moral qualities of the populace, suppressing all tendencies of parochial self-interest. The building of power is supposed to start at the most general, and hence the most abstract, level of developing the collective consensus and not by aggregating the specific interests of groups that have definite geographical domains. Even when the Chinese system is supposedly committed to "pragmatic" politics, the conflicts of geographical interests common to other countries do not arise.

We shall have more to say later about the consequences that follow from the fact that "pragmatism" in Chinese politics tends to be only a particular version of the elite's preference for consensus and not a dynamic process whereby concrete interests manifest themselves and compete with each other. But before exploring this feature of Chinese politics, we need to get a clearer picture of the Chinese concept of how power can be divorced from policy and made a central concern in the politics of factionalism. To understand the primacy of power in Chinese politics we must turn to our next general proposition.

Chapter 6

The Primacy of Power

Our fundamental hypothesis is that in Chinese factional politics, power considerations are generally decisive because power is seen as the least ambiguous and most predictive of all factors in social life.

Institutions, organizations, generational identities, and geographical affiliations all provide bases for factional alignments in Chinese politics, but while these considerations do at times suggest policy preferences, they are less important than pure power calculations. Leaders can shift their positions according to all the other considerations, but in the end they have to recognize that power is sovereign.

Given the Chinese preference for unambiguously defined situations and their comfort with hierarchical relationships, it is understandable that they place a premium on their perception of the distribution of power. Power, they like to believe, is an ultimate reality. It is noteworthy that when the Chinese had a multipolar political system, in the 1920s, the warlords did not always adhere to the classical rules of balance-of-power politics but frequently followed a distinctly Chinese pattern. Whenever a potentially dominant actor caused the lesser actors to coalesce as a balancing force, the warlords first sought to learn what they could gain from identifying with strength, and only then would they explore the payoffs of allying with the weak. The more generous the strong, the more readily they became magnets. (Note that this was precisely the way the warlord era ended, when Chiang K'ai-shek steadily bought off his opposition.) By allying with strength, a lesser warlord could greatly heighten his power status, particularly relative to those who had no alternative but to oppose the emerging threat. Thus, for the Chinese warlords, autonomy was not the ultimate value, as it was in the traditional European balance-of-power calculation; rather, they based their decisions upon associating with power.

In today's China, given the cross-pressures of political life, it is often difficult to determine the realities of power as precisely as the Chinese would like. Institutions are real and have a solid base, but it is never clear how far a particular institution can extend its influence as compared with another. Generations are readily recognizable and they provide a clear basis for status deferences, but they provide almost no guidance as to effective power. In the end, the most reliable key to evaluating relative power for most Chinese is judgment about the scope of influence of particular individuals.

Thus, when we speak of power, we shall most often be referring to the influence and prestige of individual leaders and their networks of followers, and not to institutions or offices. For example, Zhou Enlai's personal authority always extended well beyond the jurisdiction of whatever formal offices he held. The same has been true for Deng Xiaoping since Mao's death.

The inordinate importance of such personalized power in Chinese Communist politics derives in part from the absence of a system of rule by law. Cadres cannot count on each other to act predictably according to impersonal rules. To make matters worse, there is no longer the binding role of custom or tradition, which can also limit the importance of personalized power. Thus in Chinese politics the two traditional limitations on power, law and custom, are missing. And the prospect is that power is likely to become even more important because the rather fragile Communist form of restraint, that of ideology, will probably erode faster than a system of law can be established.

In Chinese politics, as in most transitional political systems, the influence of individuals often has a complicated relationship to their formal positions. Field commanders and civilian ministers of equal rank according to the tables of organization will in fact be quite unequal in the eyes of all concerned. Everyone knows that the twice-rehabilitated Deng Xiaoping is far more influential than his formal titles would suggest. Yet only those who have access to the play of power behind the scenes can judge precisely the relative power among Deng and his colleagues on the Standing Committee of the Politburo.

Outsiders who would seek to fathom the obscurities of Chinese elite power relationships can best be guided by three cardinal principles. Unfortunately, they are not consistent, but their very contradictions help to illuminate a basic source of the pervasive uncertainty of Chinese politics. (The three principles will by no means make Chinese politics completely understandable to the outsider, but this should not be cause for discouragement – as Vietnamese Prime Minister Tran Van Dong once explained to Ambassador Maxwell Taylor, "Don't feel badly about not understanding Vietnamese politics; we don't understand it ourselves.")

THREE PRINCIPLES OF POWER

The first principle of power in China is that the people tend to conceive of power relationships as a single coherent hierarchy, and therefore they try to reduce as much as possible the discrepancies between their formal and informal structures of power. (Americans, on the other hand, tend to take it for granted that congruences are unlikely between formal office holders and actual power wielders.) The most telling evidence of this feature of Chinese political behavior is the fact that of all the countries that have experienced Communist rule, the Chinese have had the greatest difficulty in maintaining the conventional dual hierarchies of state and Party. While the Soviet Union and the Eastern European countries have routinely institutionalized the dual formal and informal structures of state and Party, the Chinese Communists have been uncomfortable without a single line of authority. Deng Xiaoping's ingenious strategy of elevating himself and his followers and undermining Chairman Hua Guofeng involved turning the traditional Communist power relationship upside down and making the state control the Party. Building from his solid base in the State Council, he first made that institution the center of decisionmaking rather than the Politburo, then he gradually expanded ministerial influences on the Central Committee until finally, in February 1980, he was in a position to capture both the Politburo and its key Standing Committee. He was able to reverse the classic Marxist–Leninist pattern of Party domination of state by exploiting, first, the Chinese predisposition to attach importance to formal offices, and second, the Chinese preference for a single, orderly hierarchy of power. Unable to work with a dual power hierarchy, the Chinese – contrary to both conventional Communist practices and the near-universal fantasy about the supremacy of hidden powers – have given primacy to the more formal powers. (In doing so, they have, however, still acceded to the human propensity to mystify authority by making obscure the workings of formal, public authority.)

The second principle about power, which qualifies but does not contradict the first, is that status tends to imply power and is not treated as being merely symbolic. To be more precise, symbolic matters are treated as manifestations of genuine power, and hence status becomes power. Anyone who has been a member of a delegation visiting China in the last few years will agree that two decades of egalitarian ideology have not blunted the Chinese sensitivity to status differences. Indeed, the elimination of explicit differentiating by such obvious, though crude, measures as wealth has made the Chinese even more alert to the subtleties of status differences.

The most refined gradations of power have a vividness in Chinese politics that people attuned to other values cannot appreciate. In part, Chinese officials are actually sensitive to status differences because of their belief that nothing is accidental. To leave to chance the decision of who should have precedence over whom – as, for example, by accepting "first come, first served," or even the market – would be far too risky for people who have profound fears of disorder or confusion.

The uncompromising obligation to defer to those of higher status means that it is easy for those with superior status to act in power terms. Consequently, ceremonial appointments can be readily transformed into actual power roles if the incumbent chooses to assert authority. Old men may be appointed to high offices as tokens of respect, but there is the risk that such appointees will not be passive and will choose to exploit their potential for influence.

Paradoxically, it is this cultural tendency to equate status with power that has made it possible for the Chinese to eliminate symbols of rank in their military establishment. For people who are highly sensitized to the subtleties of status differences, the traditional categories of military rank seem crude and hardly meaningful. Once it is recognized that all generals do not hold equal rank, the difference between a general and a colonel hardly seems important. Within the Chinese military, everyone knows exactly who is superior to whom and thus there is no need for insignias of rank.

The third principle, which can operate to contradict the other two, is that power is readily transmitted through linkages of personal relationships. Indeed, the very basis of the power networks in Chinese politics is the pattern of personal bonds that are strengthened by Chinese concepts of friendship and of *guanxi*, or obligation. Although *guanxi* may not be as powerful a bond of indebtedness as, say, the Japanese concept of *on* or the Javanese feeling of *hutang budi* (moral obligation and indebtedness), which is the basis of their system of *bapakism*, it does call for concrete manifestations: Superiors must reward inferiors, and inferiors must support the interests of superiors.

This aspect of personal relations introduces an extraordinary element of uncertainty into Chinese politics: Could it be that X, who otherwise has no claim to fame, is in an honored position merely because of his old age, or could he be the ally of a very powerful figure? Is the obscure man behind the scenes wishfully pretending to be, as the Chinese call it, a wire puller, or is he legitimately an associate of one of the principals in the political game? Indeed, the initial appearance of any figure in the topmost circle, whether he be a venerable worthy or a youthful aspirant, immediately raises the question of who was the sponsor who has just demonstrated an inflation of his power. For example, when Deng Xiaoping appointed Chen Yun to the Standing Committee of the Politburo, everyone judged that Deng had strengthened his position – that is, until Chen transformed mere status into power and began to act somewhat independently of Deng's wishes.

In short, in Chinese politics names never stand alone, for they are always linked, for better or worse, with other names. Whenever a new name is added to the Politburo or the Standing Committee, everyone speculates about the newcomer's personal affiliations, and hence about whose power has risen and whether the sponsor was in fact shrewd in sponsoring such an individual.

Clearly, these three principles collectively work to complicate, and hence obscure, the realities of power for a people who believe that it is imperative to be able to read the delineations of power.

The fact that politically conscious Chinese find it difficult at times to perceive the realities of relative power and therefore are filled with anxieties about misjudging the situation does not, however, generate what might be called a paranoid style of politics. Instead, those who are confused tend to constrict their vision, ignore what they cannot fathom, and concentrate their attention on the most immediate linkages to power available to them. Thus, uncertainty strengthens personal ties, the very phenomenon that introduces the greatest imponderable into the power calculation. The result is a vicious circle.

And, of course, the importance of the third principle is precisely what contributes to the opaqueness of Chinese politics. The supposition that much must be going on that defies perception is premised on the expectation that private linkages have intruded into public affairs. At every level within the political system, anyone's power may be orders of magnitude greater than first impressions would indicate, but then again the opposite could also be true.

Hence, in spite of all the striving for certainty in the calculations of power associated with the first two principles, the third principle operates to ensure that an element of mystery constantly surrounds the facts of power in Chinese politics.

THE SEARCH FOR CLARITY EXAGGERATES
THE DIFFERENCE BETWEEN
FRIEND AND FOE

When we examine the interaction of these three principles more closely, many obscure patterns of Chinese political behavior become completely intelligible.

The speed with which leaders have risen and fallen in Chinese politics can be explained partly by the inconsistency of the three principles. A surprisingly rapid rise may occur because the routine assignments that make up one's only public record may mask more significant relationships behind the scene. We have been told about how all the members of the Gang of Four benefited from personal connections. Similarly, Chairman Hua Guofeng's rise to prominence and Politburo status from an otherwise unexceptional career has to be explained by the fact that he had the good fortune to be in key positions in the Party hierarchy.[1]

The distinctively Chinese characteristic of such cases of dramatic elevation is that they almost never depend upon quality of performance in publicly observable roles; rather, they depend upon behind-the-scene developments.[2] This is paradoxical, given the Chinese propensity to attach more importance to formal than to informal power hierarchies.

Even more distinctive is the management of the fall from power in China. In view of the deserved renown of the Chinese in dealing with matters of "face," it is surprising that they have generally been quite brutal in removing people from office and have not engaged in ritual promotions to ceremonial offices. The problem here is that the Chinese have been hoisted by their own cultural petard: Believing in rule by men and not by law, they find it difficult to define a high-status office that cannot be used as a power base, and thus it is impossible to "promote" a man to a high position that has been stripped of power by legalistic regulations.

People in high "ceremonial" positions can all too easily seek to translate status into power and use personal ties with those who command other, more literal forms of power. Furthermore, the tactic of "kicking a man upstairs" does not seem to work in Chinese politics because those who do the kicking are prone to envy, and they soon ask themselves, "Why should he get all the rewards and comforts of high station rather than one of us?"

---

1. See Ting Wang, "A Concise Biography of Hua Kuo-feng," *Chinese Law and Government,* Vol. XI, No. 1, Spring 1978.

2. One of the problems with Michel Oksenberg's account of Hua Guofeng's career is that he sought to find evidence of excellence in Hua's bureaucratic performance as a way of explaining his advancement; even when his findings indicated the exact opposite about Hua's

Throughout most of the history of Chinese Communism, the loss of power has called for disgrace and a removal from significant offices. At present, however, a change seems to be taking place, largely as a consequence of Deng Xiaoping's apparent desire to change the rules of elite relationships in order to end the system that twice stripped him of power. Apparently, at the December 1978 Central Committee meeting, Deng, returning from highly publicized trips to Japan and Southeast Asia, decided to challenge Chairman Hua Guofeng and ask for a readjustment of power relationships at the Center.[3] At the time, Deng was alone without a trusted ally on the five-man Standing Committee of the Politburo, the other four men being Chairman Hua and his ally the fifth-ranking Wang Dongxing (the former commander of Mao Zedong's bodyguards, who had performed the act of arresting the Gang of Four), and a balancing faction consisting of second-ranking General Ye Jianying and fourth-ranking Li Xiannian, both aged men, sympathetic with the policies of the Four Modernizations but somewhat distrustful of Deng.[4] We do not know exactly what took place during the prolonged meeting, but the final outcome appears to have been a compromise that only slightly favored Deng. He was not able to remove anyone from either the Standing Committee or the Politburo; but he did succeed in adding a sixth member, Chen Yun, a personal ally, to the Standing Committee, and four allies to the Politburo. None, however, had an independent power base. (Typical was the appointment of Deng Yingchao, the widow of Zhou Enlai, who could be counted on to add to Deng's prestige and hence his actual power, to the degree that she would exploit status as power.)

The much more significant outcome of the meeting was Deng's success in having Hua's allies removed from their authoritative offices while leaving them on the Standing Committee and the Politburo, dramatic

---

performance, Oksenberg failed to appreciate that what counts in a Chinese bureaucracy are relationships that are almost never open to public scrutiny.

3. Fox Butterfield, *New York Times*, December 24, 1978.

4. There is considerable evidence of Ye's and Li's distrust of Deng, but the most revealing item was the failure of either man to protect Deng after the death of his former protector, Zhou Enlai. Ye, reflecting some of the views of the military, felt no indebtedness to Deng because during the previous year Deng had cut back the military budget, and for the first time in the history of the PRC, he as a civilian had imposed his will on the Army by ordering the reassignment of several Field Army commanders. Li, whose connections were primarily with the senior bureaucrats and technicians, had a history of clashes with Deng going back to the 1950s, when Deng was in charge of the Organizational Office of the Party and had tried to control bureaucratic appointments. It was at this time that the Chinese were trying to operate with the dual state and Party hierarchies. Li was Deng's successor as prime minister in 1953, and reportedly Li complained that he had found the office in poor administrative condition.

testimony to the decline in the role of the Party. Wang Dongxing was stripped of his control of the secretive General Office of the Party and his command of the elite 8341 Military Unit that now guards the national leaders; Wu De was removed as Mayor of Peking while remaining on the Politburo; Ji Dengkui, whose career paralleled Hua Guofeng's, lost his posts in both Public Security and Agricultural Planning; Chen Yonggui was demoted in directing agricultural policy; and most significantly, Chen Xilian lost effective command of the Peking Military Region.[5]

This maneuver of first neutralizing the Standing Committee and the Politburo by dividing them into three balanced factions, and second, removing allies of Hua and Ye from administrative posts while leaving them on the Politburo was capped by a call for more "collective leadership" and an end to Hua being called "the wise leader." Although the tactic may have spared China the unsettling consequences of another major power struggle, Deng's idea of keeping disgraced leaders "only in and not out" failed to prevent later conflicts, when the assertive Deputy Prime Minister began to stumble in March 1979. For a brief period in the spring of 1979, Deng's cautious moves stimulated a significant counter-reaction from cadres who saw their champions at the top being threatened. However, at the Fifth Plenum of the Eleventh Central Committee at the end of February 1980, fourteen months after Deng initiated his maneuver, he was able to get the "resignation" of Wang Dongxing, Ji Dengkui, Wu De, and Chen Xilian. Furthermore, he finally achieved a majority in the Standing Committee of the Politburo by adding Hu Yaobang and Zhao Ziyang, and to complete his consolidation of power in the Party hierarchy he reestablished the Party Secretariat and staffed it with cadres loyal to him, under the immediate direction of Hu Yaobang.

Deng's strategy went against the rules of power in all other Communist systems. The standard approach in other countries would have been to remove any disgraced leaders first from the highest prestige position of Politburo membership while possibly leaving them in nominal governmental posts. The sequence in Deng's approach was exactly the reverse, as the four were first compromised by being relieved from their presumably secondary positions while being allowed to remain for a while nominally at the pinnacle, but then fourteen months later the vulnerable four were readily forced out of the Politburo. In the end, they were left without even the solace of symbolic posts; they all became non-people, their whereabouts and fate unknown – reminders only that those who lose out in Chinese power struggles receive no consolation awards.

The practice of leaving compromised leaders in official positions for even a brief period of time fits with the Chinese tendency to underplay

5. *Far Eastern Economic Review*, January 26, 1979, pp. 14–15.

the importance of ensuring that power and responsibility are combined. The importance of status and of personal ties has meant that people can wield considerable power without being held accountable. Leaders with high status but little administrative responsibility may erratically intervene in the policymaking process and create confusion. Politburo members without appropriate administrative duties may choose to use their high status for random interventions that they may not be able to sustain and which could provoke erratic governmental activities.

All of these causes of uncertainty in power patterns, combined with the Chinese belief that nothing is possible without understanding the realities of power, contribute to the extreme importance the Chinese attach to accurately perceiving the friends and the enemies of each principal leader. When power relations are confused, the simplest way to find order is to determine precisely who is associated with or opposed to whom, or so think the Chinese.

The Chinese propensity to magnify the difference between amity and enmity as a way of trying to bring clarity to power relations is possibly best illustrated in their foreign relationships. For example, the Chinese have gone from one extreme to the other in their relations with the Soviet Union and the United States, as though there were only the two extreme possibilities of friendship and hatred.

In Chinese culture, friendship is not just a matter of sentiment; it calls for substantive affirmations. Thus leaders will reward their friends, which leads to the obligation to ignore, if not punish, their enemies. Yet all of this must be done circumspectly, partly because of the distrust, common to all cultures, of those who are too blatant in the use of power. But there is also a peculiar Chinese need for subtlety that stems from their association of status with power. Men who hold positions of status must always pretend to be secure in their stations, yet by so acting they may also appear to be seeking real power. So they often must act as though they had no enemies, and hence no friends.

An important consequence of this rule is that senior Chinese leaders are supposed to deal only with their peers and must not show undue interest in seeking. out talent in the younger generations of potential leaders. It is the young who are supposed to seek out and support the established figures. The risks of faulty judgments are thus squarely with the aspirants for power, but, paradoxically, their decisions are also the ones that create the centers of power.

Needless to say, older leaders will at times meddle in the affairs of the next generation in order to further the careers of some over others. But they must be careful not to be too overt, for then they might be suspected of inappropriately trying to expand their power. No Chinese leader could occupy the role that Averell Harriman once played in searching for young talent for America's foreign policymaking. Leaders are supposed only to hope to be blessed with younger followers who have spontaneously rallied to them and thus have helped establish enduring power groupings without scheming or calculation. It may have been this rule of Chinese politics, rather than a manifestation of senility, which caused Mao Zedong to be puzzled when the Australian Prime Minister, searching for small talk, inquired as to how the Chairman had been able to spot the youthful Wang Hongwen and elevate him to the inner power circle. Mao would have had to deny, as he did, any knowledge of the subject, for otherwise he would have broken the Chinese rule of not displaying undue interest in younger talent.

This rule places a more than normal obstacle in the way of orderly succession arrangements. The Chinese share the universal reluctance of older men to contemplate their own passing from the scene, and they also have a distinctive problem in that retirement from power is exceedingly difficult because for them status is no different from power. Hence, since no one of high status can abandon status, no one can give up power. Without the possibility of retirement from power or of aggressive recruitment of younger followers, older leaders must deal largely with their peers in matters of power, contributing to the Chinese propensity for rule by a gerontocracy.

The problems of Mao's succession are too well known to require further comment here. At present, however, an aging Deng Xiaoping is also a prisoner of these cultural constraints. Thus in his first move to add to his strength on the Standing Committee of the Politburo, Deng had to select a man only one year his junior, Chen Yun; and all of the four he added to the Politburo at that time were approximately his own age, except for Hu Yaobang, who is eleven years his junior – an age differential that is very close to the maximum of respectability in Chinese politics. Whatever younger men Deng has been able to promote, all had to have had some previous associations with him so that their elevation could appear to be nothing more than the reestablishment of old ties and not the institutionalization of a new power structure. For example, Wei Guoqing, Deng's choice for director of the General Political Department of the Military Commission, served with him in the 2nd Army; Wang Renzhong, his choice for a vice-premier of the State Council, served with him in the Shanxi–Hebei–Shandong Border Government; and Duan Chunyi, his selection as First Secretary of the Henan Provincial Committee, served under him in the Financial and Economic Committee of the Southwest and the Administrative Council.[6]

6. "Personalities: Tuan Chun-i," *Issues and Studies*, Vol. XV, No. 3, March 1979, pp. 83.

THE PSYCHOLOGICAL BASIS FOR THE
CHINESE CONCERN WITH POWER

The Chinese concern with power and their need to treat it with such delicacy requires a psychocultural explanation. The combination of extreme sensitivity to power considerations and avoidance of explicit recognition of the facts of power suggests the hypothesis that power is associated with a form of psychological repression. And the particular repression is not hard to surmise: It is, of course, the basic human drive of aggression.

As I have argued in *The Spirit of Chinese Politics*,[7] the repression of aggression has been a central theme in Chinese culture, in contrast with Western civilization, whose central concern has been the repression of sexuality. The Chinese stress of etiquette, ritual, conformity; their anxieties over disorder, confusion, and collapse of hierarchy; their capacity to swing abruptly between the poles of disciplined order and explosive emotional outbursts; their sensitivity to affronts or criticism; and their need to vocalize their anxieties and tensions all suggest that the controlling of aggression is not only important but difficult. The Chinese preference for unambiguous situations and the comfort they find in well-defined hierarchical relationships are also reflections of concern over the destructive potential of human aggression.

The psychological dynamic of this concern is not difficult to locate in traditional Chinese culture: The absolute imperative of filial piety has traditionally meant that sons could never manifest in any manner the hostilities they might naturally feel toward their fathers.[8] This denial of man's potentially strongest feelings, when combined with socialization practices such as early teasing and then steeply heightened discipline, contributed to a tendency to divorce feelings from actions and to distrust one's own affect. The present generation of Chinese leaders are, of course, products of such socialization practices, and it does not appear that the abandonment of Confucianism will produce significant changes in the culture; young Chinese are still being taught the imperative of suppressing their own feelings and conforming to the dictates of the group. Even though the Chinese are frequently provided with legitimate targets for hatred, these targets can change so unexpectedly that they hardly provide release for normal feelings of aggression.

Thus, in Chinese culture the notion of power is directly related to a search for personal security. To overcome feelings of anxiety and insecurity, Chinese seek the protection of power, which in turn depends

7. Lucian W. Pye, *The Spirit of Chinese Politics*, M.I.T. Press, Cambridge, Mass., 1968.
8. Ibid., Chap. VI.

upon reliable personal relations in which strong and weak appreciate the need to protect each other. The more vulnerable an individual feels himself to be, the more intense will be his search for the security of reliable relationships. High officials and lowly cadres respond in the same way in searching for security, and their behavior generates power in the form of factional alignments.

These psychological insights may provide a deeper explanation for why Chinese leaders do not make an automatic linkage, as Westerners do, between power and policy questions but tend rather to associate power with ideology and hierarchical status. Our hypothesis would be that the Chinese find it peculiarly unnatural to relate power and policy, because power, being associated with the threatening qualities of aggression, has strongly negative overtones, which should not be allowed to contaminate policy issues.[9] Power needs to be enveloped and made respectable by an impenetrable veil of moral ideology; or it should be neutralized by being treated as a matter of status, analogous to the natural hierarchies of life – father and son, older and younger generations, skilled master and apprentice. At best, power should be seen as a static phenomenon, not a dynamic force capable of dictating the deliberate and sedate choices of government. Above all, policy should not be made by the vectors of contending forces but rather by the virtue inherent in each alternative possibility.

At the same time, however, power is also appreciated as a basic force in life. The universal unwritten rule of Chinese politics is the suspicion that "others are probably not as successful in repressing their feelings of aggression as I am, and therefore I must be alert to the ways in which they will use power to hurt me; and so I must protect myself by maximizing my power."

A NOTE ON THE POWER OF PERSONAL TIES

Western commentators have generally ignored the importance of *guanxi,* or particularistic personal ties, in describing Chinese cultural traits and have favored instead such other topics as the Chinese concern about gaining or losing "face" (*lien* or *mienze*). Possibly this has been because such concepts as "face" or "filial piety" have a more positive ethical quality, distinguishing as they do honorable from shameful con-

9. Arthur F. Wright, "Struggle vs. Harmony: Symbols of Competing Values in Modern China," *World Politics,* Vol. VI, No. 1, October 1953, pp. 31–34.

duct.[10] In contrast, foreigners and modernized Chinese alike have tended to see *guanxi* as a somewhat sordid form of unenlightened favoritism that should disappear once the "restoration" of Chinese culture occurs. Consequently, there has been little explicit analysis of the concept of *guanxi*.[11] Yet, even though it would be impossible to quantitatively test such an hypothesis, there is certainly considerable evidence suggesting the possibility that instead of declining in importance, *guanxi* may have increased as Chinese have experienced all the unsettling effects of revolution and social change.[12] *Guanxi* involves far more than just the Western notion of social contacts and connections related to influence. In the West, the key to the flow of personal influence in particularistic relations, say, in an "old boy network," is actual acquaintanceship; in the case of *guanxi*, it is enough that the social roles are seen as related, even though the individuals may not have previously known each other.

To a limited degree, however, it is helpful for understanding *guanxi* to think of the analogy of acquaintanceship networks in American society. As a result of increased communication, and particularly the rise of the professions, the number of people in the chain of acquaintanceships

10. On the psychodynamics of the Chinese concept of face, see Hua Hsien-chin, "The Chinese Concept of Face," *American Anthropologist*, Vol. 46, 1944, pp. 45–64; Warner Muensterberger, "Orality and Dependence: Characteristics of Southern Chinese," *Psychoanalysis and the Social Sciences*, Vol. 3, 1951, pp. 37–69; John H. Weakland, "The Organization of Action in Chinese Culture," *Psychiatry*, Vol. 13, 1950, pp. 361–370; Weston la Barre, "Some Observations on Character Structure in the Orient: II, The Chinese," *Psychiatry*, Vol. 9, 1976, pp. 215–237.

11. Studies that implicitly acknowledge the role of *guanxi* in pre-Communist China political relations include Andrew J. Nathan, *Peking Politics, 1918–1923*, University of California Press, Berkeley and Los Angeles, 1976, Chap. II; Lucian W. Pye, *Warlord Politics*, Praeger, New York, 1971; Hsi-sheng Ch'i, *Warlord Politics in China, 1916–1928*, Stanford University Press, Palo Alto, Calif., 1976, pp. 36–76.

Studies of Communist Party politics that recognize to some degree the importance of *guanxi* include William W. Whitson, *The Chinese High Command: A History of Communist Military Politics, 1927–1971*, Praeger, New York, 1973; Thomas W. Robinson, "Lin Piao as an Elite Type," in Robert A. Scalapino (ed.), *Elites in the People's Republic of China*, University of Washington Press, Seattle, 1972; Frederick C. Teiwes, *Provincial Leadership in China: The Cultural Revolution and Its Aftermath*, Cornell University East Asia Papers, No. 4, 1974; Michel Oksenberg, "The Exit Pattern from Chinese Politics and Its Implications," *China Quarterly*, Vol. 67, September 1976; and Michel Oksenberg, "Getting Ahead and Along in Communist China: The Ladder of Success on the Eve of the Cultural Revolution," in John W. Lewis (ed.), *Party, Leadership, and Revolutionary Power in China*, Cambridge University Press, Cambridge, 1970.

12. The best explicit analysis of *guanxi* is J. Bruce Jacobs, "A Preliminary Model of Particularistic Ties in Chinese Political Alliances: *Kan-ch'ing* and *Kuan-hsi* in a Rural Taiwanese Township," *China Quarterly*, Vol. 78, June 1979, pp. 237–273. Significantly, his typology of the bases of *guanxi* for studying a contemporary Taiwanese township seems applicable for the personalistic relations of early Republican China, and while he is cautious

necessary to link any two Americans has probably declined over the last hundred years. Certainly within any of the major professions, such as any academic discipline, it is usually possible for any reasonably centrally placed member of the discipline to get a "reading" on even the most obscure member with only one or two phone calls, and it is estimated that at the most it requires only six or seven people to connect any two Americans in an acquaintanceship chain.[13] In their latent state, these potential chains of acquaintanceships are essentially the same in America and China; the big difference, of course, is the purposes for which they can be used once they have been activated by an initiative: In the American case, it is true that one can, with some delicacy, go beyond merely asking for an objective "reading" of the abilities of another; in China, there is no question that greater demands can be made. It is not just that the dividing line between acquaintanceship and friendship is different in the two cultures; there is also a difference in what can be legitimately expected of even the most limited connection.[14]

The first thing to note about *guanxi* is that it is thought of as having an almost physical objective existence, and therefore it is not merely a subjective phenomenon, knowable only to participants. Thus it is perfectly reasonable for one person to inquire of another as to whether two other people do or do not "have *guanxi*," and if the answer is "yes," then it is assumed that the third party should be able to give a precise reading of the exact "quantity" and not just the "quality" of the *guanxi*.[15]

---

about generalizing to the PRC, his model would seem to be appropriate for handling the place of *guanxi* in Chinese politics as described by our Hong Kong respondents. The best case study of the role of *guanxi* in factional relations in a Chinese community is Barbara K. L. Pillsbury, "Factionalism Observed: Behind the Face of Harmony in a Chinese Community," *China Quarterly*, Vol. 74, June 1978.

13. For the mathematical model that shows that any American with 1,000 personal acquaintances can be linked to another person chosen at random by two or three intermediaries, on the average, and almost always by four, see Ithiel de Sola Pool and Manfred Kochen, "Contacts and Influence," *Social Networks*, Vol. 1, 1978-1979, pp. 5–51. See also J. Boissevain, *Friends of Friends: Networks, Manipulators, and Coalitions*, St. Martin's Press, New York, 1974; P. Doreian, "On the Connectivity of Social Networks," *Journal of Mathematical Sociology*, Vol. 3, 1974, pp. 245–258; S. Milgram, "The Small World Problem," *Psychology Today*, Vol. 22, 1967, pp. 61–67; G. Miller, "The Magical Number Seven, Plus or Minus Two," *Psychological Review*, Vol. 63, 1956, pp. 81–97.

14. An outstanding analysis of how the Chinese concept of *ganqing*, or the affect in *guanxi* relations, differs from the Western concept of friendship, see Morton A. Fried, *Fabric of Chinese Society: A Study of a Chinese Country Seat*, Praeger, New York, 1953.

15. Someone who is not acquainted with the Chinese concept of *guanxi* might, on reading Bruce Jacobs' analysis (footnote 12 above), conclude that his schematic model for measuring the value of *guanxi* was an example of mechanistic social science seeking for the illusion of quantification. In fact, however, his model is true to the Chinese spirit of objectifying and quantifying *guanxi* relations.

More important is a second characteristic of *guanxi*: It is a phenomenon whose existence or non-existence affects the behavior of not just those directly involved in the relationship – it can potentially affect all who are to any degree related to either one of the principals. Thus, if X inquires of Y whether A and B have *guanxi*, and it is established that they do and that Y has a relationship with B, then it can be assumed that X should be able to establish a claim with A. This is, of course, the nature of the latent networks among the cadres about which we have been speaking. The fact that Y has played a key role in making the network possible puts him in the highly esteemed Chinese role of being a middleman – which incidentally means that he can expect benefits from all the parties. Furthermore, the more substantive the outcome of X and A's new relationship, the more Y and B can expect to benefit. Hence there is less reluctance than might be expected for people to actively mediate so as to expand a *guanxi* network, since all the middlemen can conceivably benefit more than either of the principals who are the poles of the network.

Guanxi, however, must not be confused with the concept of patron-client relations which have recently become popular for describing well-to-do and less-well-to-do alliances in rural Asia and other third world regions. (Those who have helpfully popularized that concept have also, I believe, unfortunately stripped it of much of the richness of cultural variations in their efforts to make all cases fit various abstract models of the relationship.)[16] The patron–client relationship assumes a more

16. James C. Scott has been a leader in expanding the concept of the dyadic relationship of patron–client (landlord–peasant tenant) into a more general theory of moral economy. The basic assumptions of moral economy are that the traditional patron–client relationship, involving peasants and landlords, involved norms about justice and fairness that were the bases of the "moral" community of traditional societies, and that the introduction of market forces associated with the rise of capitalism threatened the security of the peasants, making them prone to rebellion. See such studies as James C. Scott, *The Moral Economy of Peasants*, Yale University Press, New Haven, Conn., 1976; James C. Scott, "Patron–Client Politics and Political Change in Southeast Asia," *American Political Science Review*, Vol. 66, March 1972, pp. 92–113; James C. Scott, "The Erosion of Patron–Client Bonds and Social Change in Southeast Asia," *Journal of Asian Studies*, Vol. 22, November 1972, pp. 5–37; Carl Landè, "Networks and Groups in Southeast Asia: Some Observations on the Group Theory of Politics," *American Political Science Review*, Vol. 67, March 1973, pp. 103–127; Eric Wolf, *Peasants*, Prentice Hall, Englewood Cliffs, N.J., 1966; Eric Wolf, *Peasant Wars of the Twentieth Century*, Harper and Row, New York, 1969.

The moral economy theory has been challenged by advocates of a political economy approach who hold that peasants have responded quite rationally to market opportunities, that the patron–client ties can be understood in terms of cost–benefit analysis and therefore reactions to change reflect the objective conditions and not just subjective feelings about justice and fairness. See Samuel L. Popkin, *The Rational Peasant*, University of California Press, Berkeley, 1979.

substantial difference in the resources available to parties involved than is the case with *guanxi*. In some respects, it is surprising that given the great emphasis upon hierarchy in Chinese culture, there is not a sharper sense of "patron" and "client" in *guanxi*. Yet the very essence of *guanxi* is that the relationship is in the first instance based upon a shared particularism – a common place of origin, a shared teacher, grandfathers who were friends, and the like – and thus there is a pretense at equality even as there must be a subtle recognition of superior and inferior. Also in contrast to patron–client relations, in *guanxi* there is much greater acknowledgment that the inferior can victimize the superior, and there is also much greater use of stratagems in creating feelings of responsibility and obligation on the one hand and indebtedness on the other.

In *guanxi* there is a complex blend of both affect and calculation. In contrast to Western culture, it is good form in Chinese culture to show explicit interest in the selection of the best stratagem or ploy in expanding or manipulating *guanxi* ties. On the other hand, in Chinese culture it is not necessary to dramatize or inflate the affective considerations; it is assumed that only shameless people will not honor their particularistic obligations.

VIEWS OF THE RESPONDENTS

It is difficult for most people to speak directly about the relative importance of power. Therefore, we had to explore its implications with our Hong Kong respondents through a variety of more concrete questions dealing with perceived leadership practices, qualities of superiors and subordinates, and the factors that underlie the formation of cliques. There was often considerable uncertainty in the responses of the informants, because they held sharply different views about the workings of power at the national level and at their own local level.

In general they were less sympathetic and more cynical about the behavior of leadership at the Center but relatively more tolerant of what their immediate superiors had done, even when these actions caused

---

As will become increasingly apparent, our view as to the character of the ties among Chinese officials falls somewhat between those two views about patron–client relations. Consistent with the moral economy theory, we recognize the importance of culture, but our understanding of the cultural factor is not limited to moral norms about justice and fairness; it includes all the learned behavior and practices that are deemed to give security in interpersonal relations. Consistent with the political economy approach, we recognize that there is considerable rational calculation guiding the behavior of superiors and subordinates, but we also insist that what is "rational" can be understood only in the light of cultural predispositions and not according to an abstract calculus.

them personal harm. Many tended to see power relationships in quite personalized terms; in particular, they attributed many of China's problems to Mao Zedong. But it was possibly even more surprising and significant that so many were able to depersonalize their views about power and speak of the characteristics, and more often the failings, of the "system."

The respondents were shown the statement "It is better to want to lead other men than to be a faithful subordinate," and were asked whether they personally felt it was true or false. The responses showed that 65.9 percent agreed with it, and 34.1 percent disagreed. This issue seems to have had a strong element of realism for, of those who had what the Party would call "bad family backgrounds" (parents or grandparents who were middle-class or above, educated, and hence suspect under the regime and who therefore could not realistically be ambitious), only 59.1 percent agreed; a solid 40.9 percent felt that it was all right to be a "faithful subordinate." In contrast, of the respondents with politically "good" backgrounds, 71.4 percent agreed and 28.6 percent disagreed (gamma = .27).

In some cases the positive view of leadership reflected a basically cynical attitude. Thus the son of a peasant family who had obtained secondary schooling declared, "Of course it is better to be a leader. They tell you that the loyalty and hard work of a subordinate should be rewarded and you can become a 'model worker' and be honored, but in fact they just ignore those who faithfully do their jobs. All the good things go to the leaders."

Since the former Red Guards and rusticated educated youth were generally far more cynical, it was not surprising that two-thirds acknowledged the advantages of leadership and only one-third believed in dutifully "serving the people" (gamma = .25). For some, it was precisely the Red Guard experience that taught them the benefits of leadership. For example, a girl who was caught up with the struggle in her Canton middle school said, "During the Cultural Revolution it was very important to be close to the leadership of any of the Red Guard factions, for if you weren't you wouldn't know what was going on. I decided that you had to either stay completely out of it, something which became increasingly impossible, or try to penetrate the leadership ring. To just be a subordinate was stupid."

The older and the less-educated respondents were the ones who took a positive view of being faithful subordinates. All of those who had only primary schooling or less disagreed with the statement, while 69.2 percent of those with some university experience agreed and only 30.8 percent disagreed. Among the older people and those who had not been Red Guards or sent-down youths, opinion was almost equally divided, with

54.5 percent favoring leadership ambitions and 45.5 percent the good subordinate's role. A former militia man pointed out, "There is no point in trying to become a leader because then you will only have great troubles. People will dislike you; you will always have enemies; and you are sure to be criticized for mistakes, whether they are your fault or not. It is much better to be a subordinate, keep out of trouble and just watch the leaders with their impossible problems."

Thus the general picture is quite clear: Most of the respondents, with the exception of the older and the less educated, looked positively toward leadership ambitions. To advance in the power hierarchy was generally seen as desirable. We shall next turn to two other items in the questionnaire that help to clarify the respondents' views about the personal qualities of ambitious people and the constraints surrounding leadership roles.

"An ambitious person (a) is admired or (b) creates enemies." Unfortunately, the Chinese language does not provide a truly neutral way of expressing the concept of "ambitiousness"; *xungxin* implies a virtuous quality, a "hero's heart," while *yexin*, a "wild heart," suggests all the bad characteristics. It was thus impossible to present this question to our respondents with the degree of even-handedness that is possible in English. We were forced to employ the explicitly positive term of *xungxin*.

But in spite of this tilting of the question, a surprising 50 percent of the respondents chose the second answer, "creates enemies"; 38.6 percent checked "is admired"; and 11.4 percent refused to answer because the wording was too imprecise for them.

Even more dramatic is the fact that 62.5 percent of the former Red Guards and/or sent-down youth said that an ambitious person "creates enemies," while 75 percent of those who had not had these traumatic experiences said that an ambitious person "is admired" (gamma = .67).

The extent to which distrust of ambitious people is linked to Cultural Revolutionary experiences is further revealed by the breakdown according to levels of education: Of those with university experience (who hence had escaped the worst personal consequences of the Cultural Revolution and the rustification movement), a significantly high 70 percent answered "is admired," and only 30 percent said "creates enemies"; but 61.5 percent of those with secondary school education said "creates enemies" and only 38.5 percent said "is admired" (gamma = .74).

In discussing their answers to this question, the respondents frequently showed resentment toward those who got ahead, while a few indicated bitterness over the fact that they themselves had created enemies when they were in modest leadership positions.

For example, a high-school graduate who had been sent down to be a common laborer in a commune explained, "I really wasn't ambitious to get ahead but I had no other choice but to try to get a better position. The work points did not give me enough to live on, even with the adjustment allowance, so I had to demand a better position and became an accountant at the brigade level. People didn't like to see me get this position and soon I felt I only had enemies and no real friends."

Other respondents described similar experiences, which may help to explain why 50 percent said "creates enemies," even though the positive expression *xungxin* was used. "Even though I was inspired with the virtuous sentiment of *xungxin*, others chose to misread my actions and say that I had the bad spirit of *yexin*."

With respect to their views about the nature of power, several explained that while they had gotten ahead a bit on the basis of merit, they did not have adequate protection from their superiors to ward off the enmity of their peers. This view was expressed even more emphatically in the responses to the following statement: "The most important thing in getting ahead is (a) being on good terms with the right people or (b) ignoring people and doing your very best."

This question caused the respondents considerable agony, and many asked for clarification as to whether their answer should tell what really happens or how they believe things should be. And, indeed, 9.1 percent refused to answer. Of those who did answer, 63.6 percent believed that being on good terms with the right people was most important, and 27.3 percent said doing your very best was what counted.

Thus, in spite of two decades of unrelenting propaganda about the ideals of Mao's "new man," the Chinese still seem to believe in the efficacy of personal ties. This may not be particularly surprising, given the cynicism that is widely acknowledged in China in the wake of the Cultural Revolution and the fall of Lin Biao and the Gang of Four. What is quite surprising, however, is that 85.7 percent of the respondents who had "good family backgrounds," according to the Party's way of thinking, and who might have been expected to be slightly less cynical said that getting ahead required contacts with the right people, while only 61.1 percent of those with "bad family backgrounds" took that view (gamma = .58).

Our data indicate that the experiences of the last few years may have made the Chinese more inclined to think in terms of personal relations than they were before Communism and the Maoist era. For example, only 26.7 percent of the former Red Guards and sent-down youth believed you could get ahead by doing your very best, while 40 percent of those without such experiences believed that merit would be rewarded (gamma = .29). The less-educated and the older people were evenly divided on the question.

Many of the respondents insisted that the choice was, in fact, not between the two alternatives but that there was an element of both in the way people get ahead in China. The son of a former college professor said, "You certainly need to do your best if you want to get ahead on the mainland, but merit is never enough. You also have to have someone who appreciates your abilities and will look after you and help you. That is why you have to both try your best and also try to get on well with your superior."

A young man who is now working for the Hong Kong government made much the same point when he said, "It is exactly the opposite here in Hong Kong from how it works in China. Here one needs to know people in order to find out what jobs there may be and to get an introduction, but after that it is all according to your ability. In China there is no problem knowing what possibilities exist; what you need to do is to attract attention to yourself by showing ability but after that you need to know the right people in order to keep the job and get ahead. I was able to get a good job right after middle school because of my good grades, but after that I had no hope of any advancement no matter how hard I worked because I had no special relationship with any of my superiors."

In sum, the majority of our respondents said that, for better or worse, advancement in China requires personal contacts, and therefore those who are in high positions must also have had the help of sponsors. Many of the respondents agonized over this question because of their ambivalence toward *guanxi,* or the traditional Chinese concept of obligation, which they associated with "being on good terms with the right people." All of them understood that sensitivity to *guanxi* was a sign of "feudal" attitudes that should no longer have a place in the new China. Yet in their personal dealings, they knew that *guanxi* could be both a reassuring, comforting sentiment and a source of civility. They were not sure they would like to live in a society where nobody understood *guanxi*. They were sure, however, that they did not like living in a China where the powerful denounced *guanxi* but then used it for their own purposes in their elite relationships.

In short, the respondents recognized that a valuable sentiment had somehow been corrupted by the very people who criticized its influence on society.

- A former teacher explained, "I believed the Communists when they said the old society was corrupt. In the old days people had to be selfish to survive, and those who became rich had no time for anyone but themselves. But I still think that *guanxi* is a good thing. People who know *guanxi* are kinder to others and not entirely selfish. That is why I cannot agree with the Communists that Chinese should give up all thought of *guanxi*. In fact I know that among themselves the high Party officials show *guanxi* toward each other. Oh, they certainly look after their special friends. They just keep telling the rest of us that we shouldn't have any special feelings for others. It is different from the old days, but it is still dishonest."

- A former Red Guard studying to be a nurse said, "The common people need the help of *guanxi*, for without its protection they would be alone and without friends. Powerful people don't need *guanxi* but they are always using it to become even more powerful. The powerful people, however, are always telling the common people that they should not respect *guanxi* but this is only their way of keeping the common people powerless. The way things should be is that common people should have the help of *guanxi*, while the strong people should not be allowed to take advantage of it; but the way things are is exactly the opposite. So I do not know what to say about whether or not *guanxi* should be encouraged in China."

RESPECT FOR AUTHORITY

There is an interesting and potentially significant anomaly in our respondents' views that may tell much about Chinese attitudes toward the relationship of power and authority. Whereas they are generally critical, if not cynical, about what is involved in gaining power in China, they remain remarkably respectful of established power. They seem to make a sharp contrast between the scheming opportunism and dishonest maneuvering that they associate with the process of getting ahead and the deferential, indeed often sympathetic, attitudes that are appropriate in talking about actual office holders.

This contrast is important because it suggests that the Chinese make a clear distinction between power, which is impure, and authority, which is deserving of respect; furthermore, they seem to picture authority in highly traditional terms as something given, not something sought after. People will, in their sordid ways, seek to get power, but nobody can strive for authority, for it should be inherent in the definition of high office.

The Chinese thus may be able to develop a high level of cynicism about power without an equal rejection of respect for authority in the system. One may be contemptuous of power-seekers without being hostile toward the established order. On the other hand, if persons in positions of authority were forced—for example, by the demands of factional politics—to engage in the same forms of conduct as those seeking power, there could be a dramatic loss of trust in authority in China.

The responses given by the panel to the following questions provide some insight into their attitudes about power and authority.

"Do leaders have to conform to the expectations of others or is conformity only necessary at lower ranks?" Given the pervasive cynicism of our respondents about developments in China and their views about how people get ahead, it is surprising and significant that they overwhelmingly (76.7 percent) believe that conformity is "always a necessity." Only a minority (23.3 percent) perceive leaders as being able to escape from inhibitions and become truly free. An outsider might expect that people who had experienced the heavy demands of disciplined living at their lowly stations in life would believe that those in power could do as they please without feeling the same constraints as ordinary people. Yet the view that leaders also have to conform was common to nearly all categories of respondents. Slightly more of those with "bad family backgrounds" assumed the necessity of conformity (81 percent, compared to 71.4 percent of those with "good family backgrounds"). There were no appreciable differences between the former Red Guards and rusticated youths (22.2 percent of whom said "leaders are free of conformity," and 77.8 percent said "always a necessity") and non-Red Guards (who divided 20/80 percent). Only the level of education produced significant differences, with 92.3 percent of the post-middle-schoolers seeing conformity as a necessity and only 7.7 percent seeing leaders as free, while those with primary school or less education divided 50/50 (gamma = .66).

The explanation for this surprising view is that most of the respondents were very sensitive to the fact that whatever their hierarchies, those above them faced stricter discipline than they did themselves. As we have already observed, most respondents, even those hostile to the national leadership, were sympathetic toward their immediate leaders, who they knew were always vulnerable to criticism from above. Within their own range of experience, it was true that the higher one moved up, the greater were the requirements of conformity. Those who had the greatest possibility of being free of conformity were usually the least significant members of the group, people whose behavior had to meet only minimal standards. This situation was described in many ways:

- A former construction worker said, "Our leaders had to go to even more meetings than we did, and if they made any mistakes in expressing political ideas they would find themselves in bad trouble."
- A former resident of Shanghai said, "We all knew that the higher you got in the Party the more you had to be correct in everything

you did. Leaders have to pay a price, and I am sure that this is true all the way to the top. After all, the men around Mao Zedong had to be awfully careful to always conform to his wishes."

- A former professional hunter who collected specimens for the Academy of Sciences and various museums observed, "When I was hunting all around China it was easy to talk with the common people, but just as soon as you began to deal with officials you found that they had to be very careful in everything they said. The life of a high official was probably filled with more dangers than I had even when hunting for tigers."

This unquestioning readiness to understand the constraints of leadership responsibilities did not lead to a belief that superiors were selfless and reciprocated sympathy to subordinates, however, as is clear from the respondents' answers to the following paired question: "How often do superiors try to be helpful, and how often do they just look out for themselves? (a) Try to be helpful or (b) Mostly look out for themselves." "How often do subordinates try to be helpful, and how often do they just look out for themselves? (a) Try to be helpful or (b) Mostly look out for themselves."

In what might appear to be a direct contradiction, the respondents saw their leaders as being self-centered and unreciprocating in almost exactly the same proportion as they sympathetically assumed that leaders had to conform. In all, 79.5 percent said that superiors tend mostly to look after themselves, and only 20.5 percent thought superiors were helpful. People with what the Communists classify as "bad family backgrounds" were, as might be expected, slightly more inclined to see superiors as self-interested (self-interested, 90.9 percent, helpful, 9.1 percent) than were those with "good family backgrounds" (self-interested, 71.4 percent, helpful, 28.6 percent). Much the same proportions characterized the former Red Guards and sent-down youth and those who had not had such experiences. (Red Guards: self-interested, 88.9 percent, helpful, 11.1 percent; non-Red Guards: self-interested, 81.8 percent, helpful 18.2 percent).

Needless to say, our respondents took a more kindly view toward subordinates, but they still remained basically skeptical: 46.3 percent granted that subordinates tried to be helpful, while 53.7 percent said they were self-interested. Since most of them were describing their own status, this has to be taken as a blunt statement that most ordinary people in China have to look out for themselves and cannot afford to be helpful to others, including their inferiors. Those with "good" backgrounds split exactly 50/50 on this question, and those with "bad" backgrounds were almost the same, with 45 percent responding "helpful," and 55 percent, "self-interested."

The only significant, and somewhat surprising, difference in views about subordinates was between Red Guards and non-Red Guards. Although they might legitimately feel that they themselves were mistreated subordinates, former Red Guards and rusticated youths were even more skeptical about the attitudes of subordinates: 62.5 percent said that they were generally self-interested, and 37.5 percent said that they were helpful. Those who did not have the same experiences divided in almost exactly the opposite proportions: 60 percent said "helpful," and 40 percent said "self-centered" (gamma = .43).

What do we make of these conclusions that suggest, first, a contradiction between sympathy for the constraints of leadership and skepticism about the motives of leaders, and second, that younger Chinese who have experienced the exhilaration of the Cultural Revolution and the shocks of being sent down to the countryside are more distrusting of the motivations of subordinates than are other Chinese?

A complete answer must await our analysis of "authoritarianism" and "dependency." Suffice it to say here that the contradictions in attitudes toward leaders can be explained by the ambivalent Chinese feelings about authority: Leaders are, on the one hand, important people deserving of attention, who are prepared to pay the price of getting ahead; but on the other hand, they are self-centered and often ignore their obligation to help others in lower positions. The attitudes of the former low-ranking Red Guards illustrate their belief that they were denied leadership status because those they sought to lead consistently let them down by being unworthy subordinates. Several of them were quite explicit on this point:

- "When we arrived at the state farm we were told by the head of the Revolutionary Committee that because we were educated youths we were expected to be leaders, but it was impossible. Every time I tried to tell anything to the members of my work squad who were all local people they either laughed at me or ignored me. Then I would be scolded for not being a leader. It was very unfair."
- "In 1967 I led our group of Red Guards up to Peking. I took care of seeing that they had food, a place to stay, and that they got to meet others and march through Tien An Men Square to see Mao. I looked after them all the time. After a while, after we came back to Canton, our faction was unfairly attacked by others, and those who I had taken care of became worried and didn't want trouble so they didn't stand by me."
- "I had been working in the factory for nearly three years and had been very active in all the study sessions, and I should have been put

on the political study group for our shift, and this would have put me in line to become a Party member but some of my fellow workers were jealous and said things about me behind my back which were not true."

Finally, the respondents were asked for their views about the kinds of people who become leaders, and most important of all, what they considered to be the bases for political factions: "In my experience most people who are successful leaders are: (a) brighter than others, (b) work harder, (c) are more ruthless, (d) have better contacts, (e) other, specify."[17]

The responses to this question further reveal the ambivalence of our respondents toward leaders, specifically their grudging respect coupled with distrustful scorn. The answer that received the highest weighting was "have better contacts," a sign of the respondents' particularistic approach toward most relationships and their suspicion of favoritism; yet the next highest score went to "brighter than others," indicating that they respect superiors and believe that talent in China is rewarded. Then, considerably lower, came the cynical view, "are more ruthless," at the same level as the contradictory, respectful view, "work harder." Finally, a relatively large number volunteered "other" explanations of the qualities required for getting ahead in China. The majority were of an uncomplimentary nature, such as "flattering of superiors," "agreeing to every word of the powerful," "never offending those with influence," but there were also acknowledgments of positive qualities, such as "willing to take chances," "more flexible in their thinking," "never worry about what has happened but only think to the future."

Contradictory feelings about leaders are even more apparent in the distribution of answers about each of the suggested characteristics. For example, whereas "have better contacts" was the most significant, on the basis of cumulative weighting, the quality that received the most "number one" or "most important" was in fact "ruthlessness." In all, 38.6 percent of the panel identified ruthlessness as "most important," but at the same time 31.9 percent rated it as "least important" and "next to least important." This polarized attitude about ruthlessness was matched by a similar but less extreme ambivalence about leaders being

17. The respondents were asked to rank each possibility from "most important" to "least important," on a scale of 5 to 1. (They were permitted to give equal ranking to items they felt were of equal importance.) Because the Chinese associate "number one" with "best" but equate zero with nothing, it was necessary, in order to get a raw weighting of their answers, to reverse their notations, making $1 = 5$, $2 = 4$, $3 = 3$, $4 = 2$, $5 = 1$, but leaving 0 as 0; we then added the scores, so that the possibility of having the highest total would be the most important.

"brighter" than others. This quality received the second largest number of both "next to most important" and "next to the least important" ratings.

The significance of these mixed reactions becomes clearer when we note which respondents held the different views. Of those whom the regime would characterize as having "bad" family backgrounds, 31.8 percent believed that "brighter than others" was the most important quality of leadership; but not a single respondent from a "good" family attached such importance to brightness (gamma = .31). At the same time, 45.5 percent of those from "bad" backgrounds saw ruthlessness as the most important quality of leaders, and only 28.6 percent of those from "good" families gave the same weighting. Those who came from formerly better-off families tended to see leaders as both brighter and more ruthless; in contrast, those from poorer families, who were thus favored by the regime, tended to stress hard work and "other" qualities, particularly "flattery." (There was no significant difference between the two groups about "better contacts"; on this item, gamma equaled only .02).

These figures reveal possible class-attitude differences toward leadership and power. Those with greater "cultural advantages" continue to hold the view that the elite are mentally superior, but they rationalize their own inferior status by seeing leaders as ruthless and calculating. On the other hand, those in the category of "workers and peasants," who in theory now rule China, justify their failure to become leaders by seeing people who do get ahead as more "hard-working." Both groups, however, agree on the overriding importance of better contacts, which seems to be both a traditional and a contemporary Chinese concern.

These conclusions must be further qualified, because the experiences of being Red Guards and of being sent down to the countryside appear to have significantly influenced Chinese views about leaders. Of those who were former Red Guards, 61.1 percent said ruthlessness was most important, while only 9.1 percent of the non-Red Guards agreed; and conversely, 63.3 percent of the non-Red Guards said ruthlessness was the least important consideration, compared to only 11.1 percent of the Red Guards. The degree of significance is impressive: gamma = .75. In contrast, 45.5 percent of the non-Red Guards said that leaders work harder, but only 5.6 percent of the Red Guards agreed. Indeed, 50 percent of the Red Guards ranked hard work as the least or next-to-least important quality of leadership. (Again, the degree of significance is impressive: gamma = .53.)

Our evidence strongly supports the conclusion that there is, particularly among educated people, a deep desire to respect leadership – a view that has been challenged by the experience of the last few years. Our respondents generally wanted to believe that power should be constructive and moral, but they had to accept the pragmatic fact that power could be destructive and self-centered.

"What do you believe is important in the forming of political factions? (a) similar material or power interests, (b) similar viewpoints on issues, (c) trust based on knowing each other a long time, (d) friendship (including friendship of wives), (e) co-provincials, schoolmates, etc., (f) having the same enemies, (g) other, please describe." The respondents' answers to this question dramatically reinforce the proposition that power considerations are central to Chinese factional politics and that policy matters are significantly less important. In all, 79.5 percent said that material or power connections were "most important," and only one respondent ranked this consideration below the top two categories of importance. They rated "having the same enemies" second in significance, with 38.6 percent saying it was the "most important," and only 9.1 percent identifying it as of "least importance." "Similar points of view on issues" ranked third in overall weighting, with only 11.4 percent calling it the "most important" and 38.6 percent rating it as of "middle importance."

The fact that "friendship" was considered of little importance may seem to contradict what we have already learned about the importance of *guanxi* in the minds of the respondents. When several were pressed as to whether they might be undervaluing the importance of friendship, they uniformly responded that in their view those who got to the top in Chinese politics and were instrumental in forming factions could not afford to have real friendships, but that they could share mutual material or power interests. Leaders then might help each other and work together against common enemies, but they expected to materially benefit and would not act out of a spirit of mutual friendship or obligation.

Interestingly, the respondents who came from Guangdong did attach slightly, but statistically significantly, more importance to "co-provincials" (gamma = .39) and "similar points of view on policy issues" (gamma = .30). While the Guangdong people slightly favored the more traditional Chinese considerations, they also reflected a higher degree of cynicism; for example, they dismissed as laughable the idea that friendship could be a factor in elite factional politics.

The two themes of "material or power considerations" and "common enemies" were enough to explain most of China's factional politics for the vast majority of our respondents. Those with more education did give a slightly higher rating than the less educated to the importance of "policy issues." (gamma = .23), but those who had been Red Guards or sent-down youth were significantly less prone to see policy issues as important (gamma = .54). The Red Guard or rustification experience does seem to have made the better-educated respondents more inclined to stress the importance of common enemies.

The explanations given by many of the respondents for their answers to this question tell as much, if not more, about why they placed so much importance on power and material interests and on the role of enemies in creating political alliances:

- "Right from the beginning we had two Red Guard factions in our middle school. I don't know which one came first, but they were both of the same political ideology. What separated them was just that each wanted to be all-powerful. You joined the faction which you thought would win. Then as our struggle became more intense we made alliances with factions in other schools. They would help us with our enemies and we helped them with theirs."

- "The event that made me realize how unimportant policy issues are to China's leaders and how they are only interested in power was the Lin Biao affair. Why did Lin Biao turn against Mao? Why did Mao turn against Lin Biao? They had no differences in policies. The only explanation is that each wanted more power for himself, and each came to distrust the other. They could never give us a good explanation of the Lin Biao affair. So I came to realize that our national leaders were only interested in themselves."

- "You may think that the fall of the Gang of Four was a matter of different points of view about policy questions, but that is wrong. It was really a matter of power. You see, Hua Guofeng was really close to Mao Zedong – Mao chose him – and Mao was, of course, also close to the Gang of Four. So why did Hua have the Four arrested? Not because of any policy issues but because he knew that if he didn't, they would have overthrown him. Hua was thinking only about holding on to power. And why did he bring back Deng Xiaoping? Not because they agreed on policy matters, but because Hua needed to strengthen his power with a strong ally."

- "There are factions at brigade level because the different members of the Revolutionary Committee were trying to build up their power. They would try to make contacts with people at the *xian* and even province level and learn about future plans. Then they would tell us what they knew and thus make themselves seem more important. They didn't care what the plans were, they just wanted to be powerful."

SUBJECTIVE DIMENSIONS

Although our questionnaire was not designed to explore the socialization experiences of the respondents, their answers to certain questions about how children should be brought up do provide some indication of their deeper psychological feelings about power, aggression, and authority. Even more important were their comments about why they answered particular items as they did. Indeed, without these comments it would have been impossible to appreciate why the respondents were divided exactly evenly in "yes" and "no" responses to the statement, "Obedience and respect for authority are the most important virtues children should learn." Taken at face value, the figures would suggest a relatively low level of authoritarianism (an appropriate conclusion, as we shall see in a later chapter), but it would not have explained what was really on their minds. Their comments made it clear that most of the respondents were troubled for two reasons: First, many of them said that mindless obedience was bad because it could mean obeying improper authorities and evil leaders – several said that the Party's expectation of complete obedience was one of the bad features of Communism. They felt that children should learn to distinguish proper from improper authorities before learning obedience. Second, and probably more importantly, many who said "no" were troubled over the intended definition of "children," which for them was crucial, since they generally believed in permissiveness in the early years and the introduction of discipline only with the beginning of school.

Not only is Chinese child-rearing different from Western patterns, consistent with this difference there is also a difference in the meaning of the words "discipline" and "obedience." For the Chinese, attempts to control or influence the preschool-age child are not associated with the concept of disciplining, which is reserved for much stricter and even physical sanctions. As some of our respondents explained:

- "Of course, parents try to stop their children from being naughty, but they can only shout at them, not really expecting them to obey."
- "Discipline can only come after a person has learned to reason and can remember what he has been told. You cannot expect little children to be obedient because they just know how to play."

At the same time many of the respondents felt parents could strive to instill in young children feelings of respect and awe – attitudes that in Western cultures might be taken as part of learning obedience. As one respondent explained:

- "No one is too young not to be afraid of frightening things, and these can include fathers, grandparents, and outsiders."

The responses to the statement, "A well-raised child is one who doesn't have to be told twice to do something," showed a somewhat more demanding set of standards, as 57 percent agreed (the older respondents being a bit more insistent).

In contrast with these more tolerant attitudes about early childhood behavior, the respondents overwhelmingly indicated a strong belief in the need to respect authority, as 73 percent signified agreement with the statement, "Disobeying an order is one thing that you can't excuse – if one can get away with disobedience, why can't everybody?" Thus, their attitudes of permissiveness toward young children were not inconsistent with a belief in the ultimate need to accept and respect authority in adulthood.

There is considerable psychological significance in this acceptance of early permissiveness followed by strict compliance with authority. The transition in socialization practices is thus a sharp one, accomplished abruptly in a brief span of years, in contrast to the more gradual pattern found in the West. From what we know about schools in Communist China, children are expected to be quiet, orderly, disciplined members of a group as soon as they are removed from their family setting. The further fact that our respondents experienced no doubts about childhood being the happiest period of life, when one has no cares or worries, provides a further clue to the psychological dynamics underlying Chinese views about power.

Ideally, power should provide support, as during the earlier, permissive years of life. It should never exist in any of its more aggressive forms, but since it is such a basic fact of life, it should be constantly restrained by the greater influence of shame and morality.

These attitudes are suggested by the explanations some of our respondents gave when asked to account for their tolerance of permissiveness toward children:

- A young man from Shanghai explained, "Of course, we would all like to be children who have no worries because our family takes care of us. But we have to grow up and in doing so we must learn how to behave because if we don't, others will be very hard on us. The safest thing in life is to obey those who have the right to give orders."
- A former rusticated youth from Canton said, "Once children can learn who is to be respected, then it is important for them to practice obedience. There is always the danger that bad people will influence others and that is why it is so important that only good people should be allowed to get ahead. Unfortunately it doesn't always work out right in China, but it can't be helped and so there is nothing that can be done except to obey those in power."

IMPLICATIONS FOR FORECASTING

The assertion that power considerations are of primary importance in Chinese factional politics would seem banal were it not for the fact that most writings on the subject give greater importance to ideological and policy differences. It is assumed in most societies that discussions of the "politics" of a situation will focus on power relationships, but in the Chinese case – no doubt, largely because the political process is so secretive – there is a tendency to attach greater importance to the more manifest phenomena of ideological disputation and bureaucratic policy contention.

Yet in terms of forecasting developments in Chinese politics, it is prudent to assume that there may be power struggles that are manifested in ideological phrases and policy pronouncements but which are in fact inspired by the logic of power calculations. In spite of the imperative of consensus, there will undoubtedly be contention behind the scenes whenever there is a vacuum in leadership or whenever a particular leadership element is threatening to consolidate its position and eliminate from politics all those associated with the losers.

Chapter 7

Policy Conflicts, the Symbolic Use of Issues, and Compulsive Actions

Substantive issues may divide Chinese leaders, but initially, issues tend to be of symbolic importance for defining consensus and attacking deviants.

Before further exploring Chinese attitudes toward authority and dependency, we must note the converse of the previous proposition about the centrality of power calculations in Chinese politics and seek to explain the actual role of substantive policy issues.

We shall argue, first, that while the Chinese leadership has had different views on many policy problems, the fundamental consideration in the formation of factions has been judgment about who appears to be emerging as the strongest figure and who is in the best position to provide rewards to supporters and punishment to adversaries. Second, decisionmaking does not come about in response to upward pressures from a bureaucracy seeking authoritative guidance; rather, policies emanate from grand command decisions taken by supreme leaders after they have consolidated their power. Since policy questions are often floated as a part of the process of consolidating power to facilitate the separation of friends from foes, policy discussions generally assume a distinctly symbolic nature at an early stage. (Even "pragmatic" policies are first treated symbolically and not in terms of effectiveness and value.) Finally, as we shall see in Chapter 8, once power issues are resolved, policy initiatives tend to be dramatic and highly compulsive as the successful faction seeks to assert its domination.

THE NEED FOR CAUTION IN INTERPRETING CHINESE POLICY DEBATES

In recent years the Chinese leaders have frequently participated in sustained, sometimes vigorous, but always guarded and never fully manifest debates over many basic policy questions. At times the issues have been administratively precise – for example, the issue of the proper methods for calculating work points – but more often they have reflected general ideological orientations, as in educational policies, priorities between agriculture and industry, the best forms of incentives, or whether national defense requires more technology than that at the command of the guerrilla warrior.

Therefore, substantive issues have unquestionably divided the Chinese leadership from time to time. No one would deny that public policy concerns were involved in the cases of the leaders who fell from grace during Mao's ascendancy. But it would be a misreading of Chinese political practices to assume that policy issues are the prime movers of events in China or to underestimate how facile the Chinese are in using policy issues to conceal their more basic personal clashes.

Policy issues are useful for identifying who stands with and against whom, but to assume that predictions about the outcome of such debates could be based on the relative merits of the arguments would be to turn Chinese politics completely upside down. Because the discussions are primarily symbolic, their practical aspects are often ignored. In responding to such debates, cadres and leading figures do not evaluate the wisdom of the various views, they judge the consequences for themselves of victory or defeat of various principals. Moreover, analysts must be wary of taking the significance of the issues too seriously, because the victorious faction can easily reverse its policy positions once it has gained authority.

It is necessary to keep in mind that Western analysts usually prefer to discuss factional alignments in terms of issues, possibly because they believe that such differences provide a more legitimate basis for politics. But because of the distinctively American view that holds that politics should revolve around public choices, we tend to ignore other, and often more entertaining, possibilities. There is indeed a tendency among American political analysts to employ a three-tiered scheme. At the highest and most legitimate level, there are basic issues over which "honorable men can disagree." At the next level, there are slightly more shady "interests" that may be either "legitimate" or "selfish" or both. (Public figures prefer to discuss "issues" rather than have "interests"; "issues" are dealt with by statesmen, while politicians have "interests.") Finally, at the lowest and most unspeakable level, there are personality preferences and clashes, a kind of "chemistry" in human relations that can be good or bad, the mere discussion of which borders on gossip.

The Chinese tend to see politics in almost the reverse order. In their view it is self-evident, and hence quite legitimate, that the personal qualities of a leader are critical in attracting either an honorable following or sinister "gangs." The very suggestion that people might have "interests" is taken to be a scandal; and finally, most Chinese tend to suspect that discussions of issues are merely ways of throwing dust into the eyes of the naive.[1]

It is important to keep in mind this difference between American and Chinese assumptions about the dynamics of politics in any analysis of the post-Mao era, because American analysts all too easily concluded that once the "irrational" impediments of radicals and the Gang of Four had been removed, Chinese politics would naturally right itself and become a rational, problem-solving system. Such a conclusion would completely overlook the extent to which the Chinese are capable of turning policy questions into symbolic matters that can become the bases for new personal alliances.

ISSUES AS SYMBOLS FOR FACTIONAL IDENTIFICATION

To understand the place that policy issues do have in Chinese politics it is necessary to appreciate the remarkable ability of Chinese leaders to accept complete reversals of policy gracefully and with alacrity. They can totally extinguish whatever passions they may have had for their preferred policies and stoutly deny that they ever believed what the record reports they had previously championed. As Parris H. Chang observed after carefully analyzing the struggles surrounding the Twelve-Year Agricultural Program, "It should be emphatically stated that with the exception of Mao . . . and Deng Zihui . . . most other leaders changed their positions under different circumstances and were willing

---

1. In the summer of 1977, the participants at a workshop at the University of Michigan, sponsored by the Joint Committee on Contemporary China, attempted to determine whether it would be possible to trace the role of various potential "interests" in Chinese politics. The findings of this workshop do not call for any modification of our generalization about the Chinese denial of the legitimacy of interests.

to accept the policy decided by the Party at any moment."[2] In four other case studies, Chang further documents the complex relationship between factional power considerations and policy issues. He does not make explicit the rules of inference that he used to arrive at his conclusions, but they would probably take the following form:

1. The ending or shelving of any authoritatively announced policy program signals the existence of a countervailing power group. That is, programs will proceed as announced unless countered by greater power. (The inertia of bureaucracies, combined with the uncomplaining timidity of lower cadres, will keep programs unaltered until a counterpower is exerted.)
2. A change in focus of a policy signals the existence of a contending power group that is not strong enough to be an effective countervailing power. The modification of plans rarely reflects pragmatic learning; it is a sign that a contending faction exists that wishes to humiliate the dominant group and change the basis of consensus.
3. Policies that are not workable will not be criticized or altered unless there is a contending group ready to challenge for power. Thus, leadership is only threatened by faulty policies if there is another faction seeking advancement.
4. A change in the responsibility for a program implies a shift in factional power. No group will give up authority in any domain unless it is confronted with a superior force.
5. Persistence in clinging to unworkable policies is a sign of secure power, not of mere stubbornness.
6. Any public criticism, particularly at a Party congress, must be interpreted as a challenge for power.

These six rules of inference emphasize the degree to which policy issues are seen not as technical problem-solving matters but as questions focusing on loyalties and networks. Indeed, whenever policy issues become manifest, they quickly take on a symbolic character, useful for denouncing the defeated deviants and for rallying consensus views. Issues may therefore be highlighted precisely to test loyalties and to force people to choose sides—with, of course, few wishing to be identified with politically vulnerable leaders. Many cadres no doubt genuinely opposed the policies of one, or another, or all of the Gang of Four on substantive grounds, but unquestionably a far greater number joined in the chorus of denunciations after the fall because they knew that it was the wise way to respond to "policy issues," most aspects of which they saw as largely symbolic.

2. Parris H. Chang, *Power and Policy in China*, Pennsylvania State University Press, University Park and London, 1975, p.33.

The use of particular symbolic slogans, and even more subtly, the minor alteration of established slogans, often helps to clarify political alignments and differentiate work styles even though the slogans purport to deal with policy matters. For example, in the spring of 1979, before the second session of the Fifth National People's Congress officially decreed a reduction in the ambitious goals of the Four Modernizations, the Chinese media advanced a new eight-character slogan that anyone in tune with the Chinese political vocabulary instantly recognized as similar to the one that had heralded the pullback from the extremes of the Great Leap. There was, however, a critical modification that, taken literally, suggested an even sharper break with the past than that which occurred after the abandonment of the Great Leap. The 1979 slogan was "Readjustment, reform, rectification, and raising standards," while the 1962 slogan was "Readjustment, consolidation, filling out, and raising standards." If the two slogans are read solely as guides to policy changes, the only possible conclusion would have to be that China's leadership intended the "readjustments" from the original Four Modernizations policy to be an even greater break than the 1962 policies were from the Great Leap, since the new words, "reform and rectification," obviously call for more extreme changes than "consolidation" and "filling out." Yet it seems unlikely that the "readjustments" of the Four Modernizations will in fact entail a more substantial change in policies. In the 1960s, Mao was still alive and the faction seeking change had to downplay that change in order not to provoke greater opposition, whereas in 1979 the dominant faction wished to highlight its differences with its weaker opponents. The two slogans thus explain more about power relationships than policy choices.

The 1962 slogan was advanced to mobilize support for an emerging faction – the typical way that symbols are used in Chinese politics – while the 1979 slogan was floated in a spirit of revenge against the remnants of a declining faction. In the latter case it was advantageous for the strong faction to use the slogan to proclaim the existence of an opposition. Therefore, the dominant "truth from facts faction" declared the existence of an ominous "great adverse current" composed of not only the "whatever faction" (the faction that continued to believe in the correctness of *whatever* Mao had ever said) but also the "opposition faction," consisting of bureaucrats who preferred the safety of inertia. Although the "whatever faction" was supposedly ultra-leftist and the "opposition faction" rightist, both were treated as ideologically compatible, since "as 'I am present in you, and you are present in me', the two factions find it very easy to wallow in the mire with each other."[3] The two elements of

3. "Defeat the Great Adverse Current," *Cheng Ming*, Hong Kong, June 1, 1979, in Foreign Broadcast Information Service, *Daily Report – People's Republic of China*, June 7,

the "great adverse current" were not described as ever having clear alternative policy preferences. The "whatever faction" certainly did not want to abandon the Four Modernizations and revive the policies of the Cultural Revolution, since its presumed leader, Wang Hongwen, was the very one who arrested the Gang of Four and did the actual dirty work of "smashing" them. Conversely, if all that was required in the spring of 1979 were some technical adjustments in the plans for the Four Modernizations, there would have been no need to hint darkly about a "great adverse current."

The Chinese tolerance of a significant degree of separation between power and policy opens the way to a situation in which symbols, which may initially be related vaguely to either power or policy, can readily become free-floating, available for manipulation in support of consensus or for attacking deviance. Thus, for example, when the anti-Zhou Enlai elements introduced an "Anti-Confucius" campaign in 1973, the Zhou forces picked up the campaign but diverted it into the "Anti-Confucius/Anti-Lin Biao" campaign.[4] In a similar fashion, at the spring 1979 Working Conference of the Eleventh Central Committee the anti-Deng forces proclaimed the "Four Principles," which implied a return to Marxist–Leninist orthodoxy, but which the Deng forces were soon proclaiming as their own slogan, as proof of their orthodoxy.

THE MOVEMENT OF POLICY DECISIONS FROM SYMBOLISM TO SUBSTANTIVE PROGRAMS

This, of course, does not mean that symbolism is unimportant for policy questions. The use of extensive ceremony when advancing new policies accentuates, and also explains, the symbolic uses to which the new programs can be put. The initiation of a new program usually starts with a symbolic slogan; this has been the procedure from the Three Antis to the Four Modernizations. The proclamation from on high alerts lesser cadres to what at least some elements of the elite consider to be good;

1979, p. U1.

4. Merle Goldman, who has studied the "Anti-Confucius" campaign with great care and insight, believes that the Zhou forces did not seek to so divert the campaign that in her judgment was consistently the work of the "radicals." Charles Neuhauser, in the spirit of seeking the truth and not just being diplomatic, says that we are both correct and that there were two different phases of the "Anti-Confucius/Anti-Lin Biao" campaign, one under the "radicals" and the other directed by Zhou's forces.

for example, Mao Zedong triggered off the commune movement by merely stating, "Communes are good."

We shall trace the steps following the symbolic introduction of a policy program with the concrete case of one of the Four Modernizations, the modernization of science and technology. After the initial announcement of the idea of the Four Modernizations, the policy of advancing science and technology was first given substance by the highly formal act of convening a National Conference on Science and Technology. Chairman Hua Guofeng's address, delivered in the Great Hall of the People to 8,000 cadres from throughout the nation, did not go into detail about how science and technology were to be advanced, but rather focused on the theme that the Gang of Four had opposed science and technology. Those attending the conference therefore learned that the advancement of science and technology was first and foremost a partisan political matter that called for the exposure and possible removal of all officials who had ever been associated with the Gang of Four.

The next step was for the attending cadres to return to their respective provinces to organize replica conferences for provincial cadres. At each of these conferences the message of Hua's address was repeated so that everyone would know that anyone identified with previous policies in education was in trouble. Thus, advancing science and technology became another form of "struggling" against the followers of the Gang of Four.

The third stage in the policy implementation was also largely symbolic, as it simply gave prestige to the surviving scientists. Although there was a severe shortage of trained scientists who could actually contribute to the advancement of science and technology, the Chinese leaders systematically diverted the energies of those few for essentially symbolic tasks, such as lecturing to laymen on technological subjects. The Chinese press, for example, made much over the report that "the Anhui Party and revolutionary committees have set aside time on Fridays for their staff to study science." During these sessions, professors lectured to audiences of 4,000 people on such subjects as "electronic computers, lasers, space technology, high energy physics, and genetic engineering."[5] The lay audience must surely have been entertained by this new mysterious language, after years of lectures on esoteric philosophical points in the works of Marx, Engels, Lenin, and Stalin. But how science and technology were to advance practical human endeavors was not made clear.

To the Chinese, however, it is self-evident that ceremony can advance

5. "Leading Cadres in Anhwei Study Science," Peking, N.C.N.A., Foreign Broadcast Information Service, *Daily Report—People's Republic of China,* June 15, 1978, pp. G2–G3.

policy. For example, the main item of publicity about a "science forum" held at Fudan University was that the 76-year-old president was "the first to take the floor" to read "an excellent paper" in mathematics.[6] (Presumably in China, as in the West, creative mathematics is a young man's game, but in China the aged do not retire from positions of authority.) Symbolism and ceremony were likewise used to communicate new policies in Hubei, where it was reported that responsible cadres of the provincial Party committee "have seriously grasped the work of implementing the Party's policy on intellectuals in accordance with instructions from Chairman Hua and the Party Central Committee." That is, "they have taken the lead in making friends with intellectuals and pay visits to and are talking with them."[7] The intellectuals were surely genuinely pleased by this new treatment from the cadres who only recently preferred to terrorize them; but to the Western mind, little progress seems to have been made toward the ostensible goal of implementing serious policy.

Yet this symbolic treatment of science and technology undoubtedly had the practical effect of raising the status of scientists and educators; and since status is power in China, the wishes of the scientists had to be deferred to, so the stage was set for a reversal of educational policy.

Thus, the Chinese approach was to shift from denying the authority of scientists to the sudden demand that they should assert unfettered authority and act as though their every wish could be government fiat. At the same time, these dramatic symbolic politics meant that attention was diverted from constructing an effective scientific community and achieving a technology that would be integrated into productive processes; instead, scientists were expected to behave like magicians, and since magicians work with speed, so should the scientists. There was no acknowledgment of the fact that China has periodically swung toward the worship of "Dr. Science" without much success, and no effort has been made to figure out why all the earlier attempts to capture the power of modern science have failed.

In any case, the current aging generation of Chinese scientists suddenly found themselves elevated to positions of apparent influence, and they soon compulsively sought to fulfill every wish they had been denied since the establishment of the regime. Very few seemed concerned about warning the political authorities that magic is impossible, that many of

6. "Futan University Conducts Science Forum," Peking N.C.N.A., Foreign Broadcast Information Service, *Daily Report – People's Republic of China*, June 15, 1978, pp. G11–G12.

7. "Hupeh Leader Urges Implementing CCP Intellectual Policy," Wuhan Hupeh Provincial Services, Foreign Broadcast Information Service, *Daily Report – People's Republic of China*, June 16, 1978, pp. H1.*H2*.

their attempts might not bear fruit, and that development might take more time than they have been given. The Chinese intellectuals were not, however, completely politically naive, for none made the mistake of the Hundred Flower period—none attempted to use this phase of liberalization to give vent to their social and political dreams for the country. Instead, they acted as disciplined technocrats, conforming to the state's basic objectives. At the same time, they have generally ignored the possibility that if they do not realize the goal of "modernizing science and technology" by 1985, they may become the targets of the wrath of the political class.

By the summer and fall of 1978, the enthusiasm of the liberated scientists and the urgency for administrative cadres to carry out the wishes of the supreme authority had combined to produce a frantic atmosphere and completely unrealistic expectations about the speed with which a new generation of scientists and engineers could be trained to fill the appalling gaps produced by the near total breakdown of Chinese higher education. A delegation of professors from Ohio was asked in August 1978 if their colleges and universities would admit 300 Chinese students in September—students who had only taken their college entrance examinations in July; Chinese officials spoke of sending as many as 10,000 students abroad; and the President of Peking University, Zhou Peiyuan, headed a mission to Washington where he signed an agreement with Dr. Frank Press, the President's Science Advisor, calling for the admission of 500 to 700 Chinese to American universities in the school year of 1978–1979. Fewer than 50 came.

The manipulation of symbols did, however, dramatically change the atmosphere in China so that within two years large numbers of Chinese scientists were indeed going abroad, either on official programs or through more personal arrrangements. (*Guanxi* has played a very important role in the selection of scientists for study abroad, there being no open, national competition for the opportunities.) The impression was thus created, particularly abroad, that there had been a profound change in Chinese policies. Yet in substantive terms the Chinese budget for education had by 1981 risen only 1.5 percent over what it had been when the manifestly anti-intellectual Mao was still alive.

THE REALITY OF SYMBOLS

The politics of factionalism further exaggerates the already strong Chinese propensity for hyperbole in political rhetoric.

The language of Chinese politics is a language of extremes, and never more so than when the potential for new political alignments exists. The continued need to subtly test the political waters through the use of symbols and formalized expressions has contributed to an escalation in language to the point where exaggeration abounds in proclaiming both positive and negative events, even as delicate political maneuvers are taking place. There is, of course, a basic bias for overstating the positive and an unabashed enthusiasm for uplift propaganda in favor of the regime, but the degree to which the Chinese exaggerate the negative in their political rhetoric should not be overlooked.

Given the importance the Chinese attach to symbolism, it is not difficult to appreciate the dynamics that generate their use of hyperbole. Once a new symbol has been advanced, heralding the coming of, say, a new "current," those who wish to demonstrate their commitment to the new initiative must make their support visible and must express their unqualified opposition to whoever may be against the development. And this latter imperative contributes greatly to the negative exaggerations.

For example, the ceaseless harping after 1976 about the evils of the Gang of Four would be laughable if it were seen only as explanations for policy failures, but it becomes deadly serious when viewed in the context of factional politics. Nuances in the degree of denunciation help to determine who can be rehabilitated among the victims of the Gang and who is to be saved from political damnation for once having been too much a Maoist. Thus, while the Chinese are ostensibly talking about the destructive consequences of the policies of the Gang during the "bad ten years" from 1966 to 1976, they are in fact sorting themselves out for the political alignments of the next few years. Everyone joins in using the same exaggerated language – some because they wish to tarnish their new opponents with the memories of the past, others because they feel it is premature to reveal their deviations from the presumed consensus.

There is indeed a strong cascading effect in the flow of Chinese politics, in that the sound and fury associated with one crisis of confrontation is carried over and drowns out the tumult of the impending crisis. Thus in the years after the general acceptance of the Four Modernizations it continued to be necessary to suggest that "sworn followers of Lin Biao and the Gang of Four" were scheming to revive the worst of the "lost decade," when in fact there were only disagreements about priorities and means, old scores to be settled, and above all an abundance of distrust.

For example, in April 1979 Deng Xiaoping was clearly put on the defensive at the Working Conference of the Central Committee because of what senior cadres generally recognized as the "excesses" of the wall posters on "Democracy Wall" in Peking and elsewhere. The Fifth National People's Congress had to be delayed and finally it had to convene without being preceded by the usual plenum of the Central Committee.

The Fourth Plenary Session of the Eleventh Central Committee could not be called because there were apparently too many cadres who were aware of all the difficulties in the overly ambitious program of the Four Modernizations.

Yet the Deng forces quickly resorted to the tactics of exaggeration, declaring that the "whatever faction" had now been complemented by an "opposition faction" of "left" deviationists whose "thinking is ossified or semi-ossified." Hu Yaobang, Director of the Propaganda Department of the Central Committee and Deng's appointee to the Politburo, reportedly organized a series of attacks on the "opposition faction" in the mass media, beginning with an April 13 article in the Shanghai *Wenhui Bao*, and followed by articles in the Shanghai *Jiefang Ribao*, and then in the Peking *Jiehfanjun Bao, Guangming Ribao*, and finally the *Renmin Ribao*.[8]

No clearly defined substantive issues of policy were at stake, for by the spring of 1979 there was general agreement that the initial ambitious goals of the Four Modernizations program were unrealistic and had to be revised. At the same time, nobody in positions of authority would have advocated a return to the practices of the Cultural Revolution period, and hence, to suggest that there might be such people was only another example of using exaggerated language in attacking strawmen. What did exist was the potential for disagreement precisely because concrete issues of pragmatic policy had not been fully defined, and therefore the "debate" had to revolve around symbolic statements and power calculations.

POLICY AS POSTURE AND NOT A SPECIFIC RESPONSE TO CONCRETE PROBLEMS

This style of political jousting has evolved because of the Chinese practice of reserving policy initiation for the topmost leaders, who are expected to act out of inspiration rather than in response to bureaucratically defined problems. Thus, pronouncements of policy usually occur before feasibility has been determined. The structural character of Chinese politics compels a disregard for prior staff work: The ruling elite with a monopoly of power must continue to distrust its bureaucracy if it is to preserve its authority; otherwise, the bureaucracy would expand its

8. *Wei Jan, "Investigating the Opposition Faction in Beijing," Tunghsiang,* Hong Kong, June 16, 1979, pp. 4-7, in Foreign Broadcast Information Service, *Daily Report—People's Republic of China,* June 28, 1979, pp. U2-U7.

powers as it does in all modernized societies.

It is significant that the relationship between elite policy initiation and bureaucratic operationalization was at the core of the most serious elite division in the history of the PRC. As Harry Harding has quite correctly pointed out, Liu Shaoqi and Mao Zedong fundamentally differed in their concepts of planning and policy: Liu believed that before major actions were taken, careful and detailed investigations should be made as to the feasibility, the probable consequences, and the most realistic alternatives — in short, there should be staff work before decisions — while Mao believed in boldly taking the policy initiative and then engaging in investigations to see how what had been started could best be worked out.[9] Liu's method of dealing with risk is common in most complex organizations and institutionalized governments, while Mao's method conforms to the traditional Chinese pattern of imperial direction and a court at war with its mandarin bureaucracy.

The new post-Mao leadership, while rejecting much of "Maoism," has preserved this basic element in Mao's style of rule. The initiation of policy still does not arise from within the ranks of those with day-to-day policy responsibilities, and proclaimed programs are not based on solid staff work. Deng Xiaoping has been no more ready than Mao was to trust policy formulation to his bureaucracy. Both men, like leaders throughout Chinese history, have profoundly distrusted impersonal bureaucracies, suspecting the overriding interest of officials to be the sabotaging of their master's plans. Hence, like the Chinese emperors, the current leaders feel that they must still assert their authority by autonomously proclaiming policies. Ultimately, however, the process of realistic movement from slogan to implementation requires that slogans be administratively operationalized, so that realism does gradually emerge.

This can occur only after an initial phase during which cadres are sorting themselves out as to who is safely in favor of the new current of policy and who will be identified as the enemies; then there is a second phase when those in charge must compulsively prove to their superiors that they are in fact supporting the new program. Both phases have the frantic appearance of movement, but little of substance may be taking place, and what is done is likely to be unrealistic.

This pattern of frantic but essentially ritualized initiation of symbolically expressed programs has historically characterized all major policies, from the first stages in collectivizing agriculture through the Great Leap, the Cultural Revolution, and now the Four Modernizations.

9. Harry Harding, Jr., *China: The Uncertain Future*, Foreign Policy Association, New York, 1974.

Other political systems may also have ceremonial introductions of new policies, and officials may often have to react to the spontaneous decisions of presidents and prime ministers, but the difference in degree in the Chinese case is so great as to make it a difference in kind. American presidents, for example, rarely take pride in initiating policies that have not been examined, however imperfectly, for feasibility. When new departures are announced in a presidential speech, bureaucrats do not react by immmediately seeking to glorify and exaggerate the policy statement; rather, a concerted effort is made to determine how the proposal might possibly be operationalized. The bureaucratic power struggles that take place tend to occur during the process of operationalization and not, as in China, during the ceremonial announcement of the plan.

The pattern of exaggerated and highly symbolic behavior has been quite obvious in the introduction of three of the Four Modernizations, but it has been less manifest and more muted in the fourth, the modernizing of national defense.[10] When Chairman Hua Guofeng announced the goals of the Four Modernizations at the Fifth National People's Congress he conspicuously avoided giving any details about national defense. His audience could have interpreted this to mean (1) defense had a low priority and hence could be downplayed; (2) defense planning cannot be treated merely symbolically; (3) serious disagreements over policy remained unresolved and hence little could be said; or (4) defense requires secrecy and thus it was proper to say little on the subject.

Even before Hua's announcement of the Four Modernizations, the Chinese public was alerted to the fact that some form of military policy debate was taking place. Attentive readers of the Chinese Press – and this would include most senior cadres – would have noted that with the crushing of the Gang of Four there was a dramatic decline in the attention paid the once popular "Good Eighth Company on Nanjing Road" and a spectacular rise in coverage of the activities of the "Hard-Boned Sixth Company." The first outfit had long received the accolades of the radicals, who never tired of telling of how the worthies of the Good Eighth Company were constantly devising new ways to be helping hands for nearby peasants and workers. In contrast, the Hard-Boned Sixth Company, the idol of the moderates, got its reputation from the ferocity of its fighting in Korea.[11] The change in public favor of the two com-

---

10. Jonathan Pollack will be presenting a detailed analysis of latent policy debates in Chinese military policy in a forthcoming Rand report.

11. For a typical example of how the "moderates" raised the Hard-Boned Sixth Company to be a model in the military field comparable to Dazhai in agriculture and Daqing in industry, see Chairman Hua Guofeng's speeches made during a tour of the Northeast,

panies clearly reflected the political end of Mrs. Mao and the victory of the moderates, but the policy message was slightly more ambiguous. Whereas the Good Eighth was rarely noted for having martial skills, the Hard-Boned Sixth was not entirely devoid of good works: It was proclaimed able to accomplish three days of "hard military training" in two days and so have a free day to help peasants at their work.

All of this might have been a subtle way of announcing a change in military policy in favor of greater professionalism and a decline in revolutionary posturing, were it not for the fact that the Chinese media simultaneously stopped extolling the merits of the model youth Zhang Tiesheng, whom the radicals had described as a "bristly rebel," and again brought to prominence Lei Feng, as unprofessional a do-gooder soldier as ever lived. In a lamentably short life Lei Feng compiled an awesome record of Boy Scoutish deeds: When traveling he carried a broom so he could leap from the train at every stop and frantically sweep the platform, or if time permitted, the entire station, before bounding back aboard; pictures show him "selflessly" washing his comrades' underwear; and on innumerable occasions he helped old women with their baskets and young children with their reading, writing, and arithmetic.[12] Why did the victorious moderates, who certainly favor professionalism, decide that the Chinese press should revive memories of this nonprofessional soldier? The answer lies not in speculations about the use of the media for policy advocacy but in the fact that Zhou Enlai once had some kind words for the memory of Lei Feng. Presumably everyone was supposed to know this, and therefore they could ignore the significance of the model hero's behavior and concentrate on the more esoteric issue of who had once backed which model. This was the stage of using policy issues for the symbolic purposes of distinguishing friend from foe.

Foreign Broadcast Information Service, *Daily Report – People's Republic of China,* May 6, 1977, p. E4. On the first anniversary of Mao's death, the Hard-Boned Sixth Company explicitly recognized that it had been the object of criticism by the Gang of Four, who had "stirred up an evil wind" and, "braying that consolidation meant restoration," claimed that, by "constantly paying attention to military training," the Hard-Boned Sixth "was restoring the bourgeois military line." In its own defense, the company claimed it was second to none in "forging close ties with the masses" and helping to "build the economy." In short, the Hard-Boned Sixth has been as anxious as any unit to appear to be "revolutionary" and to show that it had seen through the "ultra-rightist" character of its "radical" critics who followed the Gang of Four.

12. Most Chinese model heroes had short lives, but this fact should probably be ignored in any attempt to estimate life expectancy in the PRC, for it probably is more important in illuminating the sagacity of those responsible for creating such heroes: A living "model hero" might unforeseeably become an embarrassment in the future; a deceased "hero" is easier to manage. Furthermore, the sentiments evoked by a hero's death can touch responsive chords in the public mind, given mankind's anxieties about death and immortality.

This example also illustrates how the Chinese media operate. On the one hand, the audience is supposed to know more than what is being told, yet what is being told seems designed to obscure what needs to be known. Everyone was supposed to know that the radicals once said that the Hard-Boned Sixth Company was "a sinister example of upholding a purely military viewpoint," and that Zhou Enlai, the patron of the moderates, had once praised Lei Feng; but in the meantime the media were not permitted to give a straightforward statement about the currently correct military policy and what should now be the right mix of professionalism and revolutionary sentiment.

The Chinese press has only come up with the "Ten Should's and the Ten Shouldn'ts," a series of essentially rhetorical questions whose self-evident answers provide almost no guidance for serious defense policy planning. China would in fact be in a mess if significant numbers of influentials (or even commoners) were advocates of the obviously wrong answers to the ten, which are:

1. Should we or should we not uphold the absolute leadership of the Party over the Army?
2. Should we form leadership groups composed of the old, the middle-aged, and the young to meet the five requirements for being worthy successors, or should we not?
3. Should we or should we not set strict demands on training?
4. Should we or should we not strictly observe revolutionary discipline and rules and regulations?
5. Should we or should we not uphold proletarian Party spirit and oppose factionalism?
6. Should we or should we not stress the stability of the Army?
7. Should we or should we not inherit and carry forward the fine traditions of our Party and our Army?
8. Should we or should we not maintain the three-in-one combination armed forces system of the Field Army, local armed forces, and militia?
9. Should we or should we not have a consolidated Army?
10. Should we or should we not be ready for war?

After several million man-hours were spent on discussing these questions, it is doubtful that any serious issues of military modernization were resolved, but the symbolic issues did presumably legitimize in the public's mind the authority of the new regime to carry out whatever concrete policies it chose. All the talk and debate made the government seem fully on the side of common sense, and furthermore, it made it clear that "modernization" would not alter the political relationship between Party and Army, nor would it undermine the PLA's tradition of extolling heroism over technology.

By January 1978, the theorists at the National Defense Scientific and Technological Commission felt that the time was propitious to denounce the Gang of Four for opposing the technological modernization of Chinese forces. According to their accounts, when the Military Commission made decisions in 1975 "on consolidating the army, intensifying military training, preparing for war and improving weapons," the Gang of Four "viciously attacked the Military Commission" and "their agent on the National Defense Scientific and Technological Commission began madly and noisily to slander the situation as being dominated by the 'theory that weapons decide everything' " and a "nonsensical, malicious statement" that "satellites went up to the sky while the red flag fell to the ground."

Behind all the symbolic handling of issues, important elements in the new leadership clearly wanted to justify modernization as a normal continuation of Mao's original policies, while at the same time seeking to increase the professionalization of both the PLA and the militia, to tighten discipline, and to obtain more advanced weapons.

PURELY SYMBOLIC ISSUES

The confusion generated by introducing serious substantive issues in symbolic and subtle language is greatly heightened by the practice of using purely symbolic issues in carrying out factional politics.

Since issues can divide factions both on substantive grounds and as subjects for litmus testing, it is useful to note the function of different kinds of issues in Chinese political conflicts. In the first category are the issues that are not programmatic and hence are not limited in scope. Consequently all cadres can be expected to take a stand with respect to them. Such issues generally lie at the heart of ideological campaigns, such as the need at a certain period to oppose Confucius or to favor the "dictatorship of the proletariat," to agree to "seek truth from facts," and the like. Since people are expected to display a proper response to such issues, it is sometimes possible to discern exaggerated enthusiasms or undue apathy and thereby arrive at clues about factional positions. The unbounded enthusiasm of the pro-Deng forces in the summer of 1979 for the Four Principles that had been initiated in the spring by the anti-Deng elements was a classic case of seeking to defuse a critical slogan by excessive support of it. Unfortunately, however, Chinese culture encourages the ritualizing of emotional behavior so that most Chinese are quite capable of masking their sentiments and repeating the expected standardized phrases.

The second, and closely related, category of issues includes those calculated to smoke out and even entrap masked opponents. Such issues need not, indeed should not, have serious substantive dimensions, for if they did, some cadres might mistakenly treat the substantive aspects more seriously than the partisan ones. The Chinese have great skill in concocting such issues. They rarely make the mistake of treating trial balloons intended to test loyalties so seriously that they commit the government to foolish programs. In Chinese politics, such trial balloons are usually only symbolic allegories that provide means for partisan identification with almost no programmatic dimensions. However, those on the fringes in Chinese politics may be more anxious to appear to play the game than actually to understand it, and therefore their behavior may be unwitting. That is to say, more people respond vigorously to symbolic issues than may be informed about the meaning behind the allegories. For example, in 1974 minor campaigns were launched attacking Antonioni and later Beethoven, which the insiders understood to be veiled criticism of Zhou Enlai and Jiang Qing, respectively, because Zhou had allowed Antonioni to film in China, while Mrs. Mao had made a scene insisting that the Philadelphia Symphony Orchestra play Beethoven's Seventh Symphony during its tour of China. Throughout the country, however, lesser lights, automatically responding to their partisan cues, enthusiastically denounced a film they had never seen and music they had never heard. Still others, unaware of the partisan dimensions, joined in out of the sheer delights of xenophobia.

One of our Hong Kong respondents, a former worker in a small commune factory who left China in 1974, reports that the leaders of his commune were seriously confused over what to do when they received official notification of Henry Kissinger's first visit to Peking and the intelligence that President Nixon would soon be coming to China; their problem was not one of believing in the reliability of the information – they already knew it to be true because they had heard it over the BBC and Hong Kong radio – rather, they could not be sure how firm the dramatic change in policy was going to be, and hence they were undecided as to how enthusiastically they should report the information to the commune members. According to our respondent, all of those in the shop immediately appreciated the dilemma of the leaders on both the Revolutionary and the Party committees: The workers' discussions among themselves did not consider the merits or even the historical significance of the news; rather, they speculated on who at the Center would have favored the move, who probably opposed it, and what were their relative strengths.

The Chinese propensity for ritualizing words and actions compels their politics to revolve around who does and who does not use which particular stylized expression. The presence or absence of ritual phrases is usually the most telling test for identifying partisan alignments. Once a phrase or slogan is advanced by an element of the leadership, all cadres are expected to pick it up and use it in a standardized manner, and therefore the failure to use the phrase becomes a sign of conscious refusal and hence of direct opposition to those who do faithfully use it.

This use of symbolism can at times lead to confusion, as when participants and outside observers "overanalyze" and find significance in what are in fact unintended differences. For example, early in 1978 China-watchers noted that Chairman Hua and Marshal Ye Jianying were speaking of the need for "maintaining" the political traditions of the PLA, while Vice-Premier Deng Xiaoping spoke of "restoring" the traditions of the PLA. The apparent consistency with which they used these two key words was interpreted by some to mean that Hua and Ye were essentially satisfied with the status quo, while Deng felt a need for further changes and improvements. What seemed like a potential split was dissipated when the entire leadership began to speak about the need to "maintain *and* restore" the traditions of the PLA. Either they had resolved their differences or they had decided to signal that there had never been any.

The dominance of symbol over substance can also be seen in the approach Hua Guofeng used in trying to consolidate his authority. He called two conferences, one in December 1976 on "Learning from Dazhai" for agriculture, and the other one in the spring of 1977 on "Learning from Daqing" for industry, and he reissued Mao Zedong's "Ten Great Relationships" speech that somberly dwelt on economic and administrative matters. In a diffuse, general way, he seemed to be setting a course for basic policy, and follow-up meetings were held in every province and in every institution throughout the country to learn the same apparent messages. But although the language at all the meetings seemed to be related to policy, the Hua administration at the time was far from pragmatically resolving all the basic policy issues facing the Chinese economy. The principal priority for the new Chairman was not decisions on substantive policies but a demonstration of consensus that could be most readily realized by having the entire country learn new ritual words. Hua Guofeng was universally proclaimed as the "Wise Chairman," and his shaky rule was reinforced by the equally universal ritual of extolling the "esteemed and beloved Ye Jianying" – a symbolism obviously designed to make it appear as though leadership by Mao and Zhou had been adequately and smoothly replaced by a comparable pair of worthy leaders.[13] These moves by Hua were, however, to make him

---

13. It was this conspicuous use of symbols from Mao's rule that later made Hua vulnerable to the charge of being the leader of the "whatever faction."

peculiarly vulnerable by 1980 when Deng began his play for leadership authority. Abstract attacks on the "cult of personality" were read by cadres throughout the country as a personal denunciation of Hua; publicity that Dazhai was a massive deception and fraud became a direct challenge to Hua's authority because of his earlier praise of the brigade; and when the "model peasant" leader from Dazhai was removed from the Politburo, it was seen by everyone as a symbolic move that critically damaged Hua's power.

THE CONSPIRACY OF PRETENDED AGREEMENTS

The inhibiting effect of factionalism contributes to a compulsive style of policy implementation once opponents have been defeated and authoritative discussions seem possible.

Once a particular leadership element senses that its position is secure, it usually tries to demonstrate its mastery of power by compulsive and often dramatic acts. Dangers are overlooked as advantage is sought.

There are many cultural explanations for the compulsiveness of Chinese when they feel free to act. The gap between initial thought and action can be remarkably brief, and there is no procrastination once threats are removed.[14] When the immobilism associated with a high level of factional tensions recedes, those who feel that they are now all-powerful often choose to express their release from frustration by commanding that their wishes be done; and in Chinese culture the ultimate test of the power of a superior is the promptness of his subordinates in carrying out his wishes.

This situation contributes to the compulsive fits and starts so characteristic of Chinese politics. Orders are issued, there is much scurrying about, and the impression is created that momentous policies are coming forth. Then the unforeseen begins to happen: Problems turn out to be more complex than originally expected, and in time, retreat is necessary, sometimes in the form of merely dropping the whole matter, but more often in the form of proclamations that the policy is still in effect, as interest wanes and action is eventually replaced by a new round of manipulating symbols to create new political alignments.

Thus the smashing of the Gang of Four was followed not by down-to-earth, pragmatic policies, but rather by compulsive initiatives. Once the

---

14. I have discussed this phenomenon of China's political culture in *The Spirit of Chinese Politics,* op. cit., Chap. 8.

restraining influences of the factional conflict with the radicals were removed, Hua Guofeng, under the presumed prodding of Deng Xiaoping, emulated Mao's style of plunging ahead with announcements of policies that had not been carefully thought through. This was true not only of the broad goals of the Four Modernizations but of numerous very specific and even technical policies.

In industry, for example, there was a dramatic announcement in the summer of 1977 that wages would be raised 10 to 20 percent to provide greater incentives and thereby raise productivity.[15] The announcement was made before any decision was made as to who deserved the raises. In October it was declared that the "lowest paid" (a reasonably small, defined group) and "all those who had not received a raise for a long time" (which covered just about everybody, since there had been no significant changes in the eight-grade wage scale for over twenty years) would be the ones favored.[16] In December the government proclaimed that 46 percent of the "workers and staff" should benefit from the raises,[17] which further confused matters, since it seemed to suggest that people at all levels could expect to benefit. Managers were not sure what to do, and workers in most factories began to engage in long discussion sessions about who should be the targets of the policy; the debates and the resulting ill will actually hampered production.

The problem was further complicated by the fact (which Chinese planners readily admit) that wages in China are low because of the desire to give everyone some kind of a job that will provide income. Visitors to Chinese factories are well aware that there are more workers than necessary for production; some have judged that one-fourth to one-half of the workers have zero or even negative productivity, in the sense that if they were not around production might increase. The Chinese have thus blurred the line between industrial production and "welfare" policies to a degree unknown elsewhere. It is difficult to distinguish between a productive worker and a welfare recipient in China, because by merely dragging his feet a bit a "worker" ceases being productive and in effect goes "on welfare."

Given this situation, the propaganda announcement that the lowest-paid workers were to receive the raises meant that China would be raising the "welfare bill" without providing material incentives to improve productivity. Chinese managers and the more productive workers understood the situation and had their own ideas as to who should get the raises if the government really wanted to improve productivity. But

15. *Jen-min Jih-pao,* July 8, 1977, p. 1.
16. *Jen-min Jih-pao,* October 1, 1977, p. 1.
17. *Peking Review,* Vol. 20, No. 49, December 2, 1977, p. 3.

the government was not prepared to abandon completely the egalitarian notions of the past, and eventually each plant was left to work out its own solutions. Thus, a policy intended to provide greater incentives produced instead widespread haggling, bitterness, and recriminations, and this in turn made people feel that there had been no perceptible improvement in material standards even after over two years of Hua's rule – especially since such basic items as cooking oil, soap, and light bulbs remained in short supply, obtainable only through personal connections and the black market.

The regime also plunged into an agricultural policy presumably intended to increase the well-being of the more than 80 percent of the Chinese who live in the countryside. The program, however, was not well thought through and soon produced much the same sense of antagonism and frustration. The regime played up as a model Xiang Xiang county in Hunan, the birthplace of Mao Zedong's mother[18] and a part of the territory Hua Guofeng administered from 1952 to about 1955 when he was head of the Xiangtan District Office.[19] What made Xiang Xiang exceptional was the fact that its Party Committee had "vigorously grasped" the problem created by the "sworn followers" of the Gang of Four who had for years engaged in malpractices that placed "irrational burdens" on the peasants; after investigation, it was now "making amends" to those who had been "cheated." It was publicized throughout China that by July 1978 the production teams in Xiang Xiang county had been paid back nearly $500,000.[20] Other counties were called upon to follow suit, and some counties were identified as being laggards.

This policy, which Chairman Hua unambiguously identified in the *People's Daily*[21] as his own, clearly suggested to every peasant that he had been cheated and that he ought to receive restitution. How much he had been cheated and how much he should receive was left to local haggling, and presumably the objective was for each peasant to prove how badly he had been treated and to claim as much restitution as possible. The policy provided no incentives for future productivity; it only encouraged people to give voice to their woes.

By these actions, Chairman Hua sought, no doubt, to demonstrate that the state was concerned over the welfare of the peasants and believed that their lot should be improved. Furthermore, he demonstrated that he knew what the facts were when he spoke of "embezzlers and

---

18. Edgar Snow, *Red Star Over China*, rev. ed., Grove Press, New York, 1968, p. 134.

19. Michel Oksenberg and Sai-cheung Yeung, "Hua Kuo-feng's Pre-Cultural Revolution Hunan Years, 1949–66: The Making of a Political Generalist," *China Quarterly*, No. 69, March 1977, pp. 9–16.

20. *Jen-min Jih-pao*, August 1, 1978.

21. *Jen-min Jih-pao*, July 28, 1978, p. 1.

speculators" who used commune funds to "construct unneeded buildings" and "restaurants" and to pay for "feasts and banquets." In the fall of 1978, the Central Committee showed further sympathetic support for the peasants by ordering the leading cadres to "stop behaving like dictators" and to stop "riding roughshod over the people." In this spirit, the Shanxi Provincial Committee identified another model "negative example county," Xunyi, where cadres had used "coercion and fines" to push up production since 1974.[22]

Soon, however, it became apparent that Hua's approach of publicly proclaiming sympathy for peasants and distrust of cadres was creating sullenness among the former and paralysis among the latter, so that agricultural production stagnated. This was hardly the way to achieve the modernization of agriculture. There were probably few peasants who did not feel that they had been mistreated by their commune officials, and even fewer who would not grasp for some form of restitution if it required only the voicing of woes. As for the rural cadres, it is not surprising that after less than a year of being attacked from both above and below, they shied away from enforcing any distateful regulation.

So Hua's dramatic approach that was supposed to signal the end of the influence of the Gang of Four produced only immobilized local leaders and squabbling peasants and had to be abandoned before the spring planting of 1979. By then, two and a half years after the smashing of the Gang of Four, the leadership was finally turning to a policy of improving the welfare of the peasants by increasing the price that the state paid for grain.

We have already noted how the prestige of scientists was elevated during the initial phases of the modernization of science and technology by drama and the unrealistic goals of cultural exchanges with the United States. We need only add that as late as August 1978, officials were suggesting the impractical goal of sending *within that school year* 1,200 students to Britain, 500 each to Germany, France, Canada, and Japan, 150 to Australia, and eventually "up to 5,000" to the United States.[23]

This pattern of compulsive initiatives followed by paralysis is heightened by the structural arrangements in which lower officials must look to the top for cues as to what they should be doing, and once they are set into motion they are not allowed to communicate laterally with their peers in other "units" or bureaucracies to arrive at priorities. Priorities get sifted out only at the Center; those below are expected to plunge ahead and frantically carry out the consensus policies. Eventually, the problems of priorities overwhelm those at the top, and they must call for the slowdown that produces the paralysis.

22. *Jen-min Jih-pao*, August 3, 1978, p. 1.
23. Reuters, Peking, Aug. 3, 1978.

This pattern of compulsive initiatives by leaders on the threshold of dominant power is not limited to those who like Mao and Hua have been thought of as more ideological and "romantically revolutionary," but includes the supposedly pragmatic Deng. When Deng maneuvered to replace Hua with Zhao Ziyang, there was suddenly considerable publicity about the value of the "market mechanism," and expectations were created that enterprises would be allowed to keep their profits, invest according to their judgments, and generally abandon the practices of a command economy. By late 1980, it was necessary to pull back and acknowledge that central planning would have to remain sovereign if China was to remain socialist. Similarly, Deng's pressure to bring the Gang of Four to trial in December 1980 was a dramatic move designed to signal to all who was in charge, but rather than symbolizing the consolidation of his power, the Peking show trials stimulated dissension over what should be the historical role of Mao.

The self-defeating nature of this pattern has been demonstrated repeatedly since the establishment of the PRC, but it was most vividly dramatized for foreigners after Deng gave the signal that it was proper to import Western technology as rapidly as possible. Consequently, in 1977–1978, companies and units all over the country began making "deals" with foreign business, as though central management had been abandoned and the Bank of China had given up control over foreign exchange. It has been estimated that during that spree, Chinese officials signed letters of intent with foreign businessmen that totaled $15 billion.[24] Needless to say, the Center had to clamp down, renounce most of the agreements, and call for a general slowdown. Thereafter, provincial authorities and companies were allowed to negotiate with foreign concerns, but all allocations of foreign exchange had to be referred to Peking, where priorities are set.

It is important to appreciate that there is little risk in these compulsive and unrealistic initiatives, however, for as long as the Four Modernizations remain China's basic policy, neither Hua nor Deng is likely to be held accountable for being merely impractical. There are no mechanisms of criticism in Chinese politics for damaging leaders by comparing their words of yesterday with the developments of tomorrow. It is true that widespread disillusionment and deepening cynicism do tend to follow the cycle of elevated expectations and disappointed hopes, but such cycles have been the norm for decades. All that happens is that more realistic leaders, such as Chen Yun in this case, will in time set more realistic goals, which Hua and Deng will accept as their program.

The risks are low because such exaggerations are generally accepted

24. Statement by Dwight Perkins at a meeting of the Joint Seminar on Political Development, Harvard University–M.I.T., November 28, 1979.

as a part of the conspiracy of feigned agreement used as a weapon by the victors against a fallen faction. Compulsive actions accompanied by symbolic and unrealistic pronouncements represent only the new search for consensus. The inhibitions imposed on the system by the previous power struggle have been lifted, and suddenly there is a craving to put out of mind the dangers of confrontations that immobilize action. Yet the pretended commitment to exaggerated ends constitutes only a canopy beneath which the new factional alignments have already begun to form – alignments that will gradually introduce new confrontations and a return to sluggishness if the tensions remain modest or to paralysis if they become intense.

Those accustomed to greater accountability in politics are likely to be perplexed, and even to anticipate crisis, whenever they observe a gap between ambitious rhetoric and scurrying activities and the subsequent faltering, unimpressive performance. Because of their inclination to suppose that someone must be made to pay for unfulfilled political promises, they are likely to overlook the real issue at stake behind the ritualized promise of a golden future: the question of who will attract the greatest power, who is going to be isolated, and how enduring the new relationship will be.

Chapter 8

Authority, Dependency, and Personal Morality: The Psychological Bases of Factions

Leaders and followers have different, but essentially personal, motives for associating with each other, a fact that gives factions considerable flexibility on issues and tactics.

Up to this point our focus has been largely on the role of factions in the Chinese political process, and we have only incidentally dealt with their functions for the individuals involved. Why do people become involved with a particular faction? What are they seeking as they become identified? How do the bonds that hold factions together affect the performance of those factions in the political process?

Ironically, the most basic attraction of factions is precisely the same cultural consideration that, from the perspective of the system as a whole, establishes the imperative of consensus and therefore denies the legitimacy of factions. People are attracted to factions because of the dominance of group orientation over individual orientation, and the individual feels insecure if he cannot identify with some larger collectivity.[1] Once he does belong to a collectivity, he cannot withhold his

---

1. For sociological discussions of the importance of group orientation as contrasted to self-orientation in Chinese culture, see Richard W. Wilson, *Learning to Be Chinese*, M.I.T. Press, Cambridge, Mass. 1970; Francis L. K. Hsu, *Americans and Chinese*, Henry Schuman, New York, 1953; Hu Hsien-chin, "The Chinese Concepts of Face," *American Anthropologist*, Vol. 46, No. 1, Part 1, January–March, 1944.

commitment to it; thus his loyalty is always to a larger self.

Stated bluntly, individuals gravitate toward the illicit bonds of factions because they are seeking what the Party promises but cannot provide, the security of conformity within a hierarchical structure. In return for conformity and the rewards of loyalty, the individual expects to get the support and protection that only social groups can provide. The current Chinese national ideal, of course, is for everyone to be willing to forsake all others and dedicate himself wholly to the CCP – hence the overriding imperative of the pretended ideological consensus and the declared abomination of all lesser and more particularistic associations and loyalties.[2]

Yet the norms of the Party seem to be the very source of much of the anxiety and insecurity that propel individuals to seek more reassuring and supportive subassociations. When individuals find that they have not received the security that identification with the Party has promised, they spontaneously look for other, less impersonal associations. Once they do this, however, they know that they are violating the norms of the Party, and new anxieties generated by this knowledge lead them to invest even more emotional commitment in the informal relationships they have just sought out. Thus a vicious circle is established that produces the paradox of continued deference to the manifest consensus and increasing attachment to the latent subgroups.

This completely unplanned and undesigned process seems to have generated chains of personal and reciprocal commitments. As these fragments – cells would be much too strong a word – seek greater security for their illicit existence, they reach out and couple with other fragments. Thus, in time, informal networks of personal associations develop, and these networks of particularistically bonded individuals provide the latent structure of factions. Under either menacing external developments or internal pressures, these networks can become agitated and mobilized, thereby becoming political factions.[3]

2. The classic statement of the Communist objective of reorienting everyone toward loyalty to the Party and its norms and of making particularistic relations dangerous is given by Ezra Vogel in "From Friendship to Comradeship: The Change in Personal Relations in Communist China," *China Quarterly*, No. 21, January-March, 1965, pp. 46 – 60.

3. There is a substantial body of literature, based on careful empirical research, that reports on the existence in China of the particularistic forms of behavior that we have just described. (Generally, such behavior has been treated as the kind of deviations between the ideal and reality that one would expect in any society, and not as the seeds of significant political behavior, as we are suggesting.) Evidence for the political significance of such counternorm behavior has been increasingly provided by visitors' reports and Chinese press criticism, especially since the relaxation of the mood of China in the fall of 1978. See Martin King Whyte, *Small Groups and Political Rituals in China*, University of California Press, Berkeley, 1974; Thomas P. Bernstein, *Up to the Mountains and Down to the*

The reasons why particular individuals come to identify with one network system rather than another are usually closely associated with the circumstances surrounding their initial participation in cadre politics. Thus, geography, Party history, occupation, and above all the particular "system" or *xitong* to which the cadre was assigned all play a part in determining factional identification. In any setting, the individual soon discovers that he is more comfortable and has a greater sense of security because of his relations with some cadres in the "unit" than with others. His ties may develop with the in-group, and hence he will come to associate himself with the dominant faction in his setting; or he may feel himself to be more of an outsider and will thereby align himself with those outside the immediate chain of command.

The Party, of course, is quite aware of this potential basis for factions; thus the dossier of each cadre includes not only his detailed personal history, or *zizhuan,* but also a listing of all of his friends and social relations who might provide the basis of *guanxi* ties. At the same time, the Party, as Doak Barnett has explained, frequently transfers cadres as a part of the "regime's desire to combat 'bureaucratism' (*guanliao chuyi*), 'localism' (*difang chuyi*), and 'departmentalism' or 'vested interestism' (*benwei chuyi*), or 'excessive loyalty to one's own organizational unit'."[4] The very process of transferring cadres facilitates the expansion of networks that now can link one unit to another.

Thus the growth of the networks that give structure to factions follows the pattern of relationships inherent in both the chain of command in the various systems or bureaucracies and the career experiences of transferred cadres. Senior cadres come to trust in and value the competence of particular subordinates, while junior cadres strive for the protection of particular powerful figures in their career situations.

Several of our Hong Kong respondents described how they personally came to deviate from the impersonal standards of good Communist behavior and sought more particularistic relationships as they felt the stresses of their circumstances. One young man told about being sent out to a state farm with three other urban youths upon graduation from middle school and realizing very quickly that it was not enough to obey all the rules and profess enthusiasm for Chairman Mao. Indeed, the more he tried to be the model Young Communist League member, the

Villages, Yale University Press, New Haven, 1977; Michel Oksenberg, "Getting Ahead and Along in Communist China: The Ladder of Success on the Eve of the Cultural Revolution," in John W. Lewis (ed.), *Party Leadership and Revolutionary Power in China,* Cambridge University Press, Cambridge, 1970; Susan Shirk, "The Middle School Experience in China," Ph.D. dissertation, Department of Political Science, M.I.T., 1974.

4. A. Doak Barnett, *Cadres, Bureaucracy, and Political Power in Communist China,* Columbia University Press, New York, 1967, p. 58.

more suspicion he evoked among his new peers. "When I was new on the farm I did not know how to act and the people were not very friendly. I did everything the Party told me was right, but it did not help. The others were not sure of what my real thinking was, and I was not sure of what they really thought." Soon, however, he was befriended by one of the leading cadres who originally had also been a city person. "This cadre realized that I was lonesome and began to talk with me. He was very frank and sincere, and so I was able to tell him of all my problems. He even told me about his difficulties. Others could see that I was his friend and this made them respect me." Two of the other three youths sent down with him apparently developed personal ties with a different cadre, while the third tried not to have dealings with anyone. About a year later there was a clash in the management of the state farm involving issues in the farm's relations with both the county and the provincial committees. "We had many meetings at which the leading cadres expressed somewhat different points of view. My friend insisted that the problem was just a technical one, and that since the farm had always carried out its instructions from above, we had no reasons for fear. The other cadre said that the farm had suffered from the poison of the Gang of Four. I and several other workers spoke out for the cadre who was our friend, but it did no good. One night he had a very hard time at a meeting, and I knew after that there would be no future for me at the farm. I then began to take longer leaves to visit my family, and during these leaves I planned my escape to Hong Kong."

THE MUTUAL REINFORCEMENT OF AUTHORITY AND DEPENDENCY

The process whereby networks of particularistic relationships become transformed into factions reflects distinctive Chinese cultural attitudes about authority and dependency and their reciprocating relationship. Both leaders and followers need each other, and with about equal intensity. Furthermore, feelings of stress or anxiety on the part of either leaders or followers tend to strengthen and politicize the relationship rather than to weaken it.

As discussed earlier in Chapter 6, a surprisingly high proportion of the respondents, 54.8 percent, agreed that a "good leader expects people to decide for themselves what they should do," while 45.2 percent felt that "a good leader makes it clear to everybody what their jobs are." (American responses to these statements are sharply different, with only 15 to 30 percent in different samples agreeing with the first statement, and 85 to 70 percent favoring the second.) At first it might appear that these responses are inconsistent with the fact that an overwhelming 92 percent agreed that "if you want people to do a job right, you should explain things to them in great detail and supervise them closely." However, those whom we queried about this apparent contradiction quickly explained that they saw no inconsistency, since it was their view that those in authority should be like teachers and fathers, who explain carefully what should be done but then leave it up to those who are learning to show initiative and demonstrate their desire to do the right thing.

The inability of the respondents to see any contradiction in questions that Western psychologists have treated as contradictory reveals a significantly different concept of authority in Chinese culture. This becomes even more apparent when one examines the items on the standard scale for measuring "authoritarianism."[5] Contrary to what might be expected, our respondents revealed a very high degree of "authoritarianism" on some items, but on others they were at the opposite extreme. Although they showed "fear of uncertainty," "awe of authority," "need for strong leaders," and "anxiety over inadequate direction," they had a high "tolerance for ambiguity," they were low on "rigidity," and they did not greatly value "discipline,"[6] characteristics that are quite inconsistent with the standard measurement of the "authoritarian personality."

In short, they were authoritarian in that they placed high value on hierarchy, leadership, and clarity in human relationships, but they were anti-authoritarian in that they appreciated flexibility, could withhold moral judgment, and were not uncomfortable with logical contradictions. As we indicated earlier, this tendency to value authority without being authoritarian reflects a strong dependency upon authority.

As discussed in Chapter 1, the need for someone else to provide support and reassurance is apparently shared by both followers and leaders. Quite understandably, those who are weak tend to seek more powerful friends, but in China the more powerful also seem to have a sense of dependency that causes them to look for support not only from above but also from below.

Our respondents described many situations in which their superiors seemed to be seeking out personal contacts with subordinates. A sent-down youth said that the head of the production team on his commune

5. It is not possible to use all items on the traditional scale for measuring "authoritarianism," since several made no sense either because of Chinese culture or because of the context of life in Communist China. Therefore our measurement of "authoritarianism" involved eight key questions.

6. The responses to the individual questions have been reported in Chapters 3 and 4. For the purpose of these analyses, we have aggregated the answers that reveal "authoritarianism" and those that reveal "dependency."

"often invited several of us to go fishing with him. He had special friends with whom he discussed his problems. We listened to him and we knew he was a nice man who had problems with his superiors."

A former factory worker describing relations within his section of his shift stated, "The responsible person would talk a lot with all of us. He even showed great interest in us apprentices. He wanted to make sure that if the head of our workshop had any criticisms we workers would all defend him. Some workers were more willing to do this than others, and therefore he was more friendly toward them. I did not get on so well with him. He tried to be friendly but I could see that he was not sincere. He then became very stern with me. Later when we had a lot of criticism sessions and representatives from the workshop and the factory revolutionary committees were present, some of us attacked him. Others defended him. We were a very divided section after that."

Relationships built out of this mutual sense of psychological dependency operate at a level far removed from that of public policy. And since the bonds that hold the networks together are not necessarily related to common stands on policy issues, superiors can act with some confidence that their support will remain loyal regardless of the tactical moves they make in response to public issues. The Chinese tolerance of leaders changing their views with changing circumstances further contributes to the concept that leaders should not feel threatened if they are inconsistent on policy matters.

Thus, although it is necessary to use code-word symbols for identification purposes and to mobilize networks, which does impose a degree of consistency upon factions, the factions appear to be held together by personal sentiments that are not strongly affected by policy issues. Therefore, the unity of a faction may not be greatly disturbed by changes in the policy positions of the top leaders. This contradiction does introduce an element of uncertainty into factional politics, however, since any change in the position of a superior at any level in the hierarchy becomes a test of the loyalty and adaptability of those within his natural network.

The personal qualities of individuals, then, become a matter of major importance for the stability and strength of factions. Subordinates want to be sure that their protectors, however opportunistic they may be on policy matters, will be steadfast in looking after them; and superiors need to know that their supporters will be firm in their loyalties. Hence there is a general concern about personal morality, defined primarily in terms of loyalty. Ironically, this concern at the level of informal factions is entirely consistent with the official, consensus-level demand for moral rectitude among both leaders and followers. On the official level, the pretense is that national progress depends upon everyone being selfless and that the cause of troubles is almost always the personal failings of individuals who have not lived up to the ideals of the Party.

Thus in a particular way the question of personal failings is basic to the dynamics of both the micro-system internal to the development of factions and the macro-system of factional conflicts. From both perspectives all problems spring from personal faults.

ALL PROBLEMS SPRING FROM PERSONAL FAULTS

Factional conflicts that do surface through the blanket of conformity are usually minimized as being the deviant acts of isolated individuals.

The need to deny factionalism is so strong in Chinese politics that every effort is made to dismiss revelations of factional strife as the misguided acts of individuals. Furthermore, such revelations generally take place only after a faction has been defeated, when it is easy to single out individuals for attack.

This tendency to trivialize opposition by personalizing it made the record of inner-party conflicts from Li Lisan to Lin Biao and the Gang of Four appear as merely the deviations of isolated individuals. The initial attacks on the Gang of Four were designed to deny that profound issues of political thought were involved and to suggest that all the controversy was caused by routine human corruption.

As a part of the effort to minimize the horror of factional conflict, the Chinese tend to denounce toppled leaders for their personal misconduct rather than for their actual policy preferences, thereby avoiding criticisms of more significant activities that would have required more extensive denunciations and, more importantly, would have raised questions about the comparative merits of the policies advocated by the competing factions.

Chinese public rhetoric eschews dwelling on public crimes, such as the plotting of assassinations, which are only hinted at and which, if elaborated on, could create widespread alarm, or worse, mere cynicism. Instead, the victors count on the cumulative impact of reports of extensive private misdemeanors, the ultimate assumption being that if the person was so bad as to commit a host of improper acts, then he must be bad enough to have done the unimaginable.

The Chinese practice of destroying the public man by exposing the private man goes back to the Confucian tradition of the "Mandate of

Heaven," but psychologically it is as new as Camus's argument that Meursault must have killed the Arab because he was so callous as to smoke a cigarette at his mother's funeral.

The practice of personalizing the faults of discredited leaders is further reinforced by the logic of *guanxi* networks. To bring into doubt the personal morality of a leader is to suggest that all who have looked to him for support have been misguided. The very essence of *guanxi*, as we have noted, is that people will honor their particularistic obligations, and therefore the destruction of the personal integrity of a leader is tantamount to obliterating his capacity to attract and hold followers.

The extraordinary amount of effort that went into discrediting the personal qualities of Jiang Qing and the other members of the Gang of Four must in part be understood as attempts to suggest that all their personal ties were essentially corrupt. Indeed, the constant harping on corruption in Chinese politics should not be interpreted to mean that Chinese politicians are more venal than others; the functional need to stress corruption stems more from the need to neutralize opponents' fellowship networks and to suggest that their commitments were mistaken and that they should seek new allegiances. During the period of their power struggle, Deng Xiaoping, in spite of the nearly anarchist divisions among his rehabilitated cadres, was able to convey the public image of greater personal steadfastness than Hua Guofeng, who had to continually compromise his image in trying to appeal to diverse constituencies.

Personalization of the faults of discredited leaders has the effect of reminding all that they should improve their conduct, while preventing general debate of policy issues that might further strain the prevailing consensus. Furthermore, the stressing of individual faults may suggest that a particular faction has very few members, and they must all be wicked people. For example, as each province joined in the attacks against the Gang of Four, it was necessary to admit that the Four might have had a few local supporters, even though the standard practice was to call such collaborators vile and immoral people. The Shandong Province Committee admitted that the Gang of Four "actively supported a handful of persons in our province to establish ties independent of the Party committee leadership, form strongholds, make trouble in various meetings, engage in beating, smashing and looting and send their own men into various organizations to usurp power, thus seriously damaging revolution and production."[7]

Wang Hongwen's extensive personal failings were supposed to have begun when he "joined the Army because he wanted to evade the hard

7. Shantung Radio, Foreign Broadcast Information Service, *Daily Report – People's Republic of China*, February 1977. p. G-9.

chores of the countryside." Once in the PLA, he "did things perfunctorily, went out without asking leave and often even sneaked out alone to catch fish during wartime," and while in Korea "he was sometimes scared to death before he could even see the shadow of the enemy." After his return to Shanghai, he "dined and wined with embezzlers, thieves, and counter-revolutionary elements and accepted bribes." Finally, according to his critics, Wang joined with the other three of the Gang of Four and, "taking over the mantle of the 'green and red gangs of old Shanghai', they pulled together riffraff, thugs, rascals, thieves, and other bad elements to form a factional organization."[8]

Factions are thus ostensibly formed out of the human weaknesses of inherently bad people. Those who are seen as opponents of consensus are rarely given credit for having alternative policy preferences. Their motives have to be antisocial sentiments.

Once the leadership of a faction has been destroyed, those who had formed the basic network of the faction are put in the position of having to denounce their fallen superiors in equally personal terms. If the remainder of the network is to hold together at all, its members must minimize the extent to which they were associated on common policy or ideological terms, for if those were the bases of their identification with the disgraced leader, they would themselves be vulnerable for having such "erroneous" views. For their own safety, they must fault their fallen leaders on personal moral grounds, thereby suggesting their own innocence.

This peculiar conspiracy in which the victorious and the fallen cadres must treat the failings of the defeated leaders as entirely personal matters, however, creates a second round of problems for the victors, as they now have great difficulties in exposing and purging the fallen leader's followers.

The task of identifying proper purge victims is further complicated because of the tradition that everyone must voice the consensus of the day. Any attempt to review the public statements made by individuals before the fallen leader had been purged would only create greater confusion, since everyone, whether loyal to his faction or not, would have to voice the consensus position. Hence the only remaining alternative seems to be to dwell only on the personal, and indeed, highly private faults of the losers.

This pattern occurs not only with the purging of top leaders but also all the way down the hierarchy. Our Hong Kong respondents reflected this mode of thinking to a remarkable degree when they explained why local

8. Chou Hsin, "Wang Hung-men, Typical Representative of the New Bourgeoisie," NCNA Domestic Service, June 3, 1977, Foreign Broadcast Information Service, *Daily Report – People's Republic of China*, June 16, 1977, pp. E5–E14.

leaders whom they had known were purged. As cynical as most of them were, they did not find it convincing to say that a local leader had been purged because he had championed discredited policies or even that there was a routine need for him to be removed because his faction had lost power at the higher levels. Instead, they were quick to reiterate the personal failings of a disgraced superior and retell what must have been the official charges against his character.

In fact, the vehemence with which some of the respondents held forth on the evil ways of disgraced local leaders suggests that the practice of personalizing the faults of the fallen leader can have a cathartic effect on those harboring resentments against authority. Our respondents' explosive condemnation of the purge victims was clearly a release of aggression, since they had shown a rather sympathetic attachment to local leaders, whom they trusted more than their national leaders.

It is also further evidence of the desire for dependency and the hostility toward authority that is unable to provide stable nurturance and support. Leaders who have lost power are somehow seen as abandoning those whom they should have protected, and hence they deserve the sharpest personal criticisms. Effective leaders who can provide protection should never have to relinquish power, and those who do relinquish it deserve hatred because they inspired misplaced confidence.

Significantly, this pattern of emotionalized reasoning, which was so clear on the part of several respondents, can be found at all levels of Chinese political behavior. Even in foreign affairs, for example, the Chinese attributed personal failings to the Russians after they judged that the Soviet Union had let them down by not providing more support for China in the late 1950s. "Revisionism" became for most Chinese the general code word for a host of very ugly personal faults that were supposedly endemic among Russians. And again, the Chinese are now revealing their urge for dependency as they expect the United States to do more than it is ready to do in helping China achieve the Four Modernizations.

THE DELICACIES OF PERSONNEL POLICIES

Whenever factional strife occurs, personnel replacements are always far more difficult than changes in policy.

Paradoxically, the Chinese tend to become paralyzed on personnel questions after a factional confrontation, even though their principal method of trivializing erupting conflicts is to make them into personal matters. When tension rises and confrontation occurs and there is a need to seek order, the Chinese tend to focus on the personal faults of individuals and to avoid explicit treatment of policy. But when it is over, they completely reverse matters and explicitly treat the new conformity policies, while finding it exceedingly difficult to deal with personnel questions.

After every recent factional conflict the pattern has been the same: Leading figures disappear, and new policies are universally welcomed; but only gradually, indeed usually only after considerable time, are the personnel vacancies filled. At the verbal level, a new consensus can be readily established, but the question of who should be promoted can be agonizingly difficult. Thus normalcy may appear to be restored, even while many of the top posts remain unfilled.

This situation is made possible by the tacit understanding that policy consensus is a ritual matter that appears to be absolutely rigid but does not in fact constrain people of differing factions, while personnel appointments touch the essence of power. Behind the appearance of public agreement there may be deep factional disagreements, but the filling of important posts can only help some and threaten others, and it is certain to cause deeper divisions.

It follows, therefore, that pronouncements on policy are a less reliable guide to the outcome of political differences than the identification of those given the choice posts. Similarly, leaders who appear to have won the day because their policies are publicly proclaimed cannot be considered actually successful until they have filled all the vacancies in the top reaches of the Party and the government.

The fact that the Politburo has never been at full strength since the fall of Lin Biao is telling proof of the continuing factional tensions among the Chinese elite. With the death of Zhou Enlai on January 8, 1976, the Standing Committee of the Politburo was down to only six members; the Politburo itself had only twelve members. The fall of Deng Xiaoping, the death of Mao, and the crushing of the Gang of Four left China with a two-man Standing Committee. Only very slowly and gradually has it been possible to add members to the Standing Committee. It was not until 1979 that the membership reached six.

And, of course, even more dramatic was the difficulty the Chinese had reconstituting the Party organizations at the province and *xian* levels after the Cultural Revolution, even though the question of national policies had been officially resolved.

There appear to be both structural and cultural reasons for the great difficulties the Chinese have in replacing purged figures. To begin with, the Chinese system is not highly institutionalized, and since leadership does not operate through legally defined channels but acts as a deserving elite, the absence of officials in different posts has little effect on the processes of government. The country can easily get along without a Minister of Defense, a Chief of Staff of the Army, and a head of the Military Affairs Commission because the military is run by the top officers and Party figures "getting together." The Center can make its decisions whether or not particular posts are filled. More often, decisions are not called for, since lower officials merely feel compelled to carry on their standard practices. Given the aura of consensus, everyone acts as though he knows what needs to be done.

The Chinese seem to prefer never having to fill any posts at all. Traditionally in China people have served for years and years as "acting" this or that. Why this hesitation about making appointments official or permanent? First, the Chinese are very sensitive to the fact that once an appointment is made, it is almost impossible to dismiss the appointee without a major controversy that could destroy the consensus. One of the most striking characteristics of personnel policies in the PRC is the lack of mobility since 1949. Once an official finds his place, he usually can stay on indefinitely if he can skillfully play the game of factional politics.

Second, those making appointments assume very high risks if the appointee turns out to be unreliable and cannot maintain the consensus. The lingering tradition of a highly personalized system of human relations means that everyone tends to remember who recommended whom for what position. If subsequent trouble arises, the one who made the recommendation will have to explain away his faulty judgment. In this situation, high officials want to make very sure of the loyalties and capabilities of those they are supporting to fill any openings.

The risks are further intensified by the fact noted earlier that senior officials are not supposed to show excessive interest in identifying rising younger officials. Inevitably, however, through the movement of careers, the paths of officials cross and lower officials are seen as having ties with more senior ones. It is ofter far from clear whether a senior official should or will be tainted by the failings of a junior popularly thought to be his protégé. For example, when Song Peizhang was finally purged as First Secretary of the Anhui Provincial Committee in June 1977 for having been too close to the Gang of Four, speculation immediately arose over whether Politburo member Li Desheng might not be in trouble, since Song had been Li's subordinate some years earlier. The fact that Song fell so long after the elimination of the Gang of Four could be read as a sign of Li's declining influence; or it could be that there was no connection between the men. Regardless of what the facts may have been, the effect of the subordinate's fall was to "discredit" the superior.

Finally, and most critically, the very importance of continuing personal ties means that even though people may be hesitant to appoint their own followers to a post, they are quite certain that they do not want others to appoint theirs. Bad as it may be for one's man to fail at the job, it is much worse for another to have his man preempt the office. Consequently, appointments are only possible when agreement is achieved at a deeper level than mere consensus over policies.

The cultural and structural problem is that positions are filled not by individuals but by people who symbolize networks of associations. These networks are the realities of power in China, as we have already noted. Hence, personal appointments are pure power questions, and as such they represent the final outcome of all factional conflicts. However, as one of our respondents graphically explained, the very fact that such questions are power matters can paralyze decisionmaking:

- "In the summer of 1977 they removed the responsible person on our county Revolutionary Committee because he was a follower of important people on the provincial committee who had benefited from the Gang of Four. Then, however, they didn't know what to do to replace him. The majority of the Revolutionary Committee had been his friends, but if they picked someone from that group, then his few enemies would have been angry. Yet if they took one of the enemies it would have made the majority angry. Therefore, nothing happened as far as replacing him, and we just had a lot of meetings to denounce him."

In theory, the Chinese should have no problems in filling their posts: Lower committees are supposed to elect the members of the next higher committees – the provincial committees appoint the members of the Central Committee, which in turn selects the Politburo, whose members then choose their Standing Committee members – and, of course, the Politburo appoints the responsible state officials. In practice, however, the flow of decision is very much in the other direction as powerful leaders seek to have their supporters elected by the lower organs. Hence there are prolonged struggles throughout the country whenever the top leadership is not in agreement. If the members of the Standing Committee were to select Politburo members who could not work together, there would be true disaster, for consensus would be impossible. A divided and unruly Central Committee would be seen as threatening the unity of the whole country.

The process of purging and replacing people for particular posts can set chain reactions into motion, as "winners" and "losers" continue the struggle. The fact that eight months after Chairman Hua Guofeng moved against the Gang of Four, 14 of China's 29 provincial secretaries had been replaced does not mean that there were 14 who were loyal to the "radicals." Rather, it means that once personnel purges begin, the process of struggle at the lower levels can compromise the leadership at higher levels. The inability of provincial committee leaders to maintain the appearance of consensus can bring their downfall and thus start another series of conflicts.

Continuing waves of "struggles" that are never carried to the point of totally purging those once associated with discredited leaders have left most institutions in China staffed with people who at one time or another may have been bitter foes. The combination of the traditional Chinese attitude of "never breaking someone's rice bowl" and the Communist view that anyone can be reeducated has made it impossible for new leaders in any organization to fire those who once belonged to the wrong side. Instead, everyone has to pretend that the past is forgotten, even when everyone knows that it cannot be.

We now have massive evidence about the violence of the Cultural Revolution, but in innumerable offices and institutions the perpetrators of that violence and their victims still have to work side by side. Memories of who once did what to whom provide the motivations for the latent networks that lie at the bases of factions. In such situations, it is not surprising that the traditional Chinese values of friendship and of personal bonds or *guanxi* have endured – and indeed may have been strengthened.

Chapter 9

The Ripples When the Mighty Contend and Fall

Factional strife at the elite level is usually quickly translated into widespread anxieties that then fuel divisive tendencies.

The dynamics of factionalism in China invariably flow from the top of leadership downward, and practically never in the other direction. Nowhere is the hierarchical character of Chinese politics more apparent than in the practice of looking upward for cues as to who the acceptable figures are and which policies best "serve the people." When signals come from the top indicating that the leadership is split, all participants must calculate how they can best protect or advance their interests.

The established cadres who have positions of responsibility tend to react with a min-max strategy. They quickly need to defend their positions, ensure that they have been correct on approved policies, and strive to strengthen discipline and loyalty. Cadres with less at stake often react more daringly to the prospect of disorder and uncertainty, hoping that their big chance may have arrived but thereby leaving themselves vulnerable to charges of opportunism.

These two strategies intensify division and solidify potential cleavages among the cadres. Lesser Party members then have to respond to these developments within their organizations, and thus the stage is set for intense factional strife, which magnifies divisions among the elite and can produce the illusion that factionalism comes from within the Party.

When elite-level divisions become rank-and-file conflicts, the struggles may take on a new life of their own, and resolution of the elite divisions will no longer necessarily restore harmony throughout the Party. At that point, the bases for grudges have been established, some of the ambitious will have overasserted themselves, and some of the senior cadres will have been threatened and will feel insecure until their challengers have been humbled.

- A former accountant in Shanghai described the nervous sensitivity of lower cadres to developments at the higher reaches of the Party in these words: "Our plant manager had to be always alert to what was happening at both Peking and the Shanghai city government. He was always worried that something might happen if any changes occurred. Any new appointments at the ministry might be dangerous for him. The first thing he would ask me after he had been away for a day or two was whether I had heard any news – and by news he meant only the fate of high officials."
- A former school teacher explained: "Any change in the Party leadership could be the cause of much trouble. We knew that our provincial first secretary had excellent contacts at the Center and he was respected by the county leaders. He should have been secure, but we could not be sure how long he might last. Finally, when the Lin Biao case broke he was removed without any warning. Everyone was quite afraid because we did not know who might go next. When the big people fall many others must also go. The new leader could not trust those who worked with the former leader."

Those leaders who are successful in toppling their opponents immediately find it awkward to deal with the defeated leaders' subordinates. The pernicious influence of the fallen leader must be exaggerated in an effort to restore solidarity and consensus. At the same time, one cannot be too careful about questions of loyalty, and therefore prudence might also suggest that one should "cut into the solid flesh around the festered wound" – after all, one's own subordinates can always fill the vacancies so created.

When faced with this dilemma, the Chinese have usually proclaimed a policy of leniency while "investigating" minutely those with any connections with the fallen figure. Thus, for example, when General Yang Chengwu was purged as Secretary-General of the Military Affairs Commission during the rise of Lin Biao, the latter declared, ". . . while we oppose Yang Chengwu, we do not have to oppose all of those who worked under him, those who have had connections with him, and those who knew him. For (1) their connections were determined by historical conditions at the time; they are not a matter of personal choice; (2) he could have easily deceived people . . . . But after this has been clearly explained, we shall not tolerate anyone who fails to draw a line of distinction with him but still follows him."[1]

The CCP has had sharper reverberations and a greater potential for divisiveness than other Communist parties when experiencing a change in line, for reasons that go beyond immediate cultural factors. A key Chinese problem is that internal communications through the Party apparatus nearly always involve prolonged "struggle, criticism, and reform" sessions and not just disciplined cell meetings. The requirement for vocal participation and "mutual criticism," when combined with the historical Chinese precedent of changes in Party line being associated with dismissals in disgrace of prominent figures, seems to create an atmosphere of suspicion and deep tension. No one can be sure that a change in policies, especially one that appears to be associated with purges of the top elite, will not directly affect his future, and therefore the stage is set for aggressive behavior.[2] For Chinese underlings, this usually takes the form of "I am innocent and it was my superior's fault – I had no choice, so what could I do?" Hence the very official who has the responsibility of explaining the new line can easily become the object of criticism as some lesser cadres seek to identify themselves with the new policies and deny that they ever were in sympathy with the past policy that the unfortunate official once supported.

These attitudes and behavior patterns help to explain the three-tiered structure of reactions to inner Party struggles. The clash at the top is the fundamental one when senior officials confront each other as each seeks to build up allies among the next lower level of officials. These problems at the Center quickly touch the next level of provincial leaders. These leaders and their immediate entourages must react with caution as they strive for judgments that will balance their estimates of who is likely to win at the top, of how much room for maneuvering they themselves have without risking charges of opportunism, and how far they can move without losing the support of their subordinates. Finally, at the lowest tier, there are those who feel that they cannot afford to pass up a chance for advancement and therefore wish to see the conflict spread, since the more people are toppled from above, the more rungs on

1. SCMP 4173, p. 3, cited by William L. Parrish, "Factions in Chinese Military Politics," *China Quarterly*, No. 56, October–December 1973, p. 688.

2. For discussions of the atmosphere in these "struggle" sessions, see such first-hand accounts of the Cultural Revolution as Gordon A. Bennett and Ronald N. Montaperto, *Red Guard: The Political Biography of Dai Hsiao-ai*, Doubleday & Co., Garden City, N. Y., 1972; Neal Hunter, *Shanghai Journal: An Eye-Witness Account of the Cultural Revolution*, Beacon Press, Boston, 1969; Ken Ling, *The Revenge of Heaven: Journal of a Young Chinese*, G. P. Putnam's Sons, New York, 1972.

the ladder will be vacated and awaiting occupancy.

The middle-level cadres tend thus to be an essentially conservative force, striving always to be responsive to top-level developments on the one hand and pacifying subordinate offlcials on the other. The process of treating with ambitious and disgruntled subordinates generally opens the door to old complaints. Thus, the very structure of the Party and those arrrangements that are supposed to ensure discipline and effective communications can become an amplifying system for dissension when there is factional strife at the top.

The flow of tension downward through the Party caused by even muted top leadership struggles is often magnified by the tactics of one leader disseminating reports about the impending fall of another. Sometimes these predictions may be unauthorized rumors, while at other times they may be official, but still secret, decisions by the Politburo Central Committee. Thus six months before Zhao Ziyang replaced Hua Guofeng as Premier, the word was passed down through briefing sessions that the leader of the "whatever faction" was rapidly losing ground to Deng Xiaoping's forces.[3] Lesser cadres, aware that the power of a principal figure will shortly be less than it now appears to be, are thus given time – and indeed are tacitly encouraged – to shift their allegiances to apparently more secure leaders.

THE PROBLEMS IN DENOUNCING
FALLEN LEADERS

When a leader has been removed from power, the process of universally denouncing him is often filled with pitfalls, which can open the way to new factional divisions.

The instantaneous reaction throughout China to the fall of a leader is for all with access to the media to express indignation and hostility. The process of building the chorus of the new conformity is, however, filled with dangerous pitfalls. Any sign of underreacting or overreacting can place one outside of the new consensus. One must ascertain that he is criticizing the fallen figure for the right reasons, since not all of his policies may be discredited; indeed, in time, all of his positions may be accepted in the new consensus, and he could be remembered for views quite the opposite of those he once appeared to hold. Those who were thought of as ultra-leftists could become classified as rightists. Similarly, in most fields, China for several years followed policies once associated

3. Fox Butterfield, "Complex Hidden Network Supplies the Chinese with Vital News," *New York Times*, December 31, 1980, p. A3.

with Liu Shaoqi, while Liu himself remained a discredited figure. In short, subsequent developments may radically change the significance of anything that is said at the moment of discrediting.

The safest response, as we have seen, is to join the denunciations by merely repeating code words. Inevitably, however, some variation does creep into public denouncements of a fallen leader and the heralding of a new one. At times the variations in phrasing have no political significance, while at other times important meaning can be read into the differences in the choice of words. For example, in reacting to the elevation of Hua Guofeng to the position of Chairman, the various provincial committees did reflect in their choice of words their factional colorations of the moment. Since there is no particular advantage in gratuitously offending a new leader by appearing to be out of step or lagging in enthusiasm, failure to use the accepted language usually represents either a genuine inability to achieve agreement in drafting statements among committee members or sloppy and inattentive writing.

- One of our Hong Kong respondents told of his unit's problems in hailing the rise of Hua Goufeng as Chairman: "When we first got the news that Hua was to be Party Chairman, we were unsure of what we should do to properly honor him. It didn't seem right to use the same phrases we had used to praise Mao Zedong; but it also seemed bad to treat him in a lesser way. We waited to see what others were doing, but this was also not very clever, because some of the leaders in other units had closer connections with Hua than we did. Finally, our leading figure decided that because we did not have any special relations with leaders who knew Hua, we should be even more extreme in our praise."

The next safest approach beyond the repetition of code words is the practice of publicizing personal information, which, of course, should be bad about the fallen leader and good about the rising one. Accounts of how the leader in question once behaved in various situations and of how he treated others thus become a part of the propaganda flow that builds up the one and destroys the other.

Given the extraordinarily high tolerance for flattery in Chinese politics, there is nothing surprising about the eagerness of people to make complimentary eyewitness statements about emerging leaders. There is some question, however, as to whether any historic significance should be attached to such accounts. Many strive to have their cries of hosanna heard, but only a few are fortunate enough to be recognized. In the campaign to build up the authority of Chairman Hua Guofeng, the first-hand accounts of meetings with him tend to strengthen the impression that he was personally concerned about special categories of people – rural cadres, members of the military, and long-time Party workers. The absence of reports of Hua ever meeting with technical specialists, university figures, or foreign policy experts may be a significant clue as to whom he wished to favor, or it may simply reflect the fact that Hua indeed had few earlier dealings with the more elitist segments of Chinese society.

The publication of first-hand accounts of the bad traits of fallen leaders suggests the existence of a more complex set of calculations. The history of the last few years makes it obvious that those involved in the Chinese political process are studious in collecting evidence of possible personal misbehavior of high officials, especially any damaging evidence that might be publicized if the leader should fall from grace. Yet care must be taken that the reported misconduct fall within the standardized and appropriate middle range – it cannot be so bad that the failure to publicize it earlier would invite charges of covering up or even of conspiring with the culprit; and of course it cannot be so trivial as to suggest that one was in fact still protecting the disgraced figure or minimizing his evil qualities.

The typical solution to this problem is to cite a slight "crime" with great vigor and indignation. For example, when Zhang Chunqiao was made a part of the Peking show trials of the Gang of Four and the Lin Biao group, the people in his home county of Hongan, who had formerly taken great pride in their Long March veteran, felt compelled to announce to the nation that they "cherished an undying hatred of him and Lin Biao." One of his old regimental commanders, Fang Heming, declared that Jiang was "more dangerous and heinous" than Zhang Guotao, and "Old as I am, I will turn anger into strength and strive for the Four Modernizations to my last breath."[4] No specific crimes were identified, only anger at the defeated and dedication to the victors.

One of the most awkward problems in Chinese political behavior is deciding how to disassociate oneself from a fallen comrade. Usually former subordinates are expected to testify to the rotten qualities of their exposed superiors, but there seems to be no ritualized rule as to how far one must go in order to effectively divorce oneself from their evil influence. In general, it is sufficient for underlings to say that they were captives of their situation and that they had indeed noticed a few specific faults in their superior. Those at higher levels, however, may feel that they must boldly move from association with a collapsing group to identification with an apparently emerging force.

4. Beijing, *Renmin Ribao*, November 29, 1980, p. 3, reported in Foreign Broadcast Information Service, *Daily Report – People's Republic of China*, December 3, 1980, p. L-1.

What befell First Secretary Song Peizhang of Anhui is instructive about the cascading effects of top-level factional strife. Song's initial appointment was based on long service as a Party cadre of the pre-Cultural Revolution period, and he seemed in a secure position after the restoration of Deng Xiaoping. But after the death of Zhou Enlai and the sudden dismissal of Deng, Song sought to protect his interests by accommodation with the Shanghai leaders. When the campaign against Deng began, he attacked the "capitalist roader" and those "who would reverse correct verdicts." Ultimately, he was, however, caught on the esoteric issue of how to interpret Mao's cryptic declaration that "the bourgeoisie are right in the Party." Did the phrase mean that there were a few individual "capitalist roaders" in the Party (which would mean that it was an attack on Deng Xiaoping), or did Mao wish to purge large numbers of people who were not adequately revolutionary? In the spring of 1976, the phrase was used to mean that Mao's words were appropriately directed against particular individuals, and thus Deng. Later, however, the Gang of Four were charged with having tried to extend the phrase to cover a "stratum or class," and thus they supposedly pointed a "spearhead" against veteran cadres – that is, against all the moderates. Song Peizhang was soon being battered about like a badminton shuttlecock as subordinates anxiously sought to exploit his awkward posture of vacillation over the meaning of Mao's statement. He had quickly shifted from a narrow criticism of Deng Xiaoping to the more general interpretation preferred by the Gang of Four, but when they were crushed he found himself in a hopeless postion: His subordinates quickly attacked him for having used the Gang's interpretation of the phrase to mean a "class." Yet he could sense that Deng might still be rehabilitated by the Politburo, and therefore it would be dangerous to say that the phrase referred only to individual "capitalist roaders." It is not difficult to imagine Song's dilemma: If he had been concerned mainly about his responsibilities in the province, he should have pushed for a major campaign against the influences of the Gang, denouncing the theory that there was a bloc or stratum of bourgeoisie in the Party; but when he calculated what might be happening at the Center, it could not have seemed prudent to support what once had been an implicitly anti-Deng formulation just when it seemed likely that Deng might be restored in Peking. Finally, on June 26, 1977, Song was removed for not being vigorous enough in attacking the Gang of Four, and at a rally of over 100,000 people he was denounced by his former colleagues on the provincial committee for precisely the sin of using the Gang's interpretation of Mao's remark.[5]

5. Anhwei Provincial Radio Service, July 1, 1977, in Foreign Broadcast Information Service, *Daily Report – People's Republic of China,* July 5, 1977, p. G1.

Presumably, with Deng's restoration to all of his former posts, Song's successor, Wan Li, must have appreciated Song's dilemma and wished that he had never heard of Mao's passing comment that "the bourgeoisie are right in the Party."

QUICKLY GRASP OPPORTUNITIES, BUT BE SLOW TO SETTLE ACCOUNTS

The defeat of a leader can be exploited by others to legitimize their preferred policies, no matter how irrelevant they may have been to the position of the fallen leader.

In Chinese politics it is usually difficult for subordinate officials to draw attention to their preferred policies, and therefore, the occasion of a fall from power of a leading figure can present lesser officials with a unique opportunity to promote their own policies, even though it may have to be done primarily in a negative way. The risk is especially worth taking if the disgraced figure can be linked to policies that one would like abandoned. People do expect changes to follow a shuffling of leaders, even though the dismissal may have been occasioned by hierarchy adjustments more than policy issues.

The tactic of pressing for advantage in the aftermath of a leadership struggle is not the monopoly of any particular group. Both ideologues and pragmatic technicians can spring to action when they sense an opportunity. An example of this tendency occurred in the fall of 1980, when Politburo members were absorbed with planning the Peking trials and deciding the fate of Hua Guofeng, and therefore there were few authoritative statements emanating from the Center. Suddenly the Chinese press was filled with policy proposals and suggestions for changes in economic practices, many inspired by members of the Chinese Academy of the Social Sciences, and not a few coming close to suggesting that China should abandon socialism. Once the tension at the Center relaxed after the decision about Hua's "resignations," the press became more disciplined as lower-level cadres checked their views and deferred to the Deng–Zhao–Hu leadership.

There is always a risk, however, in trying to pin any overblown policy significance to a change in personnel, regardless of how high up the change; and if the fallen leader is either rehabilitated or charged with quite different faults, then the proffered policies can be completely discredited. A touching example of this problem occurred after Zhou's death, when Deng Xiaoping was being universally reviled. Li Yuayu of the Luta Garrison Command in Liaoning decided to draw attention to himself by vociferously charging that Deng had advocated the theory of "weapons above all other things" and "the army should fight tough battles, and really tough battles mean contests of steel."[6] Eventually, when Hua won out over the "radicals" in October, Li and all the others who had hoped to use the occasion of Deng's disgrace to oppose the modernization of the PLA, suddenly found themselves in a defenseless position. Instead of the see-saw working so that their policies might rise while Deng went down, they found themselves down while those once associated with Deng, particularly in the military, rose.

There is usually surprising restraint in Chinese factional politics in eliminating followers of disgraced leaders, but grudges, on the other hand, are long held – a pattern consistent with traditional Chinese cultural ideals.

The formal code of Chinese politics upholds the ideals of reforming rather than destroying wayward elements. The Chinese Communists have supreme confidence in their powers of persuasion and, in contrast to the Russian Communists, who accept the necessity of eliminating certain enemies, find confirmation of the merits of their ideology in their successes in converting acknowledged enemies. These cultural attitudes, combined with Mao's belief that Stalin failed in his use of terror, have made the Chinese highly sensitive to the possibility of "reform and rehabilitation" in dealing with factional foes. Although the Chinese use violent rhetoric – speaking of the need to "crush," to "beat the dogs in the water," and to "exterminate the freaks and monsters" – their struggles are, at the formal level, generally tempered, and the defeated are not publicly executed. However, it has recently come to light that the level of violence, especially during the 1960s, has been uncharacteristically high.

Victors in Chinese factional conflicts are generally inhibited in using violence against the vanquished, largely because they recognize that they could frighten off the neutrals who were not involved in the conflict but who must be won over to the new consensus. Victors must concentrate on appearing to be reliable, trustworthy leaders, deserving of the faith of the majority.

Indeed, at times the victors can bend over backwards so far to avoid appearing to be vindictive that they can sound as though they shared most of the views of the defeated faction. In criticizing the Gang of Four, it was for a time commonplace to speak of "consolidating the gains of the Great Cultural Revolution, warmheartedly supporting the new socialist things," and "expanding and strengthening the newborn forces."[7] The

---

6. Foreign Broadcast Information Service, *Daily Report – People's Republic of China,* June 15, 1976, p. L4.

7. Nanking Provincial Radio, Foreign Broadcast Information Service, *Daily Report – People's Republic of China,* December 8, 1976, p. G10.

constraint, however, is primarily in the legal use of violence. Direct confrontations of factional groups can, of course, involve considerable unsanctioned fighting and violence, which can leave deep scars. Moreover, to belong to a defeated faction is to face political ruin, a shattered career, loss of status and the perquisites of power, and economic hardships for oneself and one's family. In the tightly structured character of Chinese society, such defeats can be profoundly humiliating, producing a deep sense of loss of face.

Yet precisely because the conflicts are not usually carried to ultimate extremes, there is always the possibility of a political comeback. Although one must repent one's crimes and profess to be a part of the new consensus, it is also possible to hold a grudge and to await the time of revenge. The various twists and turns of Chinese Communist politics over the years have produced a generation of frustrated followers who must be nursing many resentments. In traditional China, men who controlled their passions and waited patiently for revenge after being humiliated were held in awe. The slighter the insult and the longer the wait, the greater the awe. The ability to control one's hatred and to have proper relations with one's enemies while awaiting an opportunity was generally seen as superior conduct and not two-faced behavior.

The Peking trials provided many examples of people maintaining civil relations as they waited for revenge. One type of "evidence" used to condemn Zhang Chunqiao was his support for You Xuetao, who purportedly organized the "244 group," named for its location at 244 Yongfu Road in Shanghai, which produced a "one-million character secret report" that was used to attack opponents of the "radicals." In the courtroom it was charged that "the wily old fox" Zhang Chunqiao did not trust his own "wolf" You Xuetao and therefore he waited until You was exposed after the Cultural Revolution to turn on him in revenge for one earlier slight; and thus "the hound was killed, once the rabbit was hunted."[8] Indeed, the formal indictment against the ten "clique" members consists of long lists of cases of their "framing" others, usually with some purpose of revenge in mind.[9]

Behind the constraints on factionalism and the emphasis on the faults of fallen leaders (combined with the apparent forgiving of the followers), there must be widespread hostility and an awareness that in time many scores may be settled. The guide to the emotional intensity of the hostilities beneath the surface should therefore be the actual damage ex-

8. Beijing, *Renmin Ribao*, December 5, 1980, p. 3, reported in Foreign Broadcast Information Service, *Daily Report – People's Republic of China*, December 8, 1980, pp. L8–L14.
9. For full text, see "Indictment of the Special Procuratorate," *Beijing Review*, No. 48, December 1, 1980, pp. 9–28.

perienced by the defeated, rather than the rhetoric of the victors. In the short run, the victors have all the advantages because they can determine the "consensus" that will mobilize all the neutral and more passive elements, while the defeated will be powerless to seek allies for fear of being charged with subversive and anti-revolutionary activities. In time, however, those with grudges will seek to act.

This explains in part why uncertainty at the leadership level is always followed by reports of widespread antisocial behavior, attacks on public property, and violence by "bad elements" – as, for example, the reports of damage to the railroad system after the fall of the Gang of Four. The difficulties in transportation were caused largely by the actions of provincial leaders seeking to consolidate their local power bases; for example, in Anhui, after his removal as First Secretary, Song Peizhang was said to have "colluded with the Gang's remnants in Shanghai, energetically going in for turning the corner and changing the leadership group in the Pengpu Railway Subbureau and [to have] dragged out 'democrats' and in the southern section of the Peking–Shanghai Railway, seriously affecting the development of economic construction in East China. This railway subbureau thus became a new hard nut of the national railway."[10] At about the same time, there were disruptions in Hankou that were said to have been caused by workers' resentment over the lack of improvement in wages after the Gang had been eliminated.

Economic difficulties usually follow political upheavals because production is hampered by the interruptions caused by criticism sessions. Such sessions tend to be protracted precisely because those in authority must seek "confessions" and "self-criticisms." This process can be complicated, since those involved are often torn between different tactics. The traditional Chinese response to charges of incorrect or criminal behavior was to plead innocence as long as possible and then seek the leniency of the authorities by emotionally overstating one's failings and asking for forgiveness. Within the Party, however, the opposite tactic often seems to work better: rapid confession to failings, while making them as trivial as possible and stoutly professing one's desire to reform. The Peking trials had examples of both tactics.

It can take considerable time to arrive at the right mix of confession, self-criticism, and group evaluation for the leadership to feel confident that they have eliminated the "poisonous weeds" and have successfully created a new consensus. The leadership can never be sure, however, whether those who were exposed and damaged will not eventually seek revenge.

---

10. Anhwei Provincial Service, July 1, 1977, Foreign Broadcast Information Service, *Daily Report – People's Republic of China*, July 5, 1977, p. G1.

BALANCING ACTS AND THE SEARCH
FOR STABILITY

Under conditions of high factional tensions it is generally easier to appraise the risks of taking extremist positions than, paradoxically, those of seeking to control the balance of consensus.

Those who have sought to exploit the advantages of being out in front on extreme policy positions have taken high, but generally easily calculable risks, while those who have sought to avoid extreme positions have not necessarily gained security. This holds true largely because the most intense political struggles have taken place near the center of the political spectrum, where a great many actors are crowding for position and hence finding themselves in direct conflicts. The "radicals," for example, were perceived as being ready to take high risks and support extreme policies, and therefore they took high but calculable risks. What has been less appreciated is that even the "moderates" have had unavoidable conflicts and a resulting lack of security.

It is easier to understand this situation if one pictures Chinese politics since the passing of Mao Zedong as being very much like a somewhat far-fetched game of king-of-the-castle on a see-saw: Those bold enough to take extreme positions and go to either end of the board can expect to rise quickly, but they may fall just as suddenly, while those who move about in the middle can adjust to all changes, no matter how extreme, but they can have little leverage over the tilting of the board. However, since so many wish to crowd into the middle, many will be pushed to one side of center or the other and therefore, quite against their wills, they may find themselves on the downside when they hoped to be on the rise.

When the "tilting" was governed by the actions of a single supreme actor, no matter how mercurial he might have been, the others could make calculated responses, either to balance his motions by moving to the other end of the board or by moving quickly with him so as to bring the whole system "down" to one side. For example, during the Great Leap and the Cultural Revolution, most cadres went to either one extreme or the other, or they sought to make whatever modest adjustments might be necessary to maintain their balance in the middle. At the time of Mao's death, the radicals sought to gain maximum leverage by boldly rushing to one end of the board to bounce the others off, but their efforts were counterbalanced, and now the crowding is taking place at the middle.

It is difficult to determine whether those who currently have either fallen or are in a precarious situation chose to move away from the center in order to gain more leverage or whether they were simply crowded out into their dangerous positions. When Deng Xiaoping returned, he squeezed into the middle and joined Hua Guofeng there in seeking to control, with great difficulty, the teetering of the board. Then for nearly two years Hua and Deng stood together and confronted each other at the middle, trying to control the teetering by responding to each other's slightest moves. Deng gradually moved away from the fulcrum and caused a major tilt of the whole system.

It is already clear that Deng's effort to squeeze back into the center has forced several people to be pushed out of the relative security of their middle positions and into precarious locations at the edge of the crowd. Apparently this is what has happened to some, if not all, of those who are now falling off or barely hanging on: Wang Hairong at the Foreign Office; Wu De, the Mayor of Peking; General Chen Xilian, Commander of the Peking Military Region; Mrs. Wu Guixian, alternate (and only woman) member of the Politburo; Mrs. Liu Xiangping, Minister of Health; and Lin Zhuanxin, Chief of the capital's security services. These people are all vulnerable because in one way or another they were seen as being less than totally loyal to Zhou Enlai and overly ready to cooperate with the Gang of Four; yet at the same time, they all tried to hold positions close to the fulcrum. The uncertain question for the future is whether Deng Xiaoping will be able to hold on as he moves more and more to an extreme in his efforts to bounce Hua and others off the board.

The process of toppling a leader is slowed down because it is not considered wrong in Chinese politics to keep silent about the crimes of a leader until after he has been discredited. The Chinese do not seem to ask why someone who has known of the shocking flaws of a leader did not speak up until after that leader had become a legitimate target of criticism. No doubt because of the sacredness of Mao, few now dare to question why he repeatedly appointed successors whom he later abandoned and denounced as having long-standing faults. It is somewhat more surprising that lesser figures can report that they have long known about scandals in the lives of leading personages without fear that they might be suspected of conspiring to conceal evidence.

There are three explanations for this phenomenon. First, the universally accepted obligation of conformity is so great that no one is expected to break the surface consensus until a leading figure has been attacked by another member of the elite. It is accepted as self-evident that common cadres will not speak out disruptively until the signs are given that criticisms are in order. Second, the Chinese doctrine that rehabilitation is always possible means that as long as a leader's current behavior is judged to be proper, it is inappropriate to bring up past failings, since presumably he has repented. Third, the cultural ideal of masterfully holding grudges is coupled with the concept that premature disclosure is a sign of weakness. One's obligation is not to instantly reveal negative information, but rather to reveal it at the most telling moment, that is, when it will do the greatest damage.

It is significant that not only do individuals with damaging information hold their tongues, organizations and even research institutions also maintain silence without risk of appearing to collaborate with the enemy. In the attacks on the Gang of Four, the Lu Xun Research Office, for example, suddenly revealed the startling fact that Zhang Chunqiao, one of the discredited Four, had in 1936 done "his best to peddle Wang Ming's right capitulationist line," and, using the pseudonym "Dick," he wrote a "sinister article," encircling and attacking Lu Xun, "the great thinker and revolutionary" who "put forward the motto, 'Beating a mad dog in the water'."[11] (Harold Isaacs remembers that the young Chinese Communist revolutionaries in Shanghai in the mid-1930s used Western first names as code names and pseudonyms, so it is not necessarily entirely fanciful that Zhang Chunqiao once used the name "Dick.")

Although in its early phases the spread of intense factional strife may appear to be random and unpredictable, once one group gains ascendancy the command decision to terminate provincial and local conflicts usually involves fine judgments and a basic appreciation of the need of legitimacy for ruling.

Logically, it might seem that when elite struggles erupt and top leaders are purged, one could easily predict where the cascading effects are likely to flow and be most disruptive. Local conflicts would normally be expected to be the most intense in those places and institutions where the fallen leaders had their greatest concentrations of followers. Yet this has not always been the case. The purging of Peng Dehuai did not result in extensive struggles within the military, and after the fall of the Gang of Four, the most serious strife in China was not concentrated in Shanghai or in those institutions concerned with culture, ideology, or the media.

Apparently, the prime bases of power of discredited leaders are immediately assaulted by the victorious forces at the Center, and all the fallen leaders' most obvious supporters are too vulnerable to put up much resistance. Precisely because the Center must mobilize its full forces against manifest trouble spots, the followers of the fallen leaders usually cannot defend themselves, so in order to survive, they must retreat and seek clemency through promises of reform and rehabilitation.

The most intense struggles appear to take place in those provinces and

---

11. Article by the mass criticism group of the Lu Hsun Research Office, "Lu Hsun Relentlessly Beat the Mad Dog Chang Chun-chiao," Foreign Broadcast Information Service, *Daily Report—People's Republic of China*, November 4, 1976, p. E1–E2.

locations where loyalties are most ambiguous, mixed, or evenly divided. In these areas, the issues that arise at the Center are immediately translated into questions of who should or should not be removed from office, and who is or is not sincere in repenting. In short, questions of loyalty to particular superiors and advocacy of particular policies are quickly reduced to the least common denominator of jobs and careers. These basic issues provide fuel for local structural conflicts that soon can take on a life of their own.

From the perspective of the operations of Chinese politics as a national system, it is impossible to predict where such intense clashes will break out following any particular factional clash at the Center. For example, if ideology was important, there was no reason to believe that the Chinese railway system would be a prime center of a disruptive struggle between the Gang of Four and the moderates. But since the intensity of local conflicts seems to depend on how ambiguous the loyalties are in the area, it follows that Liaoning had more manifest difficulties than Shanghai, and Yunnan and Fujian had great trouble, as did Sichuan.

The spread of conflict is thus beyond the control of the Center and is part of a process that would seem unrelated to the issues that are its paramount concerns. Yet this in not entirely correct. The process of local turmoil and bitter conflicts for posts and advancements is a sign of the breakdown of central authority only if it is assumed that the Chinese political system, like the Chinese economy, is centrally administered and planned. If we begin with different assumptions, however, we can see the local turmoil in quite a different light: It is a process, often of violent political transactions, by which power and loyalties are sorted out and new alignments created, so that in the end those who have the capacity to rule in the localities will have established their positions of effective strength. This process is, quite ironically, analogous to the market mechanism in economics, which is, of course, the alternative method of planning or administrative decisionmaking in allocating resources.

What we are suggesting is the possibly startling idea that the Chinese political system, under the strains of responding to elite factional strife, can be thought of as being analogous to a "mixed economy." In some areas, decisionmaking depends on administrative or centrally planned choices; in other areas, the process of allocating authority and legitimacy depends upon the outcome of localized power processes. In the latter cases, individual actors strive to maximize their self-interests and in the process they make the allocative decisions for the larger system. The "struggle" or "market" processes in the various locations operate so as to sift out local leaders who, in becoming a part of a linkage system to the national leaders, can provide the sense of legitimacy necessary to rule the huge country of China.

Ultimately it is the Center that decides that the time is right to terminate localized strife – that the legitimacy essential for ruling has been achieved. This decision hinges upon (1) the extent to which the local and provincial conflicts have produced leaders who can command authority in running the country and (2) the ability to select a new Central Committee that will be sympathetic to the will of the leadership. The act of selecting and convening a new Central Committee reflects the judgment of the leadership that the "market" process of allocating authority has gone far enough and the balance in the system can be tilted toward the ideal of a fully "planned" or "administered" system.

In creating the new Central Committee the top leadership can either accept the outcome of provincial and local-level struggles or act to remove unwanted leaders and appoint new ones. The removal of local leaders, which heralds the final preparations for designating a new Central Committee, follows a pattern with certain striking characteristics: The deposed figure instantly becomes a non-person referred to only by code words; huge public rallies are held to denounce the non-person; and out of these rallies emerges the new leader who establishes his legitimacy by expressing moral outrage at the behavior of his predecessor.

The use of code words in speaking of the removed provincial and local leaders is similar to the practice for referring to discredited national leaders. Thus, just as Liu Shaoqi became "China's Khrushchev" and Deng Xiaoping became the "capitalist roader who seeks to reverse correct verdicts," immediately before the formation of the Central Committee that would restore Deng the Chinese had "that rather influential person" of Jiangxi province and "that bad man" of Paoting Prefecture. Over half a million people were gathered in Paoting in early July 1977 to learn that "that bad man" had been removed through "tit-for-tat struggle," and that he had "dragged his feet on land reform," "colluded with Peng Dehuai during the Great Leap," schemed to "reverse his record during the Great Proletarian Cultural Revolution," and finally sought to "contact Jiang Qing" after Mao's death.[12] Thus, in spite of his having provided more than thirty years of leadership in the Chinese Communist Party, when the decision to form a new Central Committee was made, "that bad man" had to be not only removed but vilified.[13]

12. "Hopei Rally Scores 'That Bad Man' in Paoting Prefecture," Hopei Provincial Service, July 2, 1977, Foreign Broadcast Information Service, *Daily Report – People's Republic of China,* July 13, 1977, p. K1.

13. The story of "that rather influential person" of Jiangxi is very similar to that of "that bad man" of Paoting Prefecture, as both were removed from office during the politics of establishing a new Central Committee after the fall of the Gang of Four. The specific criticisms of "that rather influential person" are interesting, since they went beyond

There is no ready explanation for the Chinese fondness for using code-word names for purged leaders, but the practice seems to be related to their beliefs about the way in which legitimate authority should behave when engaged in messy and aggression-laden affairs. The procedure suggests that more is known than is being said, while what is being said is not explicit enough to provide a basis for counterattacks. Prior to coming to power, the Chinese Communists freely named their purged leaders – indeed, those very names became synonymous with different political crimes. But once in power, the Chinese Communists reverted to the practice of using political crimes or vilifying phrases in place of actual names. Presumably the use of code words suggests that the authorities do not wish to make irrevocable what would otherwise be so. For example, the Chinese in their early polemics with the Russians avoided explicit statements and relied upon surrogate names such as "Albania." And the use of a code-word name did in fact make it easier to bring back the "capitalist roader," Deng Xiaoping.

In terms of the larger process of terminating strife and reestablishing central authority through the constitution of a new Central Committee, it is significant and surprising that the Chinese attach such importance to an essentially legalistic concept. All the confusion and discord at the local and provincial levels can thus be justified as part of a necessary process of selecting that body of men who can finally give legitimacy to the new leadership and thereby make possible the ruling of nearly a billion people.

---

stereotyped railings to give a picture of local-level politics and the tactics a politically ambitious cadre might reasonably employ. According to his successors, " 'that rather influential person" sold himself out to the Gang of Four. This so-called veteran cadre long wanted to usurp Party and state power. He possessed a gilded badge of a Long Marcher and a self-made laurel crown of a 'correct representative of the Great Cultural Revolution.' . . . He regarded these two trump cards as political capital with which to acquire higher posts and power from the party and did his best to climb to higher levels. He was dissatisfied with being the provincial Party committee secretary and one of the principal responsible persons of the provincial military district. He wanted to become the No. 1 leading person of the provincial Party committee. He dreamt about it and feverishly longed for it. His ambition was not realized so he bore a grudge against the Party Central Committee . . . . In the initial stages of the movement to criticize Lin Piao and Confucius . . . that rather influential person felt his opportunity had come. He lost no time in writing a letter to Chiang Ching of the Gang of Four, in which he made false charges against the provincial committee. This letter was well received by the white-boned devil Chiang Ching, who then sent him a sinister reply clamoring that it was necessary to lift the lid off of class and line struggles . . . . When he received this sinister letter, he regarded it as a great treasure. He felt he had at last found a supporter that could give full play to his abilities." (Kiangsi Provincial Service, July 9, 1977, Foreign Broadcast Information Service, *Daily Report – People's Republic of China,* July 14, 1977, p. G5–G6.)

DENG XIAOPING'S GAMBLE

During the fall of 1980, Deng Xiaoping apparently decided that it was either safe or necessary to violate some of the prudence rules of Chinese factional politics that we have just been noting. Instead of following the principle of Chinese politics – indeed, the nearly universal rule of politics – that success in gaining power calls for conciliatory gestures to win over former foes, Deng chose to use his ascending power to intimidate cadres throughout China. At a time when it might have seemed wiser to have called for an end of mutual recriminations stemming from the Cultural Revolution, Deng pushed for the Peking show trials of the Gang of Four, five followers of Lin Biao, and Chen Boda, Mao's former secretary. The trials were designed to emphasize two points: The military should not intervene in politics, and anyone who opposes Deng will be destroyed.

The inevitable consequences of the "trials" were a further weakening of Hua Guofeng's influence and the beginning of questioning of Mao's historic role. It is possible that Deng's gamble will succeed, and cadres throughout China will rally to his leadership, hailing his protégé Zhao Ziyang as Premier, Hu Yaobang as Chairman, and Wan Li as Party trouble-shooter.[14] Yet, this historical record of Chinese factional politics suggests that the odds do not favor such a harmonious outcome. Rather, it can be expected that the search for security is already going on for the threatened cadres and they are actively strengthening their personal ties so as to survive Deng's threat.

---

14. Fox Butterfield, "The Pragmatists Take China's Helm," *The New York Times Magazine*, December 28, 1980, pp. 22–26.

Chapter 10

Communications and the Power of Words

At several points in this book we have noted the close relationship between factional mobilization and conflict and the mass media. The media in China play a critical role in factional politics. As we have already observed, the Chinese use their mass media to communicate subtle policy matters, but in their informal private communications, cadres are usually careful to repeat only the accepted versions of the consensus. We have suggested that Chinese leaders use the public media in this peculiar way to activate their networks of potential supporters and to gradually change the consensus through the introduction of ritualized code words and slogans. Sometimes the code words deal directly with policy issues, while at other times they may be highly abstract symbols that serve only as a way of helping to identify friends and foes. A leader will float such symbols in the media and watch to see who repeats them and who ignores them; his judgments about the distribution of power among cadres are then based on his observations.

The Chinese use of Aesopian language can be confusing, even for the Chinese. Sometimes the meaning is so apparent that one can only wonder why a more forthright statement could not have been used. In such cases, the purpose of the message is usually not to communicate substantive information but to push a slogan or code word and thereby mobilize factional support. On other occasions, the Aesopian language can be so cryptic as to be largely meaningless in content but significant for mobilizing purposes.

As an example, Mao Zedong jumped at the idea of suddenly requiring all the people to reflect on the "negative example" supposedly portrayed by the classic Chinese novel The Water Margin. Generations of Chinese had been brought up on the idea that The Water Margin was an anti-establishment novel, since its hero, Song Chang, was the leader of a Robin Hood-like band of rebels; but suddenly Mao announced that Song Chang had in fact been a "revisionist," a leader who on the surface appeared to be "revolutionary" but whose ultimate actions supported middle-class "bourgeois" morality. The key to the allegory was that when the founder of the band, the truly "revolutionary" Chao Gai, died, Song Chang pretended to be "as sad as if he had lost his parents," and he "cried until he fainted," but actually "these were crocodile tears and fraudulent tricks" because once he had "taken over as No. 1" he changed the "Chamber of Assembly for Justice" into the "Hall for Loyalty and Justice," clearly the act of a "revisionist" who craved the ultimate restoration of a good emperer and not success for the downtrodden. All Chinese by this time knew that "revisionism" was bad, and therefore if Song Chang was a "revisionist" he must be bad, but it was far from obvious who in the contemporary scene was being allegorically portrayed as a Song Chang. For months, millions of people throughout China taxed their brains trying to figure out who was really Song Chang. Some saw him as the Soviet Union, which had clearly gone the "revisionist" route; others thought that he might be Zhou Enlai, who presumably wished for better relations with such imperialists as the United States; still others wondered whether he might be Deng Xiaoping, soon to be the "capitalist roader who seeks to reverse correct verdicts." For still others, the symbolism was of a more general nature and therefore Song Chang stood for all who for any reason might want to reduce the tensions with Moscow. In any case, Jiang Qing made public her reading of the allegory, but when Mao was told of her theory he exclaimed, according to the Peking Review, "Shit, [she is] barking up the wrong tree."[1] Unfortunately, Mao never explained which tree his wife should have been "barking up," and therefore all the millions in China were left to mull over what they should make of the whole campaign, particularly since there could not have been a Chinese alive who did not know before the campaign began that it was profoundly wrong to be a "revisionist." In no manner could the campaign about The Water Margin have taught the Chinese anything about "revisionism" that they did not already know.

1. Peking Review, Vol. 20, No. 23, June 3, 1977, p. 22.

In the years since the death of Mao, we can find in the gradual changes in the dominant code words significant changes in the official consensus and hence in the factional alignments in Chinese politics. Initially, for example, while Hua Guofeng was seeking to consolidate his power as the heir to Mao, the Chinese media went to great lengths to sell the absurd idea that the Gang of Four were ultra-rightists; then gradually, over time, in direct proportion to the decline in Hua's dominant role, the effort was dropped and the radicals were acknowledged as guilty of "left" deviation, and cadres were scolded for believing that "it is safest to be leftist." Similarly, during the first year after Mao's death, Hua and his supporters made much of Mao's last words and especially his purported statement, "With you in charge, I am at ease." Since it had been Mao's words that legitimized Hua's chairmanship, the Hua faction jealously guarded those words and took command of publishing Volume Five of Mao's *Selected Works*. In time, the issue of how Mao's words were to be used became not just a policy question in favor of greater "pragmatism" and less "Maoism," but also a question of how much power and legitimacy Hua should command. Thus the campaign in favor of "seeking truth from facts" and, by implication, not from Mao's words was clearly an attack against Hua and his monopoly control over Mao's texts. Indeed, by mid-1979 it had become apparent that the contrived campaign against Mao's words – which involved the almost complete elimination of the public display of slogans quoting Mao – was inspired less by a continuing need to attack the Gang of Four than as a sign of factional pressures against Hua and his ally Wang Dongxing, who was once more closely associated with Mao.

In addition to the use of the media in factional politics, some other features of the communications process are equally significant for the dynamics of factionalism in China.

First there is the fact that the high value Chinese place on secrecy about politics accentuates the importance of access to information, and consequently the unevenness of knowledge intensifies distrust and slows decisionmaking.

As we noted at the outset, the Chinese have been remarkably successful in shrouding their politics in secrecy; those who are in the know demonstrate their superior status by faithfully repeating only the consensus clichés, while those on the outside have learned the prudent principle of not speculating out loud for fear of being identified as a rumor monger. Hence, it is impossible to discern from the statements issued who does and who does not know what is going on behind the scenes. This contrasts sharply with traditional Chinese politics (which also valued secrecy, partly to keep the number of aspiring participants manageable), in which all observers feigned far more knowledge than they actually possessed. When political communications in China advanced from tea-house gossip to newspapers, the style of those communications remained remarkably constant throughout the 1930s and 1940s: Reporters faithfully passed along speculation and rumors, impervious to the concept of hard news.

Yet we know that within the Party and the governmental structures there are a variety of information channels that extend to quite different networks of officials. Consequently, even among high-level cadres, information is not equally shared. It is no exaggeration to say that much of Chinese politics revolves around the question, Who knows what, when, and how?

The channels of information only marginally overlap, so that on different matters there are different sophisticates and innocents. Cadres can be remarkably well informed within their own area of responsibility but surprisingly ignorant about matters in other domains. Scientists are given access to technical information from all over the world but are kept so ill-informed about governmental matters that they are barely better off than peasants. Specialists on domestic matters will be told little about foreign-policy calculations, while those who deal with foreigners are often uninitiated in domestic matters and sound as though they know more than what they read in the press – that is, the current consensus views.

These gross inequities in access to information tend to accentuate divisions between insiders and outsiders in a wide variety of areas. Those who know that they are privy to the same information naturally sense a common bond, and they must, of course, act to exclude others from their discussions. At the same time, the overriding legitimacy of secrecy makes everyone cautious about expressing views and anxious to appear neither more nor less informed than they should be; above all, nobody ever admits to surprise in learning anything – one simply acts as though one were being admitted to a more inner circle that one always knew existed, or as though one had the information all along.

This unequal access to information explains in part why the spread of knowledge, which accompanies any new campaign of vilification, is so slow. The process of endless discussion meetings and study sessions is necessary, in part, because those meetings are the mechanism for bringing together people who have shared so little common information. Cadres, long alerted to the new developments, must work with people who never imagined what they are being told could happen. The process of smoothing over the mismatching of information takes time and thus impedes the working of the political process. The demonizing of Lin Biao and the Gang of Four involved more than just exposing them, winning over their sympathizers, and teaching others from their "negative example"; it also took time because people whose worlds were informed by different flows of communication had to be somehow integrated.

We should also acknowledge that there are certain anomalies in the organization and operations of the Chinese communications system that seemingly defy explanation. First, there is the fact that copies of the daily *Reference News*, containing unvarnished accounts of world events taken largely from Western wire services, are quietly circulated among an extraordinarily large number of cadres – some 7 million in the late 1950s and possibly 10 million today. The exposure of those cadres to such information must harden them to the idea that there is quite a gap between "classified" information and what appears in the Chinese public media. Since so many cadres have access to what the rest of the world accepts as news, one wonders why the Chinese feel that they must go to such great lengths to deny the rest of their population exposure to even small bits of that same information.

A second anomaly is that the policy of making information relatively scarce forces people to seek informal channels of communications, which in turn contributes to the building of the networks that are at the core of factions. Indeed, the practice of accentuating the different flows of communication works to create factionalism and undermines faith in the consensus.

The relationship between information and power is, however, considerably more complex, because, as our Hong Kong respondents revealed, many Chinese are apparently quite aware that those in a position to receive privileged information may use their perceived advantages to manipulate others. Consequently, there is widespread uncertainty about the reliability of information passed down by superiors, particularly given the Chinese cultural value of always appearing to be more knowledgeable than one is. (Chinese guides will rarely admit to ignorance, and equally rarely will the Chinese ask questions of a foreign visitor.)

The linkage between channels of communication and the networks of personal association behind factions is apparently well recognized, and higher cadres quite explicitly exploit their access to inside information to extend and reinforce their claims on dependent subordinates. An interesting development in this respect has been the growth since 1977 of the institution of *Xiaodao Xiaoxi,* or "by-road news." These are handwritten, usually mimeographed, accounts of inner-elite actions, often explanations for why policy decisions were taken, which are started most often by children of the leading cadres and are then passed on from hand to hand through friendship networks. They are not necessarily, or even usually, critical of the regime; rather, they provide inside accounts and esoteric rationalizations that have a somewhat greater claim to legitimacy than mere word-of-mouth rumors.[2]

The leadership's reaction to their awareness of the existence of informal channels of communication is to force all opinions into the open. Even under the "pragmatic" rule of Deng, the old Cultural Revolution ideal of everyone exposing his views persists. Thus a writer calling for the "enlightenment of people's thinking" denounced the "rampancy" of "the grapevine of hearsay" and insisted that improvement of "ideological work" required the "airing" of everybody's views.[3] Although espoused in the name of enlightenment, the demand that all information should be public and shared is, of course, a threat to the weak, for it would exclude them from any particularistic networks.

ACCESS TO, AND RELIABILITY OF, DIFFERENT SOURCES OF INFORMATION

Our Hong Kong respondents indicated that in general they had been quite serious about evaluating news and that their concept of political sophistication rested very much upon the ability to obtain information and to sift out the true and the useful from false rumors and propaganda. Thus, 62.8 percent of them said that when they read a newspaper they could usually tell when the leaders were in disagreement. Several said that while they could sometimes recognize conflicting signals in the press, they could not be sure whether those signals reflected disagreement or merely confusion, uncertainty or just an abortive attempt of some aspiring leader to be different.

A more serious problem for most of the respondents was the lack of agreement between their main sources of information and those they believed to be the most reliable. When asked to rank their sources of information from "least used" to "most used" on a scale of 5, 65.9 percent checked newspaper and magazines as being in category 1 or "most used," yet only 27.3 percent checked these sources as being most reliable.

The top ranking for reliability went to radio, which 52.3 percent iden-

---

2. Miriam London first drew attention to the existence of the "by-road news." See her "China's 'By-road' News: A New People's Channel," *Freedom at Issue*, September–October 1978, p. 9. See also Fox Butterfield, "Complex Hidden Network Supplies Chinese with Vital News," *New York Times*, December 31, 1980, p. 3A.

3. Commentator's article, "The Principle of Enlightenment Should be Adopted for Ideological Work," *Banyue Tan*, November 25, 1980, in Foreign Broadcast Information Service, *Daily Report–People's Republic of China*, November 26, 1980, pp. L8–L10.

tified as being in category 1. However, this is almost entirely a reflection of the surprisingly large number of respondents who regularly listened to Radio Hong Kong and the BBC. (Interestingly, the spread of small transistor radios, particularly those with earplugs, which the authorities have tolerated as a gesture toward an improved standard of living and better consumer products, has also made it easier and safer to listen to Radio Hong Kong in Canton.)

Wall posters were neither an important source of information nor were they seen as being particularly reliable. Only 6.8 percent ranked them in category 1, and 38.6 percent gave them a mid-ranking of 3 for use, while 48 percent classified them in the bottom two categories of reliability.

The respondents placed relatively higher value on the reliability of more personal sources of information but confessed that they received little news from these. Less than 26 percent reported friends as being the most or next most important sources of information, but 50 percent said that whatever news they got from friends was for them the most or next most reliable. The comparable figures for family members were 18 percent and 36 percent, respectively. "By-road news" seems to have been seen as being very much like face-to-face communications: Only 18 percent of the respondents had much access to this form of communication, but 39 percent gave it high scores for reliability.

This pattern is generally what one would expect in a modernizing society without a highly professionalized and autonomous system of mass communications: high reliance upon but little trust in the mass media, greater trust in the relatively less efficient word-of-mouth channels.

Most revealing, however, was the painful ambivalence of the respondents about word-of-mouth systems that were also authority systems. The respondents genuinely wanted to trust the words of their superiors, but they were acutely aware that those words were often based on ulterior motives. Similarly, they wanted to value what they learned first-hand at political meetings, but they suspected that there were calculating motives behind what they were being told at such sessions.

Clearly, what filled those two information sources with tension was that both sources demanded responses and were not simply passive conduits. People were expected to act in response to what they learned from their superiors and at meetings. Moreover, most of the respondents seemed to appreciate that these two methods of communication provided a direct means for mobilizing them into the political process.

- A former resident of Shanghai said, "It did not matter very much whether you believed or did not believe in what you were being told.

That was not the important matter, and that is why I find it hard to answer this question of yours. What mattered at political meetings was being able to figure out what your response was supposed to be to what they were telling you as news. If you simply agreed with everything they told you, you could get into trouble for being too dumb; but if you disagreed too strongly you would be in even worse trouble. You had to judge carefully how to react and not worry about how 'reliable' the information was."

- A former accountant said, "When your superior told you some news you did not ask how 'reliable' it was, but rather you realized that he must have had some purpose in sharing such information with you. Maybe he wanted you to back him at the next meeting. Or maybe he wanted you as a friend because he had too many enemies."

In short, information in China is clearly an element of power, regardless of its reliability. Our respondents described this information system as the very basic process by which they and their peers found themselves either effectively mobilized into a potential power network or left isolated and unprotected. They also explained that it was largely through political meetings and study sessions that they learned to become highly sensitive to who was using what words, and hence to what words one should respond positively or negatively.

- A former office worker explained, "I could almost always tell when there was going to be a change in the Party's policy line from just reading the newspaper. I had to wait, however, until our small group study sessions to learn how our local leaders decided we ought to react. Although in form the discussions dealt with ideological matters and what was to be the correct answer, in substance they were more concerned with their power. Many times what they said was not consistent with what I understood from the newspaper or radio, but that didn't matter because what was important was whether or not people were ready to support their leader, regardless of what he said. If I had told him that I thought he had been wrong because of what I had read in the paper, he would have thought I was trying to take his job away from him."

THE POWER OF ANGRY WORDS

The process of factional politics by its own dynamics, irrespective of who the winners and losers have been, has lowered the Marxist–Leninist ideological basis of Chinese politics and made it more pragmatic.

The Chinese are certainly technically capable of engaging in debates in the classical tradition of Soviet Communism, as Mao Zedong demonstrated in his polemics against Khrushchev. The continuing process of factional strife, however, has reduced the level of ideological criticism and produced a lowest-common-denominator form of personal attack. As we have already observed, in recent years the Chinese have almost abandoned the traditional practice of recognizing both "left" and "right" deviation by making all deviations first "rightist" and then only "leftist." Until 1978, no matter how ultra-leftist the positions of a person or faction may have seemed, it always turned out that this was only a "mask" to hide their deep rightist inclinations. As a consequence, the campaigns against people as different as Liu Shaoqi, Lin Biao, Deng Xiaoping, and the Gang of Four all ended up on the same ideological note. Since 1978, the opposite has been the case, as everyone tries to avoid being a "leftist."

To some extent, this decline in the use of the full range of ideological possibilities for criticism reflects Chinese emulation of Soviet trends. As Soviet debates have become less ideologically precise, Chinese standards have likewise fallen. For example, when the decision was made in 1976 to identify Deng Xiaoping with Khrushchev on the grounds that both were anxious to have new sayings that would replace the old quotes of Marx, Lenin, Stalin, and Mao, it also became necessary to show that Deng was as ideologically unsophisticated as Khrushchev. Deng was charged with following Khrushchev's secret attack on Stalin by opposing the "cult of the individual," which was an attack on Mao; when Khrushchev said that Communism meant "a delicious plate of goulash," Deng Xiaoping said that Communism meant "sixty catties of pork a year, half a catty of apples per day, plus two ounces of *Gaoliang* wine per capita."[4]

There has been some decline in the practice of using quotes from the Communist immortals, particularly Mao. Earlier, one of the charges against Deng was that he once cynically ordered his staff to find appropriate quotes from Marx and Lenin "by tomorrow morning" to dress up the "outline report" on education – a rare case in which any Communist Party member has ever publicly admitted to the practice of first making the decision and then seeking justification from the sacred texts.

More importantly, there has been a decline in the sustained evaluation of positions according to ideological argumentation, and this decline was greatly accelerated in Mao's last years, when a mere sentence or phrase by the Chairman was enough to provide all the necessary clues as to

4. Yun Ling, "Analysis of Teng Hsiao-p'ing's 'New Sayings'," Peking, *Kuang-ming Jih-pao*, June 17, 1976, reported in SPRCP, L129, July 6, 1976, p. 10.

what should be the ideologically correct point of view. Furthermore, Mao had become preoccupied by concerns about "revisionism," and therefore any disapproved actions were immediately interpreted as setting the stage for the "restoration of capitalism." Thus whatever the starting point may have been, every criticized activity had to be traced back in some way to prove that it supported "revisionism."

The increasingly fluid power situation caused by factionalism has also encouraged personal and moralistic attacks on individuals and policies, rather than analysis of what should be done that would require systematic ideological justifications. It is safer for all participants to settle for name-calling and concrete policy criticisms rather than to risk being identified with elaborate statements that may in time be seen as offensive by those one would like to have as allies.

A consequence of this trend has been an increase, also encouraged by Mao, in the practice we have already noted of criticism by historical allegory. Yet in spite of the frequency with which Mao used examples from Chinese history and literature to make his points, this practice was also compromised by his decision to use *The Water Margin* as a "negative example" and his statement to the Tenth Plenum of the Eighth Central Committee that "the use of the novel for anti-Party activities is quite an invention."[5] As a consequence, it is now possible to accuse someone of using even "revolutionary" materials from Chinese history to "deceive the masses and confound right and wrong," if the user of the quote is himself shown to be a "counterrevolutionary." Yao Wenyuan was charged with "humming the sinister poem, 'Watching and Waiting at Ease for the Mountain to Fall and the Earth to Split' " after the Tangshan earthquake of July 1976 and then resurrecting the Earthquake Decree issued by the "great revolutionary leader" Hong Xiuchuan of the Taiping heavenly kingdom, which begins, "All things were created by God in 6 days."[6] There was apparently nothing wrong with Hong's decree, only that Yao was the one to have exhumed it. "The 'Earthquake Decree' was a revolutionary document. [But] proceeding from their reactionary stand, the Gang of Four took over its revolutionary phrases, gave them a counterrevolutionary meaning and used them to serve their attempt to usurp party and state power."[7]

Clearly, if people can so readily change the meaning of revolutionary words and make what is in fact "revolutionary" into something that is counterrevolutionary, it is no longer either safe or meaningful to quote

5. Tung Kan, "Yao Wen-yuan's Pipedream," *People's Daily,* November 22, 1976, Foreign Broadcast Information Service, *Daily Report – People's Republic of China,* December 1, 1976, p. E7.

6. Ibid.

7. Ibid.

revolutionary texts, regardless of whether they belong to the history of Communism or of China.

The notion that words can be made to have quite different meanings than they should have is not inconsistent with the traditional Chinese awe of the power of words. Much of Chinese intellectual history has revolved around scholars seeking to illuminate the essence of particularly valued words, and the assumption always existed that wrong-headed scholars could misguide people and only the really wise man could see the truth in the mystery of key words. Indeed, instead of systematic philosophies, which would be analogous to ideological systems, traditional Chinese thought focused on making the most possible out of the analysis of particular characters, a practice not dissimilar to the current Chinese one of dwelling on esoteric words, spending hours analyzing cryptic sentences of Mao, and wondering whether correct thoughts and phrases are or are not being used.

In larger terms, the continuing factional strife has transformed the Chinese political system from one in which legitimacy was derived from a sacred ideology to one in which the right to rule emerges from a "market process" of power transactions. The decline in the place or sophistication of ideology should not be construed as a sign that the authority of the regime has in any way been weakened. On the contrary, the factional-strife process has probably provided the Chinese Communists with a stronger basis for regime legitimacy than the mystique of Marxism–Leninism–Mao Thought. Insofar as the outcome of factional conflicts at the local and provincial levels serves to bring to the top people who can effectively rule in their localities, the power of the central government has also been strengthened.

There is, of course, considerable uncertainty as to the extent to which Chinese leaders appreciate this transformation in the basis of their right to rule. Undoubtedly many leaders are anxious over the manifest decline in understanding in China, and they will probably try to recapture the magic of words. Their efforts, however, can only make the ideology ever more sterile and arcane. Other leaders will strive to make the basis of rule a more efficient administrative machine and will thus push China in the direction of becoming a bureaucratic polity. Certainly there is a strong tradition of hierarchical authority in Chinese culture that makes the ideal of an administrative state attractive to many, if not most, Chinese. And orderly and legitimate government means precisely just such a political command and control system to most Chinese.

Yet the realities of attempting to govern such a huge and diverse land suggest that the basis of legitimacy must ultimately be closer to a "market system" for allocating authority. Although the Chinese are unable to articulate the rationale for such a system of authority, are embarrassed about all manifestations of factionalism, and are clinging to other ideals about authority, they are moving in fact toward such a system.

THE EVILS (AND VIRTUES) OF MASKED REALITIES

To a remarkable degree, the accepted behavior associated with factional struggles lies at the polar extremes of contemplation and violent actions, a combination that reflects Chinese anxieties about aggression.

In their responses to factional conflicts, the Chinese Communists combine what in most cultures are widely separated activities – scholarly study and the movements of warfare. Attacks on a faction can be mounted by appeals for more "study," "deeper analysis," or "careful examination of the thoughts of Mao Zedong," all of which would suggest the need for contemplation and almost academic conduct. But attacks can also call for extraordinarily physical activities and the kinds of tactical moves associated with battlefield situations.

The campaign against Deng Xiaoping in the last year of Mao's life involved both of these approaches. A correspondent for the *People's Daily* wrote an article entitled "Only Through Penetrating Study Can We Deepen the Criticism of Deng Xiaoping," in which every paragraph stressed the theme that "studying" was a way to damage Deng and his ilk.[8] Since Deng himself had written nothing that could be studied, it was necessary, as Nan Yu pointed out, to study articles that were "big poisonous weeds, concocted under his inspiration."[9] In particular, people were called upon to "study carefully" the "Outline of a Working Report by the Academy of Science," in which Deng was supposed to have been exceptionally interested: "The moment he saw its original draft he repeatedly shouted, 'Bravo!' "[10]

The notion that one can damage another faction through studying stems, of course, from the Communist belief in the importance of ideology. In the Chinese case there are two additional concepts – first, that "studying the thoughts of Mao" can provide power through reveal-

8. Foreign Broadcast Information Service, *Daily Report – People's Republic of China,* June 24, 1976.

9. Nan Yu, "Teng Hsiao-p'ing's Opposition to 'Ultra-Left' Means Opposition to Revolution," *Survey of People's Republic of China Press,* No. 6146, July 29, 1976, p. 202.

10. The Mass Criticism Group of Futan University's Science Department, "A Counter-Revolutionary Revisionist Outline," *Survey of People's Republic of China Press,* No. 6146, July 29, 1976, p. 195.

ing correct solutions, and second, that careful study can unmask the deceptions inherent in the words of an enemy faction or a disgraced leader.

Indeed, this latter concept reveals a great deal about Chinese perceptions of how factions conduct themselves. It is necessary to "study" carefully the words of the disgraced, precisely because such statements may appear on the surface to be entirely correct ideologically, sound in reasoning, and based on accurate facts, while in fact they mask "sinister" purposes.

The importance the Chinese attach to deception provides a link between the apparently unrelated approaches of studying and warfare tactics. Much of Chinese analysis of tactical maneuvers revolves around ways of unmasking the deceptions of others and protecting one's own surprise moves.

The Chinese conception of competing factions acting militarily is well illustrated in an article in the *Xinhua Daily* of Nanjing entitled "The 'Gang' Tried to Seize Power During Confusion." It begins with the basic Chinese theme that evil forces will emerge during conditions of chaos and disorder. "In poking their noses into Jiangsu and creating chaos in Jiangsu, the Gang of Four were actually applying their counter-revolutionary tactics of seizing power through confusion. This was iron-clad proof of their counterrevolutionary crimes of attempting to usurp Party and state power and restore capitalism." (The lack of any explicit explanation from one sentence to the next follows a form of Chinese logic that is as old as Confucius.) The article then follows the Chinese classical essay form of making eight points, all of which reflect the themes of deception and military tactical maneuvers, in describing what the Gang tried to do in Jiangsu:

1. Deceive their superiors, bully those under them, and attack people at will.
2. Form cliques to pursue their own selfish interests.
3. Establish a sinister line to facilitate their command.
4. Operate bases and support strongholds.
5. Attack from both the South and North while breaking through the center.
6. Make trouble and false charges.
7. Oppose the all-out efforts to criticize revisionism and capitalism and build socialism and try to pull down the red banner of Dazhai and disrupt the movement.
8. Launch deathbed struggle and mad counterattack.[11]

11. Foreign Broadcast Information Service, *Daily Report—People's Republic of China*, February 1, 1977, p. G1.

Study and struggle, analysis and fighting are all necessary because nothing is what it seems to be, and every act can mask evil intentions. The Chinese belief in the great importance of deception in human affairs also points to the underlying Chinese cultural concern with the motives of aggression. Many Chinese cultural and socialization practices are directed toward repressing all manifestations of aggression. The psychological reaction to this repression is the diffuse introduction of the themes of aggression in all manner of situations – much as the repression of sexuality in Western culture encourages the surfacing of sexual nuances in functionally unrelated areas. Since Chinese culture places so much stress on "masking" aggression, it is not surprising that the Chinese tend to suspect that danger and hostility always lurk just below the surface. Consequently, there can be scheming behind such placid activities as "studying," and little discrimination is made between purposeful violence and random acts of violence – they are both manifestations of aggression.

In criticizing opponents' behavior, it is not necessary to suggest any precise purpose for which alleged violence might be used; it is enough to say that the others have engaged in violent acts. In spite of all the years of Mao Zedong's efforts to change Chinese attitudes about conflict and disorder and the extraordinary use of the Cultural Revolution to change Chinese political culture,[12] it is clear that the Chinese continue to see all acts of violence and troublemaking as reprehensible.

The First Secretary of the Shandong Provincial Committee, in describing how as early as 1973 and 1974 the Gang of Four had "tried to establish ties independent of the Party Committee," reported that the Gang had worked through a "handful of persons" who sought to "make trouble in various meetings, engaging in beating, smashing and looting . . . thus seriously damaging revolution and production."[13] Although in the rest of his report the First Secretary was extremely precise in explaining the significance of even the most obvious points, he apparently did not feel that his readers needed to know who was being "beaten" and "smashed" and in what context.

At the other extreme, a wall poster in Fuzhou declared that Jiang Qing had "dispatched a trusted subordinate to Fujian to enlist the support of Pi Ting-chun [the commander of the Foochow Military Region]. Pi gave

12. Lowell Dittmer goes so far as to argue that the "central purpose of the Cultural Revolution was to transform China's political culture, to achieve the same sort of 'revolutionary breakthrough' in the cultural sphere that had already been achieved in the military–political and socio-economic realms." ("Thought Reform and the Cultural Revolution: An Analysis of the Symbolism of Chinese Polemics," *American Political Science Review*, Vol. LXII, No. 1, March 1977, p. 67.)

13. Tsinan, Shantung Provincial Radio, February 1, 1977, in Foreign Broadcast Information Service, *Daily Report – People's Republic of China*, February 1977, p. G9.

no affirmative answer, but made a telephone call to Xu Shiyou, commander of the Canton Military Region, soliciting Xu's opinion. Jiang Qing learned of this and secretly sent her men to kill Pi by installing a time-bomb in Pi's special plane."[14] One might assume that such a revelation would become the dominant charge against the Gang in Fujian, but in fact most of the provincial reports were content to speak vaguely of diffuse and anarchical acts of violence at the time. The assumption seems to be that acts of violence, whether purposeful or merely random, are equally manifestations of evil conduct, since all forms of violence represent unacceptable expressions of aggression.

We must, however, note again that this undifferentiated treatment of violence extends all the way to the opposite pole, so that an activity such as studying can be assumed to mask just as vicious purposes as does physical violence. The regime's attack on the ideological journal *Study and Criticism*, published in Shanghai from September 1973 until, as the *Peking Review* says, it "conked out" with the collapse of the Gang of Four in October 1976, illustrates how the Chinese easily relate aggressive impulses and hostile acts to the manipulation of ideas and arrive at the conclusion that words can be as destructive as physical violence.

According to the *Peking Review*, the "Gang's journal," *Study and Criticism*, "under the signboard of studying philosophy and social science," engaged in "distorting facts, confounding right and wrong, and concocting rumors, . . . [and] spread a lot of political venom," so that in the end "it served as a tool for the Gang to usurp Party and state leadership."[15] The causal connection between "confusion" and the realization of power is the use of deception – specifically using "the ancient to satirize the present," "past events to disparage the present," and other forms of innuendo to damage others and thus achieve "evil purposes." The *Peking Review* gives two examples of how presumably great damage was done by subtle innuendo. "In the autumn of 1973 Yao Wenyuan made a long-distance telephone call from Peking to his trustees . . . divulging the Party Central Committee's plans to deepen the criticism of Lin Biao through the criticism of Confucius, and instructed them to write an article criticizing a prime minister of the Qin Dynasty (212–206 B.C.). . . . As soon as the article was published, Yao Wenyuan ordered the journal *Hongqi* to reprint it so as to spread it throughout the country. Later, on orders from Jiang Qing to 'criticize prime ministers', this mouthpiece of the gang churned out a series of critical articles against prime ministers of the past, euphemistically attacking Premier Zhou."[16]

---

14. Foreign Broadcast Information Service, *Daily Report – People's Republic of China*, March 11, 1977, p. G3.

15. *Peking Review*, July 15, 1977, No. 29 pp., 26 and 31–32.

16. Ibid.

Later, by merely carrying an "article about the workers' armed force," *Study and Criticism* succeeded, in the eyes of the *Peking Review*, in helping to carry out the Gang's "plot" to "turn the militia into a 'second armed force' directly under its command to counter the People's Liberation Army and make it instrumental to its usurping Party and state power."[17] It is unquestionably true that the radicals hoped that building up the militia would give them a better opportunity for political survival after the death of Mao, but any realistic evaluation of the potential of the people's militia could only have concluded that such a force could never have challenged the PLA. It could only have been politically significant if there were to be tests of force at levels of violence far below those at which the PLA itself would have been involved; indeed, the test would have to be so unthreatening to public order as not to have provoked the PLA into action.

The acceptance by Chinese political thinkers that esoteric arguments and wishful idealization of the militia can be serious power threats suggests that the Chinese are still culturally sensitive to any manifestations of aggression. This basic cultural fact stands in the way of a more open acknowledgment that conflicts and adversary relationships are not only legitimate but also must become increasingly the basis for the legitimacy necessary for ruling a modernizing country.

The importance of consensus in Chinese politics stands in striking contradiction to the inevitable increase in conflicts of interest that development will bring. Therefore, we can confidently forecast that the Chinese will continue to have great anxieties over what other cultures accept as normal and routine factional conflicts. Even as they use such conflicts to find the necessary leadership links to legitimize their rule, the Chinese will seek to sweep their existence under the carpet. The continued fear of factionalism will only be matched by gnawing suspicions that others must be masking their factional designs.

Although the general suspicion is that evil forces practice the masking of realities, it is not unknown for the virtuous to call for deceptive ploys. Thus, for example, a columnist championing Deng's and Zhao's campaign against the "whatever faction" in 1980 told the story of how Cao Cao, a powerful general at the end of the Han period, praised his military advisor Xun You as being "hopelessly stupid" because he was always "outwardly stupid but inwardly wise, outwardly timid but inwardly brave, outwardly weak but inwardly strong." Therefore, "there are people who can match him in wisdom but no one can match him in stupidity." The moral of the piece was that enthusiastic cadres were overly anxious to show cleverness in their understanding of the new leadership's new

17. Ibid.

policies, and that while there is no need in today's China to "act like Xun You who was 'worldly wise and played it safe', not to mention acting like a smooth and slick 'gentleman who tries not to offend anybody'," there would be no harm if cadres were to "keep calm" when listening to other points of view.[18]

THE DESTRUCTIVE POWER OF WORDS

In Chinese factional politics, verbal attacks rather than constructive themes are usually most effective for mobilizing power.

In all political systems the increase of power for some actors usually implies that the relative power of others must be reduced. This is generally only tacitly acknowledged, and therefore the ratio of positive and constructive statements about one's own side to negative statements about one's opponent can be high. In Chinese factional politics, however, the ratio is the other way around, for it is more openly assumed that power can only be gained at the expense of another, and thus to get ahead one must be destructive. Idealized statements about utopian goals are only useful as expressions of the consensus of the moment.

As we have already observed, the Chinese are inclined to express aggression through the written word rather than orally. Thus, published statements are likely to be more extreme than spoken words. Few cultures grant the power of the pen a more exalted status than do the Chinese. The printed word or the publicly displayed written slogan has consistently commanded great attention and cannot be easily ignored.

Thus it is not surprising that a major function of the media in the Chinese political process is to provide a vehicle for vilifying and hence "destroying" individuals. In pouring out venom against targets of abuse, Chinese writers are not only expressing the fury of their moral indignation; they also seem absolutely convinced that words of slander can truly demolish a person.

This view is closely associated with the cardinal importance of shaming in the Chinese socialization process.[19] Traditionally, parents freely practiced both teasing and shaming in disciplining children, and under Communism there seems to be even more use of shaming in schools and in criticism sessions. The Chinese have a genuine appreciation of the hor-

18. Zhang Nan, "On the Hopeless Stupidity of Xun You," *Wanbao*, November 22, 1980, in Foreign Broadcast Information Service, *Daily Report–People's Republic of China*, December 10, 1980, pp. L21–L22.

19. For a discussion of "shame" in Chinese culture, see Francis L. K. Hsu, *Under the Ancestor's Shadow*, Columbia University Press, New York, 1948; and Lucian W. Pye, *The Spirit of Chinese Politics*, M.I.T. Press, Cambridge, Mass., 1968.

ror of being singled out for public scorn. Indeed, they have, to repeat, reversed the old Western adage so that it reads, "Sticks and stones may break my bones, but words can utterly shatter me."

Over the years, in every campaign against discredited leaders, the media have been used not only to report on their crimes but actually to destroy them. And often the targets of vituperation will be charged with having used words to harm others and to weaken the "people." For example, the Ministry of Culture Criticism Group, in "Sometimes Shrilling, Sometimes Moaning – On Chu Lan's Big Poisonous Weed," declared that "big careerist Zhang Chunqiao" had a "new plan to kill people with the pen," and Chu Lan's "hack writers group" had been "holding the pen and sharpening the sword to rabidly hack the Party and the People."[20]

At times the Chinese seem to believe literally tnat spoken woras can in themselves kill, or at least that it is not necessary to prove that anything other than spoken words were used as the instrument that caused death. In the theater of political vendetta of the so-called "trial" of the Gang of Four and Lin Biao's alleged co-conspirators, Chen Boda, Mao's former secretary, was accused of "causing the death of 2,955 people and the persecution of 84,000 by giving a speech attacking a provincial party organization," but ". . . the prosecution gave no indication [as to] how the speech could have led to the alleged excesses."[21]

Media attacks are by no means used solely against top leaders who are in the process of being removed by the Central Committee. On the contrary, the lesser figures are generally the ones most seriously damaged by such public revilements. Lower-level figures are usually more vulnerable because if they were not singled out for public criticism they might escape political destruction. Yet they are constantly caught up in media attacks because of the standard Chinese strategy of offensively "killing the horse to get the rider," that is, destroying the followers to bring down the principal figure, and the defensive tactic of "expending horses and carts to protect the general."

The Chinese belief in the destructive power of words can also be seen in their acceptance of the "dumb-waiter" principle, that is, if one rides to the top by a particular formulation of words, one will automatically crash to the bottom when that formulation is discredited. Merle Goldman has documented, for example, how Zhou Yang rose in power in the context of implied attacks on Lu Xun's literary tradition, and then, when the

---

20. Peking Radio, July 1977, in Foreign Broadcast Information Service, *Daily Report – People's Republic of China,* July 6, 1977, p. E14.

21. Fox Butterfield, "Revenge Seems to Outweigh Justice at Chinese Trials," *New York Times,* December 6, 1980, p. 2A.

time came for the fall of Zhou Yang, the same strategem was used to praise Lu Xun.[22]

At the beginning of the Cultural Revolution there were numerous examples of the extraordinary vulnerability of Chinese leaders to any form of public criticism. Although in the end he was physically destroyed, Liu Shaoqi initially seemed to be numbed by the experience of being criticized in public by people he considered to be his inferiors.[23] Needless to say, the treatment the Red Guards meted out to those they would destroy, even when limited to verbal attacks, was hardly comparable to press criticism of public figures in other countries. Yet it is safe to say that current practices make China a country in which political figures can rise to the top and experience only praise and never the trauma of insult from a critical press. Whereas those who seek power in most countries must learn to live with varying degrees of public criticism, Chinese leaders do not have to pass through this form of hardening experience (they, of course, have other forms), and this may help to explain why Chinese officials seem to be among the world's most hypersensitive to suggestions of criticism of themselves or their country.

The Chinese perception of the destructive power of words and their horror of printed criticism were repeatedly revealed during the Peking show trials of the Gang of Four and the followers of Lin Biao. One of the principal charges against Chen Boda, which dominated one day's television reporting of the trial, was that Chen had written a June 1, 1966, editorial for the *Renmin Ribao* entitled "Sweep Away All Monsters," in which he had "sharply criticized honored cadres." In the same trial, Yao Wenyuan was forced to admit that he had supervised the writing of the *Red Flag* article "From Bourgeois Democrats to Capitalist Roaders," and when he tried to exonerate himself by claiming that his revisions had "lowered the tone" of the article, his "crafty trick was immediately refuted" by the prosecutor, who showed that he had "branded veteran cadres as 'old-line capitalist roaders'."

WORDS CAN UNMASK DEMONIC POWERS

The Chinese feeling for the destructive power of words is fundamentally linked to an old cultural sentiment that holds that what is

22. Merle Goldman, "The Fall of Chou Yang," *The China Quarterly*, No. 27, July–September 1966, pp. 132–148.

23. For Liu Shiao-chi's first attempts at refuting Red Guard criticisms, see Lowell Dittmer, *Liu Shiao-ch'i and the Chinese Cultural Revolution*, University of California Press, Berkeley, 1974.

hidden is usually bad, and that evil (as well as good) forces are constantly engaging in deception, but they can be utterly destroyed if unmasked.

These basic sentiments were appropriately revealed in an editorial in the *People's Daily* of June 20, 1966, that praised the introduction of wall posters at the beginning of the Cultural Revolution:

> Chairman Mao Zedong says: "Posters written in big characters are an extremely useful new type of weapon."
> The revolutionary big-character posters are very good!
> They are a monster detector to unmask the monsters and demons of all kinds.[24]

Chinese legends from *Monkey* to *The Woman Warrior* are filled with stories of ghosts and spirits who assume different guises and it is the task of heroes to unmask them and hence destroy their potency. The psychological dynamics of the power of unmasking seem to be related to the power of shaming in Chinese culture, which we have already noted. To be unmasked is to be stripped of the protective shield that comes from conforming to one's expected role. Thus, one who has experienced the humiliation of shame has also learned the destructive consequences of being unmasked.

Similarly, in Chinese politics motives are easily suspect. One must always be especially on guard against the tricks of the incorrigible, the "bourgeoisie," "former landlords," "feudal remnants," and "rich peasants" – people who can be just about anyone born after "Liberation." The Chinese political imagination permits the belief that individuals who have never owned land, had riches, or owned the material possessions associated in all other societies with a bourgeois lifestyle can somehow secretly, behind their mask of merely wishing "to serve the people," take on all the attributes of roles that were objectively destroyed a generation ago in China.

Cultures that place great importance on shaming as part of their socialization processes also tend in their legends to exploit the fantasy potentials of people becoming invisible or changing their guises. It is easy to appreciate the advantages of being able to become invisible or to change one's appearance and form in such cultures, but since the ability to do so is beyond the reach of "good" people, it is usually the "evil" ones who are most successful at it. Since Chinese culture is so shame-oriented, it is not surprising that in their political rhetoric they give free

24. Quoted in "Quarterly Chronicle and Documents," *China Quarterly*, No. 27, July–September 1966, p. 211.

play to the idea that people, especially "bad" persons, are not always what they appear to be.

The task of unmasking is never easy, because of the trickery of the evil ones, who rarely reveal their true intentions. Indeed, manifest behavior is always suspect, since it is well known that the foe practices "Waving the Red Flag to Oppose the Red Flag." Did not both Lin Biao and the Gang of Four appear to be "leftists" and "radicals" when in fact they were "ultra-rightists?" But vigilance pays off: For example, the Gang of Four could not completely hide their "sinister plans." They failed to "adhere to Lu Xun's revolutionary admonition to 'beat the drowning dog in the water,' but instead they advocated 'pointing the spearhead upward,' which could only mean that they would point the spearhead toward Chairman Mao Zedong himself."

The act of unmasking consists essentially of, first, detecting devious motives and, second, applying a new label to the person. Just as the Chinese have turned traditional Marxism on its head by stressing human willpower over objective historical forces, so they have replaced objective class categories with subjectively defined class labels. The fact that China was pathetically devoid of a significant middle class has been conveniently ignored by the simple device of inventing implausible numbers of imaginary bourgeoisie. If China in fact had had anywhere near the numbers of bourgeoisie, landlords, and rich peasants that the media have unmasked over the years, it would have been a remarkably rich country, regardless of income distribution.

In fact, however, the application of labels in the unmasking of opponents is a demonstration of the Chinese belief in the destructive power of words and not proof of objective sociological realities. Needless to say, the labels employed by the Chinese media have shattering powers.

In Chinese political culture there is a presumption that evil people will be devious merely for deviousness' sake. For example, Yao Wenyuan has been charged with helping to establish the theoretical journal *Study and Criticism* in Shanghai when he already controlled *Red Flag* in Peking. He then, in a "sneaky" and "wholeheartedly bad way," arranged for articles to be written for *Study and Criticism* that he later reprinted in the nationally established *Red Flag,* which was "completely under his editorial control."[25] When a Chinese ambassador, who was a member of a touring delegation visiting the United States, was asked why Yao Wenyuan had to follow such an indirect procedure when he was said to control *Red Flag* directly, the Chinese diplomat was nonplussed by the innocence of the American who could not instantly appreciate that the

25. *Peking Review,* No. 26, July 15, 1977, pp. 26 and 31–32.

"proof" of Yao's "sneakiness" lay precisely in his roundabout procedure in not straightforwardly publishing in *Red Flag*.

THE LIMITS OF CONSTRUCTIVE POWER IN WORDS

In Chinese politics the positive use of words is largely limited to making predictions of future states of affairs, the means for attainment of which need not be explained. In contrast to their certainty about the destructive power of words, Chinese leaders reveal considerable doubts about whether the converse holds, that is, whether the media can be used constructively to build power. This does not mean that the Chinese have not tried to use the media in this way; for example, they once used the media to build up the image of Hua Guofeng as the worthy successor to Mao Zedong, who, of course, was in his time ceaselessly extolled by all China's media. But the uninspired accounts of Chairman Hua's bland visits to communes, factories, and conferences had more the quality of dutiful acts of ritualized homage than efforts to maximize political power. The unspoken assumption seems to be that if Hua is to consolidate his power, it will not be because of any magic in the media's use of words but rather through his actual political acts. And, of course, over the years the Chinese media have, with unimaginative determination, sought to generate an illusion of power for a series of improbable foreigners, who have nonetheless remained unimportant figures. Peking's thousands of words of praise for Australia's E. F. Hill have not altered anyone's view, except possibly Mr. Hill's, that he is anything more than the leader of a trivial party with laughable revolutionary pretensions.

The one positive approach in which the Chinese do seem to have confidence is the making of attractive predictions in which the stress is entirely on the end and little attention need be given to the intended means for achieving the goals.

The symbolic importance of issues as a means of determining partisan identification encourages the Chinese to adopt postures not just about immediate matters but, more comfortably, about future ones. As a result, Chinese politics are filled with predictions about the future that are taken as having an extraordinary degree of concreteness and certainty. When, for example, Chinese leaders speak about the Soviet threat, the certainty of World War III, or any of the Four Modernizations, they deal not with specific scenarios but with matters of faith that serve as tests for determining supporters and identifying enemies. It is true that since the announcement of the Four Modernizations, and more particularly since the proclamation of "the three years of economic readjustment," the Chinese press has been filled with articles forecasting specific developments in different policy areas, but it is usually difficult to distinguish between wishful thinking, trial balloons, code-word maneuverings, and the impending introductions of firm policies.

Statements abound about what China, or the world, or particular parts of the world will be like in the future, not because Chinese leaders need to make more long-range policy decisions than other leaders, but because the very abstract and stark character of long-range predictions makes them a fine vehicle for the testing of loyalties and opinions. Agreement or disagreement about what the future holds thus becomes a useful device for judging how close leaders are to each other.

Needless to say, the inherent problem of foreseeing the future does tend to encourage a blending of wishfulness and solid judgment that necessarily amplifies the possibilities for differences of opinion. Chinese leaders, like all politicians, seek to discount the future and position themselves in what they expect will be the most favorable situation possible when that "future" arrives. They also strive for popularity by predicting what they consider the people most want for the future.

One factor running against this general proposition is the rising cynicism of the Chinese population, which has been exposed to unrelenting exhortation about the glorious future for thirty years. In the post-Gang of Four era, it is clearer than ever before that the Chinese publicists have far greater vitality and enthusiasm when they are attacking enemies than when they are trying to be constructive.

Some leaders, including Deng Xiaoping, are highly imaginative about the probabilities of change and have positive sentiments toward it, and they naturally attract similar people to themselves. Other leaders, as Mao was in his last years, are equally imaginative about the probabilities of change but they abhor what they foresee. Other leaders, such as Chen Yun, seem to welcome the notion that "necessity" will require change, while still others, like Hua, will insist that political steadfastness can overcome all concepts of "necessity."

It should be noted, however, that unlike the situation in Western politics, the principal axis for differentiating the attitudes of leaders is not the continuum from maintaining the status quo to advocating complete change—from conservative to liberal or radical. All Chinese leaders want both change and continuity in policies; they differ only in the particular changes they want. (The "radicals," it should be remembered, worried most about change after Mao's death, demanding that the Party should "adhere to the principles laid down," and even before that they wanted to preserve and return to a form of "purity" of an earlier phase in the Party's history.) This tendency reinforces a cardinal point about Chinese politics that we have made several times earlier: Policy differences are less significant than personnel questions. The sharpest division in Chinese politics is usually between those who wish to preserve the status quo of office holders, irrespective of policies, and those who wish for changes in personnel.

The Chinese practice of idealizing the future, sharply divorced from present realities, is consistent with their practice of assuming an almost magical relationship between past and present. Sudden and almost complete transformations are accepted as commonplace. Past, present, and future are stark alternatives, between which miraculous physical or objective transformations can take place; but politically, such near magic is significant only for inspiring awe and affecting the much more vital realm of subjective attitudes. The relationship between past and present is thus a series of "befores and afters"–before Liberation and after Liberation, before the Cultural Revolution and after, before the fall of the Gang of Four and after–in which instant and near-total transformations happen without a clear explanation of cause and effect beyond the occurrence of the dramatic event that divides past from present.

Although the acceptance of such magical transformations was exaggerated by Mao's voluntarism and his stress upon willpower, this tendency is not likely to disappear with his passing. Even under more "pragmatic" leaders, the Chinese will continue to adhere to their code of secrecy about the current operations of politics, and hence the future will continue to seem to be only vaguely related to the present. To the degree that the Chinese accept the legitimacy of secrecy, they also reaffirm the correctness of treating predictions about the future as subject matter for partisan concern.

Indeed, precisely because of the strong taboos about discussing explicitly current realities, Chinese political discourse is biased in favor of elaborating on either the sins of the past or the potentialities of the future. And this bias works against the analysis of objective cause and effect relationships and in favor of wishful thinking about the future and moral condemnation of the past.

Chapter 11

The Present and the Future

The combination of the inevitable succession struggle following the passing of such a major figure as Mao Zedong and the commitment of the new leadership to a new course of national development helped bring the existence of factionalism to the surface of Chinese politics. In concluding this book, it is fair to ask whether factionalism may not be a passing phenomenon. Given Deng Xiaoping's remarkable success in twice rehabilitating himself and then forcing Hua Guofeng to "resign," both the premiership and the chairmanship, will the power struggles come to an end? Is it possible that in time the new leadership will succeed in its ambitions to suppress factions?

The answer would seem to be that factionalism is likely to become more and not less a feature of Chinese politics. As we have frequently noted throughout this book, factionalism appears to originate from certain basic features of Chinese culture and personality. Furthermore, the processes of modernization are likely to exacerbate those tensions that facilitate the formation of factions. Although Mao Zedong struggled to change Chinese culture, his efforts seem only to have intensified those features that give rise to factions.

Thus, in considering the future of factionalism in Chinese politics, we shall first examine Mao's legacy and then summarize some of the basic values of Chinese political culture that will continue to shape the formation of factions.

MAO'S LEGACY

Mao Zedong left an ambiguous legacy as to the legitimacy of factions and the need for domestic enemies. Mao's personal fascination with "contradictions" and his tolerance for "struggle" and intra-Party conflicts have left the Chinese uncertain as to the proper attitude toward both intra-Party conflict and Party discipline. While Mao was alive he was the ultimate arbiter as to when internal conflicts had gone too far and what forms of antagonisms were or were not legitimate. Since his death, his heirs have been left with an ambiguous legacy of contradictory dicta. On the one hand there are all of his statements in praise of conflict and of "going against the tide," while on the other hand there is his message to the Party, "Practice Marxism, not revisionism; unite, don't split; be open and above-board, and don't intrigue and conspire."

In the post-Mao years, different leaders have used different quotations to justify their factional interest, a practice that in turn has been denounced, but also for factional advantage. Yue Xiao, for example, in an article on the "Theory of Factional Activities," said that some people in organizing "wild attacks on the Kwangtung Provincial CCP Committee" went so far as to "blatantly distort Chairman Mao's words, babbling, 'The existence of factions within the Party is a constant phenomenon', and [thereby] attempting in vain to legitimize their illegal factional activities within the Party."[1] Yue then went on to question the logic in so using Mao's words: "We want to ask several persons in our province who claim to be the opposition within the Party: 'You held that since an opposition within the Party objectively exists, that means that it is legitimate, and so you must be allowed to pursue factional activities; but, persons who carry out conspiracies also objectively exist. Do you also hold that to carry out conspiracies is legitimate? If you want to persist in such absurd logic you will certainly fall into an anti-Party mire'."[2] Yue Xiao himself had no doubts as to where such logic leads: "The several persons in Kwangtung recognized only the gang and the faction, not the Party," and therefore "they went in for conspiracy, practiced intrigues, and were very sneaky."[3]

The same Yue Xiao in another article entitled "A Reactionary Slogan Which Invites Anarchism – Refuting 'To Direct the Spearhead Upward Is the Correct Main Orientation'," pointed out that those who used some

---

1. Yue Xiao, "The Reactionary Logic of Forming a Gang and Usurping the Party – Refuting the So-called 'Theory of the Legitimacy of Factional Activities Within the Party,'" Canton Provincial Radio, 23 March 1977, in Foreign Broadcast Information Service, *Daily Report – People's Republic of China*, March 29, 1977, p. H5.

2. Ibid.

3. Ibid., p. H6.

of Mao's slogans were producing anarchy: "To wave the banner of rebelling and going against the tide in order to make trouble were . . . the tricks of those several people in our province who want to cause disorder in Kwangtung and disrupt the provincial CCP Committee. Who was rebelled against? What tide was resisted? They had their gang's words, which were 'To direct the spearhead upward is the correct main orientation'. This is a typical reactionary slogan which invites anarchism and was the conductor's baton waved by the Gang of Four to conspire to usurp Party and state power."[4] He went on to state that the Gang ". . . were also steeped in the idea of 'going against the tide', vigorously incited anarchism and attempted in vain to paralyze CCP committees at all levels. . . . Did they not clamor: 'If we do not create a little chaos, the provincial CCP Committee will not be shaken and we cannot be successful'? [They sought to create] anarchism and seize power, win victory and mount the stage amid the chaos."[5]

It is significant that while Mao Zedong clearly welcomed the emotional release associated with conflict and *luan*, he was peculiarly blind to the possibility that conflicts could become institutionalized into polarized factions, something that he abhorred. We know that during the Cultural Revolution, Mao, speaking to representatives of two polarized factions, expressed puzzlement as to why they should have become divided into factions: "There is no fundamental clash of interests within the working class. Why should they split into two big irreconcilable organizations? I don't understand it; some people are pulling strings. This is invariably the result of the manipulations of capitalist roaders."[6]

During the first months after Guo Peng and Wang Dongxing had been persuaded by Ye Jianying to arrest Jiang Qing and her three associates, but before the rehabilitation of Deng Xiaoping, the new leadership had a most difficult time dealing with Mao's statements, particularly as they related to factionalism. While Hua's entire claim to legitimacy rested upon treating as sacrosanct one of Mao's last statements, "With you in charge, I am at ease," he would have liked to dispose of such other quotes as "You are making socialist revolution and yet you don't know where the bourgeoisie is. It is right in the Communist Party – those in power taking the capitalist road." Just before her arrest, Jiang Qing had revived Mao's dictum about where the bourgeoisie was – since it seemed to damn Deng who had been labeled "a capitalist roader who would reverse correct verdicts" – and had also linked Mao's words to the proposition

4. Ibid.

5. Ibid., p. H7.

6. "Chairman Mao's Later Supreme Instructions During His Inspection Tour," *Cheng-fa hung-ch'i (Politics and Law Red Flag*, Canton, combined issues Nos. 3–4, October 17, 1967, quoted in Dittmer, op. cit., p. 81.

that "Veteran cadres inevitably become capitalist roaders," a clear reference to the old Party members, such as Ye Jianying and Li Xiannian, who had survived the Cultural Revolution.[7]

If the problem of Mao's words had been limited to the issues associated with the smashing of the Gang of Four, the problem would not have been particularly serious. But less than a year after the arrest of the Four, it was apparent that the legacy of Mao's quotations was going to create divisions among the new leadership. The aged Ye Jianying, in explaining how delicate the situation was, is reported to have said, "The Gang was like a rat beside an agate plate; if you should spring a surprise on the rat, you might have shattered the plate itself."[8] The imagery of the Gang as a rat was standard form at the time; more significant was his sense that the Party was as delicate and fragile as an agate plate.

Veteran cadres who had survived the Cultural Revolution and its aftermath were the most ready to put aside the game of using Mao's words in Party debates; those associated with Hua and Wang still had some interest in maintaining the importance of Mao's words, Hua because his legitimacy depended upon it and Wang because he physically controlled Mao's papers. Surprisingly, at the time, the rehabilitated cadres associated with Deng also had an interest in those quotes that legitimized intra-Party conflict and hence their struggle to reclaim power. Thus it was Deng's supporters who in the summer of 1977 revived Mao's statement, "Outside the Party there are other parties; inside there are groupings. This has always been the case." The *Liberation Army Daily*, which at the time was answerable to Marshal Ye, who was seeking to keep a lid on further factionalism, boldly stated that the Mao remark meant, "We should never allow . . . factionalism . . . to exist legitimately" in the Party.[9]

These struggles over Mao's legacy and the need to turn words around in the aftermath of the smashing of the Gang of Four seem to have done more to compromise Mao's image than did the shifts in substantive policies associated with the Four Modernizations. As our Hong Kong respondents repeatedly explained, the more detailed the charges against

7. For a typical example of the convoluted forms of agreement that had to take place at the time because of the legacy of Mao quotes, see Hsiang Chun, "A Complete Reversal of the Relations Between Ourselves and the Enemy," *Peking Review*, No. 14, April 1, 1977, pp. 6–12.

8. *Ming Pao*, Hong Kong, 29 May 1977, Foreign Broadcast Information Service, *Daily Report – People's Republic of China*, May 31, 1977, p. E2.

9. "Fifth Installment of the *Liberation Army Daily's* Series on the Gang's Crimes," Foreign Broadcast Information Service, *Daily Report – People's Republic of China*, July 6, 1977, p. E5.

the Gang of Four, the more it seemed to them that Mao himself was in fact the target of the criticism. Many went further and said that they had to conclude that if Mao could be cited by all sides, he could not have represented anything very substantial.

- A young man who had spent two years in Peking after the Cultural Revolution explained, "I really had to rethink everything after they announced that Lin Biao had turned against Mao. Why should Lin and Mao disagree? They both believed in the Cultural Revolution, or so I thought. They were both supposed to be heavy revolutionaries, but then they, the Party, said Lin was a 'revisionist'. If Lin could be a revisionist, then why couldn't Mao be one? Especially after he welcomed Kissinger and Nixon. Then they began to attack the Gang of Four, but how were the Four any different from Mao himself? Nobody in China, even in the most backward commune, can fail to see that Mao Zedong stood for all that the Gang of Four stood for; the Gang was strong until he died and then it collapsed – Mao was the Gang of Four. People now say it was really a Gang of Five, but really it was only a Gang of One. After all the arguing after the smashing of the Gang of Four it is clear that all the excitement is about only one thing and that is that Mao was a fool. They attack the Gang of Four, but really they are only afraid to say what they believe and that is that it was Mao who did all the crimes."
- A young girl from Canton now training to be a nurse said, "I spent many tens of thousands of hours reading Mao's thoughts, and I know that they are the same as what the Gang of Four believed and not the same as Deng Xiaoping's. Now they can all argue about what Mao said, but it is all meaningless."
- A former construction worker observed, "They still believe that it is important to have Mao on their side, but they are just pretending. Only old people who worry about death care about Mao's thoughts any more." We asked, "But people in China don't make fun of Mao, do they?" and he replied, "Of course not; but people don't make fun of old people, they don't laugh out loud at the gods or at Confucius, even though they don't believe in them."

Although these sentiments may seem too extreme to be relevant for analysis of the ongoing politics of China, they were uttered with little passion, as merely routine descriptions of the self-evident. And reports from those with first-hand experience in China's leading cities suggest that the mood of much of China's youth is similar to the mood expressed by these respondents. Mao's legacy, which has ensured the continuation of factionalism, has left China with barely a ritualistic consensus; but since the Chinese know the importance of upholding consensus, this facade is adequate for the needs of social and political respectability, even if not for devoted belief.

VICTIMS AS PERSECUTORS: DENG'S TRIUMPH OVER HUA

The dynamics of settling scores tends to ensure a continuous cycle of factionalism, for the past never disappears. Possibly the most vivid way to illustrate the manner in which past conflicts fuel new ones is to review the chronology of attempts to arrange stability in the Party since the death of Mao – each of which has been undermined by factional tensions.

The fact that the December 1980 trial by theater of the Gang of Four plus six (five generals associated with Lin Biao and Mao's secretary Chen Boda) coincided with Deng's final triumph over Hua meant that the world learned little about the circumstances surrounding the arrest of Jiang Qing and her three associates. Ironically, Hua was compelled to resign as Chairman purportedly because he was said to have been close to the "radicals" in 1976, yet it was he who must have ordered the arrest of the Four. The generally accepted version of what happened after Mao died on September 9 was that Jiang Qing sought to gain physical control of Mao's notes, which were under the guard of Mao's bodyguard, General Wang Dongxing. Presumably she intended to alter his words so as to further her interests and hence damage Hua. It seems that Marshal Ye Jianying was able to persuade Hua that he had to move decisively against the Four if he was to protect his claim to leadership, which rested on Mao's purported anointment of him.

After the arrest, Hua appeared to be secure in his dual posts of Premier and Chairman. He was the champion of all the Party members who had advanced during the Cultural Revolution, and he also had the support of many key veteran cadres. In April 1977 Deng, still purged, wrote Hua a letter praising his leadership and offering his support if rehabilitated. Other leaders apparently agreed with Hua that as a gesture of national reconciliation it would be safe to rehabilitate Deng and use his organizational and administrative talents.

After several months of behind-the-scenes negotiations, the leadership finally felt secure enough in July 1977 to hold the Third Plenary Session of the Tenth Party Congress, which was a meeting of unity and stability. Hua Guofeng was officially confirmed as Party Chairman, while Deng Xiaoping was rehabilitated and restored to his former posts after making a speech of modest self-criticism. Party unity seemed strong enough to convene the Eleventh Party Congress in August of the same year.

This meeting called for the creation of a new Politburo, which in turn starkly revealed the existence of three groups that soon were to become the bases of first three, and then four factions. Two of the five members of the Standing Committee of the Politburo, Chairman Hua Guofeng and General Wang Dongxing, represented cadres who had benefited from the Cultural Revolution and were therefore strongly supported by such Politburo members as Li Desheng, Chen Xilian, Wu De, Ji Dengkui, Ni Zhifu, and Chen Yonggui. The second pair of allies on the Standing Committee were Ye Jianying and Li Xiannian, who represented both the veteran cadres who had survived the Cultural Revolution and the military leadership. Finally, there was Deng without an ally on the Standing Committee but with potentially the largest following of Politburo members, since he could appeal to both veteran cadres and those who had been hurt by the Cultural Revolution.

During the next six months, Deng's followers became increasingly aggressive, calling for ever more thorough purging of the followers of the Gang of Four. Each wave of investigation came closer and closer, not only to the Hua supporters who had benefited from the Cultural Revolution, but also to the veteran cadres who had survived that ordeal and who now increasingly looked to Ye and Li. At this point, Deng's followers proclaimed the existence within the Party of the "swivel faction," the "wind faction," and the "fadeaway faction."

At the same time, Deng was vigorously rehabilitating cadres at all levels of the Party who had been purged during the Cultural Revolution. This campaign of rehabilitation alienated increasing numbers of veteran cadres from Deng and planted the seeds of new tensions. There is evidence that in many locations Hua's supporters joined in backing Deng's rehabilitation drive in order to turn the veteran cadres against Deng. Hua was, however, in an awkward situation: He still felt that his fortunes, and those of his followers, would be enhanced by a continuation of the old Maoist principle of "politics in command" rather than by allowing primacy to go to those skilled in economics and technical matters; yet, the more the political matters were stressed, the greater would be the search for "followers of the Gang of Four" and hence the greater the suspicion toward all who had survived or in any way benefited from the Cultural Revolution. Emphasis upon politics and ideology could thus be a two-edged sword.

It was in this atmosphere of tension that the Fifth National People's Congress was convened in February 1978 for what was supposed to be the ritual formalization of the compromise decisions of the Eleventh

Congress of the previous August. Yet in the six intervening months, Deng's faction had clearly outmaneuvered Hua's. The slogan of the day that was supposed to reflect a balanced compromise among the factions was "Class struggle, struggle for production, and scientific experimentation," but in practice the first theme was receiving little attention.[10]

By the end of February 1978, Deng had further improved his image as the ascending leader by becoming the Chairman of the Chinese People's Political Consultative Conference – an essentially theatrical event, but one that allowed for the representation of status differences. Hua's factions seemed to have been in decline, since Ye was made head of state under the new constitution at the First Session of the Fifth National People's Congress. Hua was still adhering to the somewhat absurd, but for him advantageous, view that Lin Biao and the Gang had been ultrarightists, which made cadres all down the hierarchy believe that it was still safest to be "leftist." Later in the spring, at the National Science Conference, Deng pointedly made it clear that he was not in agreement with Hua. By midsummer, Deng was encouraging great expectations about what science and technology could do for China, thus gaining the support of the Western-trained educators; and at the same time, he was dramatizing the escalating tensions with Vietnam. Hua was left with the troublesome but very basic problem of agriculture.

While Deng was being hailed abroad as China and the United States at last normalized relations, his position at home did slip a bit, and therefore he became anxious to formalize a new compromise favorable to his interests. In December 1978, at the very time that Vietnam was invading Cambodia and toppling the Peking-supported Pol Pot regime, the very important Third Plenary Session of the Eleventh Central Committee met and sought to negotiate a new balance among the leadership factions that would reflect the growth of Deng's influence. The decisions that came out of this meeting reflected both alliances and tradeoffs among the three principal factions of the leadership. The pro-Hua Cultural Revolutionist – but anti-Gang of Four – faction and the veteran cadres who had survived that turmoil were able to unite behind the decision that the Party should carry out the Four Modernizations but terminate the campaign against the Gang of Four. The tide, however, went with the pro-Deng forces: Chen Yun, who had been the economic czar behind the recovery from the disasters of the Great Leap, was rehabilitated and appointed to the Politburo and to its Standing Committee (thus briefly providing Deng with an ally). The decision on the Tien An Men Incident was reversed (which in effect cleared Deng's reputation

10. *People's Daily*, editorial, "Grasp the Three Great Revolutionary Movements Simultaneously," April 21, 1978.

and damaged that of Hua's ally, Wu De, who had been mayor of Peking at the time), and it was agreed that the Party should adhere to the principle of "seeking truth from facts."

Shortly after the meeting, all elements were praising the greatness of the Third Plenary Session of the Eleventh Central Committee but quietly attacking each other. In particular, the Deng forces were under attack, and they responded by speaking of an "adverse current" in the Party composed of a "whatever faction," who clung to whatever Mao said, and an "opposition faction" of bureaucrats who wished only to cling to their offices. Deng's forces were, of course, referring to those of Hua's supporters who still sought legitimacy based on Mao's statement, "With you in charge, I am at ease," and to the veteran cadres whose skill at the bureaucratic game had kept them in office throughout the Cultural Revolution and who had no intention of giving up power in more tranquil times.

The anti-Deng elements responded by suggesting that Deng was still campaigning against the Gang of Four as he continued to rehabilitate cadres, that his foreign policy was a disaster, especially after his "pedagogical war" with Vietnam, that he had encouraged anarchy by permitting the Democracy Wall, and that his contribution to the Four Modernizations was mainly "foolish big talk" and pretentious initiatives that had come to little. With the extraordinary Chinese aptitude for turning slogans around to damage their initial advocates, the anti-Deng elements used his "seek truth from facts" slogan to attack not the old ideologues, who saw reality in Mao thought, but the exuberant champions of the Four Modernizations, who used exaggerated rhetoric and thereby in their own way failed to find truth in reality.

By early spring 1979, not only were Deng's followers speaking of an "adverse current" in the Party, they were aggressively charging that the thinking of too many veteran cadres was "ossified or semi-ossified," suggesting the need for greater flexibility, if not more purging. The Hua – and by now, Yeh – supporters were proclaiming that "great chaos" existed throughout the land. Very significantly, the expression "great chaos" was quickly picked up in the official media of seventeen provinces, while "ossified or semi-ossified thinking" became standard in only eight authoritative places.

The balance of power had clearly shifted since the Third Plenum of the Eleventh Central Committee, and from then on it was Deng's followers who plaintively harped on the need to "uphold the decisions" of that meeting. In March, however, the Working Conference of the Eleventh Central Committee strongly backed Hua and Yeh by proclaiming that the Four Modernizations could only be realized by adhering to the new slogan of the "Four Basic Principles," which consisted of "the mass line, the dictatorship of the proletariat, democratic centralism, and Marxism–Leninism–Mao Zedong Thought." In short, the bulk of the Central Committee wanted a return to Communist fundamentals and the end of any speculation that the Four Modernizations, as pushed by Deng, might carry China in unforeseen "pragmatic" directions.

Deng's position in the spring of 1979 was further threatened when splits developed among the rehabilitated cadres. As Deng lost support among the veteran cadres, largely because of his vigor in rehabilitating purged figures, he became increasingly dependent upon those with scores to settle. He was driven to rehabilitating even the dead, lest he be charged with selfishly seeking to regain power and callously forgetting all those who had been purged with him. At the same time, however, divisions began to arise between those who were restored to positions of power and those who merely had their names cleared. Many of the former took on the attitudes of veteran cadres who were clinging to power. Many of the latter found their jobs taken by others and were left to "walk the corridors" looking for assignments, their only consolation being that they still received their former salaries.

At the same time, Deng's overly optimistic views about China's economic development were deflated when his expected ally on the Standing Committee, Chen Yun, decided that much of what had gone into the Four Modernizations was impulsive and unsystematically planned, and therefore there would have to be a three-year period of "readjustment." Chen further separated himself from Deng by downplaying the idea that China was engaged in new departures and suggesting that the country was in fact repeating what it had done after the failure of the Great Leap when Deng had taken charge of the economy. He did this by having the Politburo approve of the eight-character slogan that, as we noted earlier, was reminiscent of the slogan used in 1962, since half the characters were the same. (The 1962 slogan was "Readjustment, consolidation, filling out, and raising standards," while the 1979 slogan was "Readjustment, reform, rectification, and raising standards.")

Others of Deng's restored cadres came under increasing attack because he had assigned them to conspicuous and apparently powerful positions in which they had to cope with such intractable problems that they appeared to be impotent. For example, by the June 1979 Working Conference of the Eleventh Central Committee, there were snide attacks on "Deng's Three Hu's" and also his "Five Hu's" – the reference being to Deng's appointment of his former secretary Hu Yaobang to the impossible task of managing both cultural affairs and ideological training at a time of economic pragmatism, of his designation of Hu Qiaomu to the role of chief economic theorist when the economy was being completely rethought, and his appointment of Hu Jiwei and two others with the surname of Hu to Party administrative positions.

When the Second Session of the Fifth National People's Congress met from June 15 to July 2, 1979, it was widely recognized that there were four basic factions bringing immobilism and petty backbiting to a supposedly united Party:

1. The "whatever faction," composed of the once vulnerable but increasingly secure cadres led by Hua Guofeng who had benefited from the Cultural Revolution and continued to benefit from China's inability to openly abandon Communism and hence erase the memory of having had a Mao Zedong.
2. The "opposition faction," composed of cadres who had survived the Cultural Revolution and who wished only to hold their positions, but who would be ready to risk a "leftist" tide again if it would destroy those who were troublesomely criticizing their claim to positions. They looked for leadership to Ye and Li and were well represented in the PLA.
3. The "restoration faction," composed largely of rehabilitated cadres and some veteran cadres who believed that the Party should return to the practices of the 1950s and especially the policies of the post-Great Leap years. Their spokesman was Chen Yun and they were generally realistic, and hence less than optimistic, about the prospects for the Four Modernizations, very realistic about the limited help China could expect from Japan and the West, and convinced that the Chinese people should be told about the seriousness of their circumstances so that they would be ready to accept the harsh discipline that might be necessary to save the country from bankruptcy.
4. The "practice faction," also composed of a mixture of rehabilitated and veteran cadres who believed that all that had gone before had been disastrous for China and that new practices were called for. Their inspiration was, of course, Deng Xiaoping, and their main hope was that if China would only cast aside much of the past, near miracles could be expected. This faction above all wanted further revenge against not only the Gang of Four but also all who had in any way benefited from the Cultural Revolution. They were not prepared to allow Deng to let bygones be bygones.

Apparently, at this Second Session of the Fifth National People's Congress the "restoration faction" emerged as a dominant force, as it not only attracted veteran cadres from the "practice faction" but, more significantly, also got backing from the "whatever faction," which saw it as a preferable alternative to the "practice faction."[11] The position of the

11. Chi Hsiu, "The Class Situation on Principal Contradictions in Mainland China – An Important Theoretical Issue at the Second Session of the Fifth NCP," *Chishi Nientai,*

"restoration faction" was further strengthened by the mutually destructive clashes of the "whatever" and the "practice" factions over leadership privileges. This round of attacks was started by the "practice faction," which sought to destroy Wang Dongxing (of the "whatever faction") by charging that he had built in the Zhongnanhai compound a new house that had "eleven suites for his children, a movie theater, a gymnasium, double roofing and triple-glazed windows," at a cost of $4.4 million.[12] The "whatever faction" quickly responded with the report that 500 leading Chinese, including Deng's brother, had spent a month cruising in Japanese waters; and that Vice-Premier, alternate Politburo member, and Minister of Economic Relations with Foreign Countries Chen Muhua had arrogantly refused to allow some ill Chinese athletes to ride back to China from Rumania in her special airplane.[13] When Chen Muhua telephoned Xu Yinsheng, the responsible person at the Physical Culture and Sports Commission, to explain that the incident had been a misunderstanding caused by her incompetent secretary, and to ask Xu to hush up the story, he responded that there was nothing he could do, since "all my subordinates know of this incident."[14]

In this contest of recriminations, the "whatever faction" had a slight advantage, since those who rose during the Cultural Revolution generally had fewer scandals involving privileges than the older cadres associated with the "practice faction." Hence, not surprisingly, members of Deng's group began to strain at the decision of the Third Plenum of the Eleventh Central Committee that the campaign against Lin Biao and the Gang of Four was over. Thus began the maneuvering to revive the "Anti-Gang of Four" and "Anti-Lin Biao" campaigns. To do this, they first initiated a campaign calling for the punishment of those who killed "China's Joan of Arc," Zhang Zhixin, a newfound heroine who had been ordered executed by Mao Zedong's nephew, Mao Yuanxin – who the "practice faction" claimed was being protected by the "whatever faction" through the "devious trick" of claiming that he was dead.[15]

The split among those rehabilitated by Deng became more severe as the leadership confronted increasingly critical decisions about China's

---

Hong Kong, August, 1979, pp. 26–33, translated in Foreign Broadcast Information Service, *Daily Report – People's Republic of China*, August 13, 1977, pp. U1–9.

12. Jay Mathews, *Washington Post*, August 30, 1979.

13. Luo Bing, "The Incident of Bombarding the Woman Vice Premier and Others," *Cheng Ming*, Hong Kong, August 1, 1979, translated in Foreign Broadcast Information Service, *Daily Report – People's Republic of China*, August 9, 1979, pp. U1–U2.

14. Ibid.

15. "It is Necessary to Put Mao Yuanxin on Public Trial," *Cheng Ming*, editorial, No. 21, July 1, 1979, in Foreign Broadcast Information Service, *Daily Report – People's Republic of China*, July 10, 1979, p. U3.

economy. In particular, a cleavage grew between the economists within the Academy of Social Sciences, under the leadership of Hu Qiaomu, and those responsible officials, under Chen Yun, who were making the hard bureaucratic decisions about economic allocations. While theoretical economists could freely write, and even more freely talk, about all kinds of novel practices, including speculation about greater decentralization and greater use of market forces, the bureaucrats of both the "opposition" and the "restoration" factions felt the need for tighter controls and greater economic discipline. The "restoration faction" felt that Deng was encouraging romantic views about the actual economic choices available to China. Deng himself seemed paralyzed between wanting to be the champion of liberal experimentation and wanting to be the tough-minded implementer of hard, but necessary, policies. He chose first to waffle.

Thus, three years after the death of Mao the factional divisions within the leadership had by no means disappeared. Efforts to rehabilitate purged cadres had produced new lines of division, and the necessity to paper over the intra-Party disagreements with a consensus had produced only a host of logical contradictions. This situation was clearly illustrated in Hua Guofeng's "Report on the Work of the Government" at the Second Session of the Fifth National People's Congress in June 1979, in which he included statements that seemed designed to please each of the factions. In one sentence, for example, he said that the cadres had "basically grasped" leadership and that they "can be trusted and relied upon by the people"; but then in a subsequent sentence he said, "Evil winds and noxious influences such as becoming privileged, getting back door benefits and suppressing democracy have continued to seriously exist among cadres. . . ." In one part of his report he said that "the old exploiting class had been eliminated" and only "hostile elements" such as "criminals," "counterrevolutionaries," and "enemy spies" remain; but then he went on to say, "We admit that the class struggle has not ended," and, "We must persist in the class struggle." Thus he left ambiguous the question of whether the Chinese Communist Party was actually going to put aside Mao's warning that "the bourgeoisie is right in the Party" and no longer "take class struggles as the key link." Even on substantive policies Hua had to take contradictory positions: On the one hand, he admitted to widespread unemployment, with a total of "maybe 20 million" persons for whom some forms of make-work should be found; but at the same time, he called for the end of the "iron rice bowl" policy under which jobs are secure regardless of their usefulness.[16]

---

16. Hua Guofeng, "Report on the Work of the Government," Press Release, Embassy of the People's Republic of China, Washington, D.C., July 19, 1979. For an analysis by a sympathizer of the regime, see Yu Tsung-che, "Contradictions, Questions, and Secret Worries,"

As Hua's efforts to broaden his appeal only worked to compromise his core power base, Deng at last became decisive and aggressively sought to gain Party power. At the Fifth Plenum of the Eleventh Central Committee in February 1980, Deng forced the "resignations" of four of Hua Guofeng's key associates in the "whatever" and "opposition" factions: Wang Dongxing, from the Standing Committee of the Politburo, and Chen Xilian, Ji Dengkui, and Wu De, from the Politburo. A new Standing Committee was constituted on which Hua Guofeng now sat in lonely isolation; Marshal Ye Jianying and Li Xiannian continued to represent the veteran cadres, while Deng had three allies in Chen Yun, Hu Yaobang, and Zhao Ziyang. Confident of his new control of the Party, Deng reestablished the Party Secretariat, the office from which he had risen to power in the 1950s, and placed it under the control of his loyal associate, Hu Yaobang. During the previous year and a half in the Propaganda Office, Hu had been assigned the unenviable task of working to revive Party ideology at a time of ideological confusion and pragmatism; now he could improve Party discipline by administrative controls and the initiation of a new "rectification" program.

To further consolidate his position in the Party, and to cope with the awkward fact that his followers tend to be a generation older than Hua, Deng also tried to establish a "Council of Advisers" system, starting at the Politburo and going down to all levels of the Party. The five at the Politburo level, all septuagenarians, were three PLA marshals, Liu Bocheng, Xu Xiangqian, and Nie Rongzhen; the former Mayor of Peking, Peng Zhen; and Zhou Enlai's widow, Deng Yingchao. In theory, the system of advisers was supposed to encourage old cadres to step aside for younger blood, but as we have seen, in Chinese political culture, age confers such status that it is almost impossible to retire from a powerful position. Deng's attempted innovations only underscore the fact that his most trusted allies were aged cadres. In contrast, Hua Guofeng had been sending increasingly contradictory signals which suggested that he was unsure of his support. Those who were inclined to look to him for leadership must have gradually realized that he was not a reliable protector.

Although at the time of Mao's death it might have seemed that Hua was blessed with advantages – he had been anointed by Mao, he had solid contacts with the public security (secret police) and the rural cadres, and he had announced the grand goals of the Four Modernizations – but in fact he was an inescapably compromised leader. His closeness to Mao was compromised by his role in arresting the Gang of Four; his base with rural cadres was undermined by his identification with the early in-

---

Chishih Nientai, Hong Kong, August 1979, pp. 17–18, translated in Foreign Broadcast Information Service, *Daily Report – People's Republic of China*, August 13, 1979, pp. U5–U9.

dustrial emphasis of the Four Modernizations; at the same time, the technocratic cadres refused to respect him because of his past experiences. Thus, the more Hua tried to become a "national" leader of all the people, the more he undermined the network of earlier supporters without gaining new followers.

These vulnerabilities made it possible for Deng to accelerate his attacks. In so acting, Deng rejected the available Chinese tactic of maximizing power by seeking the role of conciliator or harmony-builder, and instead he opted for the more common Chinese strategy of pressing compulsively the advantages of the moment, for one may never again be so lucky. His purpose no doubt was to send a signal to all lower cadres that the future lay with his chain of supporters and that they should abandon their loyalties to other leaders. In this respect, Deng's tactics were the exact opposite of those employed by Hua when he had been on the ascendancy in 1976–1977 and Deng was weak. No doubt, the very fact that he had been able to rise again because of Hua's conciliatory approach made Deng believe that safety lay in always pressing one's advantages to the limit.

During the summer of 1980, Deng encouraged an aggressive campaign of not-so-disguised attacks on Hua. The Chinese press was filled with historical allegories that cadres could recognize as slandering Hua. In one article, a Tang emperor expressed his confidence in an unscrupulous eunuch in words nearly identical to those used by Mao about Hua. After rumors had been spread that Hua would be resigning as Premier, the historian Zhang Zhizhi in an August 19 article in the *Guangming Daily* debunked the theory that a Chinese premier 2,000 years ago had resigned willingly in favor of a worthy successor, and pointed out that the official had been incompetent and was later executed. Even in the attacks on Hua there was recognition that Deng's opponent had potentially strong allies. Thus in a September 1 *People's Daily* article, there was an historical account of an ambitious mandarin usurping power from an ailing emperor and then calling upon the army to help him take over the country.[17]

At the September meeting of the Third Session of the Fifth National People's Congress, Deng sought to consolidate his influence through a series of personnel changes. Hua Guofeng announced his "resignation" as Premier, retaining the post of Party Chairman. Deng also resigned as Vice-Premier to become Vice-Chairman of the Party. Six others of the eighteen Vice-Premiers resigned: Chen Yonggui, the model peasant from Dazhai, a model production brigade much praised by Mao and Hua but whose achievements had been recently exposed as blatant fabrica-

---

17. Jay Mathews, *Washington Post* and *Boston Globe*, September 8, 1980.

tions; Li Xiannian, the leader of the veteran cadres, who claimed ill health; Chen Yun, the Deng protege; and three others – Defense Minister Xu Xiangqian, General Wang Zhen, and 74-year-old Wang Renzhong.[18]

The most publicized change at the NPC meeting was the appointment of Zhao Ziyang to replace Hua as Premier. Not only was Zhao a widely recognized protege of Deng, he was also a champion of economic innovations and decentralized decisionmaking. Zhao was also the lowest-ranking Party official ever to become Premier, ranking only seventh in the Party hierarchy, after Hua, Ye, Deng, Li, Chen and Hu.

In the weeks after the NPC, the Chinese press carried extremely bold articles suggesting that in the economic field, market forces should replace centralized planning, all of which were interpreted as signs that Hua's fortunes might further decline and that Deng was indeed China's new strong man. At the end of November, Deng went further and dropped the cryptic hint to foreign visitors that Hu Yaobang was in line for a "great promotion," which was instantly interpreted to mean that he would be moving up from Party Secretary-General to replace Hua as Party Chairman. In the next week, however, after a Politburo meeting, the *People's Daily* on December 2, in an editorial that took up two-thirds of its front page, announced that it would be necessary to reimpose a larger measure of central planning and pull back from experimentations with free markets. Apparently the veteran cadres and the Cultural Revolution cadres were not as weak as they seemed when Zhao was appointed.

Deng's decision to push for a "trial" of the Gang of Four and the six further indicated his belief in the superior efficacy of intimidation over conciliation in influencing cadres. In the same spirit as he sought to "teach a lesson" to Vietnam, he made the "trials" take the form of teaching a lesson about what could happen to anyone who politically opposed him. The decision to expand the "trial" of the Gang to include the five military officers must have been inspired by fears that PLA officers, who had been complaining about the decline in defense budgets, needed to be reminded about what could happen to those who plot military coups.

18. Both Hua and Deng justified the resignations largely in terms of the need to replace aged comrades with younger officials, a problem well dramatized at the NPC meeting by the need of several of the leaders to be helped in and out of their chairs by bevies of nurses. (It appears that Chinese officials are not embarrassed by their need for medical attendants, but rather they seem, like feudal lords, to gain status gratification from the relative size and solicitousness of their respective entourages. Marshal Ye, who had the most attendants and had to have his speech read for him, officially called for younger blood in the leadership, while not resigning himself as Vice-Premier.) In spite of the explanation that the resignation reflected mainly the problem of age, the reshuffling of leaders produced a Politburo and Standing Committee of greater average age.

At the same time as the Peking trials took place, Deng worked out in the Politburo the decision that Hua should "resign" as Chairman in favor of Hu Yaobang and thus avoid further investigations into his Cultural Revolution activities. After the meeting, however, Hua apparently decided to employ stalling tactics so as to encourage a backlash against Deng's aggressive moves. He refused to attend the scheduled Sixth Plenum of the Eleventh Central Committee that had been set for late December 1980, at which his "resignation" would have become official. More importantly, he apparently persuaded Marshal Ye Jianying also to boycott the meeting, thereby causing its postponement. When the meeting was rescheduled for January, Ye left Peking for a prolonged winter visit to Guangdong Province. As the meeting was put off month by month during the spring of 1981, Deng's leadership was brought into further question by an accumulation of reports about troubles with the economy—the inflation rate was reaching double digits in the cities, capital construction had to be cut back by another 40 percent, centralized planning had to be reinforced, and many liberalization experiments with "marked practices" were ended.

The critical issue, however, was the intense debate over what should be the official Party judgment about the role of Mao Zedong. Deng's efforts at de-Maoization had generated substantial resistance, particularly among veteran cadres and PLA officers. On April 10, General Huang Kecheng, the Executive Secretary of the Central Commission for Inspecting Discipline, published the consensus article that, while criticizing Mao for "mistakes" in launching the Great Leap and the Cultural Revolution, was generally laudatory and far more positive about the late Chairman than Deng or Hu Yaobang had been.

Thus, by the time Ye returned to Peking in late May and the Sixth Plenum could finally be called in mid-June, Deng's victory in at last getting Hua's "resignation" was something of a compromise. Although Hua had to step down as chairman, many of Deng's liberalizing reforms were also ended, and the bureaucratic cadres seemed to be solidly in place. Paradoxically, the decline in Hua's status may not be politically fatal to him. Indeed, it could even help him by giving him release from the compromises inherent in his "national" leadership role and allowing him to rebuild his allegiances among his natural followers, who are both younger and more numerous than Deng's.

In the meantime, Deng seems to have hoped that his dramatic moves at the top would mobilize all cadres in support of his leadership. Aside from Hua's problems in expanding his base of support, Deng's success stemmed largely from three factors: First, and probably most important of all, he could more readily than Hua appeal to all who had suffered in the Cultural Revolution and who were inspired to aggressive political action in the search for revenge and for changes in the Chinese political system. Hua could only intellectually call for change through the policies of the Four Modernizations. Deng could insist that there had to be changes in personnel. Once the makeup of the leadership started to change, everyone expected that there would be further changes; and in acting accordingly, they steadily weakened Hua's position.

Second, Deng's success stemmed in part from his ingenious long-run strategy, unique in the history of Communism, of using state power to capture Party power. Having found himself in the minority in the top Party circles in 1977, Deng systematically built up the importance of the State Council and placed his own people in the ever-expanding numbers of vice-ministerial posts that he created. Finally, by the time of the Fifth Plenum of the Eleventh Central Committee in February 1980, he was able to capture Party leadership out of the patronage power he had created in the state apparatus, a reversal of the traditional Communist flow of power, which has always been from Party to state. He was able to do this because of the Chinese tendency, which we have noted, of thinking in terms of a single hierarchy and of treating status as power. Once Deng gained a majority in the Politburo, he quickly moved to consolidate his authority in the Party by reestablishing the Secretariat of the Central Committee, whose eleven members were expected to "look after the 'first line', or day-to-day work, while the Politburo and its Standing Committee [would] man the 'second line'."[19]

Finally, Deng was very skillful in his tactical use of liberalization at one moment and tightened controls at another. Before he had gained ascendancy over Hua, Deng appeared to be the champion of increased "democracy," which strengthened his appeal with the rehabilitated cadres. This spirit of liberalization was in fact codified briefly in the new Chinese Constitution and called the Four Great Freedoms – "speaking out freely, airing views fully, holding great debates, and writing big character posters" – activities that could only be troublesome to the established authorities in the form of the veteran cadres and the Cultural Revolution cadres. Then, as Deng's influence increased, his inclinations for liberalism decreased. "Democracy Wall" was closed in December 1980, and at the Fifth Plenum of the Eleventh Party Committee the Four Great Freedoms were eliminated from the Constitution.

While engaging in these dramatic moves within the inner-elite circles, Deng also sought to mobilize the lower cadres and the Chinese population by constantly upholding the goals of the Four Modernizations.

Yet, three years of the highly publicized Four Modernizations have

19. "The Central Committee's Secretariat and Its Work," *Beijing Review*, No. 19, May 11, 1981, p. 21.

failed to unify the leadership, so the question of the durability of the factional alignments is not apt to be answered through any formulas of national policies. The strength of factionalism lies at a more basic level of Chinese political behavior; thus, in closing our study, we must return to the fundamental motivations of Chinese political activists.

SECURITY, LOYALTY, AND RELIABILITY

As we have repeatedly stressed, policy preferences are not generally decisive factors in shaping factional ties; rather, particularistic considerations are usually more important. Furthermore, the durability of Chinese factions comes not from the reciprocity of favors common to patron–client relations but from deeper psychological needs for security that can be met only by the values of loyalty and reliability.

The chronology of continuous factional strife we have just reviewed is not the story of inordinately ambitious people seeking domination over each other, nor is it that of stubbornly committed men who would rather fight than compromise their principles. It is the story of men who are seeking security, but the logic of whose situation differs, so that what seems desirable – indeed necessary – for some becomes a threat to others.

In concluding this book we shall briefly trace the logic of the calculations that sustain factionalism as it exists for senior cadres and as it was echoed in the attitudes of our Hong Kong respondents.

THE COST-BENEFITS OF BEING INCONSPICUOUS OR OF ATTRACTING A PROTECTOR (AND/OR A FOLLOWING)

The cardinal principle of Chinese politics, as we have noted, is to successfully manage the contradiction between the imperative of supporting the consensus of the moment (even when that consensus may read "swim against the tide") and the need to be distinctive. This inherent contradiction calls for fine judgments – but fortunately, not very sophisticated verbal skills, for the Chinese political system is remarkably tolerant of banalities and can elevate to hero status those who earnestly mouth the self-evident. The successful political leader thus exploits the fact that no one will think the worst of him or consider him deficient in wits if his public statements barely escape sounding foolish, for he knows that others will assume that trite words can mask the most astute political mind, and thus shrewdness calls for unexceptional ideas, indeed commonplace sentiments and observations.

Yet at the same time there is the need to be seen as exceptional. How else is one to establish oneself in the eyes of stronger leaders who might be one's protectors? How is the successful leader to attract an ever-widening circle of followers?

In this situation, the first rule of Chinese politics is always to look upward and to act in a manner so as to demonstrate *loyalty* to some superior. Actions that show loyalty not only have the obvious merit of guaranteeing more protection from above, but equally important, they have the astonishing property of resolving the inherent contradiction of Chinese politics: They can be consistent with both conformity and self-assertion. Loyalty supports the group, and hence the consensus, and it also demonstrates the virtues of the self. Thus to be known as loyal is to be doubly secure.

Tenacious loyalty, however, can only promote this security if the group to which one is dedicated represents the principal consensus. There is the rub. Loyalty can solve all of a cadre's problems only if his is the dominant group—hence the need to struggle even over matters of little inherent importance.

In a like manner, superiors demand complete loyalty of every subordinate, not because that is the ideal but because it ensures that no one can later claim that they doubted his judgments. The concept of loyalty is comforting to all concerned, for its honoring reduces everyone's risks. If it is well known that everyone in a particular group will stick together, then not only are there no weak links, but any attempt to attack a member of the group can be counterproductive.

- A young man who was sent down to a state farm on Hainan Island explained, "I don't believe that any of the Revolutionary Committee members running the farm had any interest in the anti-Confucius/anti-Lin Biao matter, but they had to make sure that every single one of us agreed with them because they were afraid that if things later changed, those who disagreed with them might look good. As long as we all said the same thing they could be sure that their only threat came from outside. Even though I and others thought the matter was foolish, we knew that it made no sense to cause dissension, because if we did everyone else would have to criticize us. It was best for us, and for our leaders, if we all just agreed with what they said we ought to believe."

- The daughter of a college professor said, "Even after I had decided to leave, I continued to agree with my superiors, not because I really felt I had to hide my views, but because it was just a lot easier for everyone if I did not cause all the inconvenience that even one sign of doubting would have caused."

LOYALTY BASED NOT ON QUIDS PRO QUO BUT ON DETERRENCE

The virtue of loyalty unquestionably enjoys a loftier position in the Chinese political system than it does in liberal Western politics. Indeed, the extreme importance assigned to loyalty gives Chinese politics an entirely different configuration than, say, American politics, where loyalty is a value to be balanced with effectiveness, honesty, farsightedness, the appearance of high moral purpose, personal charisma, and a host of other values. In this system, loyalty represents no more than about 15 percent of the entire range of respected values in politics, while in China the comparable figure would probably be over 50 percent. This difference helps to explain why the Chinese felt they were doing the right thing in inviting a disgraced former President Nixon to visit China, while Americans thought it damaged China's reputation.

The Chinese concept of loyalty is also distinctive in that it accepts the premise that either party in a loyalty relationship may be harmed by the bond, but that even greater damage would be done by breaking the tie. In contrast, loyalty in American politics is either an absolute value (one is loyal to one's party through thick and thin, regardless of right and wrong, and there is no thought of costs or damage) or it is seen in the context of favors given and received, and of remembering helping hands. Thus there is always an element of tension at the borderline of the concept, since it easily spills over into a marketplace judgment of favors, with the less-than-honorable stigmas of being "bought out" and of questions about "staying bought."

The Chinese concept of loyalty is not entirely devoid of the notions of absolute respect or the exchange of favors. Their concept, however, stresses far more the notion of *reliability* as a means of reducing mutual damage. One person supports another through thick and thin because to do otherwise might cause great mischief and chaos, which can be self-destructive. It is in everyone's interest to reduce uncertainty and to raise the general level of predictability in political and social relations, and this can best be done if everyone understands the importance of being reliable.

Thus in Chinese politics far less stress is placed on the notion of quids pro quo that is so basic in American politics. With Americans, political loyalty is closely related to rules of reciprocity and the logic of indebtedness: For every favor given, one must be returned, and out of the balance of favors and obligations are forged basic political bonds. The boundaries of loyalties are thus set by how much one feels one should give in exchange for how little. Or loyalty is an absolute matter, filled with the exhilaration of belonging to a team, of facing victory and defeat together.

The Chinese start off on the opposite foot, stressing less the possibility of favors rendered, and more the potential for reciprocal injury. Both servant and master can grievously hurt each other, but the loyal servant keeps the family discretions, just as the master understands the human failings of the servant, keeping him on, not in spite of, but actually because of his known faults. Loyalty exists when superior and inferior each know the other could destroy him but will not because it could also bring self-destruction. The Chinese calculus is one of deterrence, particularly the negative threat of assured mutual destruction.

There is no sub-rosa marketplace of favors for winning over lesser officials in Chinese politics. Subordinates must remain loyal because they cannot readily exploit their knowledge of the faults of their superiors. As we have already observed, there is no premium on being the first to make public the crimes of a discredited leader, and there are no penalties for having long known of such faults and not publicizing them. The norms of Chinese politics require the denunciation of a leader only *after* he has fallen. Therefore, subordinate officials cannot justify going from one superior to another merely on the grounds of doing the right thing. Clearly if such practices were encouraged, Chinese politics would be inordinately chaotic, with every disgruntled subordinate holding the power to trigger off denunciations that could lead to the removal of important figures. Leaders fall because of the actions of their peers, not their subordinates.

Moreover, senior officials tend to distrust those who might be prepared to break their bonds with another senior official. The reasoning seems to be: "Since I would not trust any subordinate of mine who would do such a thing, I should not trust his subordinate when he seeks to come to me; and anyway, senior officials should never, on general principles, condone such behavior."

The loyalty transactions in Chinese politics are thus fairly durable, and the ties of loyalty are not easily severed. The initial relationship of superiors and subordinates is usually based on a deep and genuine "market transaction" in which the lesser official, after intense competition with others at his level, has proved his ability to manage affairs and therefore has the abilities needed by the superior. Loyalty is thus based on both mutual judgments of functionally relevant skills and mutual bonds of affect.

This picture of the workings of loyalty in the Chinese political process is consistent with the revelations that came out during the Cultural Revolution and during the campaign of vilifying the Gang of Four. Significantly, in all the horror stories of the dark ways of the Gang, their *modus operandi* has always been depicted as involving cooperation among like-minded, but essentially devious people; there have been no accounts of lesser officials secretly reporting to other *political* figures any of the crimes of the Gang. To the extent that worthies who were said to have become morally indignant at the actions of the Gang have been publicized, these have universally been portrayed as exemplary workers or peasants who, on reflecting what they saw, read over and over again the works of Chairman Mao and then, at great risks to themselves, went public at their regular political meetings. Or they reported the matter to the public security officials, and then were frustrated when nothing came of the investigations they had tried to initiate.

To cite only one example, consider the remarkable case of the "Martyr," Zhang Zhinxin, referred to above, whose story dominated the Chinese media during the summer of 1979 – a campaign inspired by pro-Deng rehabilitated cadres who hoped to profit from calling for a public trial of Mao's nephew, purportedly the executioner of this exemplary mother of one. With great perspicacity, Mrs. Zhang, while the Gang was still riding high, had figured out that not only were Lin Biao and Mao's wife "leftists," but also that Mao had not done right by Marshal Peng Dehuai. Yet, armed with this remarkable knowledge, which was still newsworthy even at the time of her publicized martyrdom (since Peng had just been rehabilitated), Mrs. Zhang did not try to alert potential opposition figures, she merely expressed her astonishing idea to her "political study class." In all the hundreds of thousands of words written about her martyrdom, there has never been a hint that this worthy should have used her presumed insights and knowledge in a more politically effective way.

Needless to say, it would be naive to believe that in a bureaucratic system as large as that of China there is not a great deal of peddling of damaging information and of subordinates reporting on their superiors. In fact, only a little more than a year after its reestablishment, the Discipline Inspection Commission reported that its commissions in twenty provinces had received more than 490,000 letters and visitors with complaints, and that in seven provinces there were 590 cases involving cadres at or above the county level.[20] Unquestionably, the Chinese do complain. Indeed, a central hypothesis of our study is that the Chinese

20. Xinhua Domestic Service, August 22, 1979, Foreign Broadcast Information Service, *Daily Report – People's Republic of China*, August 22, 1979, p. L-5.

tend to vocalize their misfortunes as a way of reducing inner tensions. How then is it that we can also say that they do not readily market damaging information?

This apparent contradiction brings us to an important insight into the foundations of Chinese political behavior. How do the Chinese reconcile their propensity to publicize their troubles with their reluctance to exploit damaging information in order to improve their lot? Why is it that people who are so quick to give vent to complaints of any mistreatment are not also always on the alert to find more accommodating patrons? To the Western mind it seems only logical that if someone is prepared to go public about how another has mistreated him, he must also be ready to ally with whomever is willing to oppose his tormentor. The Chinese feelings of dependency, however, produce a significantly different pattern of reactions: One publicizes one's woes, not in order to seek a new protector, but rather to shame and to humiliate the person who has done the mistreating – the wife who goes onto the street to wail at the top of her lungs about the failings of her husband is not seeking to break the relationship but rather to get help to *strengthen* her basic ties of loyalty.

THE GOALS OF SECURITY INHIBIT
THE AMBITIOUS

The tensions that cause individuals to voice their anxieties can thus best be relieved by reestablishing and improving old dependency relationships, not by running the even greater risk of seeking new ones. Even ambitious people are held in check by the awareness that they must be exemplary members of the group and model subordinates.

This means that the underlying constraint that serves to inhibit the ambitions of lesser leaders and that prevents them from constantly looking for new potential patrons is the knowledge that advancement in the Chinese system is inherently slow and that to draw too much attention to oneself can be dangerous. Thus the prime goal of security can best be realized by cultivating one's own domain, not by striving to push out one's boundaries. Those who get to the top in the Chinese system have been, almost without exception, people like Chairman Hua who avoid errors, do their assigned jobs well, gain the respect of a powerful leader, and never engage in risky enterprises. The fundamental touchstone of cadres is a sense of security that can best be fulfilled by having a clearly defined niche, a solid domain, and clear cues as to what should and should not be said or done. When such conditions are met, it is possible to mask all manifestations of ambition and claim that one "only wants to serve the people." If diligence and hard work – and above all the avoidance of mistakes – attract the attention of superiors and bring about unusually rapid advancements, the process will still be gradual enough not to be threatening to one's cohorts. Instead of being the object of envy, as is the case with those who advance spectacularly through blatant favoritism and are thus called "helicopters," the individual making such impressive but not menacing advancement can attract peers and subordinates who are eager to associate with a rising star.

The relationship that can thus develop between a secure cadre and a senior official is one based on a sense of loyalty that can be publicly defended in terms of reliability and steadfastness. This form of loyalty is comforting to all concerned because it seems to resolve the structurally inherent tension between adherence to consensus and the compelling need to seem worthy of being recognized as exceptional.

What is significant for the understanding of Chinese politics is that this pattern of individual cadre strategies, which stress the values of conformity, loyalty, and personal security, operates in a fashion that increases the potential for factional conflict throughout the system. By adhering to such calculations and by stressing the need for reliability and loyalty, informal patterns of authority relationships are built up that have the effect of creating latent divisions that can instantly become manifest whenever there is a falling out at the top.

WILL FACTIONAL TENSIONS UPSET CHINA'S POLITICAL STABILITY?

It is clear that identification with factional networks solves many basic psychological needs for the individual cadre. Furthermore, the more those engaged in power relationships feel personal insecurities, the more likely they are to seek the reassurance of dependency that can come from reliability in relations with both superiors and inferiors.

What then can we say about the prospects of the Chinese political system as a whole? Our own analysis of the needs of individual cadres and our grantedly Western tolerance for pluralism would make us conclude that the gradual institutionalization of factional politics should be a positive development for China, producing the advantages of adversary relationships and forms of checks and balances that can give stability and prevent extremism, even at the risk of some immobilism.

Against this view of the potential benefits of competitiveness, there is the uncompromising Chinese view that factionalism is an abomination, bound to create great problems and hence a frightening specter to be resisted by all right-thinking people. Thus, along with the factions composed of the various categories of cadres – the rehabilitated, the veteran survivors, and the beneficiaries of the Cultural Revolution—and their respective leading figures, there is also a chorus from all sides denouncing the existence of factionalism.

The more shrill this denunciation becomes, the more certain we can be that the factions are becoming institutionalized. On August 15, 1979, the *People's Daily* ran a special article signed by a "commentator" who was certainly a representative of the Politburo and was probably Hu Yaobang, Deng's appointee as Director of the Propaganda Department and Third Secretary of the Central Commission for Inspecting Discipline. Entitled "Resolutely Overcome Factionalism," the article said, "Factionalism is very harmful. It may disintegrate the Party politically, corrupt the Party ideologically, and split the Party organizationally. Factionalism undermines the organization, discipline, unity, and centralism of the Party . . . factionalism is an archenemy of the Party, the people, and the Four Modernizations." The article declared that, ". . . in leading bodies factions have been formed to control from behind the scenes, to lavish praise on leading cadres who act in the interests of their own factions and appoint people based on favoritism in an attempt to build up their personal influence and to exclude outsiders. In investigation work they attempted to cover up the truth, resisted investigations and shielded questionable persons; they have even struck down fine cadres who have upheld the correct line and resisted the Gang of Four. In rectifying false charges, wrong sentences, and frame-ups and in implementing the cadres policy, they have dismissed all charges against persons in their own factions and given every consideration to them. They have also deliberately delayed solving the problems of those who do not belong to their faction and have made things difficult for them. In addition, they have failed to act according to the Party's policies and have proceeded from factionalism in making job arrangements for cadres, developing Party membership, holding elections, recruiting workers, deciding on rewards, giving promotions, readjusting wages."[21]

In short, the cadres have been behaving in their factional networks in precisely the manner we have described in this book. And, just as we have said, everyone feels it necessary to denounce what is going on, regardless of whether they may have benefited from it or been damaged by it. It will be remembered that our Hong Kong respondents overwhelmingly denounced conflicts among the nation's leaders, even though they had to acknowledge that such conflicts had brought down the Gang of Four, opened the way for Deng's return to power, brought a more

21. Foreign Broadcast Information Service, *Daily Report—People's Republic of China,* August 15, 1979, pp. 1–2.

relaxed scene, and in many cases made it possible for them to leave the country. Although they could think of no way other than by factional conflicts that these positive developments could have happened, they still could not overcome their basic Chinese distaste of conflicts among leaders.

Thus the imperative of consensus continues to reign in China, even as factionalism satisfies equally basic Chinese needs. There is no way of telling whether Chinese culture will ever be able to resolve this inherent contradiction. What is certain is that with the complexities and diversification that are basic to modernization, the problem of maintaining consensus will be greater, as will be the pull of factionalism. Since Chinese political culture has survived the trauma of the Cultural Revolution, to say nothing of the entire Mao era, it seems likely that the contradiction will persist. Culturally the society is not prepared for an increase in conflicts – on the contrary, the ideology demands, now even more than under Mao, that harmony and consensus should be the norm.

Thus the most likely prospect is that the trends in China will increase the validity of the propositions we have advanced in this book to describe the dynamics of Chinese politics.

Selected Bibliography

I. CHINESE CULTURE AND SOCIAL RELATIONS

Bernstein, Thomas P., *Up to the Mountains and Down to the Villages*, Yale University Press, New Haven, Conn., 1977.

Bonavia, David, *The Chinese*, Lippincott and Crowell, New York, 1980.

Chien Chiao, "Chinese Strategic Behaviors: A Preliminary List," in *Proceedings of the International Conference on Sinology*, Taipei, August 15–17, 1980, Academia Sinica, Taipei, 1981.

Chu, Godwin, *Radical Change Through Communications in Mao's China*, East–West Center Book, University Press of Hawaii, Honolulu, 1977.

Davis-Freeman, Deborah, "Aging in the People's Republic of China," Ph.D. dissertation, Department of Sociology, Boston University, 1978.

Dittmer, Lowell, "Thought Reform and the Cultural Revolution: An Analysis of the Symbolism of Chinese Polemics," *American Political Science Review*, Vol. LXII, No. 1, March 1977.

Elegant, Robert S., *The Center of the World: Communism and the Mind of China*, Methuen, London, 1963.

Fried, Morton A., *Fabric of Chinese Society: A Study of a Chinese County Seat*, Praeger, New York, 1953.

Frolic, B. Michael, *Mao's People*, Harvard University Press, Cambridge, Mass., 1980.

Hiniker, Paul, "Chinese Reactions to Forced Compliance: Dissonance Reduction and National Character," *Journal of Social Psychology*, Vol. 77, 1969, pp. 157–176.

————, *Revolutionary Ideology and Chinese Reality,* Sage Publications, Beverly Hills, 1977.

Hsia, T. A., *Metaphor, Myth, Ritual and the People's Commune,* Center for Chinese Studies, University of California Press, Berkeley, 1961.

Hsu, Cho-yun, "The Concept of Predetermination and Fate in Han," *Early China,* Vol. 1, 1975, pp. 51–56.

Hsu, Francis L. K., *Americans and Chinese: Two Ways of Life,* Henry Schuman, New York, 1953.

————, *Under the Ancestors' Shadow,* Columbia University Press, New York, 1948.

————, *Class, Caste and Club,* Van Nostrand, Princeton, N. J., 1963.

Hu, Hsien-chin, "The Chinese Concept of Face," *American Anthropologist,* Vol. 46, No. 1, January–March, 1944.

Kessen, William, ed., *Childhood in China,* Yale University Press, New Haven, Conn., 1975.

Kleinberg, Otto, "Emotional Expression in Chinese Literature," *Journal of Abnormal and Social Psychology,* Vol. XXXIII, 1938.

La Barre, Weston, "Some Observations in Character Structure in the Orient: II, The Chinese," *Psychiatry,* Vol. 9, 1976, pp. 215–237.

Leites, Nathan, "On Violence in China," in Elizabeth Wirth Marvick, *Psychopolitical Analysis: Selected Writings of Nathan Leites,* John Wiley and Sons, New York, 1977.

Levinson, Joseph R., "The Amateur Ideal," in John K. Fairbank, ed., *Chinese Thought and Institutions,* University of Chicago Press, Chicago, 1957.

Loewe, Michael, *Imperial China: The Historical Background to the Modern Age,* Praeger, New York, 1966.

Muensterberger, Warner, "Orality and Dependence: Characteristics of Southern Chinese," *Psychoanalysis and the Social Sciences,* Vol. 3, 1951, pp. 37–69.

Munro, Donald, *The Concept of Man in Contemporary China,* University of Michigan Press, Ann Arbor, 1977.

Nivison, David, "Communist Ethics and Chinese Tradition," *Journal of Asian Studies,* Vol. 16, No. 1, Nov. 1956, pp. 51–74.

Parker, William, "Culture in Stress: The Malaysian Crisis of 1969 and Its Cultural Roots," Ph. D. dissertation, Department of Political Science, Massachusetts Institute of Technology, 1979.

Parrish, William L., and Martha King Whyte, *Village and Family in Contemporary China,* University of Chicago Press, Chicago, 1978.

Pye, Lucian W., *The Spirit of Chinese Politics,* M.I.T. Press, Cambridge, Mass., 1968.

————, *Mao Tse-tung: The Man in the Leader,* Basic Books, New York, 1976.

Raddock, David, *Political Behavior of Adolescents in China: The Cultural Revolution in Kwangchan,* University of Arizona Press, Tucson, 1977.

Shirk, Susan, "The Middle School Experience in China," Ph.D. dissertation, Department of Political Science, Massachusetts Institute of Technology, 1974.

Solomon, Richard, "Mao's Efforts to Reintegrate the Chinese Polity: Problems of Conflict and Authority in Chinese Social Processes," in A. Doak Barnett, ed., *Chinese Communist Politics in Action,* University of Washington Press, Seattle, 1968.

————, *Mao's Revolution and the Chinese Political Culture,* University of California Press, Berkeley, 1971.

Vogel, Ezra, "From Friendship to Comradeship: The Change in Personal Relations in Communist China," *China Quarterly,* No. 21, January–March, 1965, pp. 46–60.

Weakland, John H., "The Organization of Action in Chinese Culture," *Psychiatry,* Vol. 13, 1950, pp. 361–370.

————, "Family Imagery in a Passage by Mao Tse-tung," *World Politics,* Vol. 10, No. 3, April 1958, pp. 387–407.

White, Lynn T., III, *Careers in Shanghai,* University of California Press, Berkley, 1978.

Whyte, Martin King, *Small Groups and Political Rituals in China,* University of California Press, Berkeley, 1974.

Wilkinson, Rupert, *Gentlemanly Power,* Oxford University Press, London, 1964.

Wilson, Amy Auerbacher, et al., eds., *Deviance and Social Control in Chinese Society,* Praeger, New York, 1977.

Wilson, Richard W., *Learning to Be Chinese: The Political Socialization of Children in Taiwan,* M.I.T. Press, Cambridge, Mass., 1970.

Wolf, Margery, *The House of Lim: A Study of a Chinese Farm Family,* Appleton-Century-Crofts, New York, 1968.

Wright, Arthur F., "Struggle vs. Harmony: Symbols of Competing Values in Modern China," *World Politics,* Vol. VI, No. 1, October 1953, pp. 31–34.

Yang, C. K., *Chinese Communist Society: The Family and the Village,* M.I.T. Press, Cambridge, Mass., 1965.

II. GENERAL CHINESE POLITICS

Barnett, A. Doak, *Cadres, Bureaucracy, and Political Power in Communist China,* Columbia University Press, New York, 1967.

————, *Uncertain Passage,* Brookings Institution, Washington, 1974.

————, *China After Mao Tse-tung,* Princeton University Press, Princeton, N.J., 1976.

Baum, Richard, ed., *China's Four Modernizations,* Westview Press, Boulder, Colo., 1980.

————, *Prelude to Revolution: Mao, the Party and the Peasant Question 1962–66,* Columbia University Press, New York, 1975.

————, ed., *China in Ferment: Perspective on the Cultural Revolution,* Prentice-Hall, Englewood Cliffs, N.J., 1971.

————, and F. Teiwes, *Ssu-ch'ing: The Socialist Education Movement of 1962–1966,* University of California Press, Berkeley, 1968.

Bennett, Gordon A., and Ronald N. Montaperto, *Red Guard: The Political Biography of Dai Hsiao-ai,* Doubleday & Co., Garden City, N.Y., 1972.

Bernstein, Thomas, "Problems of Village Leadership After Land Reform," *China Quarterly,* No. 36, October–December 1968, pp. 1–22.

Boorman, Howard L., *Biographical Dictionary of Republican China,* 4 vols., Columbia University Press, New York, 1967.

Bullard, Monte Ray, "People's Republic of China Elite Studies: A Review of the Literature," *Asian Survey*, Vol. 19, No. 8, August 1979, pp. 789–800.

Butterfield, Fox, "The Pragmatists Take China's Helm," *The New York Times Magazine*, December 28, 1980, pp. 22–26.

————, "Complex Hidden Network Supplies the Chinese with Vital News," *New York Times*, December 31, 1980, p. A3.

Chang, Parris H., *Power and Policy in China*, 2nd ed., Pennsylvania State University Press, University Park, 1978.

Ch'i, Shi-Sheng, *Warlord Politics in China 1916–1928*, Stanford University Press, Palo Alto, Calif., 1976, pp. 36–76.

Compton, Boyd, *Mao's China, Party Reform Documents, 1942–44*, University of Washington Press, Seattle, 1952.

Dai, Bingham, "Personality Problems in Chinese Culture," *American Sociological Review*, Vol. VI, 1941.

Dittmer, Lowell, *Liu Shiao-ch'i and the Chinese Cultural Revolution*, University of California Press, Berkeley, 1974.

Fengar, Thomas, ed., *China's Quest for Independence: Policy Evolution in the 1970s*, Westview Press, Boulder, Colo., 1980.

Friedman, Maurice, ed., *Family and Kinship in Chinese Society*, Stanford University Press, Palo Alto, Calif., 1970.

Gurley, John G., *China's Economy and the Maoist Strategy*, Monthly Review Press, New York, 1978.

Harding, Harry, Jr., *China: The Uncertain Future*, Foreign Policy Association, New York, 1974.

————, "China After Mao," *Problems of Communism*, Vol. 20, No. 2, March–April 1977.

Harrison, James Pinckney, *The Long March to Power*, Macmillan, New York, 1972.

Ho, Peng-ti, *The Ladder of Success in Imperial China*, John Wiley and Sons, New York, 1964.

Imfeld, Al, *China as a Model of Development*, Orbis Books, New York, 1978.

Kau, Michael Y. M., *The Lin Piao Affair*, International Arts and Sciences Press, White Plains, N.Y., 1975.

Klein, Donald W., and Anne B. Clark, *Biographical Dictionary of Chinese Communism, 1921–1965*, Harvard University Press, Cambridge, Mass., 1971.

Lampton, David M., *The Politics of Medicine in China*, Westview Press, Boulder, Colo., 1977.

Lewis, John W., *Leadership in Communist China*, Cornell University Press, Ithaca, N.Y., 1963.

————, ed., *The City in Communist China*, Stanford University Press, Palo Alto, Calif., 1971.

Liao, Kuang-sheng, "Linkage Politics in China: Internal Mobilization and Articulated External Hostility in the Cultural Revolution," *World Politics*, Vol. 28, No. 4, July 1976, pp. 590–610.

Lieberthal, Kenneth, *A Research Guide to Central Party and Government Meetings in China 1949–1975*, International Arts and Sciences Press, White Plains, N.Y., 1976.

Ling, Ken, *The Revenge of Heaven: Journal of a Young Chinese*, G. P. Putnam's

Sons, New York, 1972.

London, Miriam, "China's By-road News: A New People's Channel," *Freedom at Issue*, September–October 1978, p. 9.

MacFarquhar, Roderick, ed., *China Under Mao*, M.I.T. Press, Cambridge, Mass., 1966.

————, *The Origin of the Cultural Revolution, I: Contradictions Among the People*, Columbia University Press, New York, 1974.

Meisner, Maurice, *Mao's China: A History of the People's Republic*, The Free Press, New York, 1977.

Oksenberg, Michel, "The Institutionalization of the Communist Revolution," *China Quarterly*, No. 36, October–December 1968, pp. 61–92.

————, "Policy Making Under Mao, 1949–68: An Overview," in John M. H. Lindbeck, ed., *China: Management of a Revolution*, University of Washington Press, Seattle, 1971.

————, "Methods of Communication Within the Chinese Bureaucracy," *China Quarterly*, No. 57, January–March 1974, pp. 1–39.

————, and Sai-Cheung Yeung, "Hua Kuo-feng's Pre-Cultural Revolution Hunan Years, 1949–66: The Making of a Political Generalist," *China Quarterly*, No. 69, March 1977, pp. 9–16.

Pye, Lucian W., "Generational Politics in a Gerontocracy: The Chinese Succession Problem," *Current Scene*, Vol. XIV, No. 7, July 1976.

————, "Dilemmas for America in China's Military Modernization," *International Security*, Vol. 4, No. 1, Summer 1979, pp. 3–19.

Rice, Edward E., *Mao's Way*, University of California Press, Berkeley, 1972.

Robinson, Thomas W., "Lin Piao as an Elite Type," in Robert A. Scalapino, ed., *Elites in the People's Republic of China*, University of Washington Press, Seattle, 1972.

Rostow, Walt W., *The Prospects of Communist China*, John Wiley and Sons, New York, 1954.

Scalapino, Robert A., "The Cultural Revolution and Chinese Foreign Policy," *Current Scene*, Vol. 1, No. 13, August 1, 1968.

————, ed., *Elites in the People's Republic of China*, University of Washington Press, Seattle, 1972.

Schurmann, Franz, *Ideology and Organization in Communist China*, University of California Press, Berkeley, 1966.

Schwartz, Benjamin I., *Chinese Communism and the Rise of Mao Tse-tung*, Harvard University Press, Cambridge, Mass., 1951.

Snow, Edgar, *Red Star Over China*, rev. ed., Grove Press, New York, 1968, p. 134.

Townsend, James, *Political Participation in Communist China*, University of California Press, Berkeley, 1969.

————, *Politics in China*, 2nd ed., Little, Brown, Boston, 1980.

Van Ness, Peter, *Revolution and Chinese Foreign Policy*, University of California Press, Berkeley, 1970.

Vogel, Ezra, *Canton Under Communism*, Harvard University Press, Cambridge, Mass., 1969.

Whiting, Allen S., *Chinese Domestic Politics and Foreign Policy in the 1970s*,

Center for Chinese Studies, University of Michigan, Ann Arbor, 1979.

Whitson, William W., *The Chinese High Command: A History of Communist Military Politics, 1927–1971*, Praeger, New York, 1973.

Whyte, Martin King, "Bureaucracy and Modernization in China: The Maoist Critique," *American Sociological Review*, Vol. 38, April 1973.

Wong, Paul, *China's Higher Leadership in the Socialist Transition*, The Free Press, New York, 1976.

III. CHINESE FACTIONAL POLITICS

Ahn, Byung-Joon, *Chinese Politics and the Cultural Revolution*, University of Washington Press, Seattle, 1976.

Bridgham, Philip, "Mao's Cultural Revolution: Origin and Development," *China Quarterly*, No. 29, January 1967, pp. 1–35.

Butterfield, Fox, "Revenge Seems to Outweigh Justice at Chinese Trial," *New York Times*, December 6, 1980, p. 2A.

Chang, Parris H., *Radicals and Radical Ideology in China's Cultural Revolution*, Research Institute on Communist Affairs, Columbia University, New York, 1973.

Dittmer, Lowell, " 'Line Struggle' in Theory and Practice," *China Quarterly*, No. 72, December 1977, pp. 675–712.

————, "Base of Power in Chinese Politics: A Theory and Analysis of the Fall of the 'Gang of Four'," *World Politics*, Vol. 31, No. 1, October 1978, pp. 26–60.

Domes, Jurgen, *The Internal Politics of China, 1949–1972*, C. Hurst and Co., London, 1973, p. 236.

————, "The 'Gang of Four' and Hua Guo-feng: Analysis of Political Events in 1975–76," *China Quarterly*, No. 71, September 1977, pp. 477–478.

————, *China After the Cultural Revolution*, University of California Press, Berkeley, 1977.

Fox, Galen, "Campaigning for Power in China," *Contemporary China*, Vol. 3, No. 1, Spring 1979.

Goldman, Merle, "The Fall of Chou Yang," *China Quarterly*, No. 27, July–September 1966, pp. 132–148.

————, "The Unique 'Blooming and Contending' of 1961–67," *China Quarterly*, No. 37, January–March 1969, pp. 54–83.

————, "China's Anti-Confucian Campaign, 1973–74," *China Quarterly*, No. 63, September 1975, pp. 435–489.

Goodman, David S. G., "The Shanghai Connection: Shanghai in National Politics During the 1970s," in Christopher Howe, ed., *The Development of Shanghai Since 1949*, Cambridge University Press, London, 1979.

Hah, Chong-Do, "The Dynamics of the Chinese Cultural Revolution: An Interpretation Based on an Analytical Framework of Political Coalition," *World Politics*, Vol. 24, No. 2, January 1972, pp. 182–220.

Harding, Harry, "China, The Fragmentation of Power," *Asian Survey*, Vol. XII, No. 1, 1972, pp. 1–15.

Hiniker, Paul, and Jolanta Perlstein, "Alternation of Charismatic and Bureaucratic Styles of Leadership in Postrevolutionary China," *Comparative Political Studies,* Vol. 10, No. 4, 1978, pp. 529–554.

Hunter, Neil, *Shanghai Journal: An Eye-Witness Account of the Cultural Revolution,* Beacon Press, Boston, 1969.

Jacobs, Bruce, "A Preliminary Model of Particularistic Ties in Chinese Political Alliances: *Kan-ch'ing* and *Kuan-hsi* in a Rural Taiwanese Township," *China Quarterly,* No. 78, June 1979, pp. 237–273.

Kraus, Richard Curt, "Class Conflict and the Vocabulary of Social Analysis in China, *China Quarterly,* No. 69, March 1977.

Lee, Hong Yung, *The Politics of the Cultural Revolution,* University of California Press, Berkeley, 1978.

Lieberthal, Kenneth, "The Internal Political Scene, *Problems of Communism,* Vol. 24, No. 3, May–June 1975, p. 7.

————, "The Politics of Modernization in the PRC, *Problems of Communism,* Vol. 27, No. 3, May–June 1978, pp. 11–14.

————, "Modernization and Succession in China," *Contemporary China,* Vol. 2, No. 1, Spring, 1979, pp. 53–54.

Liu, Alan P. L., *Political Culture and Group Conflict in Communist China,* ABC-Clio Press, Santa Barbara, Calif., 1976.

Moody, Peter R., *Opposition and Dissent in Contemporary China,* Hoover Institution Press, Palo Alto, Calif., 1977.

Nathan, Andrew J., "A Factionalism Model of CCP Politics," *China Quarterly,* No. 53, January–March 1973, pp. 34–66.

————, "Policy Oscillations in the People's Republic of China: A Critique," *China Quarterly,* No. 68, December 1976, pp. 720–733.

————, *Peking Politics,* University of California Press, Berkeley, 1976.

Oksenberg, Michel, "Getting Ahead and Along in Communist China: The Ladder of Success on the Eve of the Cultural Revolution," in John W. Lewis, ed., *Party, Leadership, and Revolutionary Power in China,* Cambridge University Press, Cambridge, 1970.

————, "The Exit Pattern from Chinese Politics and Its Implications," *China Quarterly,* No. 67, September 1976, pp. 501–518.

————, and Steven Goldstein, "The Chinese Political Spectrum," *Problems of Communism,* Vol. 23, No. 2, March–April 1974, pp. 2–9.

Parrish, William L., "Factions in Chinese Military Politics," *China Quarterly,* No. 56, October 1973, pp. 667–679.

Pillsbury, Barbara L. K., "Factionalism Observed: Behind the Face of Harmony in a Chinese Community," *China Quarterly,* No. 74, June 1978, pp. 241–272.

Rice, Edward E., "The Second Rise and Fall of Teng Hsiao-p'ing," *China Quarterly,* No. 67, September 1976, pp. 494–500.

Shen, Taosheng, "Lin Biao's Anti-Marxist 30-Word Principle," *Beijing Review,* No. 5, February 2, 1979, pp. 16–19.

Starr, John Bryan, "From the 10th Party Congress to the Premiership of Hua Kuo-feng," *China Quarterly,* No. 67, September 1976, pp. 457–488.

Teiwes, Frederick, "The Purge of Provincial Leaders, 1957–1958," *China*

Quarterly, No. 27, July–September, 1966 pp. 14–32.

———, *Provincial Leadership in China: The Cultural Revolution and Its Aftermath*, Cornell University East Asia Papers, No. 4, Ithaca, N.Y., 1974.

Thornton, Richard C., "The Structure of Communist Politics," *World Politics*, Vol. 24, No. 4, July 1972.

———, *China, The Struggle for Power, 1917–1922*, Indiana University Press, Bloomington, 1973.

Tsou, Tang, "Prolegomenon to the Study of Informal Groups in CCP Politics," *China Quarterly*, No. 65, January 1976, pp. 98–114.

———, "Mao Tse-tung Thought, the Last Struggle for Succession, and the Post-Mao Era," *China Quarterly*, No. 71, September 1977.

Vogel, Ezra, "From Revolutionary to Semi-Bureaucrat: The 'Regularization' of Cadres," *China Quarterly*, No. 29, January–March 1967, pp. 36–60.

Wang, Ting, "Propaganda and Political Struggle," *Issues and Studies*, Vol. 13, No. 6, June 1977.

———, "Trends in China: Leadership Realignments," *Problems of Communism*, Vol. 26, No. 4, July–August 1977, p. 10.

Wich, Richard, "The Tenth Party Congress: The Power Struggle and the Succession Question," *China Quarterly*, No. 58, April–June 1974, pp. 231–248.

Winckler, Edwin A., "Policy Oscillations in the People's Republic of China: A Reply," *China Quarterly*, No. 68, December 1976, pp. 734–750.

Zweig, David S., "The Peita Debate on Education and the Fall of Teng Hsiao-p'ing," *China Quarterly*, No. 73, March 1978, pp. 140–159.

IV. THEORIES OF PATRON-CLIENT RELATIONS

Breman, Jan, *Patronage and Exploitation*, University of California Press, Berkeley, 1974.

Campbell, J. K., *Honour, Family and Patronage*, Oxford University Press, New York, 1974.

Eisenstadt, S. N., and Louis Roniger, "Patron–Client Relations as a Model of Structuring Social Exchange," *Comparative Studies in Society and History*, Vol. 22, No. 1, January 1980.

Folsom, K. E., *Friends, Guests and Colleagues: The Mu-fu System in the Late Ch'ing Period*, University of California Press, Berkeley, 1968.

Jackson, Karl D., "Bureaucratic Polity," in Karl D. Jackson and Lucian W. Pye, eds., *Political Power and Communications in Indonesia*, University of California Press, Berkeley, 1978, pp. 3–22.

Lande, Carl H., *Leaders, Factions and Parties: The Structure of Philippine Politics*, Yale University Press, New Haven, 1965.

———, "Networks and Groups in Southeast Asia: Some Observations on the Group Theory of Politics," *American Political Science Review*, Vol. 67, No. 1, March 1973, pp. 103–127.

Legg, K., "Political Clientelism and Development: A Preliminary Analysis," *Comparative Politics*, Vol. 4, No. 2, January 1972.

Nathan, Andrew J., *Peking Politics, 1918–1923*, Chap. 2, University of California Press, Berkeley and Los Angeles, 1976.

Popkin, Samuel L., *The Rational Peasant*, University of California Press, Berkeley, 1979.

Powell, John D., "Peasant Society and Clientelistic Politics," *American Political Science Review*, Vol. 64, No. 2, June 1970.

Riggs, Fred, *Thailand: The Modernization of a Bureaucratic Polity*, Cornell University Press, Ithaca, N.Y., 1966, pp. 310–396.

Schmidt, S. W., L. Guasti, C. H. Lande, and J. C. Scott, eds., *Friends, Followers, and Factions*, University of California Press, Berkeley, 1976.

Scott, James C., "Patron–Client Politics and Political Change in Southeast Asia," *American Political Science Review*, Vol. 66, No. 1, March 1972, pp. 92–113.

————, "The Erosion of Patron–Client Bonds and Social Change in Southeast Asia," *Journal of Asian Studies*, Vol. 32, No. 1, November 1972, pp. 5–37.

————, *The Moral Economy of Peasants*, Yale University Press, New Haven, Conn., 1976.

Wolf, Eric, *Peasants*, Prentice Hall, Englewood Cliffs, N.J., 1966.

————, *Peasant Wars of the Twentieth Century*, Harper and Row, New York, 1969.

V. GENERAL THEORIES OF POLITICS AND PERSONALITY

Abramson, Paul, "Generational Change and the Decline of Party Identification in America: 1952–1974," *American Political Science Review*, Vol. 70, No. 2, 1976, pp. 469–478.

Adorno, T. W., et al., *The Authoritarian Personality*, Harper, New York, 1949.

Almond, Gabriel A., and James Coleman, *The Politics of the Developing Areas*, Princeton University Press, Princeton, N.J., 1960, pp. 7ff.

————, and Sidney Verba, *The Civic Culture*, Princeton University Press, Princeton, N.J., 1963.

Andreski, Stanislav, *Social Sciences as Sorcery*, Deutsch, London, 1972.

Boissevain, J., *Friends of Friends: Networks, Manipulators, and Coalitions*, St. Martin's Press, New York, 1974.

Doreian, P., "On the Connectivity of Social Networks," *Journal of Mathematical Sociology*, Vol. 3, 1974, pp. 245–258.

Eisenstadt, S. N., *From Generation to Generation: Age Groups and Social Structure*, Free Press, Glencoe, Ill., 1956.

Feuer, Lewis S., "Generations and the Theory of Revolution," *Survey*, Vol. 18, No. 3, Summer 1972, pp. 161–188.

Frenkel-Brunswick, E., "Intolerance of Ambiguity as an Emotional and Perceptual Personality Variable," *Journal of Personality*, Vol. 18, 1949, pp. 108–143.

Glenn, N. D., and R. Hefer, "Further Evidence on Aging and Party Identification," *Public Opinion Quarterly,* Vol. 36, No. 1, pp. 21–47.

Hennessy, Bernard C., *Public Opinion,* Wadsworth Publishing Co., Belmont, Calif., 1965.

Huntington, Samuel P., *Political Order in Changing Societies,* Yale University Press, New Haven, Conn., 1968, pp. 78–92.

———, "Generations, Cycles and Their Role in American Political Development," in Richard J. Samuels, ed., *Political Generations and Political Development,* Lexington Books, Lexington, Mass., 1977.

Lane, Robert E., "Fathers and Sons: Foundation of Political Beliefs," *American Political Science Review,* Vol. 24, No. 4, August 1959, pp. 502–511.

Levenson, Hanna, "Activism and Powerful Others: Distinctions Within the Concept of Internal–External Control," *Journal of Personality Assessment,* Vol. 38, 1974, pp. 377–383.

Mannheim, Karl, *Essays in the Sociology of Knowledge,* Routledge and Kegan Paul, London, 1938.

Milgram, S., "The Small World Problems," *Psychology Today,* No. 22, 1967, pp. 61–67.

Miller, G., "The Magical Number Seven, Plus or Minus Two," *Psychological Review,* No. 63, 1956, pp. 81–97.

Nettl, J. P., *Political Mobilization: A Sociological Analysis of Methods and Concepts,* Basic Books, New York, 1967.

Neuman, Sigmund, *Permanent Revolution: Totalitarianism in the Age of International Civil War,* 2nd ed., Praeger, New York, 1965.

Pool, Ithiel de Sola, and Manfred Kochen, "Contacts and Influence," *Social Networks,* Vol. 1, Winter 1978–1979, pp. 5–51.

Pye, Lucian W., *Guerrilla Communism in Malaya,* Princeton University Press, Princeton, N.J., 1956.

———, *Politics, Personality and Nation Building,* Yale University Press, New Haven, Conn., 1968, p. 16.

Quandt, William, *Revolution and Political Leadership: Algeria 1954–68,* M.I.T. Press, Cambridge, Mass., 1969.

Rentala, Marvin, "Political Generation," *International Encyclopedia of the Social Sciences,* Macmillan, New York, 1968.

Rothberg, David, "Insecurity and Success in Organizational Life: The Psychodynamics of Leaders and Managers," Ph.D. dissertation, Department of Political Science, Massachusetts Institute of Technology, 1978.

Rotter, Julian B., "Generalized Expectations for Internal Versus External Control of Reinforcement," *Psychological Monographs,* Vol. 80, No. 1, March 1966, pp. 1–28.

Sinha, M. P., and K. P. Gangrade, *Inter-Generational Conflict in India,* Nachiketa Publications, Bombay, 1971.

Verba, Sidney, "Organizational Membership and Democratic Consensus," *Journal of Politics,* Vol. XXVII, August 1965, pp. 467–497.

Appendix

The Hong Kong Questionnaire

Case Number _____

Date _____

I. Basic Data

Your age is: _____ Your sex is: Male _____ Female _____
   (26 "young"; 12 "old"; 6 no information)

Where were you born? _____ province _____ county (city)

When did you leave China for Hong Kong? _____ (year) _____ (month)

Where did your family live in China? _____ province _____ county (city)

how long? _____ years
   (28 Guangdong; 5 Shanghai; 4 Peking; remainder from Fujan, Guangxi, Hebei,
   Jiangsu, Jianxi, and Zhejiang.)

Your father's occupation was _____

Your mother's occupation was _____

What class did your family belong to? _____

What class did you yourself belong to? _____
   (30 "bad" family background; 11 "good"; 3 no information)

Where did you go to school in China?

elementary school _____(20)_____ province _____ county (city)

middle school _____(14)_____ province _____ county (city)

post-middle school ____(8)____ province _____ county (city)

How many years of schooling have you had? _____ years

Where did you work in China? _____ province _____ county (city)

_____ province _____ county (city)

---

*Marginals of the responses and summaries of biographical data are shown in parentheses.

Have you worked in the following organizations?

people's commune? __(18)_____ how long? _____

factory? _____(12)_____ how long? _____

school? _____(13)_____ how long? _____

government _____(7)_____ how long? _____

PLA? _____(2)_____ how long? _____

Other, please describe it _____

Have you belonged to any special groups?

Red Guards? _____(18)_____ Youth League? _____

Study Group: _____ Mutual Criticism? _____
("Rusticated youths" 25)

Were you ever in a position of responsibility over subordinates _____(12)_____

II. Please check (✔) if agree, check X if disagree. (These items on the philosophy of human nature test for "Trustworthiness," "Altruism," "Independence," and "Strength of Will and Rationality." All questions have been widely used.)

_____ 1. If you want people to do a job right, you should explain things to them in great detail and supervise them closely.
(Agree 38; Disagree 3; no answer 3)

_____ 2. Nowadays people commit a lot of crimes and sins that no one else ever hears about.
(Agree 20; Disagree 24)

_____ 3. The typical person is sincerely concerned about the problems of others.
(Agree 19; Disagree 24; no answer 1)

_____ 4. People pretend to care more about one another than they really do.
(Agree 36; Disagree 8)

_____ 5. Most people exaggerate their troubles in order to get sympathy.
(Agree 35; Disagree 8; no answer 1)

_____ 6. Most people can make their own decisions, uninfluenced by public opinion.
(Agree 43; Disagree 1)

_____ 7. The average person will stick to his opinion if he thinks he is right, even if others disagree.
(Agree 13; Disagree 31)

_____ 8. Most people will speak out for what they believe in.
(Agree 5; Disagree 39)

_____ 9. Most people will change the opinion they express as a result of an onslaught of criticism, even though they really don't change the way they feel.
(Agree 41; Disagree 3)

_____ 10. Nowadays many people won't make a move until they find out what other people think.
(Agree 42; Disagree 2)

_____ 11. It's a rare person who will go against the crowd.
(Agree 38; Disagree 6)

_____ 12. The average person will rarely express his opinion in a group when he sees the others disagree with him.
(Agree 39; Disagree 5)

_____ 13. If a person tries hard enough, he will usually reach his goal in life.
(Agree 14; Disagree 30)

_____ 14. Most people have a good idea of what their strengths and weaknesses are.
(Agree 23; Disagree 20; no answer 1)

_____ 15. Our success in life is pretty much determined by forces outside our own control.
(Agree 42; Disagree 2)

_____ 16. Most people have an unrealistically favorable view of their own capabilities.
(Agree 29; Disagree 15)

_____ 17. I find that my first impressions of people are frequently wrong.
(Agree 18; Disagree 24; no answer 2)

_____ 18. You can't classify everyone as good or bad.
(Agree 42; Disagree 2)

_____ 19. It's not hard to understand what really is important to a person.
(Agree 21; Disagree 22; no answer 1)

_____ 20. I think I get a good idea of a person's basic nature after a brief conversa-

tion with him.
(Agree 15; Disagree 28; no answer 1)

_____ 21. Different people react to the same situation in different ways.
(Agree 40; Disagree 4)

_____ 22. People are quite different in their basic interests.
(Agree 21; Disagree 23)

_____ 23. People are unpredictable in how they'll act from one situation to another.
(Agree 30; Disagree 14)

_____ 24. People are pretty much alike in their basic interests.
(Agree 26; Disagree 14; no answer 4)

_____ 25. If I can see how a person reacts to one situation, I have a good idea of how
he will react to other situations.
(Agree 30; Disagree 13; no answer 1)

III. Please check (✔) the right answer. (Tests for "Trust in People." These three questions
have been included in national sample of Americans.)

    1. Generally speaking, would you say that most people can be trusted or that
you can't be too careful in dealing with people?

__(5)__   Most people can be trusted

__(36)__   Can't be too careful

    2. Would you say that most of the time people try to be helpful, or that they
are mostly just looking out for themselves?

__(7)__   Try to be helpful

__(36)__   Look out for themselves

    3. Do you think that most people would try to take advantage of you if they
got the chance or would they try to be fair?

__(27)__   Take advantage

__(15)__   Try to be fair

IV. Please check (✔) if agree, check X if disagree. (Tests for "Intolerance of Ambiguity."
Have been extensively used on American samples.)

_____ 1. There is really no such thing as a problem that can't be solved.
(Agree 23; Disagree 17; no answer 4)

_____ 2. A good job is one where what is to be done and how it is to be done are
always clear.
(Agree 42; Disagree 2)

_____ 3. In the long run it is possible to get more done by tackling small, simple
problems rather than large and complicated ones.
(Agree 30; Disagree 12; no answer 2)

_____ 4. A person who leads an even, regular life in which few surprises occur is fortunate.
(Agree 35; Disagree 9)

_____ 5. It is more fun to tackle a complicated problem than to solve a simple one.
(Agree 35; Disagree 9)

_____ 6. Often the most interesting and stimulating people are those who don't mind being different and original.
(Agree 31; Disagree 13)

_____ 7. People who insist upon a yes or no answer just don't know how complicated things really are.
(Agree 33; Disagree 11)

V. Please check (✔) the right answer. (Tests for "Conformity and Sensitivity to Power" have been used on U.S. military and business men.)

1. To what extent do you believe your life goals are truly your own, and how much are they the result of others' expectations?

_(29)_ Truly your own

_(13)_ Result of others' expectations?

(2) no answer

2. It is a popular notion that in order to achieve success in an organization one must conform to the expectations of others. Is this conformity only necessary at lower levels, and will end when higher positions are reached, or is conformity necessary even near the top?

_(10)_ Conformity is only a phase, and leaders are free of it

_(33)_ Always a necessity

(1) no answer

3. How often do subordinates try to be helpful, and how often do they just look out for themselves?

_(19)_ Try to be helpful

_(22)_ Mostly look out for themselves

(3) no answer

4. How often do superiors try to be helpful, and how often do they just look out for themselves?

_(9)_ Try to be helpful

_(35)_ Mostly look out for themselves

5. An ambitious person

_(17)_ Is admired

_(22)_ Creates enemies

(5) no answer

6. Once it becomes apparent that you cannot improve your position, it is best to be content.

_(29)_ Yes

_(15)_ No

7. It is better to want to lead other men than to be a faithful subordinate.

_(29)_ Yes

_(15)_ No

8. Most of the unhappy things, misfortunes, in people's lives are due to

_(27)_ Bad luck

_(11)_ Their own mistakes

(6) no answer

9. The most important thing in getting ahead is

_(28)_ Being on good terms with the right people

_(12)_ Ignoring people and doing your very best

(4) no answer

10. There really is no contradiction between being on good terms with superiors and doing the right thing.

_(19)_ Yes

_(25)_ No

11. Obedience and respect for authority are the most important virtues children should learn.

_(22)_ Yes

_(22)_ No

12. A well-raised child is one who doesn't have to be told twice to do something.

_(25)_ Yes

_(19)_ No

13. Disobeying an order is one thing you can't excuse—if one can get away with disobedience, why can't everybody?

_(28)_ Yes

_(16)_ No

VI. Please check (✔) the right answer. (Tests for "The Media and Conflicts among Leaders." No comparative data.)

1. When I read the newspaper I can usually tell when the leaders are in disagreement.

__(27)__ Yes

__(16)__ No

(1) no answer

2. Conflicts among leaders are bad for the common people.

__(38)__ Yes

__(6)__ No

Why? _____

3. I expect that individual leaders will have to change their positions from time to time, and therefore I am not surprised or shocked when they contradict their own words.

__(40)__ True

__(3)__ False

(1) no answer

4. When leaders fall from power there is no need to be sympathetic for them.

__(29)__ True

__(11)__ False

(4) no answer

(a) If true, this is because

__(13)__ They must have done something wrong to have fallen.

__(9)__ Even if they are falsely charged, they must have done other evil things.

(b) If false, this is because

__(4)__ It is usually good people who are defeated.

__(10)__ No one should have to suffer because of politics.

From question 5 to 10, please use numbers 1, 2, 3, 4, 5 to indicate the degree of importance: "5" the most important, "1" the least important. Please use the same number if the degree of importance is considered as about the same. Please use "0" if the answer is considered as of no importance.

(All answers reported in text.)

5. In my experience most people who are successful leaders are:

_____ (a) brighter than others

_____ (b) work harder

_____ (c) are more ruthless

_____ (d) have better contacts

_____ (e) other, please describe it _____

6. In Chinese politics the following values are still important:

_____ (a) sincerity

_____ (b) propriety

_____ (c) correctness

_____ (d) concern for the people

_____ (e) ideological correctness

_____ (f) other, please describe it _____

7. What do you believe is important in the forming of political factions?

_____ (a) similar material interests

_____ (b) similar viewpoints on issues

_____ (c) trust based on knowing each other a long time

_____ (d) friendship (including friendships of wives)

_____ (e) co-provincials, schoolmates, etc.

_____ (f) having the same enemies

_____ (g) other, please describe it _____

8. Generally speaking, your political opinions were similar to

_____ (a) your parents

_____ (b) your brothers and sisters

_____ (c) your friends

_____ (d) your direct superiors at work

_____ (e) your local political authority

_____ (f) national leaders

_____ (g) other, please describe it _____

9. The major sources of your political knowledge were:

_____ (a) newspapers or magazines

_____ (b) radio or television

_____ (c) confidential documents with restricted circulations

_____ (d) wall posters

_____ (e) political meetings

_____ (f) your direct superiors at work

_____ (g) your family members

_____ (h) your friends

_____ (i) other, please describe it _____

10. Among the major sources of your political information, which did you think the more reliable?

_____ (a) newspapers or magazines

_____ (b) radio or television

_____ (c) confidential documents with restricted circulations

_____ (d) wall posters

_____ (e) political meetings

_____ (f) your direct superiors at work

_____ (g) your family members

_____ (i) other, please describe it _____

VII. Please check (✔) the right answer. (Tests for "Internal vs. External Locus of Control").

_(3)_ 1. (a) Children get into trouble because their parents punish them too much.

_(32)_   (b) The trouble with most children nowadays is that their parents are too easy with them.

(9) no answer

_(16)_ 2. (a) In the long run people get the respect they deserve in this world.

_(24)_   (b) Unfortunately, an individual's worth often passes unrecognized no matter how hard he tries.

(4) no answer

_(15)_ 3. (a) Without the right breaks one cannot be an effective leader.

_(25)_   (b) Capable people who fail to become leaders have not taken advantage of their opportunities.

(4) no answer

_(21)_ 4. (a) When I make plans, I am almost certain that I can make them work.

_(21)_   (b) It is not always wise to plan too far ahead because many things turn out to be a matter of good or bad fortune anyhow.

(4) no answer

__(6)__ 5. (a) There are certain people who are just no good.

_(37)_   (b) There is some good in everybody.

(1) no answer

_(23)_ 6. (a) One should always be willing to admit mistakes.

_(20)_   (b) It is usually best to cover up one's mistakes.

(1) no answer

_(28)_ 7. (a) In the long run the bad things that happen to us are balanced by the good ones.

_(14)_   (b) Most misfortunes are the result of lack of ability, ignorance, laziness, or all three.

(2) no answer

_(23)_ 8. (a) A good leader expects people to decide for themselves what they should do.

_(19)_   (b) A good leader makes it clear to everybody what their jobs are.

(2) no answer

_(21)_ 9. (a) People are lonley because they don't try to be friendly.

_(21)_   (b) There is not much use in trying too hard to please people.

(2) no answer

_(36)_ 10. (a) Most of the time I can't understand why politicians behave the way they do.

_(7)_   (b) In the long run the people are responsible for bad government on a national as well as local level.

(1) no answer

Index

A

Abandonment, as theme in Mao's personality, 39n
Abramson, Paul, 102n
Academy of the Social Sciences (Chinese), 26, 251
Accountability
 and ideology, 17
 and performance, 17
 and policy implementation, 181–182
 power in absence of, 135
Acquaintanceship networks, compared to *guanxi*, 139
Administration. *See also* Implementation; Policy
 informal nature of, 193–194
 leaders' role in, 14–16
 and policymaking, 15
Adorno, T. W., 114
Adversary Theory, on generations, 102–103
Afghanistan, Soviet intervention in, 36
Aggression
 and political conflict, 230

study as, 229–230
 suspicion of, 138
Aggression, repression of
 as central to Chinese culture, 137
 and code names, 213
 and deception, 228
 and filial piety, 137
 and power, 137, 138
 and suspicion, 228
Air Force, Chinese, as radical stronghold, 15, 86
Allison, Graham, 82
Almond, Gabriel A., 73n, 115n
Amateur-as-ruler, 79n
Ambiguity, tolerance for, 114
Ambition, Hong Kong refugees on, 143–145 (*see also* Power)
Andreski, Stanislav, 42n
"Anti-Confucius" campaign, as free-floating symbol, 164
"Anti-Confucius/Anti-Lin Biao" campaign, as free-floating symbol, 164
Antonioni, attack on, 175
Articulation of grievances
 as cause of conflict, 58, 59, 65

About the Author

Lucian W. Pye, one of the nation's leading authorities on the politics of Asian countries, is Ford Professor of Political Science at the Massachusetts Institute of Technology and a consultant to the Rand Corporation. He has been an advisor on foreign affairs to the Department of State and the National Security Council, a member of the Board of Directors of the Council on Foreign Relations and of many organizations concerned with U.S.–Asian relations. For a decade he was chairman of the influential Committee on Comparative Politics of the Social Science Research Council.

Professor Pye is a political psychologist whose analyses illuminate the fundamental impulses of Asian cultures and their reflection in contemporary Asian political ideology, political values, and political behavior. A major theme in his researches has been the impact of modernization on traditional Asian societies. With intellectual roots in anthropology, psychology, and psychoanalysis, as well as political science, Professor Pye has compared the political behavior and political cultures of Asian nations, including both China and South and Southeast Asian countries, in numerous published works.

Lucian W. Pye is the author of:

Mao Tse-tung: The Man in the Leader
China: An Introduction

Aspects of Political Development
The Spirit of Chinese Politics
Politics, Personality, and Nation Building
Warlord Politics
Guerrilla Communism in Malaya
Southeast Asian Political Systems

and the editor of:

Communications and Political Development
Political Culture and Political Development (with Sidney Verba)
Political Science and Area Studies
Political Power and Communications in Indonesia
    (with Karl D. Jackson)
The Citizen and Politics (with Sidney Verba)

Selected List of Rand Books

Brewer, Garry D., and Martin Shubik, *The War Game: A Critique of Military Problem Solving,* Harvard University Press, Cambridge, Mass., 1979.

Goldhamer, Herbert, *The Soviet Soldier: Soviet Military Management at the Troop Level,* Crane, Russak & Company, New York, 1975.

Hosmer, Stephen T. Konrad Kellen, and Brian M. Jenkins, *The Fall of South Vietnam: Statements by Vietnamese Military and Civilian Leaders,* Crane, Russak & Company, New York, 1980.

Hosmer, Stephen T. *Viet Cong Repression and Its Implications for the Future,* Lexington Books, D. C. Heath and Company, Lexington, Mass., 1970.

Langer, Paul, and Joseph J. Zasloff, *North Vietnam and the Pathet Lao: Partners in the Struggle for Laos,* Harvard University Press, Cambridge, Mass., 1970.

Moorstein, Richard, and Morton I. Abramowitz, *Remaking China Policy: U.S.-China Relations and Governmental Decisionmaking,* Harvard University Press, Cambridge, Mass., 1971.

Quade, E. S., *Analysis for Public Decisions,* American Elsevier Publishing Company, New York, 1975.

Quandt, William B., ed., *The Politics of Palestinian Nationalism,* University of California Press, Berkeley, 1973.

Robinson, Thomas et al., *The Cultural Revolution in China,* University of California Press, Berkeley, 1971.

Scalapino, Robert A., *The Japanese Communist Movement, 1920–1966,* University of California Press, Berkeley and Los Angeles, 1967.

Solomon, Richard H., *Asian Security in the 1980s,* Oelgeschlager, Gunn & Hain, Cambridge, Mass., 1980.

Wolfe, Thomas W., *The SALT Experience,* Ballinger Publishing Company, Cambridge, Mass., 1979.

F